P9-CBC-658

About Island Press

Island Press is the only nonprofit organization in the United States whose principal purpose is the publication of books on environmental issues and natural resource management. We provide solutions-oriented information to professionals, public officials, business and community leaders, and concerned citizens who are shaping responses to environmental problems.

In 1994, Island Press celebrated its tenth anniversary as the leading provider of timely and practical books that take a multidisciplinary approach to critical environmental concerns. Our growing list of titles reflects our commitment to bringing the best of an expanding body of literature to the environmental community throughout North America and the world.

Support for Island Press is provided by Apple Computer, Inc., The Bullitt Foundation, The Geraldine R. Dodge Foundation, The Energy Foundation, The Ford Foundation, The W. Alton Jones Foundation, The Lyndhurst Foundation, The John D. and Catherine T. MacArthur Foundation, The Andrew W. Mellon Foundation, The Joyce Mertz Gilmore Foundation, The National Fish and Wildlife Foundation, The Pew Charitable Trusts, The Pew Global Stewardship Initiative, The Philanthropic Collaborative, Inc., and individual donors.

Discovering the
Unknown Landscape

Discovering the Unknown Landscape

A History of America's Wetlands

ANN VILEISIS

Island Press
WASHINGTON, D.C. • COVELO, CALIFORNIA

Library of Congress Cataloging-in-Publication Data
Vileisis, Ann.
    Discovering the unknown landscape : a history of America's
wetlands / Ann Vileisis.
        p.   cm.
    Includes bibliographical references and index.
    ISBN 1-55963-314-X (cloth) — ISBN 1-55963-315-8 (pbk.)
    1. Wetlands—United States. I. Title.
GB624.V55   1997
    33.91′8—dc21   97-25654
                                                 CIP

Printed on recycled, acid-free paper

Manufactured in the United States of America
10 9 8 7 6 5 4 3

To Tim, my loving partner in all of life's adventures

Contents

Preface

wetland—a lowland area, such as a marsh or swamp, that is saturated with moisture, especially when thought of as the natural habitat of wildlife.
—*The American Heritage Dictionary*

In the past fifteen years, reports have chronicled the extensive loss of wetlands in America. Coverage of this once little-known landscape has been ratcheted up in newspapers and magazines. More and more people have wetland stories: "They couldn't build a shopping plaza there because it's a wetland," or "We have a wetland park in our town; the kids love to go and see the ducks." Despite all the talk, however, many people still wonder: What exactly is a wetland?

Wetlands are places where water saturates or floods the soil much of the time so that only plants specially adapted to wetness can thrive. In Southern swamps, baldcypress trees flourish in standing water. In New England salt marshes, tides wash over spartina grasses twice a day. Although cypress swamps and coastal marshes look very different, they fall under the same wetland umbrella along with other distinctive and biologically rich landscapes. All wetlands share the feature of wetness and, accordingly, have long shared human disdain associated with muck and mosquitoes.

Over the past five decades, scientists have studied wetlands and compiled a sizable body of fact on why these ecosystems are important to people. Wetlands filter pollutants; they reduce flooding; they buffer coasts; and they provide habitat for fish, waterfowl, and wildlife. With this information, Americans have shed much of their scorn and made great strides toward conserving wetlands through new laws and programs. Yet at the same time, in spite of toppling scientific evidence, our houses, roads, and farms have continued to encroach upon millions of acres of wetlands. The matter of wetlands and their conservation is not a matter of science alone—but one of culture as well.

To understand wetlands, we must know not only the science that proves their values but also the society that struggles to accommodate those values amid myriad pressing others. Such understanding has never been more urgent because Congress is currently reconsidering the laws and programs designed to protect wetlands. The outcome will have consequences for everyone who drinks water, watches or hunts birds, fishes or eats seafood, lives near a river or coast, or cares about the natural world. The final fate of wetlands must be decided not by default, ignorance, short-term convenience, personal gain, or vested interests but by careful, conscious consideration of the public values at stake.

ONE

A Landscape on the Periphery

> That man is, in fact, only a member of a biotic community
> is shown by an ecological interpretation of history. Many
> historical events, hitherto explained solely in terms of
> human enterprise, were actually biotic interactions be-
> tween people and the land. The characteristics of the land
> determined the facts quite as potently as the characteris-
> tics of the men who lived on it.
> —Aldo Leopold, *A Sand County Almanac* [1]

A salt marsh lay behind my grandmother's beach house, but I never ventured to play in its golden grasses. Somehow, as a child, I already knew the
muddy terrain was taboo. I sat on a warm black rock near the gentle surf of
Long Island Sound and peered up the glimmering creek that flowed from
the marsh. That's as close as I got.

Twelve years later, a college field trip took me to another wetland near
the Connecticut coast. Crossing a highway bridge just out of town, we saw
our destination: an expanse of reeds and cattails stretching along the Quinnipiac River, bounded by an industrial park on one end and a shipyard at
the other. We abandoned our van in the shadow of six squat oil tanks and
pulled on thick rubber boots. I didn't know what to expect when I took my
first step. Would my feet sink into stinking black muck? The wetland mysti-
fied me.

Following the lead of our ecology professor, Tom Siccama, I separated
the tall reeds with my outstretched arms and entered the marsh. With that
first step, my boot crunched brittle stalks. I didn't get stuck in the mud at
all. An earthy spring smell emanated from the rich soil and filled the breezy
air. Startling us with their commotion, a pair of blue-winged teal flew from
their protected refuge.

Our class plodded farther into the marsh to discover its inner workings.
We examined the stalks and roots of the cattails and searched for signs of

muskrats and birds. Digging a pit to investigate the soil, students by chance unearthed axe-hewn stakes that once supported hayricks, the frames used long ago for drying marsh grasses into hay. But now the grasses were gone. When bridges near the river's mouth were built, Tom explained, much of the marsh was filled in. Without the regular pulse of saltwater, cattails and reeds outcompeted the marsh grasses that had once thrived. I could see that the reeds' aggressive roots spread in rhizomatous networks, creating a thick, woven floor. Our wetland was typical of many on the eastern seaboard, where the construction of harbors, roads, and bridges had altered the ecology of salt marshes. Although cattails provide less nutritious food than the grasses they replaced, their dense stands still shelter waterfowl and wildlife. As the cattails and reeds draw water for their own biological processes, they also absorb excess nutrients and filter pollutants, helping to preserve the water quality of the urban harbor. Though changed and de-graded, the brackish wetland still serves important ecological and hydro-logical functions.

When my classmates headed back to the van, I lingered for a while, en-gulfed by marsh. When the wind blew, the reeds rustled and bent in syn-chrony. I saw only clear sky fringed by the tassels of the swaying reeds. The landscape I'd always avoided turned out to be a veritable sanctuary, not only for ducks but for me too. Here on the city's edge, I found a place apart, full of the beauty and wild intricacies of nature.

Even though a quarter million city dwellers lived nearby, almost no one noticed the marsh. After learning more about the history of wetlands, I am not surprised. Since colonial settlement, Euro-Americans have generally avoided wetlands. These landscapes have been little explored, little known, and little understood. They boast far fewer poets and champions than other more familiar terrains, such as forests, meadows, and seashores. Conse-quently, most Americans have held incomplete or mistaken perceptions of these places. Wetlands have long been a landscape on the periphery.

If people didn't shun swamps and marshes, they remade them into dif-ferent landscapes. Before industrial parks, oil tanks, warehouses, and docks girded the Quinnipiac, its mouth formed a large coastal estuary supporting abundant fisheries. The small piece I ventured into remains as a fragment mirroring the far richer wetland ecosystem that once existed. Throughout Connecticut, people have drained over 50 percent of the original wetlands, including swamps, peat bogs, and salt marshes, for cities, suburbs, and farms. Other states have suffered similar or greater losses. Louisiana has lost half of its native forested bottomlands. In the northern plains states, farmers

WETLAND DISTRIBUTION CIRCA 1780

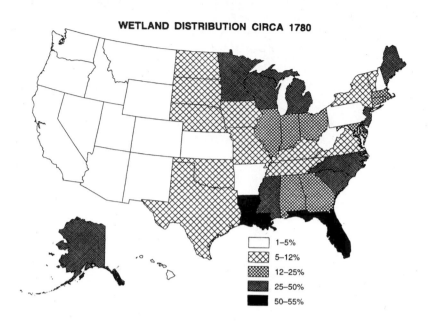

1–5%
5–12%
12–25%
25–50%
50–55%

PERCENTAGE OF BASE WETLAND ACREAGE LOST

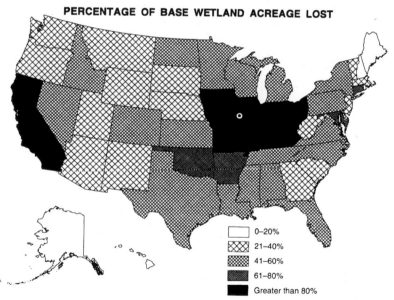

0–20%
21–40%
41–60%
61–80%
Greater than 80%

WETLAND LOSSES 1780 AND 1980S.

Scientists estimate that 53 percent of wetlands in the continental United States have been lost either to agriculture or development. With the loss of these ecosystems, there have been many consequences including increased flooding, degraded water quality, and the destruction of habitat for fish, birds, and wildlife. Not until the twentieth century did Americans begin to recognize the important natural values of wetlands. (Courtesy National Wetlands Inventory) have converted 60 to 70 percent of prairie pothole wetlands into farmlands. In Iowa, a state we rarely think of as wet, vast marshes once existed, but 89 percent of them have been drained for cultivation. Ninety-one percent of California wetlands, including much of the San Francisco Bay estuary and the once vast tule marshes of the Central Valley, are gone. Overall, 221 million acres of wetlands once graced our nation's lower forty-eight states with a rich mosaic of life.[2] More than half of these important landscapes no longer exist. And plunging acreage estimates don't address widespread deterioration of ecological functions in the wetlands that remain.

The sweeping transformation of wetlands has occurred over the course of almost four centuries, much of it happening before people recognized the values that these landscapes offer. Only in the past thirty to forty years have scientists learned that destruction of wetlands undermines natural hydrologic processes, many of them fundamental to people's lives and economy. By retarding runoff and allowing water to seep back into the ground, many wetlands have played a critical role in recharging the aquifers that people rely on for agricultural and domestic water supplies. With their spongelike capacities, wetlands have absorbed and stored water, providing natural flood control along many rivers. Wetlands have also preserved water quality by filtering excess nutrients and pollutants. But clearing, drainage, and development have compromised these services, resulting in the "need" for costly dams, levees, and water treatment plants.[3]

With the loss and degradation of wetland ecosystems, the insects, fish, birds, animals, and plants that depend on these rich landscapes have suffered grim consequences. As development has swallowed coastal salt marshes and estuaries, fish and shellfish populations have plummeted, ruining valuable commercial fisheries. Drainage of the prairie potholes, regarded as the most productive breeding grounds for ducks and geese worldwide, has decimated waterfowl populations that less than two centuries ago were said to "blacken" the skies. Remaining wetlands still provide critical habitat for 150 bird and 200 fish species, including an estimated one-third of the nation's threatened or endangered plants and animals.[4] And only in the past decade have scientists come to realize that wetlands help to preserve the biodiversity essential to our planet's well-being.

Though significant protection efforts began in the 1960s, wetlands have continued to disappear at a staggering rate. As recently as 1990, eight hundred acres—equivalent to six hundred football fields—were lost on average each day.

The ongoing destruction of wetlands has posed fundamental conflicts for our country. Despite the preponderance of scientific evidence indicating the need to preserve wetlands, efforts at regulation and conservation have been riddled by delays, misunderstandings, loopholes, and discord. As such, wetlands have become the most controversial landscape in America.

The confusion and contention surrounding wetlands did not erupt suddenly but are the products of a long and convoluted history. Americans have an abiding tradition of turning wetlands into farms and cities, yet we also have a lesser-known tradition of appreciating the many natural qualities of wetlands. Some readers may be surprised to learn that the origins of our current conflict over wetland values lie much deeper than the environmental regulatory politics of the recent decades. Only by delving further into this history can we know the very sources of our conflicting beliefs. And only by reevaluating those beliefs can we find a workable vision for the next century.

Several important themes thread this four-hundred-year story. Perhaps the most colorful strand is the way that cultural attitudes have shaped our society's understanding of wetlands and, consequently, our treatment of them. Over time, these attitudes have generally shifted from negative to positive—especially with the advent of new scientific information. But some attitudes have not changed.

The most revealing theme of this story is how Americans have long regarded wetlands as private property just like all other land. Without a clear hydrologic and ecologic understanding of these lands, early settlers saw no reason to treat them any differently. Following in their footsteps, generations of Americans have continued to misunderstand the essentially liquid nature of wetland landscapes. Although on the surface some wetlands (in the dry season) may look like any other parcel of land, they are connected to subterranean aquifers, rivers, and lakes, and, therefore, they are markedly different. If a wetland is altered, consequences reverberate throughout the watershed. For example, if a wetland is drained or filled, more runoff will flow downstream, and neighbors' basements may flood. Even beyond the watershed, there may be fewer ducks.

The Lockean tenets of labor and land ownership on which American concepts of property are based failed to account for variances in the nature of land and certainly did not account for water. Traditionally, land has been considered as private property and water as public property. Because wetlands are not only land but land *and* water, regarding them simply as real property with no other consideration has been a fundamental error in paradigm. This error long misled citizens attempting to drain wetlands and continues to mislead those who seek to conserve wetlands without violating traditional property rights.

The tricky matter is that although by customary law a citizen may survey and purchase a parcel of wetland and consider it private property, the very wetness of wetlands means that there will always be a "commons" component to them. This commons may be a public nuisance, or it may be a public good. For example, when settlers along the Mississippi River struggled against massive floods, they realized that they had to work in concert to reap the benefits of their properties. It was impossible for an individual landowner to build a single segment of levee or to drain a small parcel of swamp successfully. As engineer Arthur Morgan explained in 1910, "Many of the large drainage basins are intricately connected by overflow channels, or by large swamp areas which have served as storage reservoirs for the waters of several streams, and an effort to reclaim a small part of one of the large basins has frequently resulted in damage to some other portion, or has failed to accomplish its purpose because the small area could not be isolated for treatment."[5] In this historical instance, the wetland commonage created a public nuisance that ultimately had to be dealt with in a public manner, first by the state levee board and then by the U.S. Army Corps of Engineers. In the past, common problems posed by wetlands generated the most attention, but now the public benefits accorded by wetlands draw the most concern. Although the ways that we've understood the "commonness" of wetlands has changed through history, our response has nonetheless remained tied to the watery nature of these lands.[6]

A third theme of this story is that citizens have long looked to government for help with clarifying individual rights and responsibilities pertaining to wetlands. By their very nature, wetlands have challenged private ownership and generated confusion because many are linked to larger hydrological systems that transcend property lines and even state boundaries. To resolve such confusion, throughout history citizens have demanded that local, state, and federal governments become involved to protect against common nuisances and to preserve common values. For example, nineteenth-century farmers supported state ditch laws to prevent haphazard drainage and flooding. Over a century later, to avert a "tragedy of the commons," whereby the destruction of privately owned wetlands would degrade water quality for all, environmentalists pushed for laws to protect these landscapes.[7] A larger-scale vision, in terms of both geography and purpose, has often been needed to both develop and conserve wetlands. These themes—the role of cultural attitudes, the misunderstanding of wetlands' watery nature, and the waxing involvement of government—emerge again and again in this history.

What we can now look at as a dramatic transformation of the American landscape—the loss of over half the wetlands in the continental United States—took place in increments. The change was slow at first and then picked up pace as the prospering economy, innovations, and new laws made converting natural wetlands to other landscapes easier. For centuries, the conviction that natural swamps and marshes were worthless and troublesome went hand in hand with people's actions and government policies: citizens drained swamps, and government land grants and subsidies encouraged even more drainage.

With the striking transformation of these landscapes came a slow change in attitudes toward wetlands. By the 1860s, naturalists and influential Romantic thinkers and artists recognized that the unique beauty of the nation lay in its disappearing natural features. Their art and writing helped to inspire general appreciation and study of nature among literate Americans. Beyond naturalists, artists, and writers, late-nineteenth-century sport hunters secured the most significant attention for swamps and marshes by noticing that waterfowl populations—dependent on wetlands for nesting and breeding—were declining. National interest in migratory birds led to federal protection of wetlands for the first time.

Not until scientists learned more about the critical importance of wetland ecosystems as habitat for waterfowl, fish, and wildlife did an ecological ideology emerge and a new understanding of wetlands grow in the scientific community. In the 1950s, ecologists coined the term *wetland* to replace the imprecise and value-laden *swamp*. Despite scientific knowledge, rampant development following World War II resulted in a blitz of wetlands destruction. All in all, between the mid 1950s and the mid 1970s, 11 million wetland acres were converted to shopping centers, airports, farms, suburbs, and other uses.[8] When citizens recognized the consequences of this massive wetland transformation in their own communities, they began to organize to restore and protect those landscapes. In response to the growing grassroots environmental movement, several states passed wetland statutes to maintain open space, wildlife habitat, water quality, and flood protection. Citizen concern for environmental quality also spread to Congress, which

enacted the Clean Water Act and other laws that benefited wetlands in the
early 1970s.

Despite the growing awareness about the values of wetland ecosystems,
a traditional and powerful bias favoring agriculture and development persisted in both the institutions and the language of government and politics.
While the Fish and Wildlife Service protected wetland remnants as refuges,
other federal agencies proceeded to destroy them. When swamps stood in
the way of canal projects, the Army Corps of Engineers drained and leveed
them. When prairie potholes lay in the way of maximum crop yields, the
Department of Agriculture encouraged drainage through subsidy payments. Not until 1975 did a citizen lawsuit compel the Corps to extend
Clean Water Act protection to wetlands. And not until 1985 did Congress
finally strike from the law federal incentives to drain wetlands for croplands.
In the early 1990s, when the Bush administration and then Congress tried
to change the legal definition of wetlands, potentially removing thousands
of acres from federal protection, it became evident that a universal understanding of wetland ecosystems and their values still did not exist.

Lawmakers' inexperience and lack of knowledge regarding wetlands reflect the broader spectrum of American attitudes toward these landscapes.
Although in the past twenty years more people have come to know these
ecosystems better through parks, wildlife refuges, magazines, television,
and educational programs, wetlands still remain on the edge of most citizens' experience. Numerous state and federal laws protecting wetlands now
exist, but many individuals still evade regulations without compunction because they don't understand the aggregate effects of draining and filling
small acreages and they don't want to lose potential profits. Understaffed
government agencies cannot provide adequate public education or enforcement of protective laws. Consequently, the surviving patchwork of
swamps, marshes, and bogs remains threatened by pollution, by drainage
for croplands, and by urban sprawl. While an ecological awareness slowly
grows, 117,000 acres of wetlands continue to be whittled away each year.[9]
Only by discovering the story of these lost and beleaguered landscapes can
we move wetlands out of the periphery of our experience and into our
consciousness.

The histories of farming and city building have been recounted many
times before, but in the following chapters, you will find a story of wetlands
that reforms traditional understanding of past events and trends by focusing on the interactions between people and the natural environment.

Some interactions have been physical; farmers put considerable muscle into draining swamps for croplands. Other interactions have been more cerebral. Thoreau, for example, gained a sense of the richness of life while wading neck-deep through a cranberry bog. Still other, more complex interchanges have involved both the physical and mental. For example, early Bostonians used their natural marshes as dumps. Isolated from cleansing tides after levees were built, the severely degraded marshes repulsed citizens several generations later with odors and insects. The repugnance of the ruined landscape encouraged city leaders to restore the marshes. Such events are part of an ongoing interplay between people and the land that entails many factors including ideology, economics, law, perception, and art as well as ecological processes. Without a grasp of this back-and-forth interplay, it is impossible to know why our landscape looks the way it does today. The story recounted here will clarify our relationship with swamp and marsh landscapes and enable us to comprehend more clearly the context of wetlands loss and protection.

With its historical perspective, *Discovering the Unknown Landscape* will allow us to see that strides made in wetland conservation over the past twenty-five years are significant yet are rooted in a broader cultural continuum of appreciating wetlands. At the same time, the historical perspective enables us to see that small incremental losses of wetlands over time have become consequential. While people have always altered the lands they live on, the degree of wetland change has been tremendous and, in many cases, absolute.

Because wetlands are connected to each other across broad geography by flyways, this history considers wetlands nationwide. Delighted parents and children who watch ducks dabbling in a neighborhood pond may not realize that those same ducks depend on threatened prairie pothole wetlands seven hundred miles away. Waterfowl that breed in North Dakota's potholes have been identified in forty-six other states, ten Canadian provinces, and twenty-three other countries.[10]

To enlarge our perspective, this history also considers the nature of wetland losses over a long time span. Most of us are too young—even our grandparents are too young—to remember the true abundance of this continent, with its skies laced by endless flocks of ducks and geese, its bays filled with enormous fish and lobsters, and its estuaries embedded with succulent oysters. Because we honestly do not know the natural world that we've traded away, we settle too easily for compromised protection of what remains. As former Maryland state senator and Chesapeake Bay activist Bernie Fowler reflected, "I guess it's like sitting in a room and the oxygen is being consumed; you don't notice it until most of it is gone."[11] Although we need not revere the past landscape as a dreamy goal, we must know it well as a benchmark to guide decisions about the future.

Furthermore, understanding the history of cultural attitudes toward wetlands can help us to recognize the potency of traditional beliefs, which seldom change, even when scientific knowledge revises how we view reality. By illustrating the stark contrast between centuries of beliefs and laws encouraging wetland drainage and recent attempts to turn those attitudes and policies around, it is hoped that this history will provide insights into modern-day conflicts. For example, knowing that federal policies long encouraged farmers to drain wetlands helps us to understand the difficulty of convincing them not to drain.

The farmer's knowledge of wetlands is different from the biologist's. The ways that each of us understands wetlands fundamentally spring from some source within this story. To better understand the root of my own attitudes, when I began to write this book, I asked my mother and grandmother why our family never ventured into the marshes behind the summer beach house. "No one else went there," my grandmother explained. "It would have been buggy and muddy," my mother reasoned. "We just never even considered it." Their answers were the answers of our mainstream culture, a culture that has long despised and avoided wetlands. Slowly, these responses are changing as we all learn more about wetlands and come to understand that the "bugs and mud" play fundamental roles in nature's economy.

When a people's stories are well known, individuals lay claim to a heritage that gives them an identity and place in the broader society. The same can be true for natural landscape features. Perhaps when Americans better know the story of their wetlands, they will understand why remaining swamps and marshes at the edges of their fields, their subdivisions, their shopping malls, and their industrial parks need protection. They may even walk into such places with curiosity and wonder about the complex and beautiful workings of nature. Perhaps a newfound awareness of wetlands can inspire and nourish a vision of stewardship for these long-abused and misunderstood landscapes.

TWO

A Mosaic of Native Swamps, Bogs, and Marshes

Before we present to you the matters of fact, it is fit to offer to your view the Stage whereon they were acted, for Geography without History seemeth a carkasse without motion, so History without Geography wandereth as a Vagrant without a certaine habitation.

—John Smith [1]

With these words, Captain John Smith, in one of the earliest histories written about the land that would become the United States, explained the necessity of describing the incomparable landscape of the New World. Without presenting a literal grounding—a sense of the nature of the little-known landscape—to his English readers, Smith knew that his story would lack the force and authenticity it deserved. Over 370 years later, his words still ring true. Though as Americans we are no longer separated from this continent by a tempestuous ocean, an equally formidable gulf of time and change separates our familiar modern landscape from the one Smith found when he arrived in 1607. As such, a geographic survey of our nation's vast historic wetland estate is in order. Relying on the accounts of early European travelers and the insights of modern ecologists and anthropologists, we can begin to understand just what our country's native wetlands looked like, how they functioned, and how they were used. All told, scientists estimate that 221 million wetland acres (an area more than twice the size of California) once formed a vast life-support system for the continental United States. [2]

When considering North American topography, most people envision jutting mountains as the primary landmarks. But the low spaces lying in between form the wetland realm. Here rainwater and snowmelt collect in glacial depressions or in meandering rivers and sloughs. Where trees grow in the soaked soils, the wetlands are called swamps and bottomland forests.

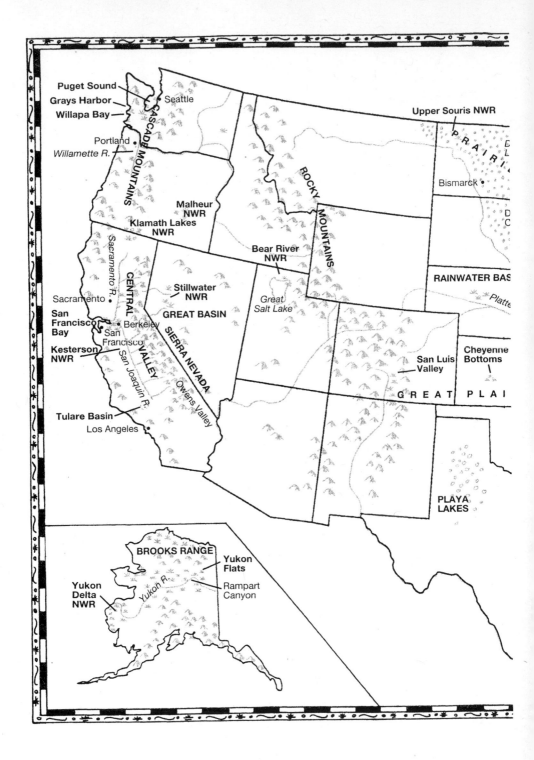

Puget Sound
Grays Harbor
Willapa Bay
• Seattle
CASCADE MOUNTAINS
Portland •
Willamette R.
ROCKY MOUNTAINS
Upper Souris NWR
PRAIRIE
Bismarck •
Malheur NWR
Klamath Lakes NWR
Bear River NWR
RAINWATER BAS
Sacramento R.
CENTRAL VALLEY
Stillwater NWR
GREAT BASIN
Great Salt Lake
Platte
Sacramento
San Francisco Bay
Berkeley
San Francisco
SIERRA NEVADA
Cheyenne Bottoms
Kesterson NWR
San Joaquin R.
San Luis Valley
Owens Valley
G R E A T   P L A I
Tulare Basin
Los Angeles •
PLAYA LAKES
BROOKS RANGE
Yukon Flats
Yukon Delta NWR
Yukon R.
Rampart Canyon

WETLANDS OF THE UNITED STATES
Locations of Sites Mentioned in Text

PEATLANDS

HOLES

Horicon Marsh

Fox R.

Des Moines

Chicago

Illinois R.

Kankakee R.

FORMER WET PRAIRIE
area of intensive tile drainage

Grafton

Wabash R.

St. Louis

Missouri R.

Ohio R.

site of former
Limberlost Swamp

site of former
Black Swamp

Geneva
Finger Lakes

New York City

Lake Erie
Marshes

Philadelphia

APPALACHIAN MOUNTAINS

COASTAL PLAIN

Sudbury R.

Charles R.
Duxbury
Green
Harbor
Sherwood Island

Boston

Hackensack
Meadows
Susquehanna R.
Tinicum Marsh
Maurice R.

Delaware Bay

Chesapeake Bay

Great Dismal Swamp
Currituck Sound
Phelps Lake
Albemarle-Pamlico
Peninsula
Mattamuskeet Lake

Cape Fear R.

Pee Dee R.
Edisto R.
Charleston
ACE Basin

Ogeechee R.
Sapelo Island
Altamaha R.

Okefenokee
Swamp

St. Augustine

St. Johns River

Mississippi R.

Lafayette

Baton Rouge

New Orleans

Atchafalaya
River Swamp

Galveston
Bay

sas NWR

es R.

Oklawaha R.

Green Swamp

Boca Ciega Bay

St. Petersburg

Caloosahatchee R.

Marco Island

Florida Bay

GULF OF MEXICO

Orlando

Kissimmee R.
St. Lucie Canal
Lake Okeechobee

Everglades

Miami

Paradise
Key

Where grasses and sedges dominate, we find interior marshes and potholes; and where wet acidic soils are present, we discover the shrubby heath vegetation of bogs. Eventually, the rivers flow to the sea carrying sediment to build tidal marshes. Despite the tremendous variety in appearance and range, all wetlands support plants specially adapted to life in water or in saturated anaerobic soils. From seaside to mountain pass, the key ingredient to wetlands has always been water.

Coastal Fringe and Eastern Swamps

Our survey begins with the Atlantic marshes, the first American wetlands encountered by Europeans. Like most colonists, Dutch settler Adriaen Van Der Donck found the extent and abundance of the golden marshes impressive. In 1656, he described the marshes fringing tidal flats at the mouth of the Hudson River: "There . . . are brooklands and fresh and salt meadows, some so extensive that the eye cannot oversee the same."[3] In the nearby Hackensack and Canarsie meadows, Native Americans derived a rich subsistence from the marshy landscape, growing maize in small plots, hunting birds, and catching fish at weirs and with nets woven from reeds.[4]

Along the north Atlantic, weighty glaciers had depressed the continent, submerging much of the coastal plain and leaving in its place a rocky shoreline subject to large tidal fluctuations. Along this rugged coast, wetlands sequestered mostly near river mouths and in small inlets, yet sizable marshes existed where sediment could accumulate. In 1524, French sailor Giovanni Verrazzano described the landscape of coastal Rhode Island as having treeless "champaigns" (meadows) seventy-five to ninety miles wide.[5] Nearly 20,000 acres of salt marsh lined embayments of the native Connecticut coast as well.[6] These northeastern marshes were vegetated largely with cordgrasses, well adapted to the rigors of saltwater life. The grasses have special root membranes that prevent most salt from entering and special glands to excrete any salt that passes through.[7] Forming a base of the food chain, the grasses eventually break down into tiny bits, called detritus, which feed small invertebrates that in turn feed small fish. Well suited to brackish waters of tidal creeks and marsh ponds, these small fish, including minnows and killifish, supplied food for larger fish, herons, kingfishers, and Algonquin Indians, who called them *mummichoa*.[8]

South of the Hudson's mouth, where glaciers had not depressed the land, more coastal plain remained exposed to the rise and ebb of the sea, creating larger tidal wetlands. Still the grandest marshes occurred in estuaries, where large rivers poured into shallow saltwater embayments, such as Chesapeake Bay. Nourished by fresh waters of Appalachian streams, hearty marsh grasses, sedges, and rushes clustered against the shores. Undulant aquatic grasses anchored to the bottom offered food and shelter for juvenile fish, including shad, bass, and herring, and a haven for rusty-headed canvasbacks and other ducks. The abundance of the native Chesapeake ecosystem was aptly described by Robert Beverly in 1702: "Both of fresh and salt water, of shellfish and others, no country can boast of more variety, greater plenty or of better." In addition to noting the great hunting potential of "the shores, marshy grounds, swamps and savannas," Beverly observed that "as in summer, the rivers and creeks are filled with fish, so in winter they are in many places covered with fowl." Overwhelmed by the wetlands' cornucopia of fish and ducks, he wrote, "The plenty of them is incredible."[9] Just to the south, Roanoke Island colonists had found Albemarle and Pamlico sounds to be similarly full of fish and fowl.[10]

South of the Chesapeake, the coastal plain widened and sloped more gently seaward, exposing more area to tidewater influence and making possible an even broader fringe of wetlands—up to fifty miles wide. Rivers flowing from the Appalachians carried alluvial sediment to the coast and deposited it on the shallow continental shelf, where marsh vegetation then took hold. Three-quarters of Atlantic tidal wetlands lay south of Maryland as part of this wide golden band. In some places, offshore barrier islands sheltered marshes from the rough surf.[11] Within the expansive marshes, upland islands called hammocks or "sea islands" supported luxuriant forests of bays, pines, and palms.

In addition to coastal marshes, there were many freshwater wetlands in eastern America. In the Southeast, moving inland and up rivers, salt marshes graded into brackish marshes, and then freshwater marshes, and eventually into bottomland swamp forests that towered along the slow-flowing coastal plain rivers. A magnificent feature of early America, the ancient forest swamps furnished habitat for birds, fish, and animals such as black bears, panthers, and wolves.[12]

On the broad, flat uplands between the large swampy rivers of the Carolina plain, another type of freshwater wetland dominated: pocosins. Named by the Algonquin peoples who lived and hunted in the region, pocosin literally meant "swamp on a hill," referring to the fact that pocosins were depressions in the uplands. Often underlain by peat, the pocosins were vegetated by acid-loving shrubs such as fetterbrush, waxmyrtle, and titi. In older, more established pocosins, pond pine, red bay, loblolly bay, and other evergreen trees reached above the shrub layer until fires once again created new clearings. The large lakes in the area, including Lake Drummond and Mattamuskeet, likely formed when raging peat fires burned out giant holes. In North Carolina alone, 2.5 million acres of pocosin wetlands existed, an area twice the size of Delaware.[13]

In swampy pockets from Florida north to New England, Atlantic white cedars stood in austere cathedral stands. Requiring dry soil and lots of light to germinate, these swamp trees generally grew in the aftermath of fires. Because native people routinely burned undergrowth and didn't suppress natural wildfires, white cedar forests flourished in precolonial America. Growing from fifty to eighty feet, lofty groves of single-age trees shaded the peaty lands below, leaving only filtered light to support a sparse understory. Some of the largest cedar stands grew in the Great Dismal Swamp, located on the border of present-day Virginia and North Carolina.[14]

Farther inland, different tree and shrub species dominated the freshwater wetlands of the glaciated Northeast. In New England swamps, red maples grew in thick clumps. When Indians burned forests to clear underbrush for better hunting, the wet swamps often resisted fire, leaving densely vegetated sanctuaries for deer and birds. Early travelers suggested that such swamps were common and extensive, "some twenty, some thirty miles" in compass, according to one. Red maples shared the seasonally soggy terrain with other water-tolerant species such as swamp white oak and black tupelo. Skunk cabbage, irises, and ferns decorated the lower stories of the swamps with their vibrant green.[15]

In interior upland valleys throughout the East, beavers created most of the wetlands. Building their dam lodges in small streams—as many as sixteen lodges per mile—beavers routinely flooded adjacent forests. As a result, many waterlogged trees died, but the forest canopy opened, allowing sunlight to warm the dammed-up water and nourish aquatic plants. Soon sedges and grasses grew along the edges of the pond. Eventually, after beavers abandoned their dam, enough organic debris and silt accumulated that marsh vegetation could colonize the center of the former pond, creating a wet meadow. With an estimated sixty to four hundred million beavers living in American streams before Europeans arrived, this dynamic process occurred in hundreds of thousands of locales, continually forming new wetlands in small valleys all across the country.[16]

Beyond providing habitat for the abundant plants, fish, birds, and animals that impressed European settlers, eastern wetlands were also the habitat of many Native Americans. Because the earliest European explorers introduced epidemic diseases that spread before them like wildfire across the continent, it is impossible to know just how many people inhabited the country before colonization.[17] One estimate suggests that 33,000 Indians lived in coastal Maryland and Virginia. Enormous midden heaps of empty oyster shells mounded around the Chesapeake remain their legacy and reveal their dependence on the wetland ecosystem. Farther south along the North Carolina coast, Verrazzano noted many settlements and fires in the 1520s, suggesting a sizable native population; historians have speculated that 7,000 people inhabited that swampy area.[18] Moreover, Algonquin languages had many words to refer to specific swamps, including *scuppernong* and *oquaphenoqua* (okefenokee), which has been translated as "land of trembling earth." All along the Atlantic, indigenous people took advantage of the varied environment for their subsistence. From the northern woodlands to the southern coastal marshes, Native Americans hunted, fished, and gathered but also farmed in small plots to supplement their food supplies. Cleared river floodplains provided fertile places to grow corn and squash. Archaeological evidence suggests that Indians grew corn even in protected clearings within heavily forested swamps.[19] Native people valued wetlands for the fish, fowl, and other food they supplied.

All told, wetlands of the Atlantic seaboard states, stretching from the glaciated Northeast south through Georgia, amounted to roughly 41.3 million acres (an area nearly eight times the size of New Jersey)—about 19 percent of the estimated native wetland estate of the continental United States.[20]

Florida's Wetland Eden

Underlain by a distinctive limestone bedrock, riddled with Swiss-cheese-like solution pockets, depressions, and sinkholes, and saturated with a high water table, Florida was wetland through and through. With roughly 20.3 million acres, the peninsula was more than half wetland—the highest density of swamps and marshes anywhere. Similar to the rest of the southeastern coastal plain, the vegetation of northern Florida wetlands graded from golden salt marshes into dense bottomland forests.

Jean Ribaut, a French Huguenot sailor who explored the wetland forests of Florida's St. Johns River in 1562, found the country to be the "fairest, frutefullest, and plesantest of all the worlde." He took note of both the abundant bottomland forest and the coastal wetlands. "And the sight of the faire medowes," he wrote, "is a pleasure not able to be expressed with tonge, full of herons, corleux, bitters, mallardes, egertes, woodkockes and all other kinde of smale birdes." Near the river's mouth, Ribaut found villages of the Timacua tribe and noted that the friendly natives took full advantage of the marshes' plentiful fish and fowl and also used marsh reeds to build their shelters. Ribaut was most amazed by the "great abundance of perlles, which . . . they toke out of oysters, wherof there is taken every [day] along the river side and amonges the reedes and in the marshes and in so mervelous aboundaunce as ys scant credeble."[21]

Farther to the south, yet another unique wetland formed at the peninsula's tip. With spring-fed flows that meandered down the Kissimmee River into shallow Lake Okeechobee, the Everglades began where the water overspilled the lake's south shore, spread out, and then slowly crept in a sheet, fifty miles wide and six inches deep. This sheet flow nourished vast sawgrass marshes, extending nearly to the Atlantic Coast and to a large baldcypress forest on the west—more than 2.3 million acres in all.[22] Warmed by its subtropical climate, the Everglades housed unusual fish, colorful wading birds, gentle key deer, and stealthy panthers, but this wetland realm was truly the dominion of the alligators.

Like dam-building beaver in more northern latitudes, alligators made their mark on the Everglades landscape by digging deep holes in marshes. When the water was high, alligators churned their long bodies like giant augurs to excavate the bottom. During dry periods, when water levels in the marsh dropped, fish gravitated to the gator holes, which then attracted flocks of hungry egrets, storks, and herons. While the holes served up easy meals for alligators, they also sustained other members of the biotic community through times of drought.[23]

Where freshwater met saltwater at Florida Bay, yet another distinct wetland ecosystem thrived. Thick mangroves grew on stilted roots, slowly colonizing the shallow waters. The roots sheltered oysters and young fish. Crocodiles also took advantage of the warm brackish environment. In the bay, aquatic grasses housed an array of fish and crustaceans, which fed countless wading birds. Like indigenous peoples in other regions, the native Calusas relied on the fish, shellfish, turtles, eels, bears, and deer of the Everglades wetlands. Archaeologists suspect that the Calusas, who depended on pine canoes to get around, dug a small canal to travel through the mangroves without having to brave the stormy Gulf of Mexico.[24]

The Great Hourglass of Potholes, Bogs, and Bottomlands

Outside of Florida, the most wetland-laden parts of the nation fell into an area shaped like a giant mid-continent hourglass. The Missouri and Ohio rivers outlined the top chamber, and the southern portion of the glass centered on the Mississippi River but fanned out to include over three hundred miles of coastal plain from the Neches River in Texas east to Florida.

North of the Missouri and Ohio rivers, glaciers scraped and scoured the land, leaving an assortment of depressions and ponds when they retreated.[25] The far western portion of this area was left densely pocked by millions of shallow bowls, each filled with snowmelt and rainwater and fringed with bulrushes, smartweeds, and wild rice. These prairie potholes dappled 6.9 million acres in the Dakotas alone, at least 5.7 million acres in Minnesota, and additional acreage in eastern Montana and northern Iowa—in total an area the size of Michigan.[26] This unique pothole landscape stretched far into the Canadian provinces of Manitoba, Saskatchewan, and Alberta.

The variety of shapes, sizes, depths, and vegetation made the potholes an ecological treasure. A teeming soup of invertebrate life, including worms, insect larvae, fairy shrimp, snails, tadpoles, and leeches, formed the base of the pothole food chain. Early each spring, enormous flocks of mallards, pintails, canvasbacks—fifteen duck species in all—from the four major migratory flyways converged in the marshy potholes to feast on these delicacies, to find nest sites, and to begin courtship rituals. Between 50 and 75 percent of the nation's waterfowl was reared in this wetland region.[27]

Just to the east of the prairie potholes, in northeastern Minnesota, the wetlands looked markedly different. From above, the landscape appeared flat but patterned, with ovoid islands of black spruce and elongated pools amid seas of heaths, laurels, and other shrubby vegetation. When glaciers receded here, the high water table of a giant glacial lake saturated the vegetation, creating an environment without the oxygen needed for decomposition. Instead of breaking down, the vegetation accumulated in layers of organic sludge to create waterlogged peat—the hallmark of bog wetlands. Covering 6 million acres (nearly the size of Vermont), these bogs of northeastern Minnesota remain the largest peatland complex in North America. Smaller bogs could also be found throughout the northern glaciated area, especially in Wisconsin, Michigan, and Maine.

The peat's high acidity made it difficult for all but the hardiest plant species to survive. Sphagnum moss, along with sedges, formed the foundation of a floating mat atop the wet peat, but other evergreen shrubs such as leatherleaf and sheep laurel flourished as well. In some places, small, acid- and cold-tolerant trees, such as black spruce and tamarack, punctuated the scrubby terrain with their stunted silhouettes. Several plants developed special adaptations to cope with the bogs' acidity and lack of nutrients. To obtain nitrogen, for example, pitcher plants attract insects, which they digest in a pool of water and enzymes created by their vase-shaped leaves.

Bogs were not the only wetlands in the glaciated North. Slow rivers meandering over the flat country also created extensive riparian marshes of bulrush, cattail, and wild rice. First Dakota and then Ojibwe Sioux inhabited the area that is now northern Minnesota. Both groups relied on wetland food plants, such as wild turnips and water-lily tubers. Locating the roots with their feet, native women often pulled the tubers in waist-deep water. Wild rice was also a staple. In late summer, Ojibwe gathered rice by arching the tops of the rice stalks and then knocking ripe grains into the bottom of their canoes with wooden rice sticks. In nearby bogs, the Sioux also harvested currants, cranberries, and blueberries. In addition to gathering the bounty of the bogs and marshes, native peoples hunted waterfowl, fish, and turtles. In winter months, Indians stalked game animals such as caribou, which grazed on the sedges and lichens of bogs, their large hooves carrying them safely over the undulant ground.[28] The Sioux also used wetland vegetation for medicinal purposes and for making baskets, mats, and canoes. According to nineteenth-century missionaries, both Dakota and Ojibwe peoples had several words to describe various wetland types, suggesting a precision of understanding based on close familiarity with the landscape. Both languages distinguished bogs from marshes and from swamps. The Indians even had distinct words for beavers of different ages and sexes and for different parts of beaver lodges and dams.[29]

In the southernmost portion of the upper chamber of the hourglass that defines the wetlands of the Midwest, tallgrass prairie spilled across most of the low-level land. Receding glaciers left their mark here as well, replacing ancient well-worn drainage patterns with ponds, sloughs, and marshes. An enormous wet prairie of sloughgrass, prairie cordgrass, and common reed spread across east central Illinois and also across the eastern two-thirds of Iowa. The wet prairie "grasses" grew to heights of eight or nine feet. One mid-nineteenth-century writer found the grass "higher than his head" as he rode through on horseback.[30] Not only were marsh grasses tall, they were vast. A French traveler canoeing the upper reaches of the Kankakee River

Rice Gatherers, BY SETH EASTMAN, 1867.
Native Americans relied on the abundance of wetlands for their subsistence. In the wetland-rich area of present-day Minnesota, Ojibwe Sioux collected wild rice using wooden paddles to knock the grains into the bottom of their canoes. (Architect of the Capitol)

in 1683 wrote about the extent of the wetlands of northern Illinois. "As far as the eye could reach nothing was to be seen but marshes full of flags [irises] and alders."[31] Wetlands along the Kankakee included both marshes and swamp forests, which the Pottowatomies used for winter hunting and then trapping once the fur trade began. In northwest Ohio, the Black Swamp, with its varied forest of maple, ash, elm, and cottonwood, girded the Maumee River, which then poured into Lake Erie, forming extensive freshwater marshes. French explorer Etienne Brulé noted in 1615 that marshes spread over one hundred miles from present-day Vermilion, Ohio, to the mouth of the Detroit River.[32] In the springtime, rain and floodwater inundated the marshes, attracting large flocks of waterfowl.

With all of its potholes, bogs, marshes, and floodplain swamps, the glaciated upper portion of the grand hourglass contained roughly 72 million acres of wetlands, an area the size of Arizona, or 33 percent of continental America's native wetland landscape.[33]

Where the wetland hourglass funneled to its stricture, the enormous

Ohio, Mississippi, and Missouri rivers joined, carrying billions of gallons of meltwater from mountains as distant as Montana and New York. From this juncture southward across the coastal plain, fluvial processes—rather than glaciation—formed the wetlandscape. The Mississippi, as well as other coastal plain rivers, flooded each spring, depositing sediments on natural levees along the shores. At the height of flooding, water overspilled the natural levees and submerged the wetlands that lay behind. Nurtured by the warm, humid climate and the plentiful nutrient-rich water, bottomland forests grew large and luxuriant. Some sloughs remained inundated year round, while others dried up for several months. Such variation in water regime enabled many different plants and animals to thrive in the forests. Some areas supported as many as forty different species of wetland trees. Bottomland-forested wetlands extended for nearly 24 million acres (nearly the size of Virginia) in the native Mississippi alluvial plain alone.[34] Viewed from above, the immense jungly treetops would have stretched from horizon to horizon—120 miles at the floodplain's widest point. As far north as Illinois's Cache River, these southern bottomland forests flourished.

In the wettest areas, water tupelo and American baldcypress prevailed. Resembling flounced velvet skirts, their fluted moss-covered trunks grew to twelve feet in diameter. The massive cypress trunks supported crowns of small horizontal branches draped with Spanish moss. Ivory-billed woodpeckers drilled into the bark of the oldest trees to find their food, the larvae of wood-boring beetles. Living for up to two thousand years, some cypress became giants.[35] Baldcypress also sent up "knees" or aerial roots near their trunks. In areas where floodwaters were deep, the tall knees helped to stabilize parent trees.

Farther from the river, where floodwaters persisted for only one-third of the year, different wetland trees lived, including overcup oak, water oak, and water hickory. In even drier areas, one could find swamp chestnut oak and the star-leafed sweetgum. Forest fires occasionally burned these seasonal wetlands, stimulating the vigorous growth of new cane shoots, which formed dense understories known as canebrakes. Native Americans of the bottomlands used the tough, bamboolike cane stalks for making spears, knives, baskets, bedding, and shelters. Cane grew more than an inch in diameter and reached thirty feet in height.[36]

Throughout their range, the bottomland forests produced enormous crops of tupelo fruits and acorns, catering an essential banquet for animals and wintering waterfowl. Birds alone, including wild turkeys and colorfully plumed wood ducks, likely consumed 10 percent of the acorn harvest. Beyond the fruits borne by wetland trees, forests dropped up to ten tons per acre of dried plant material, thus providing an endless source of nutrition to aquatic invertebrates, which in turn supplied food for the more than fifty species of fish that lived in the river-bottom swamps for at least part of their life cycle.[37] According to early explorers, three-hundred-pound catfish and sturgeon—nourished by rich bottomland waters—swam the Mississippi. Beavers, otters, and muskrats were active. In other southern rivers, fish, fowl, and small mammals became meals for larger predatory mammals, such as black bears, cougars, and red wolves, that roamed in the primeval forests.[38]

The abundant bottomland-forest habitat also supported large indigenous populations. Residing on natural levees, Chitamachas Indians traveled in dugout canoes of cypress or cottonwood and subsisted on plentiful fish and game in the Atchafalaya Basin.[39] In some places, members of the 1539 de Soto expedition found catwalks made from crossbeams attached to the trunks of trees. These walks made it easier to get around in the wet-floored forests. The resources of the swamps not only provided sustenance but inspired vital aspects of tribal culture. The Bayougoula tribe, for example, performed a special alligator dance and venerated this reptile as their totem. The nearby Houma chose the red crayfish as theirs.[40]

Beyond the Mississippi River floodplain, similar bottomland swamp forests extended up to two hundred miles inland in paralleling river valleys all around the gulf from Texas's Neches River east to Florida's Caloosahatchee.[41] Depending on local climate, different associations of wetland trees dominated, but baldcypress and water tupelo were most common.

Moving downstream toward the gulf, the bottomland forests graded into freshwater marshes composed of rushes, sedges, and grasses. Then, where fresh river waters mixed with salt, a band of brackish-tolerant species grew, including needle rush and three-cornered grass.[42] Atakapa peoples relied on this rich mixing zone to gather mussels, clams, and oysters and to catch fish and crayfish. They also hunted ducks, mink, and otters.[43] Near the delta of the capricious Mississippi, brackish marshes graded into salt marshes, in places forming a one-hundred-mile-wide band.[44] In what would become the state of Louisiana alone, there were 4.5 million acres of coastal marsh built from Mississippi River sediment (for reference, the state of New Jersey is roughly 5 million acres).[45]

All around the gulf, the sheltered shoreline harbored a wide swath of marsh. As along the Atlantic, salt-tolerant species, such as cordgrasses and salt grasses grew in marshes nearest the sea. This broad band thinned as one traveled westward, but significant marshes formed at Galveston Bay, and more marshes fringed the salty lagoons behind the barrier islands of Texas. Wetlands of the lower Mississippi and gulf states comprised roughly 78 million acres and 35 percent of estimated native wetlands in the continental United States.[46]

Western Wetlands: Playa Lakes, Snowmelt Sinks, and River Bottoms

To the west of the interior hourglass of lowlands lie arid plains sloping up to the foothills of the Rocky Mountains. Because there were far fewer wetlands in this rain shadow of the Rockies than in other regions, each one was all the more critical for the people, animals, and birds living nearby. Wetlands were primarily confined to the floodplains of rivers that meandered across the plains. In some places broad-leafed cottonwoods and willows grew into thick borders of green along river corridors. In other locales, sedges and rich grasses took hold. For example, the braided channels of the Platte River filled and spilled over into wet meadows and sloughs in the springtime. Because frequent prairie fires and flooding prevented trees from growing, riparian grasslands flourished and attracted migrating birds that found food in the lush meadows and security on the cobble-bar islands. Thousands of elegant sandhill and whooping cranes with their claret-red caps stopped to feed and rest in these prairie river bottoms.[47]

Sometimes beavers quickened the establishment of riverside marshes. As Lewis and Clark traveled up the Missouri River in the spring of 1805, they noted beavers "in every bend." The beavers, Lewis observed, would dam up "the small channels of the river between the islands and compell the river . . . to make other channels." If not flooded out by big spring freshets, these dammed sloughs eventually became wet meadows.[48]

In addition to the riparian meadows and forests, a long string of glimmering wetlands just west of the one hundredth meridian acted as a series of way stations along a route used by Central Flyway waterfowl as they migrated to and from the prairie potholes. In the southern plains, especially in the Texas panhandle, rainwater filled tens of thousands of small marsh-edged playa lakes. Although they resemble prairie potholes, the playas have no glacial heritage. Pioneers who saw buffalo wallowing in the depressions long thought that the massive animals created the lakes, but scientists believe that the flat-bottomed lakes were excavated by intense high-plains winds.[49] North of the playas in western Kansas, a 41,000-acre marsh now known as Cheyenne Bottoms accommodated migrating swans, cranes, geese, and pelicans.[50] In the Rainwater Basin of northwestern Nebraska, depressions underlain by impervious soil collected precipitation, thus supporting nearly 94,000 acres of freshwater marsh—another verdant oasis where birds, animals, and people found food and water in otherwise arid terrain.[51]

West of the Great Plains within the majestic Rockies, wetlands spread in large valleys, such as the San Luis, where heavy snowmelt saturated the aquifer and raised the water table enough to support healthy freshwater marshes. Beavers also created countless small wetlands by damming mountain streams.

Between the Rockies and the Sierra in the isolated valleys of the Great Basin, marshes abounded in terminal sinks where snowmelt pooled in late spring. Sizable marshes formed where rivers entered Pyramid Lake, the Great Salt Lake, and also in the Carson Sink. Fed by the Carson River, which flows eastward from the Sierra Nevada, Carson Sink marshes were the home of Northern Paiute ancestors, known as the Toidikadi, or cattail-eaters. Cattails and bulrushes growing in the marsh furnished not only their food but also the raw materials needed to build shelters, boats, and even duck decoys. Relying on the marsh for their subsistence in an otherwise difficult desert environment for thousands of years, these people caught fish, gathered mollusks, and hunted ducks, muskrats, and other animals drawn to the wetland.[52] Similar desert marshes emerged at the base of the eastern slope of the southern Sierra Nevada in the Mono Lake Basin and in the Owens Valley.

West of the Sierra crest, the enormous Central Valley—sprawling for a sixty-mile width between the Sierra and the Pacific Coastal Range—brimmed with wetlands. In this moister clime, clouds coalesced over the Pacific Ocean and then collided with the massive Sierra, cooling and dropping an immense snowpack in the mountains. In the springtime, a dozen rivers of snowmelt coursed down into the broad, meandering Sacramento and San Joaquin rivers, which routinely overspilled their banks and flooded the Central Valley. This annual flooding drenched the soil and nourished riparian vegetation.[53] In the 1770s, a Spanish militia captain found the San Joaquin Valley choked with "a dense growth of nettles, wormwood, grapevines, willows, cottonwoods, oak, ash, bay laurel, and the ever present tules."[54] The word *tule* (pronounced toó lee), derived from an Aztec term, was brought from Mesoamerica by Spaniards, who had been unfamiliar with the ubiquitous marsh sedge.[55] In places the captain estimated that tule marshes extended twenty miles from the river, making travel impossible.[56] In fact, Central Valley wetlands encompassed 4 million acres, nearly one-third of the valley's total area.[57] The water persisted for much of the year, saturating aquifers and supporting rich wetland vegetation before drying up. These extensive wetlands provided winter habitat for the estimated thirty-five million birds that flew in the Pacific Flyway.[58] The riparian wetland landscape also hosted large herds of deer and tule elk, and tens of thousands of beavers and otters. Even grizzly bears came to the Central Valley wetlands to feast on the abundant salmon and other fish.[59]

In the southern part of the Central Valley, the Kings River, a stream lined with cottonwoods, willows, sycamores, and thick underbrush, fed the isolated Tulare Basin. Here the water spread into sloughs and a shallow lake surrounded by dense tule marshes. Thousands of tule elk grazed in these marshes, while geese, curlews, and wading birds gathered as well. Together with Kern Lake, Buena Vista Lake, and the surrounding marshlands, Tulare Basin constituted one of the largest single blocks of wetland in native California.[60] Throughout the valley, plentiful resources supported large populations of indigenous Californians who lived in villages along the river for part of each year. From his vantage point atop the Coastal Range Mountains in the winter of 1804, one Spanish missionary counted two dozen villages within one eyeful along the San Joaquin River.[61] When trapper Jedidiah Smith camped along the San Joaquin in March of 1828, he wrote in his journal that he "was obliged to cross many slous of the River that were verry miry and passed great numbers of indians who were engaged in digging Roots."[62] The Tulare Basin had one of the highest regional population densities anywhere in aboriginal North America. Relying on the vast wetlands for subsistence, Yokut people gathered iris bulb, tule root, cattails, and salt grass for food. In the spring and fall, they hunted waterfowl that stopped over in the marshes. The Yokuts also used wetland plants to make their homes: willow pole structures covered with mats of tules.[63]

Along the precipitous Pacific coastline, the edge of the continent dropped steeply into the sea, preventing the accumulation of sediment necessary for marsh building. However, large marshes did exist in protected bays and inlets, most notably in the San Francisco Bay, where the enormous Sacramento and San Joaquin rivers flowed together with smaller rivers of the Coast Range to create an immense joint delta—a maze of some seven hundred miles of sloughs flowing through seas of bulrushes and then grading into tidal salt marshes of spartina and eelgrasses—over 1 million acres in all. In this mixing zone, many types of animals, crabs, clams, snails, waterbirds, and 120 species of fish flourished.[64] Fifty different indigenous tribes made their livelihoods in this region, hunting and fishing in the marshes of San Francisco Bay. Early Euroamerican travelers to the delta claimed that salmon runs were thick enough to walk on.[65] Even in the mid nineteenth century a traveler riding a steamboat through the delta reported being "greatly annoyed, by the almost deafening, tumultuous and confused noises, of the innumerable flocks, of geese and ducks, which were continually flying to and fro, and at times blackening the very heavens with their increasing numbers, and making the aerial region ring, with their tumultuous croaking and vehement squaking."[66]

Other significant estuaries along the California coast included Mission Bay in southern California, and Tomales and Humboldt bays in northern California.

Adjoining misty rain forests of the Northwest, tidal marshes formed near the mouth of the Columbia River, in Coos Bay, Willapa Bay, Grays Harbor, and Puget Sound. In the interior Northwest, snowmelt from the volcanic Cascades Mountains ponded in valleys to the west, creating extensive freshwater marshes. A variety of sedges, grasses, and shrubs blanketed lowlands in the Willamette Valley and east of Puget Sound. These coastal and inland wetlands hosted Pacific Flyway waterfowl and vigorous fish populations, which native northwesterners relied on for their subsistence.

Farther to the north and west, yet another distinct wetland region existed in Alaska, where 175 million acres (an area larger than Texas), roughly 43 percent of the enormous, present-day state, was wetland. In interior and northern Alaska, permanently frozen soil underlay most of the land. Each summer, rainwater and the melted-out surface layer of soil pooled atop the frozen "permafrost" to make countless wet depressions in all lowlands. In many areas of central Alaska, the vegetation was not much different from the bog vegetation of northern Minnesota. Spindly black spruce occupied the driest areas, while sedges and scrub alder thickets dominated the wetter areas. Grizzlies found millions of cranberries and blueberries to sate their ursine hunger. In the tundra region north of the Brooks Range, grasses, sedges, moss, and lichen carpeted the permafrosted Arctic Coastal Plain, where caribou roamed. In addition to permafrost-melt wetlands, enormous rivers like the Yukon meandered across flat, wide floodplains, leaving many wetland sloughs and abandoned channels. The Yukon and Kuskokwim rivers both formed giant estuary complexes on the west coast of Alaska, which served as breeding grounds for Pacific Flyway waterfowl. Even the distant wetlands of the Yukon have long been connected by flyway to wetlands in the lower forty-eight.[67]

From the resilient salt marshes of the Atlantic to the potholes of the plains, from the fertile Mississippi bottomlands to the acidic northern bogs, wetlands were an important feature of the presettlement landscape. Covering 11 percent of the forty-eight contiguous states, native wetlands made a fundamental network of pools and sponges tempering the flow of water across the continent. Whether influenced by tides, rivers, or glaciation, these terrains supported a variety of distinctive vegetation adapted to local hydric conditions. In many cases, decaying material from wetland plants formed the fundament of food chains that sustained whole communities of living creatures. These rich landscapes provided vital habitat for fish, birds, animals, and Indians. While the wetness of these lands made them a marvel of biological wealth, that very same quality would in due time provoke disdain and misunderstanding from European colonists, who brought a different view of wetlands to America.

THREE

A Nation Founded on Wetlands

> This *Miry slow,* is such a place as cannot be mended: It is the descent whither the scum and filth that attends conviction for sin doth continually run, and therefore it is called the *Slow of Dispond.* . . .
>
> —John Bunyan, *The Pilgrim's Progress*[1]

When Reverend William Blaxton set up his farm on the Shawmut Peninsula in 1625, he did not intend to establish a colony. He had just left an unsuccessful settlement to the south and was content to find a homesite with a reliable spring on the narrow, knobby peninsula. The grassy hills of the Shawmut were substantial; the tallest reached 138 feet. He built his modest dwelling on a hillside and planted orchards and vegetable gardens nearby. From atop the hill, later known as Beacon, the Reverend enjoyed quite a view and could see anyone approaching from miles around. The peninsula jutted like a fist from its narrow connection to the mainland out into the blue waters of Massachusetts Bay. At high tide, this slender strip was often covered by sea water. To the north, he could see where the Charles River flowed into the salty bay. Golden tidal marshes stretched north and south along the mainland and nestled in the many inlets and coves of the peninsula's shoreline as well. In these extensive wetlands, Blaxton fished and hunted for plentiful game. In summertime, a cool ocean breeze kept mosquitoes at bay. The small, quiet farm at the continent's edge was a suitable home for this thoughtful, hard-working man.[2]

But Blaxton's pastoral refuge changed abruptly when he was joined in 1630 by the Puritan colonists of the Massachusetts Bay Company. Led by Governor John Winthrop, the Puritans had zealously planned a utopian settlement grounded in common spiritual beliefs and obedience to God. During their transatlantic passage aboard the ship *Arabella,* Winthrop explained to his fellow colonists that their new community should "be as a city upon a hill," a place above the squalor and vice they had left behind in

England. With this image, Winthrop immediately projected a moral landscape onto the physical landscape of the New World. Before they even set foot in America, the Puritan colonists understood the topographic tension between pious and pure hilltops and the dark, dismal lowlands. Negative impressions of the malarial fens and marshes of their motherland reinforced their belief. Consequently, the Puritans chose to settle, quite literally, upon a hill on Shawmut Peninsula. They soon proclaimed their settlement the town of "Boston."[3]

Even though indigenous Americans had long used the land, disease had decimated them fifteen years prior, so few Indians inhabited the coast when the Puritans arrived. The land's emptiness and wildness helped the Puritans to justify converting it to patterns of European ownership and use. Unlike the Indians, who had used the land in common for subsistence, Puritans and other European colonists sought to go beyond what they regarded as bare-bones existence by gleaning products from the land to sell in the free-market economic system brought with them from Europe. Owning land would be the cornerstone of economic opportunity and prosperity, and successful commercial ventures were integral to the larger moral project of civilizing the wilds of North America.[4]

To European settlers, the coastal marsh landscape appeared pastoral and less threatening than dense forests. The Puritans realized right away that the hearty cordgrasses would provide indispensable forage for their livestock and thatch for the roofs of their humble cottages. The marshes' abundant heath hens and waterfowl also supplied staple food sources.[5] The industrious settlers made full use of the marshes in their efforts to create homes and communities in Massachusetts.

Colonists put salt marshes to good use in other coastal settlements as well. Large rivers that made the best harbors also deposited silt near their mouths, providing the substrate necessary for marsh growth. With their extensive Low Country draining and diking experience, the Dutch founded New Amsterdam in a marshy area at the mouth of the Hudson.[6] English colonists built substantial parts of Baltimore, Philadelphia, and Charleston on marshland as well. In villages between the large seaports, such as the ones scattered around Delaware Bay, colonists relied on wetlands more directly, subsisting on cattle grazed in the salt marshes and fish caught nearby.[7] Reports of the high forage quality of cordgrass were common throughout the colonies. In the 1600s, titles and deeds to land on Long Island typically boasted of "meadows, marshes, hunting, fowling," and "hawking" as valuable attributes of properties changing hands. Towns that owned salt marshes routinely leased haying rights by auction to local farmers.[8] In the Chesapeake Bay region, most marshy shoreline was parceled out for settlement by 1669. Colonists depended heavily on the natural resources of marshes for their sustenance, eating a variety of seafood, turtles, waterfowl, and small mammals that inhabited the wet-lands.[9] Although English colonists knew about the unhealthy reputation of the marshes and fens in England, they found American marshes to be different. Captain John Smith assured readers that he had not seen "large Fenny unwholsome Marshes," and that the marshes and swamps in the colonies were "more profitable than hurtfull." Medical historians agree that malaria was not present in America until Europeans imported it.[10]

Colonists soon discovered the values of freshwater marshes located along rivers as well. As early as the 1630s, along the Sudbury and Concord rivers of Massachusetts, local farmers harvested the meadow hay to feed their livestock. Although the fertility of upland fields was rapidly depleted, marshes were continually replenished by spring freshets that carried rich sediment. Farmers transferred this renewed nourishment from the marshes to the fields in the form of manure. As one farmer explained, the Concord River wet meadows "required no labor but that of reaping the harvest, no fencing, no fertilizing, but . . . on the contrary, they filled our cow-yards and barn-cellars with the best of fertilizers for our uplands."[11] Nearly every farmer owned or leased a strip-shaped lot in the meadows from which they mowed hay. Freshwater meadows were critically important for agriculture throughout the Northeast. When a settlement west of the Connecticut River at Hadley, Massachusetts, petitioned to form a new and separate town, for example, Hadley argued against the separation, contending that the tract west of the river did "not afford *boggy meadow or such like,* that men *can live upon,* but their subsistence must be from their home lots."[12] People considered it undesirable and unsafe to start a community where there were not adequate marshlands.

Though Native Americans and early colonists recognized natural marshes as good habitat, new concerns overshadowed the traditional subsistence value of marshes as interest in commercial endeavors grew. On the tiny Boston peninsula, marshes hindered development. Only 1,185 acres of dry land were available for new businesses, shops, and residences, but 485 acres of salt marsh and 1,570 acres of mudflats and shallow water lay vacant around the booming metropolis. The religious zeal of the Puritan settlers was superseded only by the commercial zeal of a thriving, secular, merchant class. By 1640, Boston's population had reached twelve hundred, and people needed more elbow room, so the industrious Yankee colonists began to see the marshy inlets and irregularities of the shoreline as potential space.[13] If only they could create new land out of the marshes, they could accommodate growing businesses and demand for housing. As early as 1641, the town granted the rights to Bendeels Cove to a group of entrepreneurs for the purpose of building wharves and warehouses to improve ship commerce. In 1643, the town granted another group of businessmen a cove and its adjoining marshes on the condition that they dam the cove to create a millpond and erect gristmills. Little by little, citizens traded pockets of natural salt marsh for other services needed in the town. By 1645, Bostonians had manipulated all the natural marshes that had initially existed within their small city's boundaries.[14] Salt marshes in other growing cities were similarly filled to make land or excavated to enlarge harbors.

By 1700, Boston's population had surpassed seven thousand people. Pressures of growth inspired entrepreneurs to build still more land from the marshes.[15] Some began to look at the local hills as a source for fill. In 1758, one Bostonian turned a parcel of land he owned on the side of Beacon Hill into a gravel pit. By 1764, laborers had removed so much gravel that the landmark feature was severely disfigured.[16] Yet the project of creating new land for development by filling the marshes remained paramount.

By 1747, the colony's population had increased so much that there was too little salt hay to feed everyone's livestock. One Bostonian explained that early farmers who settled by marshes had "found so much mowing Ground more than thay had Occasion for, that they Improved only such Parts as were best and nearest at hand, and let the Rest lie, and when by the increase of People, they wanted more, they made use of what had been before Neglected, without any tho't or care to provide more; and Meadows not being easily or speedily bro't too, many are drove to great Straits."[17] Because the marshes seemed inexhaustible, colonists took them for granted. Already conflicts between the natural values of wetlands and their apparent hindrance of development opportunities arose.

Yet the opinion of the merchant class prevailed. Even farmers closest to cities began to recognize that their profits could be greater if they grew crops instead of salt hay. Because it was difficult to drain lands as an individual landowner, farmers in the Northeast formed meadow companies to drain wetlands collectively. Such arrangements were legally sanctioned for the first time in 1788, when the New Jersey legislature enacted its statewide drainage law. This allowed groups of landowners to elect officers to manage and oversee drainage projects with funds collected from company members. Such laws became common.[18] As marshlands closest to urban centers were drained and converted to truck farms or filled for commercial development, still-needed salt hay was produced in more distant marshes and then transported on flat-bottomed gondolas to markets in Boston and New York. Farther away from big cities, farmers disliked the new idea of marsh drainage, and so the practice was uncommon. In Maine, for example, marsh lots were already divided into parcels of less than 5 acres each for haying. To effectively dike and drain, a single landowner would have to buy and consolidate the small lots, or farmers would have to create cooperative drainage associations. These seemingly newfangled options were less feasible in the hinterlands, where people depended more directly on their own land and valued tradition and self-reliance highly.[19]

Yet the marshes surrounding Boston and New York were readily transformed as those cities grew and as people demanded more space and food. This pattern of development would repeat itself again and again as coastal towns everywhere grew. Although marshes were initially recognized as valuable resources in colonial America, their traditional importance declined when the commercial economy began to thrive. People—especially merchants—came to regard marshes as a hindrance to prosperity. Within the framework of the new market economy, marshes were devalued. But swamps were another story.

Evil Swamps

While the abundant grasses and sedges of coastal and riparian marshes presented colonists with familiar pastoral landscapes, the swamps they found in the interior had an entangled, foreboding appearance. When Puritans arrived, they knew little about the physical swamp landscape. In fact, English-speaking settlers had no ready-made word for these places because the forested wetlands of England had long been eliminated. "Swamp" and sometimes "dismal" became the terms settlers used to describe the wooded wetlands.[20] Although the colonists were unfamiliar with the physical nature of swamps, they did know that swamps violated their norms of orderliness and presented an incomprehensible, chaotic landscape—in contrast with the familiar English countryside and the pastoral landscape that they sought to re-create in New England. Because there was so much land available, colonists could initially avoid settling near swamps. But, ultimately, the need for firewood and lumber drew Puritans farther up rivers and into forests where swamps abounded in the glaciated landscape. Because they couldn't see beyond the twisted and tangled branches and had difficulty traveling in the muck, colonists usually chose to go around or turn back. But the qualities of swamps that repelled the Puritans also fired their fearful imaginations, so they brought back stories and warnings to support their strongly moralistic and dualistic worldview. Swamps were clearly sinister.

William Bradford, governor of the Plymouth colony, expressed this common impression of swamps when he related a story about Native Americans. The Indians, he explained, "got all the Powachs [medicine men] of the country, for three days together in a horrid and devilish manner, to curse and execrate them with their conjurations, which assembly and service they held in a dark and dismal swamp."[21] Because Puritans associated Indians with the evil, sinful, and fearful, they attributed Indians' familiarity with swamps as a sign that the landscape itself was evil as well.[22]

The colonists' perceptions of swamps as wicked places grew stronger as hostilities between increasing numbers of settlers and remaining indigenous peoples escalated during the late 1600s. With colonists encroaching further upon favorite Indian hunting and camping grounds, sporadic conflicts intensified. Eventually, tensions exploded into a war between the colonists and the Narragansett, Wampanoag, Pocasset, and Nipmuck tribes. In response to Indian raids during the winter of 1675, colonists organized and pursued tribal leader King Philip and his warriors to an Indian village nestled in a frozen swamp near present-day Kingston, Rhode Island. Then colonists set flames to the place. By one estimate, three hundred warriors and over three hundred women and children were killed in the truculent massacre, known as the Great Swamp Fight. About eighty Englishmen perished in the campaign as well.

King Philip's War continued for more than a year, pushing the tenuous colonies to the verge of ruin. More than half the towns in New England suffered substantial damage: one out of sixteen men of military age was killed; many women and children were captured or killed; and with so many hands drawn away from fishing and farming, the economy collapsed.[23] In this context, the terrifying story of pursuing Indians into a swamp became material for contemporary cultural legend because it resonated in the psyches of the Puritan colonists, who already feared the Indians and wild lands that surrounded their settlements. Stories of the Great Swamp Fight and of other frightening battles in Pocasset and Hopewell swamps were recounted numerous times in Puritan New England and always with an emphasis on the dreadful features of the wet landscape.

In his interpretation of one swamp battle, Boston preacher Increase Mather saw nature colluding against the colonists. The Indians fled into the swamp, withholding from battle, he explained, until "they should have the leaves of trees and swamps to befriend them." Once in the swamp, Indians had great advantage because they were "so light of foot that they [could] run away . . . through inaccessible Boggs . . . and thickets."[24] Most terrifying of all, in the swamp confused soldiers could not discern between fellow Englishmen and Indians and so mistakenly killed their compatriots. Mather interpreted the war as both a test of the colonists' virtue and as divine punishment for New England's backsliding from its intended piety.[25] He was not alone in associating Indians and swamps with evil.

Boston merchant Nathaniel Saltonstall sent a letter to a friend in London emphasizing the wetland terrain as a dominant aspect of the war. "This Pocassit Swamp is judged about 7 or 8 miles long, and so full of Bushes and Trees," he wrote, "that a parcel of Indians may be within the Length of a Pike of a Man, and he cannot discover them; and besides, this as well as all other Swamps, is so soft Ground that an Englishman can neither go nor stand thereon, and yet these bloody Savages will run along over it, holding their guns and shooting too."[26] Saltonstall's description focused on the terror of not being able to see or travel easily in swamps while being stalked by those who could see and run agilely. From his perspective, the Indians seemed to have a mysterious connection with the swamp landscape. Roger Williams even suggested that the Indians did not fear the colonists because they anticipated assistance from Satan when they fled into swamps. Everything that the colonists experienced and learned confirmed their belief that the swamp landscape was dangerous and wicked.[27]

In his extremely popular book, *The Pilgrim's Progress,* published in 1678, John Bunyan seized upon the pervasive imagery of swamps as sinful places in recounting the allegorical story of Christian, a man searching for true salvation. As Christian tries to run from the city of Destruction, he falls into the "Slow [slough] of Dispond"—a mucky obstacle on his path to redemption. The "miry slow" not only presents a physical hindrance but metaphorically embodies the spiritual impediments of doubt and fear as well.[28]

The common perception of swamps as sinful also became a motif in the popular captivity narratives, which enjoyed a large circulation for centuries.[29]

In these gripping narratives, colonists—mostly women—recounted their horrific experiences of being captured by Indians. As part of her story, Mrs. Sarah Gerish described being taken "through horrid Swamps," where she had to climb over enormous fallen trees. Another woman and her eight children were surprised by Indians in a swamp and then enslaved.[30] After her capture in 1675, Mary Rowlandson wrote about being taken into a "vast and desolate wilderness," filled with numerous swamps. She described one swamp where she camped with Indians as "a deep Dungeon."[31] For the earliest Puritan colonists, who strove to bring order to wild nature as part of their providential mission, swamps symbolized the ultimate chaos to tame, the ultimate evil to right—both spiritually and physically.[32]

A similar suite of beliefs concerning swamps developed in English settlements in the South, where Puritan ideology was absent, but where numerous coastal plain swamps presented greater challenges. In 1728, Colonel William Byrd II set out to survey the Virginia–North Carolina state line, which passed straight though the Great Dismal Swamp. Surveyors could travel only short distances each day, taking ten days to progress fifteen miles through the thick baldcypress, gum, pine, canes, and briars. While Byrd praised the extensive stands of timber, he was less pleased with the general character of the landscape. "The foul damps ascend without ceasing, corrupt the Air, and render it unfit for Respiration," he observed.[33] Byrd labeled the swamp "dismal," a word derived from Dismus, the name of the thief crucified with Jesus; for Christians, "dismal" readily signified an alliance with Satan.[34]

Although associations with evil discouraged colonists from straying into swamps, they nonetheless took advantage of swamp resources. From the outset of settlement, a European taste for beaver hats had fueled the fur trade. English colonists, "being not patient to lay a long siege" in wetlands, avoided hunting for beavers themselves but rather relied on Indians, who accepted "trifles" in exchange for the pelts.[35] In New England nearly every stream was occupied by beavers before Europeans arrived, but extensive hunting for the fur trade began as early as the 1620s, when more than ten thousand beaver were killed in Connecticut and Massachusetts. From 1630 to 1640, about eighty thousand beaver a year were taken from the Hudson River and western New York, and demand increased when King Charles II in 1638 decreed the use of beaver pelts mandatory in hat making.[36] Beavers' low rate of reproduction and long parenting cycle made them particularly susceptible to overhunting. Owing to the mild southern winters, pelts from that region were less thick and initially less sought after. But southern colonists traded with Indians who either traveled farther west and north or traded with other Indians for thicker beaver pelts. Between 1699 and 1714, the Virginia colony exported an average of two thousand pelts per year. By the early 1700s, the practice of using steel traps scented with musky castoreum extract that attracted the animals grew widespread and ultimately decimated beavers. Without even stepping foot into wetlands created by beavers, the colonists with their beaver-fur market altered the natural processes of wetland ecosystems throughout the interior. Lacking beavers and their dams, the unleashed streams flowed faster and cut deeper, increasing erosion and flood damages to communities developing on the floodplains.[37]

The need for timber and the desire for commercial profit eventually compelled colonists to overcome their swamp repulsion and to consider the economic potential of these wetlands. While cultural disdain delayed development in some areas, the same scorn eventually fueled an unrestrained transformation of the landscape. Though profits were undoubtedly the primary motivation for logging and draining swamps, most colonists held beliefs about swamps similar to those of the Puritans. Taming chaotic American wetlands into a physically ordered landscape was not only a religious obligation but a fundamental part of the colonists' worldview. The swamp landscape became at once an opportunity for spiritual salvation, public service, and commercial success.[38]

Redeeming the Southern Swamps

While northern economies focused on the commerce afforded by excellent harbors, southern economies capitalized on the agriculture made possible by the region's mild climate. Because the southern coastal plain had so many wetlands, agriculture in that region required extensive drainage. Initially, farmers built their plantations in upland areas, but many recognized that the rich soils of the wetlandscape would be an asset for growing water-loving rice. After a series of unsuccessful attempts, intensive production finally began when South Carolina planters imported a suitable variety of rice from Madagascar in the 1690s. As the legend goes, when a storm compelled a Madagascan ship bound north to land in Charleston, planter Landgrave Smith asked the ship's captain if he could have some rice to try growing in the low areas of his plantation. The captain obliged, procuring a small bag from the ship's cook. Smith successfully sowed the seed, which produced large, palatable grains, and then distributed it to neighboring planters. Before long, the Madagascan rice became South Carolina's staple crop.[39]

Even more significant than importing suitable rice, southern planters imported slave labor. Because the onerous and costly tasks of clearing and draining swamp forests for rice cultivation could not be accomplished by individual farmers, planters relied on African slaves to do the work.[40] According to Jedidiah Morse in South Carolina, "No white man, to speak generally, ever thinks of settling a farm, and improving it for himself, without negroes."[41] Africans had stronger resistance to diseases such as malaria and yellow fever that had gained footholds in the American South by the mid 1600s. This resistance enabled them to work in flooded fields with less risk of infection than whites. Furthermore, slaves from West Africa had experience growing different kinds of rice on floodplains of the Congo and Niger rivers. Because most planters had little knowledge of rice cultivation, they depended on the expertise of their slaves to develop a profitable agriculture.[42]

South Carolina Governor John Drayton specifically identified the contributions of the slaves to the reclamation of that state's wetlands. If not for slaves, he wrote, "the extensive rice fields which are covered with grain, would present nothing but deep swamps, and dreary forests; inhabited by panthers, bears, wolves and other wild beasts. Hence the best lands of this state would have been rendered useless. . . . "[43] Because most southern colonial governments required landowners to improve land either through cultivation or by clearing and draining several acres in order to gain title, even acquisition of land depended on slaves.[44] If not for slavery, landowners would not have been able to own or to reap the benefits of their wetland properties.

Initially, the planters and slaves grew rice in impounded freshwater swamps, but by the mid eighteenth century, they began to experiment with cultivation in the tidewater zone. If a plantation was located just above the extent of saltwater, yet still within the area where tides exerted force on the fresh river water, a planter could use the rise and fall of tides to alternately drain and irrigate rice fields when necessary. Beyond irrigation, with "water culture" the planters could use river water to subdue weeds and insects, to discourage grain-eating birds, and to replenish the fields with rich sediment. After some trial and error, tidewater planters' yields increased up to

50 percent. By the last decade of the eighteenth century, almost all rice planters had relocated their plantations along the ten- to twenty-mile reaches of tidally influenced freshwater rivers from North Carolina's Cape Fear to Florida's St. Johns, the niche where water culture was possible.[45]

Wresting rice farms from river swamps was a slow process. Before cultivation could begin, slaves cleared thick forests of baldcypress and tupelo and built ditches to drain the land. Clearing was usually done in winter, when the soils were drier and the risk of snake bites less. Sometimes planters would forgo the value of their lumber for expedience, but most often timber was floated downstream to mills.

After the land was cleared, slaves constructed the necessary dikes, check banks, and floodgates. An 80-acre plantation required 2¼ miles of dikes and check banks and 12 miles of canals, ditches, and quarterdrains. To build these structures, slaves, standing shin-deep in mud and using only shovels and axes, had to move over 39,000 cubic yards—the equivalent of 117,000 wheelbarrows—of river-swamp muck.[46] When the banks were built, woodworkers constructed flood-control gates that closed automatically when the river rose. When necessary, a gate tender could either let water into the fields or drain it out. After the fields were created, slaves sowed and then cared for the rice. In the summer, they worked standing in water and muck. Women fastened their skirts up above their knees with a cord. At the end of the season, the slaves cut rice with sickles and then bundled the stalks into sheaves to be threshed and winnowed after picking more perishable crops. During harvest, malaria was most prevalent, so planters routinely retreated to less dangerous climes, leaving the plantations to be run by industrious slaves and slave drivers who knew the lands well.[47]

Because the work of clearing, weeding, irrigating, and harvesting rice fields was so varied, a distinctive labor system evolved in the tidewater region. Rather than work in gangs under the direct supervision of an overseer, as was common on cotton plantations, tidewater slaves were assigned specific tasks each day. When the tasks were complete, the slaves had time for themselves. In their free time, many slaves procured food to supplement plantation fare, including waterfowl, fish, deer, and even alligators, which reminded them of crocodiles in African rivers. Some even gathered items such as Spanish moss to sell at nearby markets for mattress stuffing. Some built dugout canoes to travel more easily up and down rivers to market or church. Although state slave codes restricted slaves from moving about freely, local custom permitted such travel in the tidewater province. The

A RICE PLANTATION ALONG THE OGEECHEE RIVER NEAR SAVANNAH, GEORGIA, SKETCHED BY A. R. WAUD.
With the work of slave labor, southern planters put tidewater wetlands along every river in South Carolina and Georgia to use growing rice in the late 1700s. Fields were flooded and drained with the aid of tidal flows and special gates. (From *Harper's Weekly*, January 5, 1867, reprinted by permission of Beinecke Rare Book and Manuscript Library, Yale University.)

labyrinthine river swamps would have made enforcement of those codes impossible anyway. For tidewater slaves, the swamp and marsh landscape offered a refuge from the oppression of their owners and an opportunity for a certain degree of autonomy.[48]

South Carolina, with its favorable tidal variations and climate, became the nation's leader in rice production. By 1790, an estimated forty thousand acres of tidewater plantations produced rice crops; in 1842, seventy thousand acres were devoted to growing rice.[49] Georgia, with its enormous tracts of level marshland and milder climate, followed closely behind. When the state ban on importing slaves ended in 1749, rice cultivation rapidly spread south, and the population grew quickly. In 1750, roughly one thousand slaves and two thousand white people inhabited Georgia; by 1773, there were sixteen thousand slaves and eighteen thousand white people.[50] With such an enormous workforce amassed, the transformation of wetlands on the coastal plain was just a matter of time.

As planters altered more lands and waterways to grow more rice, the wetland landscape changed. After several growing seasons, the fertility of the formerly swamp fields was sharply reduced, but planters successfully used their water-control systems to flood fields with fresh sediment and to leave fields fallow as fish ponds in order to restore the depleted soils. Some changes in the land had broader effects. For example, natural riverside wetlands had formerly absorbed excess spring runoff and tempered floods. But by holding water in rice fields during the spring, planters left nowhere for floodwaters to collect and so increased the chances of flooding and property damage downstream. Consequently, by 1787 both South Carolina and Georgia had passed regulations that required all rice dams to be open in the spring to prevent accumulation of runoff. Recognizing the outcomes of unrestrained wetland cultivation, these early state regulations limited what individual property owners could do in order to avoid the public nuisance of flooding.

But some alterations were not so easily reversed. When planters constructed rice-milling dams on waterways, they impeded both commerce and fish passage. Most significant, when planters cleared new lands and built new canals, they altered local hydrology, sometimes allowing saltwater to intrude and inundate their own or their neighbor's fields. On the Ogeechee and Cooper rivers, planters' manipulations caused saltwater to intrude upstream for three miles, lowering farmland values to one-tenth of their original value. Some planters wanted to widen the Santee River for shipping, but others feared the risk of salinization. One Charleston engineer warned a planter who wanted to build a new navigational canal: "Nature in the formation of her works has acted for the general welfare of man. It therefore behoves us to consider well the consequences before we deviate from, or counteract her ways."[51] As planters altered the wetland landscape to grow rice, they discovered that their actions could backfire in unanticipated ways, but they didn't generally recognize the subtle effects of changing the landscape until it was too late.[52]

In many places, forest industries grew hand in hand with the development of rice culture. When lands were cleared, timber was floated by river to mills, where it was turned into shingles, barrel staves, and lumber. Many of these products were exported to the West Indies by the decade of the 1760s. By 1775, Georgia alone exported ten million shingles, thirty-six million staves, and twenty-one million board feet of lumber, much of which came from the bottomland swamps of the coastal plain.[53] By the latter half of the eighteenth century, entrepreneurs identified even more remote wetland areas for their investment potential.

Despite William Byrd's disparaging descriptions of the Great Dismal Swamp in 1728, the potential profitability of timber and agriculture eventually attracted investors, including the young George Washington. Unlike Byrd, Washington, who surveyed the perimeter of the two-thousand-square-mile swamp in 1763, was impressed with the natural beauty of the Great Dismal, describing it as a "glorious paradise" abounding with fowl and game. In 1764, Washington applied with five partners and the backing of one hundred other investors to the Virginia assembly to obtain a charter for a new company: "Adventurers for draining the great Dismal Swamp." The investors were most interested in timber revenues but fully intended to profit from fertile farms that would be established after the forest was cleared. The company's name, "Adventurers," referred to the capital "adventured" but also revealed the investors' attitude toward the swampland: the landscape presented an unknown challenge that they would vigorously confront.

Of course, it was the slaves owned by the company who would actually confront the adventure of draining the wild swamp. Housed at a small settlement known as Dismal Town, slaves began digging ditches and canals to facilitate logging. In the late 1760s, they dug a canal five miles long and twelve feet wide from the swamp's edge to Lake Drummond at its center. During the following decades, they built many more canals to gain access to different areas of the swamp. By the time of the Revolutionary War, the swamp produced eight million shingles for export annually. The company abandoned its initial plans for agriculture and focused primarily on producing shingles from the enormous baldcypress trees.[54]

To the southeast of the Great Dismal, on the swampy Albemarle Peninsula, another group of entrepreneurs identified Lake Phelps as an area suitable for timbering and agriculture in the 1780s. Because the nearby Scuppernong River was lower than the lake, they planned to build a connecting canal to drain the lake and expose its rich soil for agriculture. The Lake Company formed in 1784 and sent a ship to West Africa to procure slaves for the job. In the summer of 1786, the slave ship arrived back in the Edenton port. No time was wasted putting the young African men to work. The digging took two grueling years. According to one account, the overseer built cages around slaves as they dug, making them pass the muck out through the bars. While building canals, many slaves died from either respiratory disease or overexertion. They completed the six-mile canal in 1787, lowering the level of the lake enough to allow farming on 10,000 acres around its margin. The canal was also used to transport timber to a company sawmill. By 1790, 113 slaves worked cutting and preparing timber, maintaining the canal, and preparing the farmland for rice cultivation.[55]

While profitable to successful planters, tidewater rice cultivation and swamp logging were not without their problems. Both created pools of stagnant shallow water that fostered the reproduction of mosquitoes. Although anopheline mosquitoes were likely abundant in the South before settlers arrived, they became transmitters of malaria only after settlers brought the *Plasmodium vivax* parasite in their bodies from England. At first, the odds of introducing the cycle of malaria were low; a mosquito had to bite an infected person, then live long enough for the infection to develop within its own body, and then bite again. For this reason, malarial outbreaks became frequent only where large numbers of people settled in areas with many mosquitoes, such as in the tidewater or along coastal plain rivers. By 1650, malaria had become endemic in the Chesapeake Bay, and by 1680 it had taken hold along South Carolina's Ashley River. In the late 1600s, more virulent malaria strains came to America in the bodies of African slaves. Slave ships also brought *Aedes aegypti* mosquitoes that transmitted deadly yellow fever. The first American outbreak occurred in the slave-ship port of Charleston in 1699.[56]

At the time, people did not understand that mosquitoes carried the diseases; rather, they attributed the pervasive illness to unhealthy air produced by stagnant water in marshes and swamps, known commonly as "miasma." The anonymous author of *Animal Husbandry* identified the tidewater region as "one of the most unhealthy climates in the world" because most of it was "spread with stagnating waters." From the mud of these "stinking sinks and sewers," he claimed, "the heat exhales such putrid effluvia as must necessarily poison the air." Such miasmic air, he continued, could not "but prove prodigiously injurious to the health of the human body."[57] This widely held understanding of wetlands prompted local governments to get rid of the marshes and lowlands around settlements. In 1766, for example, an "Act to Remove a Nuisance in Baltimore Town," required landowners to wall off and fill a "large miry marsh giving off noxious vapor and putrid effluvia."[58] Although their theory of pathogenesis was incorrect, Baltimore leaders recognized in miasmic gases the "commons" aspect of wetlands.

Only if landowners owning wetland property were directed by law to join and drain their lands could the public be protected from the scourge of disease.

The causal linking of wetlands and disease became more and more entrenched as America's nascent scientific community began to research and write about the topic. One popular theory, which accounted for the preponderance of disease in populated wetland areas, suggested that cultivation unleashed the miasmic gases. As one proponent explained: "These exciting causes of disease lie dormant in the native state of new countries, . . . but when the ground is cleared and its surface broken they are put into immediate activity."[59] The actual parasitic origins of malaria and yellow fever would remain unknown for more than a century.

Disease-causing parasites were not the only invisible travelers that came to North America as shipboard stowaways. Exotic plant and animal species hitched rides as well. Ships required ballast to sail efficiently on their transatlantic voyages to the colonies. When there was no marketable ballast, boat crews frequently scooped up sand and gravel from European tidal flats to fill their keels. When the ships arrived at American ports, they dumped this foreign ballast material into harbors, along with waste hay, bedding, and manure that had been used to tend to livestock. In this assemblage of organic matter, seeds often found passage. The showy purple loosestrife came from Europe this way during the colonial period and subsequently spread up watercourses and canals. Eventually, over the course of several centuries, the loosestrife established itself in wetlands nationwide, disrupting existing ecological cycles by displacing native plants.[60]

From Swamps to Shingles and Sugar

While English colonists struggled with eastern swamps and marshes, French colonists dealt with the difficulties attendant to settling on one of the world's largest river deltas. In 1717, Jean Baptiste Le Moyne, Sieur de Bienville, traveled from the existing French outpost at Biloxi on Mobile Bay to the mouth of the Mississippi. There in the vast bottomland forest, he found richer timber stands, more abundant furbearers, and greater agricultural potential. Along the river, Le Moyne found well-developed natural levees of sediment that had been deposited during spring floods. He chose for his new town site one such crescent of highland along the lower river. Without even knowing that the enormous river drained two-thirds of the continent, an insightful engineer protested Le Moyne's floodplain choice, but then reluctantly laid out building sites, insisting that each have its own drainage ditches and dikes. Enormous trees of the bottomland forest were cut to carve out a space for the town. By 1727, New Orleans had a levee over one mile long, one yard high, and eighteen feet wide at the top to keep floodwaters out. By 1738, over forty-two miles of earthworks lined both sides of the river.[61]

At first, owners of the fertile riverfront were held responsible for maintaining their own sections of levee. But as more settlement occurred behind the levees, riparian landowners resented the obligation required by their deeds to maintain levees on their land for public benefit. Consequently, maintenance suffered. In 1735, a large flood destroyed most of the young town's levees.

Yet despite its flood-prone location, New Orleans grew. Most people traveling to the interior passed through the port town, and its role as a commercial hub continually enlarged. The colony's French allegiance made it a sanctuary for French-speaking refugees. After expulsion from Canada, the Acadians arrived in Louisiana between 1765 and 1785. Shortly thereafter, in 1791, a slave revolt in Haiti prompted Creoles to migrate to Louisiana as well. Both groups re-created their communities and cultures in the remote bayous of southern Louisiana. Depending on the rich swamp fishery for subsistence and trade, they found freedom and peace in the remote swamp landscape.[62]

The immense bottomland forests attracted the timber industry to the lower Mississippi Valley early on. The swamp forests presented a seemingly inexhaustible supply of giant trees—especially baldcypress. Because its wood resisted rot, the plentiful tree became a popular source for roofing shingles. During winters, farm slaves often rived shingles in the swamps. Numerous small sawmills also opened to supply building materials to booming New Orleans. By 1722, the French colony was exporting baldcypress lumber from bottomland swamps to pay for basic foodstuffs.

Timbering in the swamplands presented new problems. Known European methods for logging in uplands didn't work in the wet bottomland forests. For example, swampy conditions precluded the help of animals. Instead, timber companies constructed canals to drain land and to make working by boat easier. Because canal building was such a brutal job, Louisiana entrepreneurs were reluctant to risk the lives of their valuable slaves to disease and overexertion. Instead, they hired Irish and later Asian immigrant laborers, who risked their own lives at no expense to the business

owners. In 1720, immigrants dug a small canal between the Mississippi and
Barataria Bay to gain access to timber close to New Orleans.[63] Canals penetrated many upstream swamps as well. Yet even when the canals were
built, heavy, sap-filled trees would not float once felled. By 1725, loggers
developed a new method to avoid this problem. In autumn, crews of slaves
would gird trees that then dried out during the winter. When the high water
of spring came again, the dry trees were cut and floated to the mill.[64] After
the logs were milled into lumber, slaves assembled them into enormous
rafts and floated with them downriver to market.

New Orleans soon became the fastest-growing city in all the South. Even
its own sawmills couldn't keep an adequate supply of lumber in town. Local
lumberyards had to buy bottomland lumber from mills in Pensacola,
Florida, and in Texas to meet heavy demand.[65] By the 1830s, logging had
progressed up the Yazoo River valley, one of the largest stands of timber accessible by sloughs and creeks. At a giant oxbow on the Mississippi River
just below the mouth of the Yazoo, rafts containing tens of thousands of
logs and covering acres of river and slough were assembled and displayed.[66]
When the water was high enough, crews floated the rafts downriver to mills
and markets.

With forests sheared off, the bottomlands were ready to farm.
Louisianans experimented with several crops, including rice, but sugar fast
became the favorite. Sensitive to freezing, sugar demanded the most tropical climate possible, and south Louisiana came closest to providing the
necessary warmth, regular precipitation, and fertile soil. Soon after the
Louisiana Purchase, droves of hopeful Americans moved to Louisiana with
dreams of successfully farming sugarcane. The alluvial levees of rich soil
sloped gently away from the river, providing a degree of natural drainage.
Slaves ditched and cross-ditched fields to carry water off more quickly.[67]
Sometimes they built levees at the rear of the fields to protect the crops
from rising swamp waters. Like tidewater rice planters, sugar growers used
river water to irrigate when necessary but also drained fields—sometimes
with horse-powered pumps. When granulation techniques were perfected,
growing sugar became even more profitable and spread throughout
southern Louisiana. The thin levees of land formed by Bayou Lafourche
and Bayou Teche, distributaries of the Mississippi River, became primary
sugar-producing regions. In order to open up even more lands to sugar cultivation, wealthy sugar planters displaced the Acadians and Creoles, who
retreated deeper into the bottomland swamps.[68]

Within a hundred years, many bottomland swamps were transformed into landscapes of agricultural wealth. In 1818, traveler Estick Evans described lands that were once swamps: "For about one hundred miles above New Orleans, both banks of the river are under a high state of cultivation. The country continues thus cultivated for twenty miles below the city. The plantations within these limits are superb beyond description."[69] Both the desire to profit and the drive to order swamps into civilized lands prompted early conversion of bottomland forests into sugar and rice fields.

A Wealth Squandered

By 1800, great cities such as Boston and New Orleans had been built upon marshes and swamps. Wetlands' wealth had enabled colonists first to subsist and then to engage in the commerce that helped to win the colonies' independence from England. Rich wetland soils became the foundation for remarkable agricultural productivity in both the North and the South.

Initially, conventional wisdom governed the colonists' response to wetlands: familiar marshes were used as pasture (especially in the Northeast where there was less malaria), and fearful swamps were avoided. Then as colonists grew accustomed to the country and as demand for resources grew, their beliefs changed; they began to convert marshes into cities and wharves and swamps into farm and timber lands. Traditional attitudes helped to fuel this commercialization of wetlands. Not only did colonists profit from the furs, timber, and agricultural products they extracted from swamps and marshes, but by draining wetlands they believed they were eradicating disease and clearing the way for trade and civilization. Many saw reclamation as their duty to God. Ideals of improving public health and of better ordering the unruly wetlands corresponded well with the growing feasibility of developing these marginal lands. Eventually, the religious ideological underpinning that supported the drive to rid the country of unhealthy marshes and wicked swamps was replaced by the realization that wetlands simply and physically stood in the way of commercial progress.

With so many reasons to abhor wetlands, it is no wonder that colonists little recognized natural marshes and swamps as the sources of their wealth. Some observers did notice how settlement changed the nature of the landscape. Eighteenth-century tidewater rice planters certainly lamented tinkerings that transformed their rice fields into brackish marshes. By the time Swedish botanist Peter Kalm traveled through the Northeast in 1750, many coastal marshes had been converted to farms or towns, so colonists had only the remaining fraction to use as hunting grounds. Swedes and English settlers born in America told Kalm that "there were not nearly so many edible birds at present as there used to be when they were children." The birds' decrease was "visible." According to Kalm, "They even said that they had heard the same complaint from their fathers."[70] Kalm noted a particularly American mentality that resulted in the obliteration of resources. Writing about the Philadelphia area, he observed, "People are . . . bent only upon their own present advantage, utterly regardless of posterity. By these means many swamps are already quite destitute of cedars."[71] Because they required a rare dry seedbed for germination, the Atlantic white cedar forests could not reestablish themselves readily after indiscriminate cutting. In the lower Mississippi Valley, Le Page DuPratz, who traveled between 1718 and 1734, noticed a decline in that region's bottomland forests: "The cypresses were formerly very common in Louisiana, but they have wasted them so imprudently, that they are now somewhat rare."[72]

With the removal of forests for both local use and export, habitat for wildlife vanished rapidly. By 1731, Mark Catesby had recognized that black bears retreated "as the Inhabitants advance[d] in their settlements." Other animals also withdrew or were killed by white and Indian hunters, who sold their pelts for profit. By the late eighteenth century, beavers had become noticeably scarce. In the mid 1770s, William Bartram found only "a few beavers" remaining in the southern coastal plain, and in 1802 South Carolina Governor John Drayton wrote that east of the Appalachians, "The beaver is but rarely to be met with."[73] Habitat destruction along with market hunting and trapping became major factors in the decline of wetland animals.

Changes in wetlands could be observed most markedly near cities. To accommodate the metropolitan expansion of Boston, developers widened the thin neck connecting the Shawmut Peninsula to the mainland by filling in adjacent salt marshes to make new land. At a town meeting in 1804, citizens voted to fill in the fifty-acre millpond that had been built in the marshy North Cove by the earliest settlers. New land was in far greater demand than power from mills.

The need for fill continued to direct attention to the hills. John Hancock's heirs, who owned land on Beacon Hill, sold it as fill for the millpond. When the massive excavation threatened to undermine the foundation of a sixty-foot monument commemorating the Revolution, the town simply relocated the statue from its prominent hilltop spot; and the resculpting of the landscape continued. For twelve years, men dug up and carted away rock and soil until the 138-foot hill was nearly leveled. Material from Beacon Hill provided fill for a number of projects around the peninsula. In addition to earth from the hill, the colonists used street sweepings, oyster shells, and other garbage to fill in the millpond.

With the conversion of the millpond to land, demand for power grew once again. Entrepreneur Uriah Cotting petitioned to build a newer and larger millpond and turnpike road by constructing a new dam, 50 feet wide and 1½ miles long, from Boston to the mainland through the Back Bay, an area of tidal mudflats and salt marshes. Cotting would also erect a perpendicular cross dam from Gravelly Point Peninsula to divide the Back Bay into two basins. The upper basin would fill at high tide, and then let water pass into the empty receiving basin, powering numerous mills built along a sluice on Gravelly Point. The lower basin would then drain back into the Charles River at low tide through a small gate in the main dam.

When Cotting's tidal hydropower project received its charter in 1814, one insightful citizen asked his fellow townspeople in a newspaper editorial: "What think you of converting the beautiful sheet of water which skirts the Common into an empty mud-basin, reeking with filth, abhorrent to the smell, disgusting to the eye?"[74] His dire speculations about the project were right on target.

After Cotting completed the dam and mills in 1821, the receiving basin and its salt marsh grasses dried. Clouds of fine dust blew over the city and created such a disturbance that a new sluice had to be built to keep the mudflats covered with water at all times. By the end of the decade, the receiving basin became a dump where ashes and other refuse were thrown by the tipcart full. One neighborhood's sewer outlet entered the basin.[75] The foul odors caused by the garbage, the sewage, and the lack of natural tidal cleansing conspired to make the wetlands repugnant. Through use and abuse, the salt marshes that Bostonians had once valued became a landscape of contempt.

But even as some settlers noticed how the landscape was changing, none understood that the changes had repercussions beyond what was readily apparent. While they knew that marshes were good places to hunt waterfowl, they didn't realize that the abundance of waterfowl was integrally linked to the expanses of healthy marsh. While the French recognized the bounty of the Mississippi Delta, they didn't realize that when they built levees and cut the trees, fish and game would have fewer places to live.

People frequently remarked that if only they could get rid of the water, they would uncover a superior landscape hidden underneath; they didn't realize that it *was* the water that helped to nourish the enormous trees and the abundant waterfowl and furbearing mammals. The colonists lacked understanding of the interconnections between resources they sought and the ecosystems where those resources thrived. The plenty of the land was so great that even though degradation occurred, the environment remained far richer than what people had left in Europe. Even as the land changed, a strong sense of abundance persisted. Despite their exhilaration at the vast natural wealth of America, colonial settlers began the misguided task of annihilating the very source of that abundance.

FOUR

Exploring the Unknown Landscape

We see things not as they are, but as we are.
—Henry Major Tomlinson, *Out of Soundings* [1]

The paramount focus of the English colonial period was establishing profitable, self-sustaining outposts in the New World, but once the colonies became well established, people began to wonder what lay beyond the edges of settlement. At first, their curiosity was piqued by the potential for remunerative resources. Then as the colonies prospered, learned citizens pursued their curiosity through science. Centered in Philadelphia through the 1700s, a vibrant intellectual circle viewed the unknown natural world as an enticing topic of inquiry. As botanist to the king of England, John Bartram was an esteemed member of that scientific set.

Under John's careful tutelage, young William Bartram had learned much about the natural history of North America, in particular about "the vegetable kingdom." The father and son conducted an exploratory trip collecting plant specimens in Florida. Then in the early 1770s, the young Bartram was commissioned by an English doctor to do his own expedition, a systematic investigation of the "rare and Useful productions" of nature to be found in the semitropical climes of Florida and Georgia. Possessed with ebullient curiosity and a thirst for learning, Bartram envisioned the trip as an opportunity to make a name for himself. He dreamed of discovering plants in the unknown territories that would be useful and important to society. [2] With his gentle heart open to new experiences, William Bartram set sail from Philadelphia to Charleston in the spring of 1773. When he left his family home on the banks of Schuylkill River, he left the refinements of that colonial city behind for nearly five years in exchange for a grand and rugged adventure in the wilds of the Southeast.

Although the patchwork of colonial settlement reached well up Atlantic watercourses by the late eighteenth century, the wetlands where Bartram traveled remained largely unknown. Despite centuries of Spanish exploration, much of the swampy southern wilderness was still labeled "terra incognita" on maps. Maps typically identified human settlements and routes of travel, such as towns and watercourses, but left other areas blank. In the case of wetlands, cartographers often used a universal symbol of sedges growing in water, ⊻ , even in uncharted areas, to warn travelers like Bartram of the morasses they would face.[3]

In addition to his stack of empty notebooks and sturdy wooden trunks— filled with trinkets for Indian trade and intended for storage of specimens he would collect—Bartram brought to the southeastern landscape particular beliefs about the natural world that invariably influenced his experiences in the wetlands through which he ventured.

Carrying beliefs to unknown places was nothing unusual. All travelers have expectations. These expectations, made from an unconscious collection of images and beliefs, inform travelers' impressions of the landscapes they encounter. Like different sets of eyeglasses, preset notions enable people to see the same places in markedly different ways. For example, Puritan settlers wore spiritually charged lenses through which swamps appeared evil and chaotic. Later colonists wore utilitarian lenses through which wetlands appeared as resources to be converted into commodities. In the late eighteenth and early nineteenth centuries, when travelers and explorers began to penetrate wild, new terrain, they too carried particular ways of understanding and explaining the natural world. Travelers most often viewed wetlands as impediments to their progress, but they drew on other perspectives as well.

While Bartram donned many of these typical lenses during his trip, he usually saw the wetland landscape in ways quite different from his contemporaries. Having grown up amidst a cadre of naturalists and Enlightenment intellectuals who believed that all creation was a divine manifestation of Providence—wetlands included—Bartram gained interest in the incredible diversity of life. In his way of thinking, nature was a book created by a divine author, all parts worthy of reading and comprehending, all parts worthy of praise and reverence. Any new plant fascinated him. When he had to wade through swamps, the discovery of new species made the difficulties bearable. He was "continually impelled by a restless spirit of curiosity" to learn the beautiful intricacies of creation.[4] Learning about the natural history of the colonial borderlands was for Bartram a way to discover the untouched natural world as God had made it. It was a way to feel closer to his Creator.

Familiar with aesthetic theories of his day, Bartram also brought the Romantic categories "sublime" and "picturesque" to wild wetland places. Seeing leafy vegetation, riotous vines, flowers, birds, and alligators, he reflected that his view needed only an Indian and a wigwam to complete its portrayal of picturesque and wild nature. Although swamps were not usually considered beautiful, Bartram managed to find in them attributes typical of conventionally picturesque scenes and so became one of the first Americans to see aesthetic value in swamps.[5]

From the port city of Charleston, South Carolina, he embarked on his journey throughout the South. He explored Georgia's Altamaha River and then ascended Florida's St. Johns River. He wandered across northern Florida, along the gulf coast, and finally up the lower Mississippi Valley to Baton Rouge before returning to Charleston. He wrote about his adventures in an entertaining monograph, published in 1791, which became known simply as Bartram's *Travels*. Because he encountered many coastal plain swamps and marshes, his detailed book offers a glimpse of both the wetland landscape of the 1780s and the complexion of contemporary public sentiment regarding wetlands.

In describing swamps, Bartram most frequently used the adjective "rich." In the mind of a collecting botanist, "rich" signified an area where the most robust, unique, and varied specimens could be collected—a meaning akin to the modern definition of "biodiversity." For example, Bartram labeled a large swamp near the mouth of the Tombigbee River as the "richest" he had ever seen. He identified the trees there—baldcypress, ash, sycamore, cottonwood, sweetgum, and many others—as "by far the tallest, straightest and in every way the most enormous that I have seen or heard of." He provided evidence of the "extraordinary fertility of the soil" by describing the thick undergrowth of canes, many of which exceeded thirty feet in height and grew thick as a man's arm in diameter. Bartram also noted the bounteous fish and waterfowl present in many swampy areas. Finally, in describing the lot of the Seminoles, he regarded the swampiness of their south Florida territory as an asset; the swamps provided them with secure retreats from invasion and, most important, with copious supplies of game. According to Bartram, "No other part of the globe so abounds with wild game and creatures fit for the food of man."[6]

Aside from generally characterizing southeastern swamps as rich, Bartram recorded specific details about the unusual attributes of many swamp species. With his usual reverence, Bartram suggested that the "majestic stature" of the baldcypress trees was so surprising that on approaching

them, "we are struck with a kind of awe." Describing their unusual pro-
truding knees and immense trunks, enlarged near the bases by "prodigious
buttresses or pilasters," he explained the baldcypress's preference for
growing in two to three feet of standing water for much of the year. Figuratively climbing up the trees' trunks with his thorough account, he explained
how Carolina parakeets loved to nest in cavities and feed upon the trees'
seeds. He noted that streamers of Spanish moss hung from stout horizontal
branches and that birds such as cranes and storks roosted in the treetops. In
addition to the baldcypresses and their associates, Bartram told about the
various snakes, turtles, frogs, and fish he observed. Rather than projecting
any repulsion onto these oft-reviled creatures, he commented on the beauty
of several snakes, including the coach whip. He often referred to species as
tribes, attributing to them the human traits of loyalty, relationship, and
camaraderie.[7]

Beyond making detailed observations, Bartram ascribed beauty to the
natural world and recognized its divine creation. When he serendipitously
discovered a pond covered with a floating field of yellow water lilies at the
edge of a sweeping savanna, he became wholly engaged in contemplating
the "unlimited, varied, and truly astonishing native wild scenes of landscape and perspective." He could not help but be amazed by the "display of
the wisdom and power of the supreme author of nature." His mind for a
moment was suspended in meditative reverie, then filled and impressed
with awe.[8] The *Travels* reveal Bartram as one of America's first spiritual
naturalists.

Although slogging through wet and buggy terrain on horseback must
have been unnerving, Bartram described the thickest swamps and canebrakes as merely "troublesome."[9] He recounted his experiences in a matter-
of-fact manner without passing judgment on the landscape. He preferred,
however, to travel through wet country by canoe, his "bark," as he called it.
While waterways made for easier travel, there were few suitable places to
camp in the watery bottomland forests.

Bartram's most memorable adventure occurred in such a wetland forest
when he ventured alone in his bark up Florida's St. Johns River. After
searching for hours, he eventually found a campsite on a crescent-shaped
ridge next to the river. He landed in a cove formed by the high ground, set
his bedroll under a sprawling live oak, and prepared to fish for dinner. As he
did these chores, he noticed that alligators "began to roar and appear in uncommon numbers" in the waters and along the shores of his cove. Then

two enormous alligators engaged in a tumultuous wrestling brawl in the center of the lagoon. Bartram noted that "clouds of smoke"—later clarified as vapor from their breath—issued from the reptiles' dilated nostrils.

Pink light filtering through the forest and growls from his empty stomach signaled the day's end, so Bartram decided he better fish quickly. He pushed off in his canoe toward the mouth of the cove, but when he reached the center, the large alligators tried to overturn his boat. He clubbed the saurians with a stick and quickly made his way back to shore, jumped from his boat, and scrambled to the highest ground, evading the giant reptiles.

Bartram was again and again approached by the rogue alligators. Finally at nightfall, he learned why the reptiles had congregated in his cove. Looking upstream, he saw a solid bank of fish finning their way down the river but bottlenecked at the narrow spot near the lagoon's mouth. Through the night, Bartram was kept awake by the alligators' frenzied plunging and chomping in the fish-laden waters, only somewhat relieved that he was no longer the sole object of their aggressions.

Despite his frightening experience, which might have created a profound fear of swamps, Bartram proceeded the next day to investigate nearby mound-shaped nests where female alligators had laid hundreds of eggs. After being kept awake by alligators and hooting owls for several nights, he characterized the swamp with the only mildly derogatory adjective "dreary."[10]

With its exciting adventures and detailed accounts, Bartram's *Travels* soon gained the attention of educated people on both sides of the Atlantic, informing not only naturalists but distinguished English writers such as Samuel Coleridge and William Wordsworth. Bartram's vivid descriptions of pristine nature became the manna of these Romantics, whose writings would later influence American thinkers struggling to understand their wild estate.[11]

Audubon at Large

Perhaps the most acclaimed American influenced by Bartram was John James Audubon, a man who became renowned for his magnificent, lifelike bird paintings. Audubon devoted himself to painting birds at age thirty-five. In 1820, the self-taught artist left his wife and children in the temperate Ohio River valley and moved to New Orleans, where he intended to hunt and paint the colorful birds of the semitropical bottomlands. To support himself and his young assistant, George Mason, Audubon painted portraits

and taught private art lessons. Unable to acquire birds easily in the surrounding swamps as he had hoped, Audubon nonetheless proceeded with
his work by purchasing dressed game birds at the bustling French Market.
He hit the shops at dawn to procure the best specimens of many different
and unusual birds sold there, such as purple gallinule, blue grosbeak, great
blue heron, trumpeter swan, and whooping crane. The following New Year,
the ambitious artist resolved to paint ninety-nine birds in ninety-nine days
and hired market hunters to bring him new specimens directly each
morning.[12]

Through drawing and painting hundreds of birds in Louisiana, Audubon
improved his techniques and capabilities. Unlike other naturalist painters of
his day, he portrayed more than just stiff, silhouetted figures. Many of his
dynamic paintings show birds in their natural habitat engaged in their routine activities, such as eating fish or protecting chicks. Audubon's ecologically true style required that he first observe birds in their natural settings.
He then shot (or purchased) the birds, stuffed them, threaded them with
flexible wire, and placed them in animated natural positions. After he rendered the birds, Mason painted the backgrounds, also based on observation
of nature.

After spending three years in Louisiana, Audubon ventured to Philadelphia, still the cultural center of the nation, to find a publisher for his first
collection of paintings. Despite the quality of his artwork, he gained little attention in the city, where his backwoods persona clashed with the refine-
ment of the urban savants. Audubon then took his portfolios to London,
where he found tremendous interest in his work and readily located a publisher for *The Birds of America,* a series of hundreds of plates bound in large
format. The volume was expensive, but Audubon managed to sell several
subscriptions while in England.

With new commitment and resolve, he returned to the United States
and embarked upon a journey to Florida in 1831. Having read Bartram's
Travels, Audubon anticipated finding many new birds. He hired a taxider-
mist and a Swiss landscape painter, George Lehman, to go along.

Audubon's accurate representation of the habitats and behaviors of the
birds he painted was his greatest contribution as a naturalist, so it is ironic
that he relegated the task of painting backgrounds to other artists. While
Mason had painted primarily the sprigs of vegetation on which Audubon's
first collection of painted birds perched, George Lehman rendered many
of the more complex landscape scenes found in *The Birds of America.*

Yellow Shank, BY JOHN J. AUDUBON, 1836, ROBERT HAVEL, ENGRAVER.
As John J. Audubon searched for new birds to paint, he explored Southern swamps and marshes firsthand. Though best known for depicting birds in their natural habitat, Audubon usually left the backgrounds for his assistants to paint. (Gift of Mrs. Walter B. James, ©1996 Board of Trustees, National Gallery of Art)

Lehman's backgrounds included native vegetation and landscapes seen in the field, but also structures, such as distant plantation homes, subtly documenting the encroachment of civilization into the wild realm of the birds. Often Lehman and Audubon worked together closely to represent the behavior of a bird interacting with its habitat. In the portrait of the whooping crane, for example, Lehman painted a small striped crocodile in the bird's slender bill.

Although Audubon had hunted in the backwoods of Kentucky and near New Orleans, the trip to Florida was his first painting expedition. He arranged to travel on a naval ship to Saint Augustine, where he set out with his assistants to retrace routes that Bartram had explored nearly sixty years earlier.

Abundant and varied bird life attracted Audubon first to the coastal salt marshes of the Halifax River, a locale that hadn't interested Bartram from a botanical standpoint. In a letter to a friend, he described the daily routine of his party: "We get into a boat and after a hard hour of rowing, we find ourselves in the middle of most extensive marshes, as far as the eye can reach. The boat is anchored and we go wading through mud and water, amid myriads of sand-flies and mosquitoes, shooting here and there a bird, or squatting down on our hams for half an hour, to observe the ways of the beautiful beings we are in pursuit of. This is the way in which we spend the day."[13] Awake and ready before sunrise, the three men worked in the field until dusk. In the evenings they skinned birds, cleaned guns, and made notes.

Audubon, however, did not find particular beauty in the swamps and coastal wetlands of Florida. Although as a naturalist he recognized that the richness of these wetland landscapes supplied him with birds to paint, he saw marshes and swamps mainly as essential drudgery. Unlike Bartram, he experienced the Florida wetlands primarily as a series of travel frustrations.

In addition to the persistently annoying insects, Audubon wrote about the difficulties presented by the salt marsh tides and mud. One day he went out into the marshes with a crew including his assistants and several slaves whose services a local plantation owner had donated. At dusk, when the temperature began to drop, the party found itself beached in the midst of a mudflat surrounded by marshes, so they decided to sleep the night in the bottoms of the boats. When frigid morning dawned on the still-beached boats, they realized that "the only resort was to leap into the mire, waist deep" and push the boats to a nearby, marshy shore where they could build a fire with the wood of a single small tree. After warming around the fire, the party again struggled through the mud and eventually found enough water to float their boats. As if in retribution for their irksome night, they then set the salt marsh ablaze for entertainment and watched all the "marsh rabbits, scampering from the fire by the thousands." The group seems to have projected its anger and frustration onto the landscape rather than concede the marsh's value to their studies. Audubon soon thereafter wrote a letter to his wife, Lucy, requesting that she send fresh socks to replace his worn ones, as the "salt marshes through which I am forced to wade *every day* are the ruin of everything."[14]

Not only was Audubon disappointed with the coastal marshes, but he disliked the wetland forests he found along the St. Johns River as well. Because physical experiences dominated his perception of the landscape, Audubon was dismayed. "The general wildness, the eternal labyrinths of waters and marshes, interlocked and apparently never ending; the whole surrounded by interminable swamps—all these things had a tendency to depress my spirits," he wrote to Lucy.[15]

But Audubon recognized that his disappointment stemmed in part from his grand expectations of the Florida landscape. He recollected that as a young man he had "consecrated in [his] imagination" the image of Florida as a garden, drawing specifically upon descriptions from Bartram's *Travels*. Audubon made clear that his own accounts of Florida would not corroborate the botanist's "flowery sayings." He redefined Bartram's definition of Florida as a garden: "A garden where all that is not mud, mud, mud, is sand, sand, sand; . . . where in place of singing birds and golden fishes, you have a species of ibis that you cannot get when you have shot it, and alligators, snakes, and scorpions."[16]

While Bartram clearly viewed Florida with more reverence and romance than Audubon, it is also likely that during the sixty years between their expeditions, changes in the landscape changed the gardenlike character of the place. A lieutenant with the ship that Audubon sailed on noted the ruinous techniques of planting along the St. Johns River: Farmers cleared land, planted it for two to three years without replenishing the soils, and then moved on and cleared more land, leaving behind desolate, denuded wastelands.[17] Audubon commented on the sixteen plantations that spread along the Halifax River between St. Augustine and New Smyrna. He also noticed that waterfowl in that area were extremely gun shy, making it difficult for him to approach and observe them. He noted that birds were reportedly less skittish farther south, away from the encroaching settlements. With the clearing of many new lands and with the increase in commercial and millinery hunting, the natural bounty of Florida was already diminishing. Unknowingly, the painter witnessed a fallen garden.

While Audubon was disappointed by not finding his imagined paradise, he did collect 550 skins, boxes of shells, and numerous seeds—testament to the natural abundance of early-nineteenth-century Florida. He also made twenty-nine drawings.[18] Furthermore, his Florida paintings had far-reaching and persisting value. The habitats represented in the backgrounds of the well-known water-bird paintings became some of the first artistic renderings of the wild wetland landscape of the Southeast. As the paintings gained wider recognition in the following century, they would become a fundament of the body of information and images that informed Americans' vision of wetland landscapes.

The Eye of the Pioneer and Traveler

By reading William Bartram's book, Audubon had developed preconceptions about Florida wetlands long before he ever traveled there. But where did other travelers' expectations of swamps originate? These preformed images were foremost rooted in traditional beliefs and experiences but also in the literature and stories brought back from travelers who had documented their own experiences.

For people who read, images of places were likely based on the writings and sketches in books and magazines. Washington Irving, whose chilling stories gained notoriety in the first part of the nineteenth century, frequently used swamp landscapes as backdrop to heighten suspense and terror. In "The Legend of Sleepy Hollow," it was near a swamp that the headless horseman appeared.[19] In "The Devil and Tom Walker," the rendezvous with Satan took place in a quagmire "where the green surface often betrayed the traveller into a gulf of black, smothering mud."[20] Several contemporary writers used the swamp landscape as a metaphor for fright, deceit, and evil to elicit fear and to titillate their readers with the exotic. In one story, branches of swamp trees intercept light, teaching the day "to counterfeit the night."[21] Swamp images also appeared with increasing frequency as engravings in magazines and other printed materials.[22] The publication of fictional, exaggerated, and misleading depictions of mythic marshes and swamps helped to shape the reputation of wetlands. Because few people had firsthand knowledge of the landscape, the wetland lore and legends became accepted and integrated into the dominant Euroamerican culture.

Literate people frequently adopted the colorful metaphoric language of popular writings in their own descriptions of swamps. In her personal journal recounting several years spent in Georgia, Fanny Kemble called Spanish moss the "banner of death" and described the baldcypress as "a gigantic tree of monstrous cobwebs." Kemble figuratively associated the swamp landscape with death and decay in the same way that contemporary authors did. Travel experiences tended to strengthen preconceptions rather than to change them.[23]

Beyond the naturalists, soldiers who fought in the War of 1812 were among the first travelers to gain firsthand experience with swamps and marshes. In order to recapture Detroit from the British, the United States deployed soldiers and maintained supply lines through northwest Ohio, but no one realized that the fifteen-hundred-square-mile Black Swamp lay en route. In journals and letters written home, soldiers recounted their confrontation with the wetland. For example, Robert Lucas, in his June 10, 1812, journal entry wrote that he "encamped in what is Called the Black Swamp, had a Disagreable night of wet and Musketoes." Other soldiers complained of travel "mid leg deep in mud" and mud "ancle deep in our tents."[24] Twenty-three years later, soldiers fighting in the Seminole Wars were dispatched to Florida's Everglades. In the *St. Augustine News* in 1840, one soldier described "a vast sea filled with grass and green trees, and expressly intended as a retreat for the rascally Indian."[25] By associating Indians with wetlands, his description echoed those of Puritan fighters two centuries earlier. With their firsthand accounts of the landscape, soldiers continued to form opinions and understanding of the frontier swamps and marshes.

Just on the heels of the military, surveyors and pioneers traveling westward began to encounter wetlands as obstacles to progress. Those who traveled by foot were best able to describe the landscape in visceral detail. Surveyors like John Tipton, who surveyed the Illinois–Indiana boundary in the late spring of 1821, had to slog through mud. Crossing back and forth across the Kankakee River, Tipton described the area as a "most dreadful swamp," which necessitated "wadeing . . . four hours . . . to our waist." Tipton's party was also tormented by the "merciless attack of the muschetter [*sic*] who almost darken the sky with their nos [*sic*]."[26] Harry Wiltse, who surveyed swampy terrain in Wisconsin in 1847, wrote that "during four consecutive weeks, there was not a dry garment in the party, day or night."[27] A drainage engineer who later surveyed a line across south Florida's Everglades for the Tamiami Trail described similar troubles traversing swampy terrain. "As one foot is pulled out, the other one continually sinks, making progress almost impossible. . . ."[28] Aside from bemoaning the difficulties of travel, surveyors typically noted the wet nature of land to inform pioneers about its poor agricultural potential. A surveyor traveling from Ohio to Indiana observed, "The country is so wet that we scarcely saw an acre of land upon which a settlement could be made."[29]

But surveyors weren't the only ones who experienced wetlands on foot. On her way to build a new home in southern Michigan, sixty miles northwest of present-day Detroit, Mrs. Caroline Kirkland traveled through many wetlands. At one marsh, she was disappointed to find a causeway made only of round logs laid in a row—known as a corduroy road—with a "slough of despond to be crossed in order to reach it." Although she began to cross the marsh in a wagon, the rocking and jiggling became too unpleasant, so she decided instead to walk "over its slippery eminences to the utter annihilation of a pair of [her husband's] shoes."[30]

Writing in great detail about setting up a household on the frontier in her book *A New Home: Who'll Follow?*, Kirkland described many encounters with wetlands. One time, she ended up in a bog when her husband mistook its floating green vegetation for solid ground. The bog engulfed horse, carriage, and passengers and coated all with mud. Another time, the lead horse came loose right in the center of a marsh, and Kirkland was stranded in the carriage with her children for several hours until her husband could return with another horse. "The expanse of inky mud which spread around us was hopeless as to any attempt at getting ashore," she lamented. Creeping down the wagon's tongue, she tried out "one or two of the tempting green tufts, which looked as if they *might* afford foothold; but alas! they sank under the slightest pressure."[31] Despite these troubling encounters with marshes, Kirkland described her experiences with good spirit and humor. In fact, wetland experiences were the primary elements of comedy in her book, which was reviewed favorably in magazines and eagerly read by prospective pioneers.[32] Readers likely formed their own expectations of prairie wetlands based on Kirkland's story.

A road through Ohio's Black Swamp was finally built in 1827. Despite its reputation as "the worst road on the continent," westbound travelers routinely took this sole route through the morass. For those who lived nearby, hauling stuck wagons and horse teams out of the mudholes became regular employment.[33] After emerging from the Black Swamp, pioneers invariably met up with wet marshes in the unfamiliar low country to the west. After getting stuck once or twice, most savvy travelers learned to avoid black grass, which grew tall in moist and poorly aerated soils. Another less hydric prairie grass was known as compass plant, because pioneers tied scraps of cloth to its tall stems to indicate to other travelers the safest route of passage around swales and sloughs.[34]

Frequently, settlers arrived in a new area in late summer and built on a flat, rich-looking, grassy area only to find their farm inundated with floodwaters the next spring. One guidebook for pioneers, J. M. Peck's *Guide for Emigrants,* published in 1831, warned about this potential occurrence:

"The emigrant may mistake [*sic*] in the dry season, and fancy he has a rich, level, and dry farm in prospect, but the next spring will undeceive him."[35]

Despite such warnings, the prairies continued to seduce pioneers. In 1837, a group of Norwegian families settled in an area 113 miles south of Chicago. Four men, who examined the land late that summer, were pleased to discover its flatness, rich soils, and abundant tall prairie grasses. They purchased the land, and through the winter the families worked on establishing new homes. But come spring, floodwaters deluged the entire settlement for as far as the eye could see. In addition to the tragedy of the pioneers losing their new homes to floods, the receding water left swampy areas unhealthy with malaria. Many of the Norwegian settlers who tried to rebuild, including the leader of the party, died by autumn. Most of the remaining emigrants abandoned the place.[36]

Such pioneer experiences with malaria throughout the Midwest and stories generated by the devastating illness perpetuated the traditional reputation of wetlands as miasmic and unhealthful. According to Illinois Governor John Reynolds in the early 1800s, "The idea prevailed that Illinois was a graveyard."[37] The incidence of malaria in the state had skyrocketed as early as the 1760s, when Mississippi River boat traffic picked up. During the 1820s, a potent strain of malaria killed 80 percent of the population of Pike County, nestled between the swampy Mississippi and Illinois rivers. One doctor deemed all of central Illinois "a gigantic emporium of malaria."[38]

In less virulent form, the disease, with its recurring fevers and chills, became so common that most pioneers stopped regarding it as an illness and began thinking of it as an inevitable part of acclimatization. They began referring to their ashen-faced, afflicted neighbors as "not sick" but just troubled by "the ague."[39] Undeterred by sickness, pioneers found choice fodder for their livestock in the marshes. As one south Michigan farmer wrote in a letter to *Cultivator* magazine, "To new settlers, these marshes have proved invaluable, by enabling them from the first to support their own stock with scarcely any cost."[40] Prairie homesteaders recognized both the danger and the value of their wetlands.

Once settled in new areas, pioneers could learn the whereabouts of marshes and swamps and then avoid them or build corduroy roads across them, but dodging wetlands was not always easy. The midwestern terrain was so flat that after spring rains, water accumulated to depths of three feet in many places. One visitor to Chicago in 1848 noted that "on the outskirts

of the town . . . the highways were impassable, except in winter when
frozen, or in summer when dry and pulverized into the finest and most pen-
etrating of dust. At all other seasons they were little less than quagmires."[41]
In the poorly drained area surrounding the city, horses might have to
struggle knee deep in mud and water—taking a day to travel less than twelve
miles during the wet season. In the city itself, plank bridges were laid down
on pilings to keep roadways elevated above the water that would rise with
the level of Lake Michigan in the springtime. In the most severely flooded
locales, people simply suspended travel and trade during the wet season.
One merchant closed his dry goods shop and went hunting on balmy spring
afternoons, since "people from the country, never thought of coming to
Chicago during the neigh of mud, except for very urgent reasons."[42] Areas
covered by water for more than half of the summer were known by pioneers
as "slashes."[43] The seasonal waxing and waning of natural wetlands in the
Midwest were a routine part of people's lives for decades until trains and
newer roads improved travel conditions and widespread drainage dried up
the land.

Although a traveler might expect to feel safe from the elements sitting in
a cushioned stage coach, passengers routinely had to help push their carriage or wagon out of the mud in swamps. Francis Hall, an English officer
traveling near the Pee Dee River of South Carolina in 1816, for example,
wrote that his party lit pine branches for torches and proceeded through the
swampy woods "with crash, whip, and haloo. Such an equipage, in such a
place, with the torches, and negroes, and harsh sounds, more resembled
a vehicle for the transport of the damned to their infernal dwelling, than a
stage coach in a rational country."[44]

Railroads provided a presumably more comfortable means of travel, but
the early cars and tracks by no means insulated travelers from swampy sur-
roundings. Perched upon pilings, railroad tracks often cut straight through
swamps. After riding a train from New Orleans to Osyka, Mississippi,
during the 1850s, Amelia Murray reported that "the train danced up and
down on the line more than was pleasant from the boggy nature of the
ground." On that same trip, the locomotive derailed and "ran off deep into
a quagmire."[45]

When the travel was not so calamitous, trains enabled many passengers,
through the safety of their windows, to view swamps for the first time. En
route to Georgia, for example, Fanny Kemble took a train that skirted the
edge of the Great Dismal Swamp. Its sight shocked her. "To describe to you

the tract through which we now passed would be impossible," she wrote, "so forlorn a region, it never entered my imagination to conceive." But, in fact, Kemble's imagination leapt at the opportunity to describe the swamp with vivid details. The Spanish moss, she wrote, hung "about the dreary forest like a drapery of withered snakes."[46]

A canal built through the Great Dismal Swamp in 1820 also afforded pleasure-boat travelers, including many journalists, an intimate glimpse of the swamp. Sternwheelers stopped at the well-known Half-Way House, a novel hotel straddling the state line in the midst of the swamp. Articles about the canal appeared in several magazines. The travel route became so well known that a lithograph by Thomas Williamson depicting the swamp, the hotel, and a boat of travelers adorned various paper currencies in Virginia, New Jersey, and Delaware in 1837. Usually appearing in a suite of images symbolizing progress, the widely circulated lithograph gave more people a sense of what swamps looked like and delivered a message that they could be successfully developed.[47]

Although the majority of travelers to unknown wetlands were struck most by foot-soaking, body-jarring, fearful experiences, some were impressed most by the abundance and life of the landscapes. Peter Pond, a Connecticut shoemaker-turned-fur-trader, had set out for the upper Midwest in 1765 before most white men made it into the interior. He described the abundant resources enjoyed by the Menominees near the mouth of the Fox River at Lake Michigan. According to Pond, large quantities of wild rice grew in the bay near the river's mouth and along the placid margins of the meandering river. At a shallow lake, he noted that the "Wilde Oates ware so thick that the Indians Could Scarse Git one of thare Small Canoes into it to Geather it." Noting even more remarkable evidence of the plenitude, Pond described how "the Wild Ducks When thay Ris Made a Nois like thunder."[48]

Another early trader and Indian agent, George Croghan, observed the "prodigious" richness of the forested bottomlands farther south along Illinois's Little Wabash River in 1782. Having seen numerous buffaloes, deer, and bears in the swampy woodlands, Croghan deemed the area as an "exceeding fine hunting ground."[49]

In 1841, German doctor Frederick Wislizenus, traveling across the plains of western Kansas, remarked on the abundance he discovered at the marsh now known as Cheyenne Bottoms. He mistakenly wandered from his party and spent several days thrashing across the marsh. Despite the difficult experience, which nearly killed his horse and threatened to separate him permanently from his traveling companions, he was struck most by the bird life of this marsh situated on the Central Flyway. "All sorts of water birds swarmed from all sides. Never have I seen such quantities of swans, cranes, pelicans, geese, and ducks as were here, and they seemed to feel themselves so safe that I could have killed hundreds of them with . . . my double-barreled weapon."[50]

Farther west in 1849, Captain Howard Stansbury described the birds at the Bear River marshes in the northeast corner of the Great Salt Lake. "Thousands of acres, as far as the eye could reach," he wrote, "seemed literally covered with them, presenting a scene of busy animated cheerfulness, in most graceful contrast with the dreary, silent solitudes by which we were immediately surrounded."[51] Vivid images of waterfowl were frequently recorded by explorers and pioneers, many of them dependent on hunting ducks and geese in their travels or new prairie homes.[52]

The Farmers' View

Although travelers and pioneers had different experiences with swamps and marshes, they most commonly viewed wetlands from an agrarian perspective—seeing in natural wetlands the potential for farmland. Because most Americans farmed or believed that farming formed the nation's economic and moral backbone, this agrarian outlook predominated.

The agrarian view of wetlands found a voice in the agricultural press, which had become active in the early 1800s. By mid century, more than four hundred farm journals were published, and in 1840 the most successful thirty had a combined circulation of more than 100,000. On the eve of the Civil War, the fifty top journals had a combined circulation of 300,000. According to historian Paul Gates, "No other economic group . . . was the recipient of so much free advice, practical as well as impractical, as were the farmers." The agricultural press was a nineteenth-century version of mass media.[53]

While journals tackled all facets of farming, drainage was of particular interest. New Orleans's *DeBow's Review* regularly featured articles promoting drainage of Louisiana. One article in 1847 identified the potential for growing rice in the bottomlands. "Suitable dykes or levees, proper ditches, both for draining and flooding the fields, with the addition of drainage wheels . . . is all that is necessary to secure millions of acres for this

object that are now solely tenanted by every worthless specimen of the am-
phibious, vegetable, and animal creation."[54] Drainage, it seemed, could
magically create valuable lands from worthless lands, a prospect that
matched expectations of unsurpassed opportunity in America. Other journals, such as the *Country Gentleman* and the *Farmer's Monthly Visitor* began
to advance specific techniques for draining lands as well. The agricultural
press became the primary means of exchange and education for farmers
living in remote areas.

One of the best-known advocates of drainage in the South was Edmund
Ruffin, founder of the popular *Farmers' Register.* He routinely traveled to
farms throughout the region investigating theories and techniques of cultivation. Owing to his excellent reputation, Ruffin was commissioned by the
state of North Carolina to make recommendations about its partially
drained and unsalable swamplands.

The apparent successes of agriculture at Lake Phelps and other swampy
areas in the Albemarle-Pamlico Peninsula in the late 1700s had prompted
the state to begin considering its swamps as valuable resources. In 1819,
North Carolina established a Board of Internal Improvements that promoted drainage. Most important, in 1825, the legislature assigned all un-
claimed swamplands, 1.5 million acres, to the State Literary Fund, expecting that property sales could generate money for education. Not until
twelve years later did the state have adequate funds to begin drainage work.
From 1838 to 1842, canals were dug at Alligator and Pungo lakes, draining
70,000 acres. Lake Mattamuskeet was also drained. Despite such efforts,
land sales languished because of incomplete drainage, the lack of roads, and
a strong fear of disease. It was in reference to these Literary Fund lands that
the state needed Ruffin's expert advice in the 1850s.[55]

When he explored the swamps of the Albemarle-Pamlico Peninsula in
1857, Ruffin saw through the eyes of a scientist farmer. With so little
change in elevation, it was impossible to remove water from land without
conveying it for several miles. As a result, the few established farms in the
area were only partially drained and still harbored swampland. According
to Ruffin, "Proper drainage alone would double the productive value and
profit of the whole great area." Even with only partial drainage, Ruffin
found the lands to have "fertility rarely exceeded anywhere."[56] In his 1861
report to North Carolina, Ruffin recommended techniques for properly
draining swamps. Recognizing the difficulties of clearing wet terrain with

dead roots and half-buried logs, he described the first generation of steam
dredges being used to drain the nearby Great Dismal Swamp. Ruffin called
the machines, which boasted enormous beams that held forty-cubic-foot
iron scoop boxes, "monster ditchers."[57] With mechanized help, a farmer
could improve his land considerably. In conclusion, Ruffin declared, "No
where is there a region where agricultural improvement is more needed,
and is more available, and offers more prospective profit; and no where
have the great advantages offered by nature been more neglected, or seem
to be less known."[58]

While Ruffin chiefly saw swamps from a farmer's viewpoint, he recognized other wetland values as well. Although the tidal marshes of nearby
Currituck Sound seemed useless for cultivation, Ruffin realized that their
richness lay in the habitat they provided for waterfowl. In the sound, he
noted the ducks "congregate in numbers exceeding all conception of any
person who had not been informed."[59] To capitalize on this resource, he
suggested that landowners lease shooting rights to hunters or hire gunners
to deliver ducks to market. He also recommended using the marshes for
grazing.[60] Ruffin imaginatively transformed the natural bounty of the wetlands into a marketable commodity.

While Ruffin wrote about the efficiency of the monster ditchers with enthusiasm and the hunting potential of marshes with zeal, he also described
wetlands with a Romantic, aesthetic tone at times. Canoeing through the
Great Dismal Swamp, he reflected that "the swamp forests . . . present
scenery of solemn grandeur and of rare and peculiar beauty . . . a combination of the gloomy sublime and the beautiful of Nature that is rarely
equalled elsewhere."[61]

Although different types of travelers and observers saw wetlands primarily from perspectives particular to their own preconceptions and experiences, most held multiple impressions of wetlands. Both Bartram and
Ruffin recognized natural beauty but also the agricultural potential of wetlands. Wislizenus recognized the difficulties of plodding through Cheyenne
Bottoms but also the abundance of that marsh. Pioneers and early farmers
could recognize the bounty of natural wetlands and still choose to convert
them into farms. The abundance of the young nation was so great that one
did not have to choose between rich waterfowl and green squares of farmland. It seemed that people could transform wetlands into farms, homes,
and cities and still retain the benefits of natural wetland wealth.

While it seemed that no choice had to be made, the dominant lenses through which people regarded wetlands all focused on the same ends: to rid the nation of pestilence and travel difficulties, and to make good use of rich resources. Most everyone could agree that wetlands best served the needs of the country by vanishing and becoming well-ordered, nonthreatening, productive, cultivated lands.

FIVE

The Drainage
Imperative Codified

The first and fundamental interest of the Republic is cultivation of its soil.

—Solomon Downs [1]

When in New Orleans, Louisiana Senator Solomon Downs roomed at the fashionable St. Charles Hotel. From there, he could easily stroll to the city's levee and drink in the view of an enormous brown river, roiling and frothing. There on the banks of the Mississippi, Downs at once saw the fundament of his state's wealth—an unsurpassed artery of commerce and fount of incomparable soils—but also an uncontrollable monster swallowing up the labor, wealth, and dreams of the state's residents with its increasingly frequent floods.

Carrying snowmelt and rain from lands rimmed by both the Appalachians and the Rockies, the Mississippi River for centuries had meandered and overflowed its channel every spring, recharging riparian wetlands and creating a floodplain more than thirty miles wide. But the river's aggressive overflows did little to discourage settlement throughout the watershed. Along upper tributaries, pioneers girded, cut, and burned oak-hickory woodlands to make space for their new farms and to supply themselves with lumber for homes, barns, and firewood. As lands throughout the watershed were denuded by the mid 1800s, the soil and water previously held in place by forests and understory vegetation washed into streams during spring freshets. The swollen stream waters accumulated in large rivers, including the Ohio, the Illinois, and the Wabash and eventually funneled, silt laden, into the Mississippi. The enormous river flooded downstream bottomlands with growing severity. This became a problem as more settlements developed on the river's banks.

Because bottomland swamps along the river routinely flooded, people confused cause with effect and blamed these lowlands for the flood problems. They decided that the solution lay in eliminating the culpable swamps. By building levees along the river's banks, settlers believed they

71

could prevent the Mississippi from deluging and overflowing into riparian wetlands. Then after drainage and "reclamation," new settlers could inhabit and cultivate the fertile lands. If wild swamps could be converted into well-ordered farms, people believed that the rampages of nature would no longer afflict them. Their self-serving theory was not unlike that of pioneers on the Great Plains who believed that rain would follow their plows.

Owing to their generally undesirable qualities, however, extensive tracts of swamplands remained unsold and in federal ownership. Because such large-scale drainage could not be accomplished by small landowners, and because better lands could still be found elsewhere, there was little chance that settlers would purchase the marginal bottomlands. With no jurisdiction over those vast bottomlands and few available funds, the Mississippi valley states could do little to remedy their plight.

Their only recourse was to take the circular problem to the U.S. Congress. Prompted by devastating floods, Louisiana and Missouri Democratic delegates proposed the first Swamp Land Act in the winter of 1849. Under this bill, the national government would transfer ownership of federally held swamplands to states with severe flooding problems in the lower Mississippi River basin. States could then sell the swamplands within their borders to generate funds necessary for drainage and levee building. Low prices would encourage individuals to buy and farm the bottomlands. New settlement would increase local tax bases, allowing the states to build even more levees with the proceeds.[2]

Legislators used their rudimentary understanding of hydrology to argue that upstream development worsened downstream flooding. Because the problem extended beyond any single state's authority, southern lawmakers thought the federal government had a duty to respond. In his striking Irish brogue, Louisiana Senator Downs explained the workings of the Mississippi watershed to his Senate colleagues: "It is reasonable to suppose that the whole country is now more rapidly and thoroughly drained into the Mississippi than when in a state of nature. Then no doubt, a great quantity of water was collected in pools and swamps, and there remained until carried off by gradual evaporation."[3] But since upstream lands were opened to cultivation, he contended, the water had discharged more quickly into the river, boosting its volume. Along with leading engineers of his day, Downs recognized that upstream drainage shunted more water into the river. He also realized that upstream levees funneled surplus waters more quickly downstream.

But despite their understanding of the river's hydrology, congressional delegates proposed still more drainage and more levee building to keep water out of downstream areas. Even though they knew that additional cultivation and new levees would aggravate flooding potential by constricting the river's volume and speeding its increased flows, lawmakers thought that the water could be conveyed safely to the Gulf of Mexico. Although Senator Downs noted the flood-abating qualities of swamps in past times, strong belief in drainage precluded any consideration of this natural wetland benefit.

Because the first swamp grant bill ultimately included lands only in Louisiana and appealed to widely accepted agrarian values, both the House and the Senate readily approved it in March 1849. By the next year, though, other congressional delegates demanded grants of the public swamplands within their states' borders.[4]

As the question of what to do with swamplands progressed from a circumscribed local matter to the broader issue of dispersing federal lands throughout the public domain, legislators found themselves not only defining various types of swamplands but also reassessing the controversial balance of authority between state and national government.

Understanding the Nature of Swamplands

The swamplands bill brought the struggle to understand wetlands from the experience of individuals to the collective national fore. During congressional hearings, legislators grappled both to comprehend the physical characteristics of swamps and to develop for the first time a legal definition for these lands. Initially, the legislation sidestepped the problematic definition of swamps altogether by ceding lands "known and designated on the plats of the General Land Office [GLO] as swamplands." Advocates assured their incredulous northern colleagues that "swamplands" was a technical surveyors' term referring to "all lands habitually wet." But the GLO soon advised Congress to change it because the survey plats—recorded during the driest seasons—usually failed to show swamplands accurately. Reworded in accordance with GLO recommendations, the new bill incorporated a clause that revealed more precisely the primary problem with swamps: The bill granted states "all swamp and overflow lands made *unfit thereby for cultivation.*" A New Hampshire senator fumed that the amended language made the swamp grant too vague: "There is nothing to ascertain what these lands are. There is no criterion given; the whole is loose and indefinite, and uncertain!"[5]

The greatest difficulty in formulating language appropriate for swampland legislation was that the word "swamp" evoked a variety of images for lawmakers living in different regions. Beyond flood damages, senators familiar with the inundated lands of the Mississippi River valley focused attention on the unhealthy aspects of swamps. A Mississippi senator, for example, described swamplands as "generative of noxious influences" and "injurious to human health," while an Illinois senator told colleagues that his constituents called swamps "fever and Ague lands." A Missouri senator deemed the lands "pestilential," while an Arkansas senator concurred that the swamplands were "prolific of disease and inflicted a curse. . . ."[6] Because epidemics devastated the country during the mid nineteenth century, disease evoked fear and offered a persuasive justification for drainage.[7]

Although the southern legislators agreed upon the sickly character of swamplands, legislators unfamiliar with the lower Mississippi Valley persistently questioned the bill's definition of swamps. Connecticut Representative Chauncey Cleveland, for example, expressed skepticism about the nature of overflowed lands. Reflecting upon his own experience of landscape in the seasonally flooded Connecticut River valley, Cleveland argued that overflowed lands were often the best suited for cultivation. He feared that the swamp drainage bill gave away useful and fertile lands—"the very Egypt of America"—to southern states. Cleveland was not the only lawmaker perplexed by the nature of swamplands. Regional variations in experience with wetlands resulted in perennial misunderstanding of the physical nature of the lower Mississippi swamp landscape.[8]

No matter where they came from or what they knew about swamps, legislators regularly drew upon the familiar and common language of agrarianism to understand wetlands. For example, language recommended by the GLO to define swamplands, "made unfit thereby for cultivation," clarified the reasoning behind the swampland grants: to make swamps suitable for farming.

For nineteenth-century legislators, agriculture was not merely a means of production; it provided American culture with a fundamental system of beliefs and values as well. Championed by Thomas Jefferson as a means to attain American goals, the ideology of agrarianism had been tightly woven into the young nation's purpose, identity, and ideals. According to tenets of agrarianism, every freeman had the right to hold land. Furthermore, because land ownership and the independent, land-based nature of farm work engendered virtue and health, independent farmers ideally functioned as moral pillars of the egalitarian democracy. Finally, farm production formed the very basis of the nation's wealth. Therefore, it was imperative that the national political system encourage development of a farming class to maintain both the morality and the economy of the country.[9] As a result, natural landscapes—wetlands included—were evaluated primarily in terms of their cultivability.

Agrarianism endured as a guiding political principle even when the nation's expanding industrial economy encouraged a significant demographic shift away from rural areas by the middle of the nineteenth century.[10] Though increasingly mythic, a potent vision of virtuous farm life persisted and influenced social and political discourse.[11] To understand the uncertain swamp landscape, legislators debating the swampland grant readily drew on the language and images of idyllic farm life.

Louisiana Senator Downs, for example, appealed to the economics of agriculture to solicit additional drainage funds for his state. He reminded the Senate, "The first and fundamental interest of the Republic is soil." According to Downs, cultivation represented the "sole fountain of the capital or wealth which supplies every channel of industry." Therefore, developing agriculture more fully in Louisiana's (and in other states') swamplands would economically strengthen the country.[12]

The senator also argued that drainage and cultivation of swamplands would help the nation to attain its moral goals by favoring the "increase of population, the augmentation of wealth, the cultivation of virtue, and the diffusion of happiness." By hoarding swamplands and failing to provide means for drainage, the federal government had instead limited opportunities for farmers to own land and thereby blocked the development of the independent farmer class so essential for egalitarian democracy. Harkening back to traditional colonial beliefs, Downs and other legislators frequently labeled swamplands as "evils" in need of "redemption." Again and again, they claimed that the national government was "morally bound" to expedite drainage and agricultural settlement, emphasizing the ethical nature of the obligation.[13]

Legislators also used utilitarian logic to understand swamps. Missouri Senator Thomas Hart Benton, for example, described swamps as "a refuge for wild animals that prey upon the stock of the people of the country." He further complained that swamps acted as "impediments to progress of the people in going from one part of the state to another."[14] By hampering the spread of farms and pasturelands and by obstructing access to markets, swamps precluded the realization of agrarian ideals.

Besides informing economic, moral, and utilitarian reasoning, agrarianism also underlay a popular aesthetic sensibility. When requesting additional funds for flood control along the Mississippi, Senator Downs conjured a resplendent agrarian image. With flood control, he explained, "The whole of both shores of that magnificent river, to which the world has nothing equal . . . will be one continued succession of plantations, lawns, villas, gardens." Downs imagined that the beauty and utility of the transformed landscape would attract "equally the admiration of the lover of nature and the man of taste and . . . the philosopher and the political economist."[15] In his plea for appropriations, Downs painted a pastoral image that significantly excluded natural wetland landscapes; the contemporary aesthetic ideal lay in the material prosperity of well-ordered agriculture.

Beyond all else, agrarianism predicated a particular relationship between humanity and nature. Not only did land exist primarily for human use, but citizens were obligated to improve nature by transforming its chaotic wildness into an ordered garden. Such thinking had evolved directly from the beliefs of the original Puritan settlers. Lawmakers often suggested that swamps simply covered the earth and could be easily removed like a blanket from a bed. For example, one Missouri senator compared the agricultural potential of low-lying swamplands with adjacent productive highlands. Also, legislators routinely referred to swamplands as "sterile"—an unlikely word to describe the lush vegetation of the lower Mississippi—because swamplands failed to produce crops. Legislators thus voiced their beliefs that lands remained valueless unless cultivated.[16]

Rather than recognize that excess water in swamps *supplied* bounteous riparian forests, vast flocks of waterfowl, and other natural riches, legislators, along with most citizens, thought that surplus water prevented lands from being even more abundant. Furthermore, nascent scientific understanding of the southern environment failed to provide precise information and language to define swamplands and to explicate their processes.[17] Rather than understand swamps as topographic features inherently wet for reasons of geology, geography, and climate, legislators regarded swamps as afflicted and agriculturally barren lands in urgent need of human ingenuity.

Swamp Visions Enacted

Beyond allowing lawmakers to adopt a familiar understanding of swamps, the lens of agrarianism provided a unifying ideology and language that enabled legislators to align opinion in the otherwise contentious political climate that preceded the Civil War. By the early 1850s, tensions regarding the role of the national government had escalated. While Northern Whigs and Republicans envisioned an activist federal government setting national policies on future land development, transportation, and social issues, Southern Democrats held fast to their vision of government that gave priority to the rights of individual states. While Northerners sought to prevent the spread of slavery to western territories, Southerners sought to maintain their right to use forced labor in new territories. As a result, the Swamp Land Acts took on decidedly larger meaning in the context of sectional conflict. The legislation, however, appealed to both groups for different reasons. Southern politicians considered the swamp grants an opportunity for states to gain control over more lands held in the public domain. Northern delegates saw the legislation as a means for federal involvement in land distribution and public health policy; some even hoped to engineer the law as a means for limiting the spread of slavery.[18]

Over a year after Congress granted swamplands to Louisiana, it approved a similar grant in September 1850 known as the Arkansas Act, which gave federal swamplands to several wetland-laden states. Altogether, fifteen states benefited from swamp grants: Louisiana, Arkansas, Missouri, Mississippi, Alabama, Florida, Ohio, Indiana, Illinois, Michigan, Wisconsin, Iowa, and California. Congress extended the grant to Oregon and Minnesota in 1860. The Swamp Land Acts, as they were commonly known, directed the secretary of the interior to compile lists and plats of swamplands and then send them to the governors of the participating states. If the larger part of a section was swampy, then the whole section would be classified as swampland. Sections with less than half swampy area would be excluded from the grants.[19] The very process of swampland selection with its square concept of land reveals a fundamental misunderstanding of wetlands and their irregular, water-determined boundaries.

The legislation directed states to pick one of two methods for choosing their swamplands. Selections could be made on the basis of federal surveyors' field notes, which most often included land descriptions, or states could oversee their own surveys to select swamplands, which were then reported along with affidavits as proof of their swampiness to the surveyor general for final approval. Most states adopted the latter plan.

Though Congress ceded federal swamplands primarily to ensure their drainage, drainage seldom occurred. Reasons for failure were manifold. Most states had little capital and unsophisticated laws to deal with public trust issues. Swamplands in different regions presented a variety of challenges for drainage engineering. Riparian bottomlands of the Mississippi

Valley, for example, differed from wet prairies of the Midwest and from the vast tule marshes of California's Central Valley. Furthermore, techniques for effective drainage were just emerging, making expertise difficult to find—especially in frontier communities. Because states placed swamplands on the market at an economically inopportune time for farmers, many fell into the hands of speculators who had no intention of investing in drainage. Finally, because states disseminated the authority to select and distribute swamplands so widely, the program was easily and extensively abused.

The Great River Delta

It was no surprise that the Louisiana congressional delegation spearheaded passage of the Swamp Land Acts. For the citizens of Louisiana, in particular, the federal donation of swamplands to the state was a very urgent matter. For decades, residents of the lower Mississippi sat like ducks before a loaded gun as the river repeatedly discharged its floodwaters. The numerous floodplain swamps could not be effectively drained without first controlling the overflow waters. Swamp drainage and flood control were essentially two sides of the same coin. The Swamp Land Acts finally provided the capital necessary for both improvements.

Unlike other beneficiaries of the act, the lower Mississippi states had more than a century of experience trying to drain swamps and protect lands from flooding. Since French founders first built New Orleans in the midst of a swamp, levee laws had relegated the building and maintenance of levees to owners of the rich, riverfront lands. Some planters used drainage wheels powered by steam engines that bucketed water out of drainage canals and deposited it into backwater swamps behind the fields.[20] Drainage wheels and simple earthen levees worked well early on, when settlement in the Mississippi watershed was concentrated near the river's mouth. But as people settled upstream and built levees to protect *their* floodplain settlements and croplands from the natural inundation regime, more water was more quickly funneled downstream. In particular, the flood of 1828 precipitated a wave of upstream levee building. As State Engineer A. D. Wooldridge explained, "Had nature never been interfered with, the annual overflow of our streams would not only have raised very greatly the general level of the delta, but have provided us with levees as would, ultimately, have made inundations little to be dreaded. We have however, placed ourselves in an unnatural position . . . and it now develops upon us to protect and defend ourselves in a position from which we cannot retreat."[21]

With more levees upstream, bigger floods became an annual occurrence, and it became apparent that riverfront landowners could no longer provide flood control. In order to recoup the benefits of the riparian lands, collective planning and financing would be necessary. With the colossal floods of 1849 and 1850, however, Louisiana had no funds in its state coffers and was at a loss about what to do. Floods deluged rich farmlands and threatened plantation mansions along the river between Baton Rouge and New Orleans. All that Louisianans had struggled to create from the swamps they settled was at risk of being taken back into the realm of the wild by the Mississippi River.

With passage of the first federal Swamp Land Act, citizens pushed the Louisiana legislature to implement the grant as quickly as possible. In 1852, the legislature divided the state into drainage districts according to topography and hydrology so that citizens in each district would share a common interest in the building and maintaining of levees. Then they established a Board of Swamp Land Commissioners with representatives to oversee drainage and reclamation in each district. While this seems a simple proposition today, at the time such division of lands and establishment of additional governance was revolutionary. It required citizens to accept a whole new vision of the proper role of state government.[22] The revenues generated by the sales of swamplands would be appropriated to the board. Then each commissioner would decide upon the most needed projects in his district, hire the lowest-bidding contractor, and make certain that the projects were completed. The board began by implementing the most urgent projects: repairing crevasses in principal levees.

But difficulties abounded from the start. Frequently, levees were built too close to the river or with too little a base, so they easily washed away during spring floods.[23] The board also lacked adequate baseline hydrologic and engineering expertise to develop coherent plans. For example, one engineering controversy arose between those who advocated a system of drains that allowed the river to flow through outlets and distributary bayous, and those who believed that building solid banks of levees would encourage the river to downcut and carry floodwaters more rapidly to the gulf. Most important, the piecemeal approach of the commissioners— guided more by the power of individual landowners than by a hydrologically sound plan—simply did not work. For example, several small levees might be patched to protect the frontage of an influential plantation owner, but an upstream levee crevasse might remain unrepaired, threatening the work below.

Because the river rose each spring like clockwork, contractors had only a limited period of time to secure the levees. If problems, such as malarial outbreaks, prevented them from hiring adequate labor, the necessary work remained incomplete, endangering the entire levee system. Spring flooding inundated and destroyed important earthworks nearly every year.[24]

Because progress occurred slowly, and audits revealed poorly kept records and sloppy monetary transactions, the reputation of the Board of Swamp Land Commissioners soon fell into disrepute. One district had purchased an expensive dredge boat, which auditors deemed "an extravagant piece of furniture."[25] When board members decided to sell the boat to raise money for more drainage work, they were compelled to cut a gap in a secure levee in order to extricate the dredge boat from a canal. Neighboring landowners appealed to the board to fill and repair this breach, but funds were unavailable. The untended fissure eventually caused further damages. Such apparent ineptitude along with the growing list of unsuccessful projects scarred the board's credibility.

Furthermore, citizens wanted more than just new levees for flood control; they wanted drainage as well. But more heavy rains in 1856 damaged many of the early projects. Then, owing to flooding in 1858, sugar planters lost 20 percent of their crop.[26] By 1860, it became evident that the Board of Swamp Land Commissioners had accomplished little in the way of securing property from flood damages. The board offered many legitimate excuses, including the difficulty of finding labor, the onerous regulations imposed by the legislature, and the lack of funds. The board also had to experiment with various possible engineering solutions, many of which didn't work.

But perhaps the most plausible explanation of all was that the grand Mississippi proved unrelenting in its inundations. After big floods in 1858, State Engineer Louis Hebert opposed plans to close off Plaquemine Bayou with levees. Hebert insisted that the Plaquemine must remain open as an outlet of Mississippi floodwaters. He concluded that an effective flood-control plan would require the state to maintain some of its swamplands in a natural state to absorb Mississippi floodwaters. In Hebert's view, safeguarding the valuable lands bordering the Mississippi was worth the trade-off of leaving some swamps to accept floodwaters. While he echoed the advice of previous state engineers and gained support from the legislature's House and Senate Committees on Internal Improvements, the minority members of those committees backed the position of the Swamp Land Commissioners—that the swampland grant moneys were intended to drain swamps, and that was what most needed doing. Because this solution led rhetorically to the outcome that most citizens supported—a high and dry Louisiana—the "levees-only" policy became dominant without much further question as to its feasibility.[27]

The Civil War prevented further progress in flood control and swamp drainage throughout the South. Many of the established and secure earthen levees were breached or allowed to fall into gross disrepair during the course of the war. In Louisiana alone, more than 107 miles of levees were destroyed. In fact, alluvial lands were less protected from floodwaters in 1869 than they had been in 1854 when riverfront stewardship of levees remained the custom in many places.[28]

When the war ended, the state established a new Board of Levee Commissioners to begin repairing the neglected and crevasse-ridden levees. With borrowed money, the commissioners successfully established more uniform levees. However, floodwaters from large storms ruptured the Morganza and Grand levees, causing more damage to new dikes downstream. To maintain the integrity of the flood-control system, the board estimated that it needed at least $1 million annually—a large amount of money for a state whose very tax base had been repeatedly quashed by floods.[29] When the levee board's failure seemed imminent, the state began to petition the national government with more urgency to help with flood control. By the 1870s the state sent constant pleas for aid to Washington, D.C. While Congress willingly offered emergency help to victims in the form of food and shelter, members declined to fund local infrastructure improvements unless necessary for general navigation, a responsibility that fell more clearly under federal jurisdiction.[30]

The state tried yet another scheme to control flooding. The governor established the Louisiana Levee Company as a semiprivate corporation to take responsibility for diking the Mississippi. Within its first year, the company succeeded in building almost 2.5 million cubic yards of levee. However, citizens so severely criticized the high property tax imposed to fund the effort that it was lowered, reducing the amount of levee work possible. In the following year, powerful floodwaters streamed through large crevasses, once again eviscerating the levee system.[31]

By the late 1870s, it seemed that there was little hope of containing and controlling the Mississippi River, let alone draining the swamps along its banks. To raise revenues for the attempted reclamation work, the state had sold large tracts of swampland into private ownership, oftentimes into the possession of timber companies.[32] Despite persistent efforts, spending over $11 million and building over twenty-two million cubic yards of levee, flood control plans had failed miserably.[33] To top it all off, an epidemic of yellow fever, which people still attributed to miasma, swept through the valley in 1878.[34] The feeling of defeat and hopelessness was well expressed by a joint resolution of the Louisiana legislature requesting from the U.S. Congress not only an appropriation to build Mississippi River levees but also the passage of a law that would provide for "the assumption by the General Government of the Mississippi River . . ." and its lower tributaries—an improbable move for a southern state not long after the Civil War.[35] Eventually, in 1879, the federal government created the Mississippi River Commission to coordinate navigation and flood-control work, but the swamps remained, and the mighty river continued to flood routinely.

Undrained Marshes of the Midwest

At the same time that Mississippi Delta states received swampland grants to help reclaim their chronically flooded wetlands, states in the upper watershed received swampland grants of their own. Glaciers had left the Midwest flat and poorly drained, enlaced by sloughs and meandering rivers that divided potential farmlands into chaotic patches. Experts estimate that the swampy areas of the eight midwestern states once amounted to almost 64 million acres (larger than the state of Oregon).[36]

Because Illinois and Indiana sat squarely on westward travel routes, their wetlands had been among the earliest encountered and settled by pioneers. Indiana's largest wetland region lay in its northwestern corner. Often flooded by the braided Kankakee River, it contained both flat and marshy terrain, along with some large forest pockets. In his assessment, federal surveyor Jeremiah Smith characterized the Kankakee region as "rather uninviting to the capitalist and speculator." While he recognized the value of the lands for pasture, Smith advised that, without drainage, the area would remain "a most dreadful swamp."[37]

Illinois hosted 8.3 million wetland acres—nearly a quarter of the state—some occurring adjacent to rivers, but most spreading across the east-central portion of the state known as the wet prairie.[38] Considering the prairies unhealthy, Illinois settlers initially relegated them to growing wild hay and grazing livestock during dry months. Only when all preferable river valley lands were occupied did midwestern pioneers begin seriously to consider draining the swamplands.[39]

In Illinois and Indiana, extensive settlement predated the federal swamp-land grants, so the states had already developed some means for governing their inundated, malaria-ridden lowlands. Drainage presented challenges to all swampland settlers. To prevent rivers from overflowing into riparian wetland areas, landowners built levees. To drain the waterlogged prairie soils, they dug ditches across the flat landscape. Ditches, however, could not function properly without effective outlets, which often required se-curing rights to build drains across the property of neighbors. Indiana solved this problem by passing the first ditch law in the Midwest in 1832. Modeled after road right-of-way laws, the ditch law directed township jus-tices of the peace to appoint twelve "respectable" landowners to ascertain whether proposed ditches were "necessary and proper." Illinois passed a different type of law in 1845 that authorized landowners of adjacent farm-lands to form "field committees" to oversee the construction of cooperative ditches, fences, and dikes.[40] Both laws recognized that the watery nature of wetlands necessitated cooperative efforts.

While state legislatures designed these laws to govern early drainage at-tempts, little swampland reclamation actually occurred through the 1840s. An Indiana farm journal explained in 1845 that no reason existed for a gen-eral plan to drain the state's wetlands yet because "many farmers have al-ready more arable land than they can till to advantage." The article went on to explain, "Land redeemed from a slough would not pay for itself in many years."[41]

The economics of the situation changed with the 1850 Swamp Land Act. Congress gave nearly 15 million acres to midwestern states alone. In-diana received nearly 1.3 million acres of swamplands, and Illinois received almost 1.5 million acres.[42] Both states chose to rely on their own surveys to identify swamplands, but they picked different administrative methods to disperse the properties.

Indiana chose to hold title to its swamplands. During its 1851–1852 ses-sion, the state legislature hammered out a procedure for selecting, re-claiming, and selling the lands. Each county would have a surveyor identify qualified swamp parcels. After a state auditor and GLO officials verified the county lists, public land auctions could occur. Under Indiana's procedures, settlers purchased swamplands for a minimum of $1.25 per acre, with the understanding that the state would drain them at a future date. In this manner, the "desolate waste" of Indiana would be transformed into a "habitat for industrious, healthy, and happy people."[43]

To oversee drainage, the governor appointed for each county a swamp commissioner, who consulted with engineers, accepted bids, and then proceeded with the least costly work. Because swamp sales initially brought large revenues to the state coffers, the Indiana legislature fell to the temptation of spending the funds for other purposes. In the meantime, local swamp commissioners continued to let drainage contracts commensurate with land-sale income in their counties.[44]

By 1855, Indiana could no longer afford to finance drainage projects, so the governor halted all contracts until new swamp sales raised more funds. The spending freeze, however, precipitated a dramatic decrease in sales. Prospective purchasers regarded the governor's action as repudiation of the state promise to drain its wet lands. The worried governor explained to his swamp commissioners that many people had invested in swamplands "under the confidant expectation that the work of draining and improvement would be carried on vigorously and promptly." "Justice to them, and the faith of the State," he implored, "require that work should be prosecuted by all means."[45] But little money was available to resume drainage.

By 1859, the whole Indiana program teetered on the brink of collapse, so the state senate set up a special committee to investigate the dispersal of swamplands. In addition to uncovering gross corruption and ineptitude, the committee discovered that only 10 percent of contracted swamp drainage projects had ever been completed, and "in a majority of cases a spade ha[d] never broken sod."[46] Furthermore, huge parcels of land had ended up in the grip of speculators.

Although 1,257,588 acres of federally granted swamplands had passed into private ownership in Indiana by 1860, few permanent residents actually worked or inhabited the state's wetlands.[47] Not until the later establishment of cooperative drainage enterprises and the advancement of technology would Indiana's wetlands be transformed into farmlands.

Illinois's swamp dispersal program did no better to accomplish the drainage objectives of the federal swampland grant. In contrast to Indiana, the Illinois legislature decided to turn over swampland titles to counties straightaway. Along with the titles, the legislature gave counties all authority for dispersing lands. Consequently, counties often sold large parcels of land (ostensibly expecting them to be drained) to speculators. Illinois's eight wet prairie counties sold 56 percent of their swamplands to nonresidents. But speculators most often bought the land for a short-term investment or for large-scale cattle operations. For example, in Iroquois County, 47,000 acres went to one New York investor with the understanding that he would drain the wet lands, but the large landowner, later found to be in collusion with a county judge, never intended to drain the swampy land.[48]

Because swamplands held by outside business interests generally remained marshy and uncultivable, local residents hostilely opposed acquisition by speculators. As one editorial in the *Central Illinois Gazette* commented: "We consider every acre that goes into the hands of a nonresident, non-improving speculator as a positive detriment to the people." The editorial went on to castigate speculators: "Our hard working farmers consider *you* an unmitigated evil, and wish that you and your sharp bids and your money making calculations were at the bottom of the Dead Sea."[49]

Only Livingston County favored resident buyers by offering them liberal credit terms: no down payment, no principal for five years, and 5 percent interest, with the title contingent on drainage. But high costs prevented owners of small parcels from draining effectively, so lands were routinely sold three to four times before title was finally passed. In general, counties used few of the funds accumulated through swamp sales for drainage; rather, they spent the minimal income for other expenses.[50]

In the Midwest, neither the system of maintaining state authority tried by Indiana, nor the method of spreading responsibility to counties tried by Illinois worked to accomplish the goals of drainage and cultivation envisioned by the drafters of the Swamp Land Acts. Although hundreds of thousands of acres of wet prairie and forested bottomlands passed into private hands in the twenty years following enactment of the law, most remained natural through this period. Though encumbered by fences here and there, the splendor of the midwestern wetlands still lay undrained and marshy, hosting its abundance of wildlife.

California's Wetlands Besieged

At the time Congress ceded swamplands to California, that territory had only just become a state, owing to the influx of thousands of people looking either for gold or for a profitable part in the boom. In 1852 alone, seventy-seven thousand newcomers arrived in San Francisco, where Telegraph Hill was blasted and dumped into the marshy inlets and coves of the bay to create more dry land for the swelling metropolis.[51] Optimistic about the promise of the new state's wealth, Californians built three-foot levees and established their capital city along the flood-prone banks of the navigable Sacramento River, located halfway between the San Francisco seaport and the mountain gold mines.[52] Aside from their choice of bay and riverside townsites, the first California settlers, like settlers in the East and Midwest before them, avoided wetlands. Consequently, in 1850, the state's natural wetland landscape appeared to be largely intact. Despite appearances, however, the ecosystem had already been heavily tampered with. Since the days of Spanish settlement, cattle had roamed river valleys, displacing the native mule deer and tule elk. Trappers had depleted beaver and otter populations decades earlier. By 1833, Canadian trapper John Work had noted that the country was already "so exhausted that little [could] be done."[53] Furthermore, indigenous peoples that had once lived more or less in balance with the richness of California's wetlands had been exterminated almost entirely by disease or violence.[54]

One journalist viewing the landscape from the vantage of a steamboat chugging between San Francisco and Stockton in the 1850s observed an "apparently interminable sea of tules extend[ing] nearly 150 miles south, up the valley of the San Joaquin."[55] Tule wetlands also stretched northward up the Sacramento River valley. All in all, more than 1 million acres of tules spread through both valleys, known collectively as the Central Valley, and joined together in an enormous delta just east of San Francisco Bay. Settlers soon learned that river overflows completely flooded the Central Valley wetlands in the spring and early summer, but much of the year the land remained dry.

The sporadic hydrologic nature of the lands along the Sacramento and San Joaquin rivers caused some to note their suitability for growing rice. As one observer explained: "The tules invite the planter to convert them into rice fields."[56] But because the initial focus of California settlement was gold mining, and because a strong, individualist, laissez-faire sensibility dominated state politics, there was no impetus for legislators to develop a plan to administer the federally granted swamplands just yet.

Initially, the California legislature did little to act on its federal swampland impartment of nearly 2.2 million acres except to make one experimental grant of 640 acres on Merritt Island in the Sacramento–San Joaquin Delta in 1851. Legislators directed the new owners to drain and cultivate the swampy island and then report back to the state. Their successful reclamation set the precedent for the state to transfer the responsibility of drainage to swampland purchasers. Not until 1855 did the legislature finally pass a plan to select and sell the rest of its swamplands. Since the GLO had not yet surveyed much of the state, California chose to direct its own survey so that it could begin selling swamplands immediately.[57]

To discourage speculation, the state required purchasers to pay the costs of surveying and limited parcel size to a maximum of 320 acres with restricted frontage on rivers, streams, and lakes. To gain title, settlers had only to pay interest, to drain one-half of the land, and to remit the full price within five years. In the meantime, the grantee could cut wood or graze cattle for only the minimal cost of interest. If the terms of the contract were not met, the land reverted to the state for resale in its used condition. Because people took advantage of the program as a leasing arrangement, the generous credit terms actually prevented the drainage of many lands.

State and federal squabbles over what constituted swamplands led to numerous misunderstandings. Often the same lands were sold twice: by the state as swampy, and by the federal government as arable. As a result, settlers avoided buying swamplands from the state, fearing that they would have to pay the federal government a second time to gain legitimate title. In some instances, the state sold swamplands that were subsequently improved by drainage before the GLO completed its official plats. Federal surveyors then recorded the lands as cultivable—not as swamplands—placing titles in question once again. Colusa County surveyor Will Green explained: "Men dislike to invest money in land when the title is in so *chaotic* a state as is the present title to swamplands in this state."[58] As a result, by 1860 the state had failed to sell many swamplands and had drained little land.

Hydraulic mining along upstream tributaries also clouded the certainty of titles, making individual investment in drainage even riskier. As miners wielding high-pressure water jets literally disintegrated hillsides in search of gold, mountains of silt and mine tailings washed into river channels. Downstream in the Central Valley, the swollen rivers deposited higher beds and then overflowed newly erected levees, re-inundating the purportedly drained swamplands. Although the silt and mine tailings caused flooding that damaged many valley farms and an important fishery, farmers and fishermen voiced few complaints. They relied on miners as their primary market. Also, people held a strong belief that citizens—upstream miners included—could do whatever they wished with their private property. The enormous quantities of silt, however, did prompt an article in the *Sacramento Daily Union* warning that, in addition to calamitous flooding, gold mines might cause the state to lose evidence of title to the swamplands being filled by mine tailings.[59]

As flooding worsened, public support for swamp drainage grew. State political sentiments also became more sympathetic to the concept of infrastructure planning espoused by the antislavery Whig party. In 1861, the state legislature recognized that individual enterprise was inadequate to successfully drain swamplands and appointed a Louisiana-style Board of Swampland Commissioners to resolve land title controversies, to manage funds from swampland sales, and to supervise drainage projects. Despite the revolutionary nature of the statewide reclamation program, by the end of the board's first year, twenty-eight hydrologically based districts in twelve Central Valley counties had signed up. The commissioners would provide engineering advice and administer funds to groups of landowners who formed drainage districts. If the estimated expense of drainage cost less than the money paid into the fund by swampland owners, the project could proceed. But in many instances, large portions of drainage districts remained unsold or were only half paid for. No district had enough money to pay for all its drainage projects.[60]

Furthermore, several landowners still resisted drainage. Cattle ranchers, for example, relied on the rivers' seasonal overflows to grow tules for livestock feed. The state surveyor general in his annual report for 1856 remarked, "It is well known the tules are extensively used in the dry season for food by cattle, and swine fatten in them better than elsewhere."[61] Even some grain farmers recognized that the rivers' overflows fertilized the valley with rich nutrients. One long-time Colusa County resident explained, "The best crops of grain ever raised upon prairie lands . . . were after they had been overflowed by one of the heavy freshets which have occurred every few years, and without such overflow no dependence can be put on raising a good crop of grain."[62] Opposition intensified when the legislature authorized counties to collect additional taxes to fund drainage projects in 1862. Despite friction, demands for flood control won out. A newly appointed Board of Commissioners then tried credit financing to fund drainage projects—but with little success.

By 1865, citizens began to criticize the swampland commissioners for not reclaiming enough overflow lands. At one estimate, the commission had supervised draining only 15,000 acres of swamplands. The reasons for the board's failure were many. Commissioners lacked necessary hydrological data, technical expertise, and credibility. Moreover, revenues generated from swampland sales did not begin to cover drainage costs. Then heavy rains in the winters of 1862 and 1863 caused floods that destroyed levees and foiled planned projects. Finally, post–Civil War racism shifted political sensibilities in California against federalism; locally, this antigovernment anger was directed at the swamp commissioners.[63]

Particularly unimpressed with failed drainage attempts near Sacramento, the state legislature disbanded the Board of Commissioners in 1868 and instead turned the job of selling swamplands over to counties, which then sold the land without acreage limitations. During the first three years that counties sold lands, nearly all the state's swamp holdings passed into private ownership. Thus began the long tradition of large landowners in the Central Valley. For example, Miller and Lux cattle operations acquired 900,000 acres in the San Joaquin Valley, most of it swampland available for less than one dollar per acre.[64]

Private ownership did little to further drainage. The sharp angles of the new property lines made watershed planning more difficult. The individual efforts of large landowners frequently resulted in the flooding of adjacent and downstream lands. Many landowners had trouble draining their lands because levees were not uniform. Furthermore, substantial acreages of swamplands passed straight to absentee speculators, who had little concern for local flood issues. In fact, in California the term "swamplander" came to refer derogatorily to fatcat speculators.[65]

Without consensus, piecemeal efforts at levee building failed. If hydraulic mining disgorged more tailings or if swamp owners built levees upstream, landowners downstream needed newer, higher levees. In many ways, the difficulties of draining California's wetlands were similar to the difficulties of irrigating the state's arid lands. In both cases, individual efforts repeatedly failed because of large capital requirements. Landowners of both wet and dry lands throughout watersheds had to assent to either a drainage plan or common water laws to make reclamation projects work. Furthermore, the technologies of both drainage and irrigation were still evolving. Early levees were built without surveys or technical supervision, often by Chinese laborers who worked with shovels, wheelbarrows, and horses shod specially for muck; only the desired length and width of the levee need be specified.[66] Finally, in mid-nineteenth-century California, laws, financing opportunities, and expertise remained limited.

In 1874, the editor of the *Sacramento Daily Union* derided private swampland owners for building levees of their own accord, "with a sublime disregard for any unity of plan or action, and in many cases with the smallest consideration for the most ordinary principles of hydraulic engineering."[67] Many others agreed.

State Engineer William Hammond ("Ham") Hall, in his 1880 report to the legislature, criticized the lack of coordination in levee construction and the unbridled mess of mining debris. He noted that the state's swampland policies encouraged conflict between landowners when, in fact, people needed to cooperate to build successful levee and drainage systems. In Hall's estimation, "The general works designed for the prevention of overflow in this State generally have failed."[68] Though most of California's interior wetlands were privately owned by 1880, they remained largely undrained.

Wetlands Reprieved

While the Swamp Land Acts infixed attitudes toward swamps, codified the cultural imperative to drain wet lands, and transferred over 60 million acres into private ownership, the legislation failed to drastically change the face of the land.[69] Though Congress intended to transform swamps into farms, little drainage actually occurred under the auspices of the acts.

Because the definition of what constituted swamplands confused citizens and surveyors as much as it perplexed members of Congress, the swamp grant law was subject to great distortion and graft. In Mississippi, where surveyors were compensated on the basis of how much swampland they entered for the state, one reportedly dragged a canoe over acres of dry pinelands, expecting that passability by boat would be sufficient evidence for swampiness. Such disingenuousness was typical.[70] In 1857, the surveyor general wrote that he received lists of sworn swamplands "situated amongst and embracing portions of the Ozark Mountains." Federal field surveyors had previously described the same lands as "too mountainous and hilly for cultivation."[71] To keep fraud in check, the GLO eventually employed special agents in the field. Upon one reexamination, an agent found only 7,500 acres of a 50,000-acre parcel claimed by Illinois to be actual swampland.[72] Out of 64,360 acres claimed in five counties in Iowa, only 7,400 were swampy. One agent auditing Iowa reported that of fifteen tracts he inspected one day, "nine could not in any sense be claimed as swampland . . . some of it is high, dry, and arable; and in successful cultivation, and among the best lands in the country."[73] Taking corruption into account, the federal swamp grant probably included many lands that would not be considered wetlands today.

Most significant, through the 1850s and 1860s the technological, legal, and financial groundwork necessary for successful drainage did not yet exist. Historian Margaret Beattie Bogue has suggested that the whole of drainage problems and scandals would have been minimized if states had only waited two decades for the improvement and widespread dissemination of tiling techniques.[74] During those decades of technological trial and error, infrastructure would develop, state governments would forge necessary laws, and financial institutions critical to funding drainage projects would grow.

But in 1872, the commissioner of the General Land Office concluded that the swamp grants had not yet fulfilled the commendable goals that "its projectors hoped for."[75] Although the Swamp Land Acts did not accomplish the drainage its authors envisioned, the engineering experience gained in trying to implement the acts laid the foundation for successful drainage projects undertaken later in the century. Furthermore, many legal and legislative concepts established with the Swamp Land Acts became permanent fixtures in the realm of drainage and flood-control policy.[76] For example, the concept of local quasi-governing bodies collecting taxes for specific services grew more familiar and acceptable. In particular, the idea that wetlands were property with finite boundaries just like all other property became further entrenched without any heed for their common hydrologic attributes.

In privatizing the nation's swamps, Congress gave away its ability to oversee a systematic approach to drainage planning and also eliminated the possibility of protecting the many public values not yet understood to be provided by wetlands.

Tide Marsh Trials

While states with swampland grants puzzled over appropriate ways to drain and cultivate their wetlands, citizens of East Coast states, most of which had sold off wetlands a century earlier, struggled with reclaiming their privately owned tidal marshes. In a few locales, such as the Delaware Bay and along New Jersey's Maurice River, landowners had formed cooperative reclamation companies necessary to drain tidal marshes. But effective drainage was the exception.

Early on, tidal marshes had been divided up into small parcels. Generations of farmers had harvested salt hay for fodder, and in many coastal towns, there was strong reluctance to give up this customary land use. Aside from cutting hay, people hunted wild fowl, dug clams in marshes, and caught fish in tidal creeks, which also served as travel routes and generated power by turning waterwheels. The long-standing success of this multiple-usage pattern made it unlikely that small marsh owners would assent to drainage. Some farmers even quoted scripture to argue against salt marsh reclamation. They regarded it as a new idea that threatened their traditional way of life.[77] Aside from cultural considerations, few farmers had surplus assets to invest in risky drainage ventures.

When entrepreneurial farmers did attempt to drain small marsh parcels, burrowing muskrats or high tides usually undermined the inadequate dikes. Expressing the frustration of many, James Bill of Connecticut explained: "Now, after expending $40,000 . . . I don't feel like saying one word to induce others to fool away their money upon those old worthless salt meadows."[78] According to David Montgomery Nesbit, who conducted a national survey of tide marshes for the USDA in 1885, the litany of failed attempts discouraged most tide marsh owners from considering drainage any further. "A burnt child dreads fire," he wrote, and so many small marsh owners bitterly opposed reclamation efforts.[79]

Aside from the evidence of failure, the prospect of draining marshes raised many questions about competing rights of landowners and other marsh beneficiaries. For reclamation to be profitable, large tracts had to be protected from saltwater by single massive dikes; otherwise, costs would easily exceed profits. If one marsh owner refused to cooperate, drainage efforts might not succeed. Some questioned whether it was fair for one person to hold up progress that could benefit the entire community—especially considering the public health benefits of drainage. Yet, on the other hand, if an individual marsh owner wanted to continue harvesting salt hay as he had always done, it wouldn't be right to force him to do things differently. Such ethical enigmas routinely prevented small marsh owners from pursuing drainage. Furthermore, most states did not yet have laws to clarify the rights of various owners.[80]

Even when all marsh landowners agreed to drain, the livelihoods of other community members might be adversely affected. In many coastal towns, for example, tide mills relied on the outflow of rivers for their power; if the rivers were blocked, the local miller could no longer operate.[81] Draining tidal marshes could also affect fishermen. In Marshfield, Massachusetts, for example, a group of marsh owners sought to drain their lands by building a dike across the outlet of a tidal river to prevent inundation with saltwater at high tide. From the beginning, fisherman and waterfowl gunners who depended on the anchorage at Green Harbor for their livelihoods opposed the dike. They feared that closing the outlet of the river would diminish the outward scour at low tide and cause the harbor to shoal up. After years of debate, the state legislature, reflecting society's traditional bias toward agriculture, approved plans for the farmers to build their dike with the provision that they dredge up any shoals that clogged the harbor.

With completion of the dike in 1872, farmers successfully excluded saltwater and began to grow vegetables and English grasses, such as timothy, redtop, and rye. Within thirteen years, the value of the lands increased from six dollars an acre to forty dollars an acre. But as fishermen had feared, soon after the dike blocked the outlet of the Green Harbor River, their harbor shoaled up and farmers refused to dredge it. Unable to resolve the squabble locally, the fishermen requested relief from the state. Despite a legal order from the Board of Harbor Commissioners and a special appropriation from the legislature to enforce the original stipulations of the law, the marsh owners still made no effort to remove accumulated material. Bitter feelings between the "dikers" and the fishermen grew. Vigilante fishermen attempted to blast the obstructive dike with dynamite—five times.[82] Not until 1898 did the legislature resolve the contentious dispute by using taxpayer moneys to build jetties and dredge a new harbor. Because shoaling was an ongoing process, maintenance of the harbor would endlessly continue to drain state funds.

In 1908, the legislature directed a joint board of harbor and land commissioners to investigate the feasibility of removing the dike altogether and returning the harbor to its natural conditions. In its final report the joint board admitted, "The experiment of reclaiming the marshes above the present dike has been costly to the Commonwealth, of slight benefit to the marsh owners who built the dike, and a source of undoubted injury to this small harbor."[83] Nonetheless, owing to marsh subsidence, the commissioners warned that removing the dike would only destroy "much valuable property" and create a "serious nuisance to the whole neighborhood." Instead, the engineers recommended continued dredging and more jetties, or a plan to install more sluices in the dike to allow for scouring releases. In either case, public funds would be needed to remedy the consequences of the marsh owners' experimental drainage project.

After reviewing all the conflicts associated with drainage in tidal marshes in 1885, USDA surveyor David Nesbit, from his reclamation-favoring perspective, suggested that "all private rights inimical to greater commercial or other public interests should be extinguished at public cost."[84] In this way, the larger project of drainage could proceed unimpeded by the knotty issues of individual rights. Nesbit saw the government's power of eminent domain as a legitimate tool for communities seeking to drain their marshes. Of course, at the time, he didn't realize that "public interests" associated with marshes extended far beyond farming. Despite Nesbit's agrarian vision of a drained eastern seaboard, the bias against new methods of farming in traditional communities coupled with the availability of fresh farmlands in the West left most of the Atlantic and gulf coast marshes in their natural state, used for grazing, fishing, and fowling.

While the persistence of customary marsh use generally discouraged large drainage projects in Atlantic marshes, coastal states still had to grapple with many of the same problems attendant to wetland development in the western swamp-grant states. Because the water and land nexus of wetlands defied traditional understanding of land and land use, all states had to develop legal and financial means to facilitate cooperative drainage. Only through joint enterprises, usually districts created by or provided for by state law, could individual swampland and tideland owners reap the benefits of drainage and cultivation of their wetlands. Yet even with new laws in place to encourage cooperation, individual landowners often failed to understand how the interconnectedness of wetland hydrology made collaboration necessary. Some resisted paying drainage taxes or tried to do reclamation work on their own. Usually such attempts failed and undermined other efforts as well.

Although the drainage laws ostensibly conceded something different about the nature of wetlands by fostering cooperation between owners, they still treated these landscapes fundamentally as land. Not until well into the next century would people gain a better understanding of wetland hydrology and recognize the public values of wetlands. In the meantime— until states developed laws to make drainage and financing easier, until technology improved, and until people agreed to work together—America's wetlands remained largely intact.

SIX

Wetlands Portrayed and Envisioned

> Hope and the future for me are not in the lawns and the
> cultivated fields, not in the towns and cities, but in the im-
> pervious and quaking swamps.
>
> —Henry David Thoreau [1]

As the Mississippi rose in mid June, fearful, sweat-browed residents
patched levees to keep floodwaters from pouring into their swamp-wrested
farms. But in New England, in a patch of maple woodlands just west of
Concord, Massachusetts, one man experienced the wetland landscape in
an entirely different manner. The heat and humidity of the early summer
compelled Henry Thoreau to plunge into the cool water and mud of a local
swamp. Suspending all traditional preconceptions of what swamps should
be, Thoreau eased his wiry body into the pungent mixture of decomposing
leaves, stagnant water, saturated sphagnum, and mire. His feet stopped in a
thick layer of muck threaded by long-fallen branches. Submerged to his
neck, he squatted further to be less conspicuous. With only eyes and nose
above the water, he proceeded through the small wetland, observing intimately all the life present in this place unknown to his fellow Concordians.

Later that day, June 15, 1840, Thoreau recorded the invigorating experience in his journal. "Would it not be a luxury to stand up to one's chin in
some retired swamp for a whole summer's day, scouting the sweet-fern and
bilberry blows, and lulled by the minstrelry of gnats and mosquitos?" he
mused. "Surely, one may profitable be soaked in the juices of a marsh for
one day, as pick his way dry-shod oversand."[2]

Well mentored in Romantic and transcendental thought by his neighbor
Ralph Waldo Emerson, Thoreau took those ideas further by literally im-
mersing himself in the natural world to an intense and original degree.
Beyond enabling him to learn about nature, Thoreau's explorations led
him to question the values of contemporary society. Although he initially

wrote about swamps in a conventionally derisive manner, using them as metaphors to criticize society's ills, he soon realized that the landscape worked better as metaphor for the vitality and exuberance of life. The very fact that swamps were so strongly disliked by society prompted him to rein-vestigate and develop his own understanding of them. What began for Thoreau as an exercise in social critique blossomed into an intimate and fertile relationship with natural swamps.[3]

For Thoreau, like William Bartram, the complexity of the natural swamps was evidence of divine design, and closeness to that landscape meant a closeness to God. Throughout his journals Thoreau characterized wild swamps as spiritually significant places because they had remained vir-tually untouched by humanity since creation. He praised wetlands for their wildness and beauty, though he acknowledged being the only person in his town so inclined.[4] But most important to Thoreau, swamps provided a refuge from modern society—a place where people could retune themselves to harmonious natural songs.

While Thoreau's journal did not become available to readers until the following century, essays published posthumously in the *Atlantic* in 1862 presented his new ways of looking at the swamp landscape to a broader au-dience. In his well-known essay "Walking," Thoreau wrote: "When I would recreate myself, I seek the darkest wood, the thickest and most interminable and, to the citizen, most dismal, swamp. I enter a swamp as a sacred place, a *sanctum sanctorum*. There is the strength, the marrow, of Nature."[5] To Thoreau, the swamp epitomized wild nature. Actually, in nineteenth-century New England, about the only unused and unmanipulated land-scapes remaining were the swamps still tucked along the edges of farm fields and rivers.

Thoreau's revision of swamps was unique, but it was not all that far off the mark from other contemporary thinkers. Literate people had begun to question, for example, whether it was always so clear that some things were unequivocally bad and others good. Was it not possible and exciting to con-sider alternative perspectives? With an increasing secularism and greater willingness to abandon old-fashioned puritanical values, topics long held as taboo were open for consideration. Although traditional ways of under-standing swamps still dominated, by the middle of the nineteenth century, educated people began to reexamine the previously eschewed landscape.

A contemporary of Thoreau found his solace in another wetland land-scape. Martin Johnson Heade painted the expansive salt marshes of the

Atlantic Coast as his primary subject. Although other painters occasionally included marshes as backdrop, Heade was the first to paint salt marshes for their own sake. Introduced to coastal wetlands on a duck-hunting excursion, he began painting marshes in 1860 at age forty after a full career painting portraits and other landscapes.

While Thoreau had bent transcendentalism to his own vision of embracing the wild complexity of nature, Heade tempered transcendentalism with aesthetic theory to a more meditative end. Like many painters of the day, Heade sought to evoke a sense of the sublime with his art, but rather than render craggy peaks, he found that tranquil salt marsh scenes accomplished his goal. Because marshes prompted one to gaze across their monotonous, grassy expanses to the horizon, for Heade they were the perfect vehicle for conveying the transcendental, awe-inspiring state experienced when contemplating infinity. Heade frequently added approaching storms to heighten the drama of his marsh compositions. To exaggerate the horizontal and better represent the infinite, he made most of his canvases two times as long as they were tall. Often including graceful stacks of salt hay in the foreground of an otherwise simple view, Heade depicted the marshes as pastoral, comfortable scenes—honoring the common landscape that so many small communities had founded their livelihoods upon. Even the familiar haystacks receded into the distance, ultimately guiding the viewer's eyes to experience transcendence by gazing toward the horizon.[6]

When contemporary landscape painters of the leading Hudson River School encouraged fellow artists to document the beauty of nature before it was despoiled by the ravages of expanding industry, Heade painted marshes. In these landscapes, he saw that a balanced relationship between people and the natural world persisted. In many coastal towns, people still worked quietly reaping salt hay without destroying the marshes, in sharp contrast to the new railroads, farms, and towns that leveled and destroyed forests farther west. Working in salt marshes in Massachusetts, Rhode Island, Connecticut, Maine, Long Island, New Jersey, and eventually Florida, Heade disregarded negative associations with the marsh landscape and instead found in them a refuge for the contemplation of the spiritually profound. In his association with the Hudson River School painters, he enjoyed small acclaim but never achieved mainstream recognition.[7] Yet the subject of salt marshes riveted him until his death at age eighty-four. He completed more than one hundred known marsh paintings, and art historians suspect that there were many more.[8]

Although Thoreau's essays and Heade's paintings suggested new ways of envisioning backyard swamp and marsh landscapes as spiritually significant, they enjoyed only limited popularity among the cognoscenti. Another contemporary writer, however, managed to intrigue a wider audience with his exotic swamp adventures.

In September of 1856, readers of *Harper's Monthly* enjoyed a narrative journey to Virginia's Great Dismal Swamp. Journalist David Hunter Strother, well known to his readers by the pen name Porte Crayon, recounted a tale of swamp adventure in the popular magazine. Traveling by canal boat, Strother could focus on what he saw and heard while floating easily through the terrain that 130 years prior had sucked the shoes off William Byrd's surveying party. Being able to travel through wetlands with greater ease would become very important to the changing perceptions of these places.

Without the difficulties of travel to overcome, Strother was struck visually by the unusual features of the swamp. As character Porte Crayon journeyed down the canal, he described how the vegetation enclosed the waterway: "Lofty trees threw their arching limbs over the canal, clothed to their tops with a gauze-like drapery of tangled vines; walls of matted reeds closed up the view on either side, while thickets of myrtle, green briar, bay and juniper, hung over the black, narrow canal, until the boat could scarcely find a passage between."[9] But at times, the thick vegetation gave way, allowing Porte to glimpse deeper beyond the confines of the canal to "extensive pools of black, slimy water, from which rose the broad-based cypress, and . . . those strange contorted roots, called knees, gnarled and knotted like stalagmites in a cave."[10] Though highly descriptive, the language Strother used in his article was not moralistic.

For hours, Porte floated through the canal, watching the unusual vegetation as he passed. When he finally arrived at the center of the swamp in Lake Drummond, he sang a ballad well known to nineteenth-century Americans, "The Lake of the Dismal Swamp," written by Irish poet Thomas Moore in 1803. Porte recalled that the song was sung to him as a lullaby, probably as it was sung to many children. The ballad was so popular that another writer later claimed that the name of the Great Dismal was "almost as familiar as Niagara or the Rocky Mountains."[11] The ballad told of a man who became crazed when the woman he loved died. In his madness, he raved that she had not died but gone to the Dismal Swamp, where she paddled a white canoe; so he followed there in search of her.[12]

The Barge.

Readers of *Harper's* became acquainted with the Great Dismal Swamp through the adventures of David Strother's colorful character, Porte Crayon. Traveling by barge enabled Strother to float through the swamp with ease. Unencumbered by difficulties of travel, he reported about the landscape as a curious and intriguing place. (From *Harper's New Monthly Magazine,* September 1856, reprinted by permission of Special Collections Department, University of Virginia Library, Charlottesville.)

While Moore's poem had associated the Great Dismal Swamp with traditional attributes of death and mysterious apparitions, the journey of Porte Crayon portrayed the swamp in a wholly different manner—as curious object, as aesthetic object. In fact, in mid-nineteenth-century context, the ballad formed part of the allure of the place. Porte's journey represented a new relationship with the exotic landscape: one in which the traveler was no longer threatened or overwhelmed by real dangers and conventional associations. Swamps simply fit next to other landscapes, such as mountains and beaches; and there was no question that they—like the other landscapes—should have their own literature. The very characteristics of swamps that in the past had repulsed people now seemed to generate intrigue.

The adventures of Porte Crayon reflected a growing interest during the mid nineteenth century in armchair travel to exotic places. With growing secularization, mid-Victorians were fascinated by the new and different. The experience of bizarre and horrific was not spurned but rather experimented with as titillation. It was in this context that the swamp landscape was taken out of the back closet and brought into the open for closer scrutiny. Art and literature provided the safest and easiest ways for people to explore the little-known swamp landscapes.

While it may be difficult for modern readers, barraged with multimedia, to comprehend the influence of painting and popular literature on the American consciousness during the nineteenth century, these mediums formed important referents with which people made sense of their lives—perhaps in the way that television now provides viewers with a common denominator for discussion. It was not uncommon for literate people to refer to art and literature when describing their own experiences. For example, when explorer George Preble canoed through the interior of south Florida in 1842, he used an art metaphor to describe the landscape in his diary. Camping amidst baldcypress, bay, and cabbage palms, he wrote, "The beautiful moonlight contrasting with the dark recesses of the forest, and our campfires' glare upon the gray mossy beards which draped the trees, and our rough and rugged men in their careless costumes and still more careless attitudes, combined to make our bivouac a scene which Salvator Rosa would have been glad to have copied."[13] Rosa was a well-known Italian painter whose name had become synonymous with picturesque landscapes. By comparing the swamp hammock he visited to Rosa's artwork, Preble invested greater meaning in his own description of the landscape; the view clearly exhibited the aesthetic qualities of a good painting. More important, Preble's familiarity with art enabled him to experience a particular reverence for the landscape. In the same way that Salvator Rosa's paintings made an impression on Preble, the writings of Thoreau, the paintings of Audubon and Heade, and the adventures of Porte Crayon would similarly impress and influence others.

Literary magazines gained tremendous popularity in the mid nineteenth century. *Harper's Monthly,* for example, enjoyed a circulation of 200,000 readers before the Civil War, prompting one commentator to note, "There is not a village, there is scarcely a township in the land into which [Harper's] has not penetrated."[14] And so, there was scarcely a locale where Porte Crayon was unknown. By 1860, Porte Crayon had become a household name.[15]

Beyond Crayon's jaunt in the Great Dismal, literate Americans became acquainted with a number of swamps through the popular press. *Harper's New Monthly* magazine published several other stories about swamp adventures. In the anonymous "Ibis Shooting in Louisiana," a bird hunter and collector led readers on a journey through the bottomlands of the Mississippi Delta in search of a scarlet ibis. In a small skiff, the hunter paddled through black-water bayous deep into the marshy swamps. When he finally saw his desired quarry at the end of an island, he delightedly shot it and then ran across the island to retrieve it. Only when he held the bird in his hands and looked back did he realize that the boat had floated away. The hunter immediately realized the peril of his situation. He couldn't wade or swim because alligators wove back and forth in the water surrounding the island; and nobody would realize that he was missing. He fell into a stupor of sorts until night when he was shocked back into awareness as the giant reptiles attempted to snuggle up to his warmth. For days, he was unable to sleep because the alligators came near him whenever he lay down. "Even when I lay for a few minutes motionless," he explained, "the dark reptiles came crawling round me—so close that I could have put forth my hands and touched them."[16] Willingness to even consider the titillating chance to touch the rough, black, saurian skin was a newly admissible topic, but *Harper's* audience approached such encounters with curiosity and relish. Like Strother, the anonymous hunter provided descriptions of the swamp and its denizens but attached little moral meaning to the landscape. After several trying days, the hunter claimed to have escaped on a raft of inflated alligator innards.

Swamp adventure stories appeared in other popular contemporary magazines as well, including the *Atlantic Monthly*. Even the *Ladies' Magazine of Literature, Fashion and Fine Arts* featured an article entitled "Rambles in the Swamps of Louisiana," which endeavored "to investigate the social, political, scientific, and religious condition" of that state's swamps.[17] Landscapes clearly held profound meaning for inquisitive nineteenth-century readers.

In addition to articles in popular magazines, literate Americans became more familiar with swamps through Henry Wadsworth Longfellow's landmark poem *Evangeline*, first published in 1847 and ultimately published in many editions. Even though Longfellow had never traveled in southern swamps himself, his poem made a local Louisiana legend into the national rage. Longfellow first heard the tale from a Louisianan student at Harvard. Intrigued by the story of a woman separated from her lover when the

Acadians were brutally banished from Canada, Longfellow decided to write a poem about her. After a long search that culminates in descriptive verses about her trials in Louisiana's swamps, Evangeline finds her beloved Gabriel in the bayous, where the Acadians had remade their homes. In order to describe the swamps accurately, Longfellow studied the landscape through books and through correspondence with people more familiar with the Louisiana bottomlands.[18] He portrayed swamps as inviting places of refuge.

The growing popularity of landscape painting in both Europe and the United States generated further interest in the tremendously varied American lands. As American artists and writers struggled to create their own homegrown art and literature independent of European influence, the wild natural landscape formed an inspiring and truly American subject. The American landscape became a font of nationalism, and knowing the landscape became a favorite project for nineteenth-century Americans.[19] In fact, numerous books—both picture books and travel books—chronicled the various landscape types.

One such book, *Romantic Landscapes,* authored by T. Addison Richards in 1855, described the varied American landscape through the eyes of a group of travelers, one of whom spoke about swamps of the Southeast with particular relish. "My favorite haunts are the dark and poisonous lagunes which lead into the mysterious heart of the ghostly swamp," Mr. Blueback explained. "Creeping in my canoe through these dismal passages—their black waters filled with venomous snakes and lurking alligators, and shut out from the light of the day by the intervening branches of the cypress, the dark foliage of the magnolia, and the inextricable veils of rampant vine, with the gray trailing moss pendent everywhere in mournful festoons—my fancy has run riot through a thousand wild and dreary imaginings which it would harrow up from your soul to hear."[20] The very qualities and characteristics that had always turned people away from swamps held for Mr. Blueback and for other landscape enthusiasts a new fascination.

Beyond curious and exotic features, the wildness of swamps also captivated the Romantics. Although the swamp landscape itself had not yet changed much, the ratio of wild lands to cultivated lands in the East had shifted markedly; and few wild lands remained. Romantic regret for the loss of those pristine places, where one could know the earth of God's creation firsthand, inspired at least part of their interest in the enduring swamplands.

With their writing and artwork, Romantic landscape enthusiasts challenged the long-standing tradition of considering swamps as worthless wastelands.

The Swamp as a Metaphor for Slavery

The mid nineteenth century saw an awakening receptivity not only to aesthetic swamp images but to rhetorical ones as well. While Romantics chose to investigate the sensual and exotic attributes of swamp landscapes, abolitionist intellectuals revived the Puritan habit of projecting moral meaning onto landscape and bolstered conventional associations with swamp landscapes—but to a particular purpose. Their swampy Southern landscape embodied a moral and physical wasteland linked with the evils of slavery. As sectional tensions mounted, this rich swamp metaphor became commonplace.

After finishing the popular and influential *Uncle Tom's Cabin* (1852), Harriet Beecher Stowe wrote *Dred, A Tale of the Dismal Swamp* (1856), using the landscape as both physical and allegorical backdrop for her anti-slavery novel. Although Stowe had never traveled to the South, she managed to provide a typical rendition of cypress swamps, based largely on descriptions given by her friend Frederick Law Olmsted, who traveled through the South in 1852.[21] But beyond her conventional portrayal, Stowe quite explicitly invested symbolic moral meaning into the Southern swamps. "The wild, dreary belt of swamp-land which girds in those states scathed by the fires of despotism," she wrote, "is an apt emblem, in its rampant and we might say delirious exuberance of vegetation, of that darkly struggling, wildly vegetating swamp of human souls, cut off, like it, from the usages and improvements of cultivated life."[22] Beyond dreariness and evil, Stowe's Southern swamp landscape represented indolence and uncontrolledness that directly threatened the Northern social standards of industriousness and moral propriety.[23]

In an 1863 book, *Out-door Papers*, T. W. Higginson, an *Atlantic Monthly* writer, corroborated Stowe's symbolistic view. "But there lingers upon this continent a *forest* of moral evil more formidable, a barrier denser and darker, a *Dismal Swamp* of inhumanity," he wrote, "a barbarism upon the *soil*, before which civilization has thus far been compelled to pause,— happy, if it could even check its spread."[24] The entangled, pestilent, and confusing swamp symbolized the indecipherable and unresolvable moral conflict presented by slavery.

While the dominant metaphoric use of the swamp landscape emblema-
tized moral turpitude, Stowe's narrative also portrayed the swamp in a different light—as a refuge for runaway slaves. Describing Dred, she wrote:
"To walk knee-deep in the spongy soil of the swamp, to force his way
through thickets, to lie all night sinking in the porous soil, or to crouch, like
the alligator, among the reeds and rushes, were to him situations of as much
comfort as well-curtained beds and pillows are to us."[25] While it is unlikely
that any slave was as comfortable living in swamps as Stowe suggested, her
idealization of Dred's "communion with nature" is significant. Although on
one hand she linked wild swamps to the evil of slavery, she also characterized them as a Romantic repository of spirituality that nourished Dred's for-
titude.[26] Henry Wadsworth Longfellow, who shared the same political sentiment and social circle as Stowe, published another popular swamp poem
in 1855 along the same theme, "The Slave in the Dismal Swamp." This
motif also became the theme of several paintings, including Thomas
Moran's *Slaves Escaping through a Swamp,* which depicts a slave couple
trudging through a pool of water surrounded by entangled swamp vegetation. In the background, dogs and hunters trail them in pursuit.[27]

At the same time Northerners came to understand swamps as both
symbol and sanctuary, the notion that runaway slaves congregated in
swamps aroused fear of slave uprisings among Southerners. The imaginative linking of fugitive slaves with swamps had became common in the aftermath of the 1831 Nat Turner rebellion, when Turner and his cohorts retreated to the Great Dismal Swamp after their violent revolt.[28] In fact,
Stowe likely modeled her character Dred after Turner. Southern author
Sam Warner, however, wrote about Turner and his fellow insurgents in a
less sympathetic manner. Warner thought it incredulous that "within the
deep recesses of this gloomy Swamp, 'dismal' indeed, . . . subsisting on
frogs, tarripins, and even snakes! . . . there could be found an individual of
the human species, who, rather than wear the goading yoke of bondage,
would prefer becoming the subject of so great a share of want and
misery!"[29]

Later, Louisiana author George Washington Cable, in his historical
novel *The Grandissimes,* further perpetuated this scare. According to a
legend—told to him by a black porter in a New Orleans cotton brokerage—
the king Bras Coupé was brought from Africa in chains. Maintaining his
regal integrity, he could not stand to labor as a slave and so escaped into
nearby swamps. With voodoo powers, he cursed his master's land, which

consequently fell into low productivity. Coupé then terrorized fishermen and hunters who ventured into his swamp domain. As such, the black fugitive lurking in the swamps became a symbol of white fear.[30] This concept was particularly unsettling for white Southerners who had come to regard swamps as a symbol of regional alliance. The swampy Southern terrain knit the region together with common experience and knowledge that no outsiders shared.[31]

In addition to writing and art that portrayed swamps metaphorically, at the time of the Civil War, Union soldiers brought back firsthand descriptions and stories of their own experiences in the Southern swamps. In a series of popular articles covering the war for *Harper's Weekly,* writer and illustrator A. R. Waud presented descriptive images of the swamps of Louisiana. Waud's interpretation of the landscape was multivalent. On one hand, obstacle-ridden swamps with fearsome snakes and alligators presented Union soldiers with extra difficulties in their battles. But on the other hand, Waud recognized that the bizarre terrain offered much of interest. He described eighty-foot cypress trees "draped with [Spanish moss] in the most fantastic style," the fragrance of the luxuriant water lilies, and the brilliant colors of the birds. In this vein, Waud portrayed the swamps as sanctuary for the soldiers as well. "Inhospitable as they are," he wrote, "these swamps formed a secure place of refuge for many a persecuted Union man during the rebellion; and were, on the other hand, silent witnesses of more than one martyrdom to the Union cause."[32]

More than his language, Waud's illustrations conveyed memorable visual images to *Harper's* readers. An engraving entitled "Cypress Swamp on the Opelousas Railroad, Louisiana," which appeared in *Harper's Weekly* on December 8, 1866, included all predictable denizens of the swamp. Leaving little room for the Union soldiers whose experiences he recounted, Waud crowded alligators with enormous claws, large insects, spiders, snapping turtles, snakes, and a lone heron into the rectangular window of the illustration. He also included strange-looking cypress knees, pendulous Spanish moss, decaying tree trunks, shelf fungus, and lily pads. His image typified the contemporary understanding of the swamp landscape as intriguing yet still frightful.[33]

The Images of Reconstruction

As Americans became reinterested in their nation's landscape after the Civil War, writers and thinkers began to reconsider swamps with open minds once again. After the abolition of slavery, swamps could no longer be cloaked in neo-Puritan associations of evil. In fact, following the war, a greater number of Northerners traveled to the South as tourists to enjoy the warm climate and the different landscapes. As new attitudes toward Southern politics and culture developed, new attitudes toward the Southern landscape developed as well.

Even Harriet Beecher Stowe, who had heaped the most repugnant descriptions upon the Southern landscape, saw things in a new light when she became a Floridian after the war. In her 1873 book, *Palmetto Leaves,* Stowe referred to the swampy land around her home as "the most gorgeous of improprieties."[34] Then in a letter to friend George Eliot, she described the luxuriant vegetation of the swamp as a personal refuge: "the place to forget the outside world and live in one's self."[35]

Some writers and artists who had spent time in the South during the war were drawn back to the unusual landscape. In an 1871 article for *Every Saturday* magazine, journalist A. R. Waud, who had covered the war for *Harper's,* expressed new reverence for the swampscape as he neared "the thick solitude of the magnificent old cypresses." Echoing Thoreau's sentiments, Waud described the swamp as a religious temple where "all the feathered and reptile brethren in their vast cathedral went on with their beads and paternosters reckless of the intrusion or possible heresy in their midst."[36] What during the war Waud had portrayed as obstacle now became solely the object of curiosity—much in the way that David Strother had depicted the Great Dismal in his Porte Crayon stories before the war.

Painter Joseph Rusling Meeker had spent the war in Southern swamps working as a navy paymaster on a Union gunboat that traveled the length of the Mississippi. Having completed all the appropriate training for a painter of his day, Meeker had set up a studio in St. Louis before the war. His experiences on the river, however, turned his artistic interest toward landscapes. From the gunboat, he collected sketches of swamps that became the basis for his later bayou paintings. Meeker worked steadily in St. Louis from 1870 until 1889, returning to the swamps at times to make more sketches. Many of his paintings shared similar compositions, iridescent colors, and a particular quality of mystery and of light. Meeker frequently painted canvases that were taller than wide, which enabled him to include the entire height of a cypress tree from its fluted trunk and burly knees to its top. Meeker also painted several large canvases depicting Longfellow's popular *Evangeline,* down to minute descriptive references, such as a garland of

A Florida Swamp.

Engravings portraying the curious and exotic features of swamps such as this one, which appeared in the popular travel book *Picturesque America,* introduced many nineteenth-century Americans to the Southern swamp landscape. (From William Cullen Bryant, *Picturesque America,* vol. 1, New York, 1872, reprinted by permission of Special Collections Department, University of Virginia Library, Charlottesville.)

"roses, trumpet flowers, banners of moss, and grapevines" suspended like a "ladder of ropes" from willows and cypress trees. Innumerable details inhabit both poem and paintings.[37] Although Meeker never gained national fame, his artwork remains a unique testament to the contemporary aesthetic intrigue of Southern swamplands.

In addition to those writers and artists who expressed their personal fascination with the Southern swamp landscape, others took advantage of growing national interest. As more entrepreneurs, sightseers, and invalids seeking a healthier climate traveled to the South, travel guidebooks were written to accommodate their interests. *Picturesque America,* edited by William Cullen Bryant and published in 1872, featured in its roster of more typical scenic spots three swamp landscapes: the lower Mississippi River and Florida's Oklawaha and St. Johns rivers. Struggling to describe the swamps of the lower Mississippi in language parallel to the other spectacular landscapes, one author wrote: "Destitute though it be of the charm of mountains and water-falls, with no distant views, no great comprehensive exhibitions, it nevertheless inspires a sort of awe which it is difficult to define or account for." He further explained to readers that in a swamp, "all objects are upon a water level; and when you look aloft through the gloom of the towering trees, you feel as if you were in a well, and below the usual surface of the earth, and that the place is born of the overflowing waters."[38] A series of engravings provided readers of *Picturesque America* with even more visual images to enhance their understanding of the unusual swamp landscape.

Another popular writer, Edward King, found the same difficulty expressing the beauty of swamps. King traveled twenty-five thousand miles through the South reporting on post-war conditions for *Scribner's* magazine. In 1875, he published a compendium of those articles and other writings in *The Great South,* the first book to provide Northerners with a comprehensive look at the issues and landscape of the region. Particularly impressed with Florida's St. Johns River, King wrote: "It is not grandeur which one finds on the banks of the great stream, it is nature run riot. The very irregularity is delightful, the decay is charming, the solitude is picturesque." Because the swamp landscape did not lend itself to conventional aesthetic responses, writers had to forge a new aesthetic sensibility, relying more upon emotional responses the landscape elicited than conventional scenic cues. King recommended that "one should see such a swamp in October, when the Indian summer haze floats and shimmers lazily above the brownish-gray of the water; when a delicious magic in the atmosphere transforms the masses of trees and the tangled vines and creepers into semblances of ruined walls and tapestries."[39] Drawing upon more traditionally understood motifs of beauty, King encouraged readers to see the swamp landscape with a new aesthetic lens.

Through popular literature and art, the developing canon of American landscapes slowly expanded to include swamps. By the close of the nineteenth century, it was common for writers and thinkers to consider swamps with curiosity and intrigue. While few immersed themselves as completely as Thoreau had, it was through the originality of these thinkers that the nation's understanding of swamps began to be revised. This revision of understanding, however, occurred most predominantly in arts and letters and so remained subject to the whims of creativity and language. A more complete knowledge of swamps and marshes was yet to be discovered, but not before an unprecedented transformation of wetlands began to reveal its consequences.

SEVEN

Machines in the Wetland Gardens

The coming age is to be an age of conquest, the conquest
of nature, the reclamation of swamplands . . .
—John C. Gifford, 1911[1]

As America turned the corner from the nineteenth to the twentieth century,
the country's transition from a rural, local society into an urban, national
society touched every aspect of life. Looking beyond traditional small-farm
livelihoods, farmers envisioned tapping into expanding commercial markets and "getting rich." Additional railroad lines made large markets accessible, and technological innovation spurred new industries. Waves of ar-
riving immigrants and children of rural families streamed to the crowded
cities seeking jobs in new factories. The American dream of prosperity
gained a fresh prominence, and more people than ever before sought
growing opportunities. By 1890, America was one-third urban and well
over one-half urban in the Northeast.[2] The urbanization and industrialization that profoundly restructured America's culture and economy in the
late nineteenth and early twentieth centuries also altered the natural environment on an unprecedented scale. Wetlands figured prominently in the
American dream—not as they were, but as what they might become.

Growing urban populations needed more agricultural products and
housing. Along the northern New Jersey coast, where farmers had historically diked vast acreages of marsh to harvest salt hay, industrialization reduced the demand for hay to feed working horses. But with quick accessibility to New York City via ferries and railroads, the marshlands were
converted to truck farms and in some cases remade into residential neighborhoods.[3] In the District of Columbia, developers filled wetlands to make
adequate space for the nation's capital city.[4]

The demand for farm products and building materials generated by
urban growth affected more than nearby wetlands. Railroad lines fingering
into the nation's interior guaranteed that even farmers who broke lands in

remote areas had access to metropolitan markets. With the wave of settle-ment completed to the Pacific Coast, attention turned to reclaiming mar-ginal lands that had been passed by earlier. By making commercial farming more lucrative, railroads encouraged farmers to break these marginal soils. For example, the arrival of the railroad in the Tulare Valley of southern Cal-ifornia in 1872 opened a door to new markets and thereby prompted farmers to convert local marshlands into bonanza wheat farms.[5] In the South, railroads—by ensuring entrée to larger markets—fostered a logging boom in the bottomlands as well. By linking remote rural areas to populous cities, the rails encouraged the extraction of more commodities from the natural landscape.

In addition to carrying agricultural products and lumber to wider mar-kets, the railroads themselves devoured swampland timber resources, using wood for ties, trestles, and fuel. In the state of Ohio alone, the "iron horse" consumed fuel at a rate of one million cords annually. To meet this demand and supplement their incomes, many local farmers cut timber in Ohio's in-famous Black Swamp. In paying for wood, railroads provided local farmers with the capital to drain and remake the cutover swamplands into crop-lands. By 1885, elms and ashes of the rich Black Swamp had been con-verted into hours of smoky train travel.[6]

While railroads imposed new market relationships on natural landscapes, other innovations affected the land by boosting the efficiency and prof-itability of farming and lumbering. Steam-powered dredges and dragline excavators, for example, made drainage more feasible. Beyond machines, a cadre of well-trained professional engineers and scientists emerged and of-fered their expertise to the scene. The most conspicuous and influential groups were those affiliated with the Army Corps of Engineers. Although the institution had been established for a century, the Corps developed greater prestige and presence after the Civil War by opening offices in nearly every state to supervise and maintain river navigability, which was increas-ingly threatened by industrial dumping.[7] To keep shipping channels open, Corps engineers blocked sloughs, built revetments, removed snags, and dredged shallow areas. All of these activities systematically reduced the ex-tent of riparian floodplain wetlands.[8] The expertise of the Corps, along with that of private engineers and scientists, provided not only new information but also the confidence and optimism that were necessary to garner capital for large-scale drainage reclamation projects.

While markets, machines, and technical expertise advanced, new ideas about efficiency and management evolved in both government and business. The Progressive Era, ushered in with the presidency of Theodore Roosevelt, embodied a new vision that national government, with access to scientific expertise, could solve resource problems more efficiently and effectively than haphazard local efforts. For Progressive reformers, depletion and rampant waste of natural resources exemplified the public costs of industrialization; only Progressive government could counter abuses of unrestrained private enterprise. In many places, a tension between traditional laissez-faire politics and the ascendancy of powerful government institutions on local, state, and national levels ensued. Progressive politics would have direct consequences for wetlands.

In wetlands, Progressive local governments found one of their earliest successes. Through the 1880s and 1890s, swelling urban populations demanded the drainage of nearby wetlands to control diseases they thought sprang from the air over swamps. With more and more people packed into cities, greater numbers risked contracting malaria. According to sanitation advocate George Waring in 1890, few neighborhoods within thirty miles of New York City were free from the life-endangering "scourges."[9]

When medical researchers finally cracked the mysterious pathogenesis of malaria at the turn of the century, they discovered that parasite-infected mosquitoes, not miasma, transmitted the disease.[10] Armed with scientific authority, recently organized city and state health boards spearheaded drainage and mosquito eradication programs with new resolve. Between 1910 and 1920, the New York City Health Department began a massive mosquito elimination program, including a public information campaign of billboards and pamphlets that warned against letting water accumulate anywhere—even in discarded tin cans. The city employed hundreds of workers each summer to dig drainage ditches and build tidal gates in nearby marshes.[11] In neighboring New Jersey, mosquito-control ditching began in 1902. Eventually, the state required local governments to create their own "county mosquito extermination commissions." By 1924, the Bergen County Mosquito Control Commission alone maintained 1.5 million feet of ditches in salt marshes and adjacent uplands. By 1926, 130,000 acres of coastal salt marsh were ostensibly rendered free from breeding mosquitoes. In the South, the federal Public Health Service began an antimosquito campaign because population densities were too small to fund local efforts.[12]

After ditching, tidal waters washed in and out on a daily basis and prevented the pooling of stagnant water that mosquitoes needed for breeding.

But the practice also lowered water tables, thereby altering vegetation and ruining habitat for birds, fish, mollusks, and crustaceans.[13] In addition to ditches, the public health agencies promoted spreading oil on still waters each week to smother mosquito larvae, a practice that poisoned many wetlands.

While state and local governments sponsored large-scale drainage and oiling projects in urban and coastal areas, where many wetlands were publicly owned, regulations became the primary means to eliminate malaria in areas where private ownership predominated. Many states and local governments adopted laws and ordinances that recognized places where mosquitoes bred as "public nuisances" and held landowners responsible for eliminating the problem. For example, an ordinance in Des Moines, Iowa, deemed it the "duty" of the owner to drain or fill depressions where mosquitoes bred.[14] While many laws identified easily emptied receptacles, like rain barrels and tin cans, other laws specifically identified "sunken lots or marshlands" as nuisances.[15] If a landowner refused to comply, the board of health would get rid of the offense and then put a lien on the property. Local governments clearly conceived of it as the duty of the landowner to prevent public harm and nuisance by draining or oiling wetlands.[16]

Although many of the wetlands where mosquitoes bred were privately owned, because infected vector insects could fly beyond property boundaries, malaria essentially became a commons component of the wetlands— a nuisance. Beyond the direct health hazard, the presence of mosquitoes lowered land values, thereby reducing local tax bases. Only by enacting laws that required landowners to control mosquito breeding on their own parcels of land could states and local governments effectively deal with malaria and maintain property values.

Although ditching and oiling damaged many wetlands, those practices succeeded in their aim of eliminating infected mosquitoes and thereby extinguishing malaria. Between 1900 and 1914, there was a 64 percent reduction in malaria mortality nationwide. In some locales, the reduction was far greater. New York City reduced its malaria mortality by more than 86 percent. In Jacksonville, Florida, malaria mortality declined by 80 percent, and in Key West, malaria deaths declined by nearly 94 percent.[17]

While progressive local government successfully solved mosquito problems, new ideas about management and efficiency in business affected wetlands as well. Small companies recognized the benefits of collaborating with their competition, allowing for the development of cooperative institutions and eventually large corporations. Greater accessibility to markets also allowed for new mass-marketing schemes. With the success of growing businesses, entrepreneurs amassed large amounts of capital, which they reinvested in newer technology and in larger-scale operations. Scientific management principles provided savvy businesses with guidance on how to maximize profit.

The story of the cranberry industry illustrates how organized business, expanding markets, government expertise, and technology transformed natural wetlands into mechanized managed landscapes. Settlers had long gathered the wild cranberries that grew in the sandy freshwater marshes and peat bogs of the New Jersey coastal plain. In fact, the berries were so popular that the state legislature had passed a statute in 1789 forbidding people to pick them before they fully ripened. Soon locals began to cultivate the cranberries to sell. What began as a small-scale endeavor burgeoned in the mid nineteenth century when two railroads routed their tracks through southern New Jersey. Counting on quick access to new markets, residents in Ocean County invested one million dollars in diking and clearing freshwater marshes for cranberry cultivation. In 1868, the local paper reported, "Vast swamps are being cleared and the prospect is that thousands of acres will be planted. There is no doubt that there is money in it."[18] By 1873, farmers set nearly 5,000 acres to vine in four coastal counties along Delaware Bay, producing 110,909 bushels of cranberries. By 1881, the railroad carried more than 30,000 bushels annually to Philadelphia alone.[19]

The nascent industry received a boost when prominent growers organized the American Cranberry Growers' Association in 1871 to better promote and sell the berries. Their cooperative promotion scheme worked well. Association members distributed cranberry cookbooks and boxes of free berries to help crack new markets and create greater demand for their products. Their most successful publicity coup was hooking the queen of England on their tart berries, which helped to open the British market. By shipping their fruit in uniform barrels and boxes at uniform prices, members of the association profited from efficiencies of scale and maintained good prices for their product.[20]

The growers' association also provided a forum for the exchange of ideas about how to improve cranberry culture and how to deal with pests and diseases that had begun to infest the rapidly expanding acreages of cranberry monoculture. The group also persuaded the U.S. Department of Agriculture to set up a Cranberry Experiment Station in Whitesbog, New Jersey, to help farmers with technical advice. Cranberry growers in Cape Cod and Wisconsin followed suit, creating local growers' organizations and gaining their own federally supported agricultural stations.[21] The largest and most successful national cranberry cooperative would eventually become well known by its trade name, Ocean Spray.[22]

While the organization of growers and their development of new markets nurtured the cranberry industry, innovations that sped harvesting boosted it to an even larger scale. Because the berries had to be picked quickly when ripe, the key to a successful harvest had long been hiring lots of workers. Large Italian families from Philadelphia came to the Jersey shore for several weeks each fall and lived in bunkhouses; even young children helped with the harvest.[23] At the turn of the century, the invention of the cranberry scoop changed that. The steel-toothed boxes allowed berry pickers to comb through the vines more efficiently but were too heavy for women and children to use. A cranberry-sorting machine, which bounced the fruit down a series of steps to separate out soft berries, also streamlined and mechanized the harvesting process, further reducing needs for labor. As a result of the more efficient operations, wetland acreages under cultivation increased. Workers diked, cleared, and planted more and more natural wetlands. Between 1872 and 1899, annual cranberry production in New England, New Jersey, and New York grew nearly fivefold, from 46,666 to 211,666 barrels of fruit.[24] Much fish and wildlife habitat was lost.

Over and over, all across the country, the same strategies that sealed the success of the cranberry industry were adopted by other industries. Entrepreneurs amassed capital and organized. They profited from new markets opened by the railroads. They relied on scientific knowledge and new technology. They enlisted the help of government—both state and federal—for either legal purposes or expertise. Doing business more efficiently and profitably meant that the wetlands, long protected by their remoteness or by their apparent marginality, were now vulnerable. During this period of industrialization and intensive management, Americans changed their wetland landscapes more profoundly than ever before.

The Big Trees

While Northern farmers and entrepreneurs capitalized on the tiny red fruits of their wetlands' wealth, entrepreneurs in the South used similar strategies to transform the natural bounty of giant bottomland forests into profit. No other tree—indeed no other symbol of any kind—signified the magnificence of wetlands in the South more than the baldcypress.

Although logging operations had edged into the expansive domain of the baldcypress for more than a century, the antebellum industry had remained small, employing no more than nine hundred workers. The methods of logging were still primitive, relying on spring floodwaters to move the logs to sawmills. As a result, loggers cut only the most readily harvestable trees along waterways. The Civil War had also slowed the sales of Southern swamplands and timber. By the time that Grant and Lee met at Appomattox, towns and plantations had been destroyed, but most of the enormous cypress forests of the southern river swamps stood intact.[25]

The war had demonstrated to Southerners the weakness of their agriculturally based economy, and amidst the rubble that remained, a desire to emulate the active, industrialized economy of the North took hold. Because the extensive bottomland forests were the region's most readily available resource, Southerners looked to these big trees as the foundation for future economic and industrial growth.[26]

To initiate post-war reconstruction, Southern leaders pushed the U.S. Congress to pass the 1876 Timber Act, which fostered the sale of large parcels of federally owned forestland and provided tax breaks to lumber developers. With supplies of wood in the northern forests surrounding the Great Lakes region giving out, Timber Act incentives attracted Northern investors looking for more wood and primed for easy profits in the South.[27]

At the same time, Charles Sprague Sargent, arboriculturist of Harvard's Arnold Arboretum, attempted to inventory the nation's forest resources. In his resulting report, published with the 1880 census, Sargent estimated that a massive 333 billion cubic feet of timber remained available for logging in the South.[28] Chicago author William H. Harrison, in his book *How to Get Rich in the South,* further spread this notion of plenty, claiming that the South's timber supply was "inexhaustible."[29] Excited by such prospects, northern lumber companies sent out "cruisers" on special trains from Chicago to Mississippi and Louisiana to assess the potential of the delta forests.[30] Much of the timber, however, grew in swamps. Undaunted, logging companies bought up large parcels. In the Atchafalaya Basin, for example, big timber companies purchased several holdings larger than 10,000 acres.[31] In Louisiana, Northern purchasers secured deeds to well over 1 million acres between 1880 and 1888. Historian Paul Gates estimates that under the Timber Act, the government sold off 5.7 million acres of federal lands in five Southern states by 1888. This figure does not include the millions of acres of "swamplands" still being sold by the gulf states to private individuals for prices as low as twenty-five cents per acre.[32]

The sale of these vast acreages of forest and swamplands and the building of new sawmills constituted an enormous injection of capital into the Southern economy. In addition to money, much needed technical expertise flooded into the South. In 1888, the *Northwestern Lumberman* put out "A Call for Technological Innovation," to make the vast amounts of remote bottomland cypress trees more accessible to sawmills. "There is a grand opportunity," the journal goaded, "for some ingenious Yankee to invent some way to get cypress timber from the marsh to the bayou . . . where it will float."[33] The answer to this call came from Horace Butters of Michigan. Butters took the overhead logging cableway steam skidders designed to remove logs from the wet kettle holes of the Great Lakes to North Carolina to see if they could be adapted to harvest swamp trees.[34] Although his system worked tolerably, it was inefficient because it used tower trees for aerial support and had to be re-rigged for each operation.

William Baptist of New Orleans improved on Butters's skidder system in 1889 with the "pullboat," which ultimately revolutionized cypress logging in the South. The pullboat consisted of a steam engine mounted on a barge anchored with cables to pilings or stumps. The engine operated two spools: the larger one carried a thick steel cable that could winch logs 5,000 feet out of a swamp; the second one held a wire rope used to return the cable to the harvest site. From the central position of the anchored pullboat, loggers cleared straight runs through the forest like giant wheel spokes 150 yards apart. Trees were systematically pulled from this enormous radius to a location where they could be floated to the sawmill. Baptist also invented a steel nose cone to place over the ends of logs so they wouldn't snag as they were dragged down the long straightaways. The more clever practice of "sniping" or trimming the end of a log into a point was suggested by one of Baptist's black workers and eventually superseded the nose cones. By 1891, the pullboat was in general operation, and ancient cypress, some thirteen hundred years old, were felled on a scale never before known in the bottomlands.[35]

Other technological advances included the use of steam-powered circular saws and then band saws at mills. The full suite of efficient mill machinery that had grown up with the industrial mechanized logging of the

PULLBOAT LOGGING WITH A NOSE CONE, CA. 1880.
The swampy terrain of the southern baldcypress forests made logging difficult. Northern capital and innovative logging techniques developed in the late nineteenth century, including the use of nose cones as pictured here, finally made it possible to cut and clear. Entrepreneurs drained and converted much of the cutover forest lands into farmland. Near the Mississippi River, however, chronic flooding made it difficult to reclaim the bottomlands. (From the Collection of the Louisiana State Museum, New Orleans)

North helped to speed lumber processing in Southern forests as well. By the 1890s, narrow-gauge railroads built on fill and timber cribworks enabled swampers to penetrate stands of cypress that had previously been too far from waterways to be logged even by pullboats.[36] The narrow-gauge lines connected with the Louisiana Railway and Navigation Company, which provided rail service from New Orleans to Shreveport, where it linked with other main lines to the interior.[37]

While Northern capital, know-how, and innovation propelled the cypress industry, continual shortages of labor hindered logging in the remote forests. By 1890, nationwide advertising campaigns promised workers the highest wages in the timber industry, company housing, stores, schools, and full reimbursement of travel costs.[38] Although the folklore of logging generally depicts loggers as independent bachelors following seasonal work opportunities, the southern climate allowed year-round work and so enabled loggers to bring their wives and children with them.[39] Full-service "skidder" towns were set up on floating barges near the cypress-harvesting sites. Some companies hired women and children to do chores. New workers, including immigrants and former slaves, flocked to the Louisiana swamps to partake in the cut. As a result, the population of the Atchafalaya Basin grew 10 percent between 1890 and 1900. By the turn of the twentieth century, the Louisiana cypress industry employed about eleven thousand people.[40]

Beyond capital and technical know-how, Northern timber companies brought with them new ideas about how businesses should be conducted. As the cypress-logging industry grew, lumbermen recognized that individual companies could benefit from collaborating much as cranberry growers had. In 1906, fifteen large cypress manufacturers formed the Southern Cypress Lumber Selling Company. The group established a grading standard for cypress timber, developed uniform prices, and branded a special trademark into the highest-quality wood.[41]

Most important, the trade association took on the responsibility of coordinating sales and marketing cypress lumber throughout the world. For years, the cypress market had been limited primarily to humid regions, where the rot-resistant qualities of the wood were well known and where lumber could be transported by ship. The gulf states exported nearly all their lumber to Latin America and other overseas markets.[42] When railroads began to provide inexpensive transportation to the interior of the United States, whole new markets became available. The Southern Cypress Lumber Selling Company started to aggressively promote their product domestically, dubbing cypress lumber as the "wood eternal" because of its superior rot-resistant qualities. Sales representatives entertained visiting groups of retailers aboard elegant Mississippi River steamships. In 1910, the trade group pushed to make cypress the theme for the National Lumber Manufacturers Association convention. Even the cover of the convention program resembled the rich reddish grain of cypress wood. In all, the trade association distributed 85 percent of the cypress harvested and milled in Louisiana.[43]

In 1912, the selling company reorganized as the Louisiana Red Cypress Company. To broaden its markets further, the group trained and employed fifty salesmen to promote the wood eternal throughout the nation. As a result of their work, sales in eastern cities grew by 40 percent in 1914 alone. Interest in cypress continued to grow as suburban development kindled demand for high-quality shingles. Cypress lumber was also sought: new oil companies in Pennsylvania wanted to construct their tanks from cypress; the city of Denver wanted to use cypress in its street railway system; and the Pullman Palace Car Company wanted to build its luxury railcars with cypress. The mills could barely keep up with all the orders coming in, and there weren't enough trains to transport lumber around the country.[44]

By the turn of the century, Northern investment, technology, and know-how had paid off, and the cypress industry enjoyed enormous profits. More new mills were built, and logging went on at an ever increasing pace. To pay off the large debts accrued through capital improvement, mills operated continuously, and cypress production throughout the South rose to about one billion board feet per year from 1905 to 1913.[45]

While the cypress industry savored its success, timber workers who labored harder to meet the increasing demand saw little additional gain for themselves. Toiling eleven-hour days on round-the-clock shifts for modest wages, workers became frustrated, but attempts to organize, such as the strike of cypress mill workers in the summer of 1903 and the strike by the Brotherhood of Timber Workers in 1910, failed. By blacklisting, dismissing union workers, and even breaking up meetings, the organized timber industries suppressed unrest and kept their mills running profitably.[46]

Logging reached its apex between 1910 and 1914 and then held steady, despite a wartime dip, into the mid 1920s, when nature seemed to conspire against the cypress business. Two years of drought made moving around in the swamps very difficult. Then in 1926, a powerful hurricane downed many trees, clogging channels used to float logs. Finally, in 1927, a big flood on the Mississippi swept away expensive equipment and damaged mills.

But the most significant blow of all was the industry's own doing; by the mid 1920s old-growth trees were all cut. Timber scouts from the eastern portion of the Atchafalaya Basin combing the area for suitable timber began meeting scouts from the western part of that enormous swamp, which people had long thought inexhaustible. Because loggers had used pullboats and skidders, the mucky forest floor had been scoured and disrupted to such a degree that young trees could not germinate in the place of the felled ancients.[47]

Although Northern capital, markets, and expertise created a profitable cypress lumber industry, it was not the long-term economic boost that Southerners had hoped for. As in all extractive industries, the economic benefits lasted only as long as the natural resource lasted. Because the capital for timber investment came mostly from outside the region, businesses had little interest in sustaining the industry over the long term. The timber barons simply moved on, taking their money with them. While Louisiana baldcypress logging had supported 150 mill towns in 1915, the number dropped to 90 five years later. By 1940, only four cypress mills hung on; the final one ceased operation in 1956.[48] For its remaining, numbered days, the heavy-handed yet ephemeral industry moved to the few cypress pockets left in Florida.

Ironically, despite the timeless qualities of its "wood eternal," over 1.6 million acres of cypress bottomlands in Louisiana alone were liquidated in a matter of decades.[49] The natural riches that had taken hundreds of years to create vanished. And with the primal forests went the black bears, the panthers, the ivory-billed woodpeckers, and countless other creatures of the swamps. The lasting legacies of the cypress industry were the beautiful and resilient structures built from the cypress wood it supplied and the vast acreage of mucky, lifeless cutover left in its wake.

Tiles, Draglines, and Drainage Districts

While cranberry growers and cypress loggers took advantage of wetland resources, others looked beyond the wetland to envision the agricultural fruits of a wholly transfigured landscape. Although people had experimented with draining land by digging open ditches, a major breakthrough came with the innovation of tile drainage. The seminal tiles were first imported to the United States in 1835 by John Johnston, but it was the manufacture of tiles decades later that made widespread drainage of farmlands economically and technically feasible.

When Johnston came to the United States from Scotland in 1821, he settled on a farm near the new Erie Canal in Geneva, New York. Neighbors warned that his plot of land was one of the least productive in the county, but the persistent and resourceful Scot set about making it into a premier winter wheat farm. For fifteen years he experimented by adding manure and lime to the earth with excellent results. In the course of his work, Johnston realized that poor drainage plagued much of his land; so after reading several articles about the successes of tile drainage in Scotland and England, he decided to try it on the wet and waterlogged portions of his own farm. He would have to bury horseshoe-shaped tiles in long lines; then, like gutters, those underground conduits would carry surplus water away from his fields to ditch outlets.

Because tile drainage, also known as underdrainage, was not practiced at all in the United States at the time, Johnston sent away to Scotland for a drain-tile pattern. When the U-shaped pattern arrived in the winter of 1835, he eagerly brought it to his friend Benjamin Whartenby, a manufacturer of earthenware crocks and jugs in nearby Waterloo. Before winter's end, Whartenby had crafted a set of earthenware tiles by hand. Because huge numbers of tiles were needed to shunt water from wet lands, the hand-made tiles proved too expensive for large-scale projects, so Johnston and Whartenby fashioned a crude tile-molding machine that lowered the cost.[50]

In the spring, Johnston began to dig a network of ditches 2½ feet deep, and then he laid the drain tiles, but not without the skepticism and ridicule of his neighbors. One remarked, "John Johnston is gone crazy—he is burying *crockery* in the ground."[51] Others warned that the tiles would poison the soil. But instead, Johnston's farm productivity rose dramatically. In an 1849 article for *Cultivator* magazine, Johnston optimistically speculated that drainage could double the yield of wheat crops.[52] By 1851, he had managed to lay sixteen miles of tile on 320 acres of his farm.[53] "The more I drained," he wrote, "the more I was convinced I was right . . . my fondest anticipations have been realized."[54] Although to most bystanders, tiling seemed a large and unnecessary expense, Johnston's success sparked the interest of other farmers. Popular agricultural journals regularly featured stories about drainage and the success of the Johnston farm. Farmers came from all over the country to see how Johnston's drainage worked, while even more wrote to him asking for advice.[55] Soon testimonial letters declaring the successes of newly underdrained farms filled the pages of the leading agricultural magazines.[56]

With more local farmers wanting to use tiles, Whartenby's machine could not keep up, so Johnston, together with other Seneca County farmers, imported a new tile-making machine from England. The Scragg's Patent Tile Machine could produce twelve thousand tiles—enough for approximately 3,600 feet of drainage—in a day at less than half the price that farmers had been paying.[57] Whartenby set up the new machine, and by working through the winter, he accumulated enough stock to supply farmers early in the spring. In less than ten years, there were nearly a dozen tile manufacturers operating within a ten-mile radius of Whartenby's and

several more running throughout the poorly drained Lake Erie plain of upstate New York.[58]

As farmers buried thousands of the clay tiles, drainage progressed
rapidly. By 1864, they had laid 6,060 miles of tiles in addition to building
nearly 13,000 miles of stone drains and 7,460 miles of open ditches. In
New York state alone, farmers constructed enough drainage ditches to en-
circle the earth.[59]

Along with the news of tile drainage successes, use of tiles spread rapidly
from upstate New York to the Ohio and Mississippi river valleys. Increased
demand for tiles prompted the small tile-manufacturing industry to move
westward. By 1867, Ohio boasted five hundred steam-powered tile-making
machines that produced 2,000 miles of drain tiles annually. By 1880, 1,140
drain tile factories operated in Ohio, Illinois, and Indiana, while nearly a
hundred more operated in Michigan, Iowa, and Wisconsin.[60] As the manufacture of tiles became widespread, farmers everywhere could afford to
drain the marginal agricultural areas on their farms. By 1882, Indiana
farmers had laid more than 30,000 miles of drainage tiles.[61]

Once a tile drainage system was buried and began to work, the hydrology
and ecology of the wetlands changed. Instead of pooling in soggy soils,
water was conveyed to ditches and then to outlets in streams and rivers.
Areas that had grown sedges and rushes dried out, were cultivated, and
began to look just like the other farmland. In a matter of generations,
farmers would even forget where the tiles were laid unless they kept their
grandfather's drainage plans in a desk drawer or unless an obvious problem
revealed itself.

In addition to the improvements in efficiency and the reduced costs of
manufacturing drain tile, midwestern farmers developed innovative ways to
lay tile. When John Johnston first laid his tile, he had hired Irish laborers to
shovel out the relatively shallow ditches by hand. By the mid 1850s, some
farmers had invented horse-drawn machines that excavated soil and deposited it in mounds on both sides of the trench. Not until the 1880s did
these machines—the most popular of which was the Pratt Ditch Digger—
become available commercially and come into general use. Still they required farmers to make several passes over the same line in order to create
ditches deep enough and wide enough for the tiles. In the early 1880s, the
Pratt-style ditch diggers were supplanted by a new horse-drawn machine.
The Blickensderfer Tile Ditching Machine manufactured in Decatur, Illinois, dug four-foot trenches with only one pass. But the greatest revolution

came with steam-powered ditch-digging machines. The most highly sought, known as the Buckeye Trencher, was introduced in 1892 in Findlay, Ohio. For $1,125, a farmer or group of farmers could purchase this steam-powered, wheel-type trencher capable of cutting 1,320 to 1,650 feet of 4½-foot-deep trench in a day. In 1908, the revolutionary steam engines were themselves superseded by gasoline-powered engines.[62]

The invention of the dipper dredge facilitated construction of larger public drainage outlets as well. By the turn of the century, steam-driven floating and land dredges had become the most widespread and economical excavation equipment. Within the decade, the dragline excavator eclipsed dredges and became the universal excavating machines because they could be made in many sizes.[63] With each innovation, the promise of drainage was made available to more farmers, who enjoyed greater profits, which they reinvested in newer machines and in turning more acres of wetlands into croplands.

Regardless of strides made in drainage technology, drained water still had to go somewhere. Midwestern states had pioneered the first ditch laws to provide a legal means for securing drain outlets across private property. But the success of more extensive landscape-scale drainage hinged on broader planning. Furthermore, when costs of tiles, ditches, outlets, and maintenance were taken into account, the prospect of draining large areas was still financially daunting. For these reasons, farmers had to approach large-scale drainage as a community endeavor rather than as a series of individual projects.

Because common law did not give landowners adequate legal powers to organize on a voluntary basis, state legislatures passed new statutes authorizing the creation of drainage districts, which became the cornerstone institutions for successful large-scale conversion of swamplands. Most significant, the new laws vested drainage districts with the authority to tax landowners in order to pay for drainage works and maintenance. Many states gave districts the right to force the acquisition of land for projects through eminent domain. Most laws also required that the benefits of drainage outweigh the costs and that the projects serve public health, welfare, and utility.[64]

Even so, drainage districts, with their taxing and land condemnation powers, were a radical concept. There was little precedent for creating such layers of local government, except for boards some states had started to implement the Swamp Land Acts. Although state legislatures set the ground

THE HOLLAND, 1918.

Technical innovations made it possible to drain and develop swamp and marshlands that had been too difficult to drain before. Dipper dredges like this one, with names like Hercules and Goliath, made it possible to build substantial levees to keep flood-waters from overflowing into the Sacramento–San Joaquin Delta. (Department of Special Collections, University of California Library, Davis)

rules, districts were generally initiated at the local grassroots level by a peti-tion of landowners. A majority of landowners or property owners holding the majority of the land within a proposed district had to sign on. Then a special board of reviewers assessed and collected drainage fees in propor-tion to the benefits that a landowner was expected to receive. With revenues generated, drainage districts could hire expert engineers and construct the necessary public drains and outlets.

At first, many landowners dragged their heels about paying more taxes. In California, for example, a drainage district law that passed in 1880 was repealed the following year in response to political pressure from swampland owners who refused to pay. But by 1900, drainage districts had proven successful. Between 1870 and 1900, twelve states passed the necessary legislation, and over 14.5 million acres of wetlands came under the auspices of drainage districts—mostly in the Midwest.[65] As early as 1888, one writer noted, "Progressive Agriculture has removed the unsightly ponds and marshes from the farm by tile drainage, and has converted the proverbial ague seats of Indiana into a most salubrious climate."[66]

During the first decades of the twentieth century, drainage district activity peaked as the economy prospered, farm prices rose, precipitation rates soared, and the Progressive passion for efficiency rippled into rural communities seeking to better themselves.[67] For example, by 1911, fifty-three districts, covering over 700,000 acres, had organized in North Carolina.[68] Nine more states enacted drainage district legislation by 1920, and another thirteen followed suit in the next decade.[69] The 1920 census revealed that nearly 66 million acres of poorly drained land nationwide were part of active drainage districts, though much of this remained undrained.[70] Beyond the technologies of clay tiles and ditch diggers, it was only through drainage districts that farmers could generate the cooperation, expertise, and capital necessary to cope with the drainage difficulties they shared in common.

The widespread drainage of wetlands rewarded midwestern farmers amply. Drainage promoted the breakdown of organic matter that had been prevented by water, releasing new fertility. In Illinois, for example, drainage increased corn yields by 50 percent. The value of lands typically rose 500 percent after drainage. Furthermore, as tiling spread, the incidence of malaria in rural areas decreased.[71] But negative effects of drainage became apparent, too. Wells went dry as tiles artificially lowered water tables, and waterfowl populations declined markedly. One ornithologist noted that sandhill cranes nested in Iowa for the last time in 1894.[72]

Nevertheless, by 1920, the machinery of drainage had picked up unstoppable momentum. According to USDA surveys, between 1906 and 1922, nearly 9 million acres of swampland were drained in just seven states. Illinois, Indiana, and Iowa lost nearly 30 percent of their wetland acreage during this sixteen-year period.[73] In north central Iowa, only 1 percent of swampland remained.[74] Vast areas that had escaped the plow owing to their wetness were finally brought into cultivation, and the glacially variegated wetlands of the Midwest became a homogenized grid of square-edged farms.[75]

Big Rivers, Big Problems

While tiles did wonders for draining low-lying wetlands of glacial origin, the flood-sculpted wetlands of the lower Mississippi and California's Central Valley presented a different hydrological problem. Yet the solution lay in similar requirements for capital, technological innovation, and institutionalized cooperation.

To turn flood-created wetlands into croplands, farmers had to first build levees to keep river water out. Only then could the land be ditched and drained. But keeping river water off traditional floodplains was a mammoth task. In the northern part of California's Central Valley, for example, the Sacramento River carried voluminous snowmelt from the Sierra Nevada, each spring overflowing into a veritable "inland sea."[76] After the state turned swamplands over to counties in 1868 and large parcels were sold off, private swampland owners blundered with expensive, piecemeal levee construction. But when one landowner built a levee to keep water off his property, the flood simply spilled onto lands across the river. Or if landowners constricted the river with levees on both sides, the resulting faster, larger flow would inundate property downstream. If one town had bigger levees than another, then the small-leveed town was flooded. A spiraling war of fortification between large swampland owners and communities went on for decades. Each party strove to have the highest levee, but whoever lost suffered tragic deaths and extensive damage to homes and farms.

Although the massive floods routinely blasted levee efforts, when the legislature passed a drainage district law in 1880 to encourage broader planning, many individual swampland owners resented being taxed and told what to do by the state's engineers. The following year the law was repealed, but the debate between laissez-faire management and a centrally planned drainage and flood-control system designed by the state's engineers picked up steam.[77]

Upstream hydraulic mining amplified California's drainage and flooding problems. Mines discharged tons of sediment into the tributaries of the Sacramento River. According to state engineer "Ham" Hall, the mine debris coupled with the haphazard collection of levees built by large landowners reduced the carrying capacity of the river considerably and thereby worsened spring floods. Modest levees built by smaller landowners didn't stand a chance. Eventually, valley farmers and residents formed an Anti-Debris Association in 1878 to shut the troublesome mines. But despite extensive damage to downstream properties and to navigability, the laissez-faire sentiment of the state government prevailed.[78]

In the meantime, debris continued to exacerbate flood problems. While the chronic overflows prevented the conversion of Central Valley wetlands into farms, the mine-induced floods damaged even the natural floodplain. Rather than inundate the land with nutrient-rich soils and nourishing waters, the floods scoured the fertile ground and deposited a desert of cobbles where lush riparian trees, tules, or crops had grown. Over 39,000 acres of rich alluvial farmlands were buried under the gravel, and natural wetlands were choked by rocks and silt.[79] Downstream in the San Francisco Bay, the massive debris reduced the magnitude and volume of tidal flows, affecting marshes and fisheries there as well.[80]

Not until 1884, after several court cases and more devastating floods, did farmers finally gain an injunction to stop hydraulic mining with the landmark *Woodruff v. North Bloomfield* case. Even after mines closed, the tailings that remained tumbled down rivers for years, and problems continued. Enormous floods in 1892 destroyed many levees built by counties and landowners. Furthermore, an economic slump caused by a drop in grain prices (resulting from overproduction on the Great Plains) created a national movement to inflate the value of currency, thus stimulating new demand for gold. California saw the agricultural promise it had counted on fall, while the prospects for its outlawed hydraulic mining industry soared. The desire to reopen the profitable mines together with the need to protect people from frequent floods prompted Californians to consider a centrally planned water project that might accommodate the needs of both miners and farmers. The time was ripe for a plan that would eliminate the inefficiencies and dangers of individual efforts.[81]

In 1892, California asked the U.S. Congress if it could tap the expertise of the Army Corps of Engineers to develop a plan for reopening the mines while at the same time maintaining shipping channels of the Sacramento River, protecting valley farmers from floods, and opening up new croplands. Congress responded by creating a special federal panel made up of Corps engineers, the California Debris Commission (CDC), to work in conjunction with the state public works office. The commission first addressed the debris problem by requiring mines in the Yuba River watershed to build special dams to contain tailings. Although the CDC initially focused on reopening mines and keeping river channels open, the continued failure of local flood-control and drainage efforts ultimately compelled the commission to broaden its scope.[82]

Calling for a total of five hundred miles of riverbank and bypass levees, the CDC designed one of the first watershed-scale projects ever with its Sacramento Flood Control Project. The new levee system would be funded by landowners, the state, and a new financial partner—the federal government. In 1911, the state legislature unanimously supported the CDC plan and created a State Reclamation Board to supervise the millions of acres of private lands included in the flood-control project. The board would require landowners to build levees on their own properties in accordance with CDC standards. The board could also assess fees to pay for collectively beneficial structures, such as bypasses to funnel water away from towns. Despite the enormous benefits to landowners subsidized by the federal government, property owners still balked, filing over one hundred lawsuits against the Reclamation Board when assessed for their share of costs. This time the courts upheld the position of the state.[83]

Because Congress debated the principle of using tax moneys for purposes that favored only people living in particular localities, the federal portion of the funding was delayed. Federal purse strings were further tightened when World War I broke out. Not until the Flood Control Act of 1917 did Congress formally give the Army Corps of Engineers responsibilities and funds to develop flood-control projects—and not just navigation projects—on the Sacramento and Mississippi rivers. In the meantime, California pushed ahead with the CDC's plan by dredging a huge outlet for the Sacramento River at Horseshoe Bend.[84]

With the CDC's Sacramento Flood Control Project in progress, the low-lying lands of the Central Valley seemed secure from flooding for the first time, and swampland owners reclaimed their lands with new confidence and purpose. As demand for agricultural products grew during the war, farmers converted more tule marshes into croplands. In the Sacramento–San Joaquin Delta, locally invented, long-boom clamshell dredges, with names like Thor, Hercules, and Goliath, replaced the labor of Chinese immigrants, who had built earlier levees with shovels and wheelbarrows. Most important, dredge technology made it possible to build levees quickly with river alluvium rather than less reliable peat soil. Caterpillar-styled tractors, also locally invented, made farming the peaty soils possible as well.[85]

New railroad routes in the Central Valley, together with the opening of the Panama Canal in 1914, gave California farmers cheaper access to eastern markets. In the reclaimed delta islands, rice culture boomed; in 1916, farmers produced 2.5 million sacks of rice at a value of $5 million.[86] In the valley proper, orchards replaced less profitable grain crops altogether. In 1918 alone, private landowners spent $2 million on levees and drainage.[87] By the end of the year, 700,000 acres of lands had been reclaimed by private landowners working with drainage districts to carry out the CDC's plan.[88] With the apparent danger of flooding eliminated and the prospect of farming drained lands, the population of the Central Valley grew rapidly. The conversion of swamplands into croplands in California skyrocketed during this period.[89] By 1922, 70 percent of the state's wetlands were gone.[90]

Drainage and flooding problems along the floodplains of the lower Mississippi River were similar to those in California but larger in scale and political complexity because the river's giant watershed spanned dozens of states. Swampland owners and municipalities there had also vacillated between laissez-faire and expert-planned flood control and drainage. But frequent enormous floods had finally convinced lower-basin states of the need for a broad watershed plan in the 1870s, when they beseeched Congress to take responsibility for the river. In 1879, Congress responded by creating the Mississippi River Commission (MRC), composed of Corps engineers, to tackle the multifarious problems. By the turn of the century, MRC was fully engaged in building and maintaining a massive system of main-line levees along the Mississippi to preserve navigation channels and to control floods.[91]

With the apparent success of this flood-control program, Louisianans—free from the fear of annual inundations—began to drain swamplands and marshlands behind the levees with more assurance. With the Army Corps providing public drains and large outlets, hundreds of drainage districts formed in the lower Mississippi River valley around the turn of the century.[92]

At the same time, the timber industry sold off its cutover lands at low prices, offering opportunities for small farmers and entrepreneurs alike. One speculator who took advantage of this chance was Edward Wisner. Not a typical carpetbagger, he came to Louisiana from Michigan to convalesce from an illness, but the cheap marshlands, some selling for as little as 12½ cents per acre, seduced him into launching a business venture. Ultimately acquiring 1.5 million acres, Wisner formed the Louisiana Meadows Company, choosing to use the word "meadow" rather than "marsh" for its pleasant, pastoral connotations. Wisner started his first drainage project at LaBranch on the Illinois Central Railroad about fifteen miles northwest of New Orleans. Using steam-powered machinery, he quickly cleared, leveed, and installed the pumping plant necessary to drain his very wet lands. The success of corn and truck crops convinced many would-be investors of the property value, and Wisner's project became the hub for swamp development.[93]

In addition to its reclamation efforts, the Louisiana Meadows Company opened publicity offices in Chicago and other northern cities and began a sophisticated marketing campaign directed at lakes-states and Corn Belt farmers. Persuasive pamphlets boasted of alluvial black soils "rich as the bottomlands of the Nile." Comparing swamp and bottomland fertility to that of the world-renowned Nile became a cliché widely used by salesmen to invest familiar value into the unknown wetlands.[94] One pamphlet even contended that "artificial drainage is as much better than natural drainage as irrigation is better than rainfall."[95] Because northern farmers had many preconceptions about the insalubrity of the southern climate, sales pamphlets specifically highlighted the area's low rates of infant mortality and included comments from settlers that confirmed the area's healthfulness. The Louisiana Meadows Company even shipped boxes of dirt all over the country to show prospective settlers the quality of its peat soils.

Railroads also took an active part in publicizing reclamation projects in Louisiana, offering low fares to potential settlers and distributing their own promotional materials. The Louisiana Department of Agriculture and Immigration contributed as well by sponsoring trips for newspaper reporters and business leaders to view the successful drainage projects. Even the U.S. Department of Agriculture offered engineering assistance to developers.

The Louisiana Meadows Company took orders for small family farms at prices ranging from $150 to $600 per acre depending on the location of the lots.[96] The confidant Wisner speculated, "Judging from the progress that is being made by the Louisiana Meadows Company . . . with the assistance of others interested in this matter, all the present swamp in Louisiana will be drained in a comparatively short time."[97] His comments reflected a widely held optimism prevalent during the first two decades of the twentieth century that tremendous development would follow on the footsteps of drainage in the lower Mississippi Valley. Before the rush to reclaim marshlands was over, between twelve thousand and fifteen thousand people had visited the pump-drainage projects, and five thousand had purchased lands, as either investors or settlers.[98]

While land developers, with their skillful administration and access to the technical expertise of engineers, had initial success in draining the Mississippi bottomlands, those who purchased drained swamp parcels usually had little understanding of the land they bought. Most development projects were legally organized as drainage districts, so they levied hefty taxes on the new owners to pay off bonds that had financed the drainage. Oftentimes lands beyond the sample lots were not fully drained and so yielded disappointing crops. Furthermore, once plots in a district were sold off, responsibility for their maintenance, including operation of the pumps and upkeep of the levees, fell to a group of commissioners elected from the new farm owners. Most had no inkling of how to keep the complex system of pumps and levees in working order. As a result, most pump-drained development projects in southern Louisiana ultimately failed.[99]

Although the Corps of Engineers built drain outlets and the USDA's limited staff provided technical help to several drainage districts, many farmers wanted more federal assistance. When the national government got into the business of irrigating arid lands in the West with the Reclamation Act of 1902, many southern farmers believed that similar federal involvement in drainage would be useful, and only fair. In 1906 and 1907, states with large swamp areas, including South Carolina, Georgia, Florida, and Missouri held a National Drainage Conference to lobby for a government program to finance drainage projects. In 1910, the Arkansas State Farmers Union issued a resolution to garner more state and federal aid for drainage.[100] But not all interests agreed on how to proceed, and their efforts went nowhere.

According to engineer Arthur E. Morgan, it was the overall lack of coordination that repeatedly undermined drainage efforts in the Mississippi Delta. Despite interest in planning, drainage districts had remained local in scope. In 1910, Morgan wrote, "It has become apparent to many landowners, public officials and engineers that the method of digging ditches here and there in these large areas, without having a well-defined plan of procedure, will result in the waste of a large amount of money, and will secure only a part of the benefit desired. . . . If success is to be secured, each large division of the Delta which, because of its geographical and topographical characteristics, presents a single and indivisible drainage problem should be improved by a single well-drained and comprehensive plan." However, he continued, "This conclusion has not been reached in all parts of the Delta at the same time. . . ."[101] In the contest between laissez-faire and expert-planned drainage, the power of inertia won out. Ultimately, the reluctance of local drainage districts to consider the type of large-scale planning advocated by Morgan stood in the way of successful drainage.

Although the federal government spent $30 million and local levee districts spent $90 million building Mississippi River levees between 1882 and 1916, their haphazard efforts were ineffective. In the wake of massive floods in 1912, 1913, and 1916, many levees gave out; partially drained farm tracts were reclaimed by the river and started to become swamplands once again as new forests of fast-growing, bottomland hardwoods—tupelo, gum, ash, willow, and water-loving oaks—rooted themselves in the inundated muck of the cutover.[102]

The Great Florida Land Giveaway

Despite the run of obstacles and pitfalls, farmers, loggers, developers, and engineers gained greater proficiency in drainage, and the growing record of success gave boosters reason for optimism and confidence, even where it wasn't warranted.

In the 1870s, the Everglades of south Florida remained an inviolate wetland frontier. Its remote 3,500-square-mile expanse was still a mangrove-fringed, palm-clad bastion of wildness where only alligators, panthers, wading birds, and those who dared hunt such creatures trod. But the wetland became less remote as Florida's tourism industry grew. Guidebooks, such as Bryant's *Picturesque America* (1872), heralded the wondrous Eden that travelers would discover in Florida and attracted many wealthy northern travelers looking to experience a tropical landscape and climate through a Romantic lens. While few visitors strayed from the main tour up the St. Johns and Oklawaha rivers, young Hamilton Disston's interest in fishing drove him deeper into the interior. There, in the winter of 1878, he first saw the vast sawgrass marshes of south Florida. Looking beyond Romantic appreciation of the exotic natural world, the gears of his entrepreneurial brain started grinding, figuring the profits and acclaim to be had if the tropical swamp could be drained and put to good use.

Disston's dream of draining the Everglades became financially possible the next year when his father died and left him heir to America's largest saw and file manufacturing company. So when Disston presented a formal proposal to the governor of Florida and to the state's Internal Improvement Fund (IIF) in 1881, they quickly accepted his offer. Since the federal Swamp Land Acts had granted Florida 22 million acres—59 percent of all land in the state—the IIF had struggled with its mission of draining wetlands.[103] Before the Civil War, it sold less swampy lands to investors such as the New York and Florida Lumber and Land Company, which bought 1.1 million acres for 10 cents each. The state granted another investor the right to purchase 6 million acres of Everglades for 6.25 cents each in exchange for building a small canal. But the land giveaway was stifled by scandal. Rather than spend money generated through swampland sales for drainage, the state earmarked the funds to guarantee railroad construction bonds. After the Civil War, when railroads went bankrupt, bond holders demanded payment. News of the lawsuit soured most of the land deals that Florida tried to make.[104]

Although several speculators had approached the IIF trustees with proposals, Disston's plan had something new and compelling. It was backed by northern wealth. When Disston promised to drain all of the swamps overflowed by Lake Okeechobee and the Kissimmee River in exchange for one-half of the reclaimed land, the trustees jumped at the offer despite his inexperience. In addition to the drainage proposal, Disston made an outright land purchase of $4 million, filling the state treasury with enough money to pay off railroad bond litigants right away. Identified as the largest single land purchase ever, Disston's deal gained national attention. The *New York Times* praised the project, explaining that canals would "entirely drain the swamp, reclaiming from ten to twelve million acres of the richest land in the world."[105] The well-publicized purchase opened the door for more northern speculators and business leaders, who brought promises of capital, know-how, and innovation in the form of railroads, canals, luxury hotels, and other services. Disston's capital marked the beginning of a stream of investment flowing into Florida on a much grander scale than ever before.

After two years of working near the Kissimmee headwaters, Disston's company announced its successful drainage of 2 million acres. President Chester Arthur, along with an entourage of journalists, visited in 1883 and confirmed the achievement.[106] With the approval of the state engineers, Florida deeded over half the land to Disston. By the end of the decade, small plantations produced corn, rice, and sugar cane at impressive yields.[107] But the honeymoon did not last long. Critics charged that much of Disston's land had not been swampy to begin with and that years of abnormally low rainfall had accomplished more of the drying than any drainage efforts. While the boosterish state administration initially suppressed criticism, the legislature eventually called for an investigation. In 1887, a special committee reported that only 50,000 acres had actually been drained. The resulting bad publicity and the financial panic of 1893 slowed Disston's land sales so much that he could not keep up with his drainage expenditures. Unable to pay workers, he had to stop dredging and was compelled to default on bonds and loans.[108]

The insurmountable difficulties of draining such persistently swampy land proved too much for the young developer. In 1896, with his dream of reclaiming the Everglades floating out of reach, the humiliated Hamilton Disston filled the porcelain bathtub of his Philadelphia home with water, climbed in, and shot himself. Before his suicide, however, Disston had succeeded in building a linchpin canal to drain Lake Okeechobee through the Caloosahatchee River—the first significant step in draining the Everglades. Eventually, much of Disston's wet land reverted to the state or was sold by his family, who had long disliked his risky Florida ventures.[109]

Disston was not the only northern capitalist to make a deal with the IIF. Other investors proposed to build an intracoastal waterway along the state's east coast in exchange for land. Numerous railroad developers, including magnate Henry Flagler, requested land in exchange for pushing their lines deep into the wilds of Florida. But by the turn of the century, the political winds, which had been pro-railroad for fifty years, began to turn away from big business. With Disston's failure, Floridians grimaced at the idea of giving more land and power to unreliable northerners. The same skirmish between laissez-faire individual efforts and organized state attempts at swamp reclamation that had occurred in California and the lower Mississippi Valley erupted in Florida as well. But this time populist thinking took hold with the administration of Governor Napoleon Bonaparte Broward.

Broward saw giving land grants to the railroads as turning over control of Florida's wealth to outside speculators and tycoons. He proposed that the *state* should earn the profits by draining the swamplands itself. Shortly after taking office in 1905, the governor toured south Florida by steamboat. Conceiving of the enormous Everglades ecosystem as a simple basin, Broward thought that the state could easily lower the level of Lake Okeechobee by "knock[ing] a hole in the wall of coral and let[ting] a body of water obey a natural law" by flowing toward the sea.[110] Broward determined that 6 million acres could be reclaimed by diverting more lake waters into rivers that flowed to the sea. According to his grandiose plans, drainage would bring up to $60 million into the state treasury, financing not only itself, but the state government and school fund as well. The reclaimed land could then meet all of the nation's sugar needs.[111] It was a Progressive dream: Engineering expertise put to good use by well-run government would generate wealth and benefits for the people of the state—not just for rich outsiders.

Because half the land in south Florida already belonged to railroad companies, Broward proposed creating a new drainage commission with authority to levy a five-cent-per-acre tax on swamp owners. As Broward envisioned it, the taxes would finance long-term drainage projects. The legislature approved his plan by passing the Drainage Act of 1905, not unlike drainage acts passed in many other states. In the meantime, Broward dipped into IIF funds and ordered dredges from Chicago to build the New River Canal from Lake Okeechobee to the Atlantic.[112]

As in other states, railroad interests and swamp owners didn't take the new tax lying down. They filed lawsuits questioning the constitutionality of the new tax and refused to pay. Pro-railroad newspapers did their best to discredit the governor's plans, accusing him of misspending school funds. The legislature tried to placate the railroads and developers by passing a revised drainage act that reduced the scope of the drainage district, but swampland owners still refused to pay, arguing that the proposed projects would benefit only a small percentage of the lands.[113]

Before long, lawsuits stacked up, and IIF funds dwindled. Broward had initially planned to finance drainage with tax revenues and to hold as much land as possible to sell after reclamation at higher prices, but resistance to drainage taxes made it necessary to sell lands up front in order to keep the dredges at work. Furthermore, the IIF finally began to recognize the enormousness of the project. By the end of 1907, two dredges had excavated only 4½ miles, draining only 12,000 acres. Broward's critics charged that, at that rate, it would take a hundred years to reclaim less than half the Everglades. Broward left office with only a fraction of his drainage ambitions realized.[114]

One of the largest land deals made by the Broward administration while it struggled to keep its drainage plan on track was the sale of 500,000 acres of Everglades to New York tycoon Richard Bolles for $1 million. Bolles founded the Florida Fruitlands Company and cleverly promoted his Everglades land with fancy brochures depicting sugar cane, orange trees, and happy farmers. Land could be purchased as part of a package that combined the ease of paying in small installments with the thrill of gambling. For every $240, payable in twenty-four monthly increments, each investor received a lot in the proposed model community of Progresso—just north of Fort Lauderdale—and a farm in the Everglades. The excitement came with a special lottery that would determine the exact size and location of the lots when all the land was sold. Some of the lots promised to be very large. Slick salesmen proffered the swamplands nationwide.

Like most developers before him, Bolles soon discovered that swamp drainage was far more difficult and expensive than anticipated. By the time he finished selling his lands, Bolles had drained only a few parcels, but he planned to conduct his lottery as promised nonetheless. In the winter of 1911, hordes of small land investors flocked to southern Florida to be on hand for the Progresso lottery. Thousands of contract holders arrived by train in Fort Lauderdale, where they packed into overflowed hotels and set up tent cities on the sandy coastal ridge.

For most Florida Fruitlands Company investors, seeing their Everglades land was disheartening and enraging. They had been promised farmland richer than the valley of the Nile, of course, but instead they saw before them nothing but expanses of sawgrass—much of it still unsurveyed and still under water. One disillusioned Iowan lamented: "I have bought land by the acre, I have bought land by the foot but, by God, I have never before bought land by the gallon."[115]

Most of those who fell for land schemes in Florida—which would later become a cliché for gullibility—went home in disgust. Angry contract holders sued Bolles and other swamp promoters for the return of their money. Newspapers in forty-three states covered the "Florida Scandal." At a trial in Kansas City, prosecutors showed that Bolles had twelve thousand contract holders committed to paying $2.88 million. The federal circuit court ruled that Bolles could keep the $1.4 million he had already obtained but could collect no more until the promised drainage was complete.[116]

In the meantime, Broward's successor, Governor Albert Gilchrist, tried a more temperate tack to gain corporate backing for the state-sponsored drainage project. Companies agreed to pay back drainage taxes on the condition that future taxes be reduced to only three cents an acre. With the new funds, dredges could start work again, and land developers could collect money from their investors. The whole system operated on a faith that drainage efforts would soon pay off. But by 1913, publicity from scandals had once again eroded the necessary faith. There were few new buyers, and many small investors stopped paying their installments, which prevented the developers from paying their taxes. With little income, the state's entire reclamation program nearly collapsed, much to the dismay of promoters, whose lands would never sell undrained.[117]

One developer, V. W. Helm of the Everglades Land Sales Company, decided to take the situation into his own hands and hired three independent engineers to investigate the Everglades problem. Their 1912 study revealed that the state's drainage work actually hurt more than it helped because water from Lake Okeechobee flowed into unfinished canals and overflowed surrounding lands.[118]

Governor Park Trammel followed up the next year by hiring his own expert New York engineering consultants. The engineers corroborated Helm's report but recommended that the state concentrate on widening and deepening the St. Lucie Canal. To finance the work, the legislature created a new Everglades Drainage District that levied taxes on a sliding scale based on benefits to landowners. The district then managed to sell $3.5 million in bonds to an Ohio corporation, which provided immediate funding. At the request of Governor Trammel, the U.S. Department of Agriculture established an experiment station to provide local farmers with advice on how to cultivate the region's peat soils, which after drainage, it turned out in this ongoing fiasco, dried and released toxins that killed many of the new crops as they began to grow.[119]

The state's new focus on dredging the St. Lucie Canal, coupled with many years of light rainfall, created moderate success for the drainage projects. Despite the initial trials of farming peat soils, by 1920, 34,000 acres were under cultivation and twenty-three thousand people resided in the Everglades Drainage District. More railroads, new highways, effective drainage, improved agricultural methods advanced by the experiment station, and the coming of big sugar farms all contributed to a boom in the mid 1920s. By 1927, 46,000 acres of Everglades land—more than ever before—were farmed, and ninety-two thousand residents inhabited the district. With the combination of engineering expertise, the authority of the state government, and support of the local drainage district, the inviolate Everglades were slowly changed.[120]

While the overall picture of wetland drainage between 1880 and 1920 was one of entrepreneurial success, new technology and institutional sophistication did not always manage to conquer wetlands. In most instances, the challenges wetlands presented for those who would develop them demanded all of the advances that the new industrial society could dish out. Wetlands in the Central Valley, the Mississippi Delta, and the Everglades did not easily succumb to arrogant optimism. Oftentimes farmers could only partially drain their lands and then had difficulty maintaining the new drainage systems.

In some locales, drainage attempts failed completely. In northern Minnesota, three counties invested tremendous capital to drain their peatlands. By 1928, more than fifteen hundred miles of ditches were built in Beltrami County alone, but the peatlands remained wet, and the high costs of ditching left the counties bankrupt.[121] On North Carolina's Albemarle-Pamlico Peninsula, an entrepreneur invested a fortune in the world's largest pumping station to drain Lake Mattamuskeet in 1923. Hundreds of miles of ditch were built to carry lake water to the four-steam-engined station, where it was pumped into Pamlico Sound at a rate of one million gallons per minute. Despite such grand efforts, after four years of cultivation, the industrial-scale project went belly up owing to excess water, poor soil conditions, and technical difficulties. The lake bed filled with water and once again became a home for migrating tundra swans.[122]

Guided by the appeal of cheap land, entrepreneurs and farmers in all regions displayed a zealous persistence for draining wetlands, in spite of tremendous difficulties, risks, expenses, and failures. Although the wettest of wetlands stubbornly remained unchanged, millions and millions of acres were drained, dried up, and transformed.

Drying Up the Wetlands

As America entered the twentieth century, the face of its landscape had changed. All over the nation, natural wetlands were converted on a massive scale to human purposes. From the cranberry bogs of New Jersey to the cypress forests of Louisiana, from the wet prairies of Illinois to the mangrove resorts of Florida, from the tules of California's Central Valley to nameless wetlands around every major city, the growing American population was flexing its muscles, using its capital, its innovativeness, and its new institutions to make more elbow room, more food, and more money. This process profoundly restructured the natural environment.

In many regions, wetland losses were heaviest during the first decades of the 1900s. Farmers drained 69 percent of Iowa's wetlands and 68 percent of Missouri's wetlands by 1922. In California, more than 70 percent of wetlands were reclaimed.[123] With new farms and developments came new roads and people, and with new roads and people came more farms, developments, and roads. As this spiral endlessly twisted, it sucked countless natural wetlands into its vortex. Wetlands throughout the country were invaded, incised, and parceled out more rapidly than the speed of the locomotives that made it all possible.

While expanding markets, technical expertise, innovation, and efficiency shaped the dominant response to wetlands during this period, there were other responses as well. These new responses were voiced by people who recognized not only the plentiful fruits of industrial progress but also the less favorable side effects. It was these people who would begin to give voice to the case for wetland conservation.

EIGHT

New Voices for the Wetlands

Indeed there are many beauties that adorn these marshes.
. . . The play of light on the flat mud near the water, the
scarlet sky reflection on the little waves, the amethystine
hue made by a flow of wind rippling the surface of the bay,
the splendor of the sky, the radiance of the white
clouds . . .

—John C. Van Dyke, (1898)[1]

When construction crews dug up Napoleon Avenue in downtown New
Orleans to make way for a drainage canal in 1913, they unearthed unexpected quarry: a ghost forest of massive cypress stumps from trees cut by
the city's founders two hundred years prior. Many residents were surprised
to learn that their cosmopolitan city had been built where a primeval forest
had once stood.[2] Within two hundred years, people had forgotten how city
forebears changed the land. To most, the stumps were artifacts of progress,
just like the stumps left by the more recent boom in the cypress logging
industry. In much of Louisiana where majestic giants stood only forty years
earlier, nothing was left but partially drained cutover lands.

The extensive cutovers of industrial logging had shown that American
forests could indeed be exhausted. In response, President Theodore
Roosevelt created a new system of National Forest Preserve lands, with
the assistance of Progressive forester Gifford Pinchot. As an alternative to
unbridled deforestation, Pinchot championed the idea that American
forests—especially those in the West—should be replanted and
scientifically managed to produce a sustainable yield of timber to meet the
country's needs into the future. According to Progressive thinking, not
only forests, but all natural resources should be conserved for use by both
present and future generations. In promoting their policies, the
Progressives implanted the idea of conservation in the minds of the
American people for the first time.[3]

But in the South, only a few lone voices spoke out against the destruction of that region's forests. Recognizing that the timber industry would not
last long, lumber company owner Henry Hardtner favored reforesting cutover pine lands and successfully planted saplings on lands clearcut by his
company. Hardtner's fervent belief in reforestation attracted the attention
of his cypress industry colleagues.

In 1908, the Southern Cypress Manufacturers' Association created a
"Committee on the Utilization of Cutover Cypress Swamp Lands" to
investigate the possibility of replanting. But at a meeting two years later, the
committee chair explained that the slow-growing nature of baldcypress
made waiting for a second cut unprofitable. After measuring the growth of
young cypresses, he had determined that it would take at least seventy-five
years for the trees to attain suitable logging stature. Instead, he recommended converting the cutover cypress stands into farmlands. The state
commissioner of forestry suggested alternatively that other water-loving
trees, such as tupelo and willow, would grow quickly on cutover and could
provide the additional benefit of protecting the lands and levees from
erosion.[4]

That same year, reflecting the growing interest in forest conservation,
Hardtner was appointed president of the newly established Louisiana State
Conservation Commission. In that capacity, he pushed for reforms,
including a new conservation fund and incentives for replanting. But of most
immediate concern to lumber companies—especially cypress companies—
was the existing property-tax system. Because timberland owners were taxed
on the value of their lands, it was in their best interest to log as quickly as
possible and then either sell or abandon the cutover, rather than to log slowly
while new trees grew. Hardtner advocated a severalty tax that would be paid
when the trees were cut.

Speaking to the Louisiana legislature in 1910 as an industrialist-turned-
conservationist, Hardtner drew upon the latest scientific information to
emphasize the crisis at hand. "Forests were intended to protect us from soil
erosion, cyclones, climatic changes, and hurricanes. Shall we destroy that
protection?" he demanded. "We are doing it, and so rapidly that inside of
twenty years, Louisiana will be the poorest state in the Union unless measures are adopted to prevent these calamities." Hardtner directly indicted
the lumber industry: "What has the lumber man done? Proceeded to cut up
these forests just as fast as he can, not leaving even seed to reforest his lands;
running his mills night and day; producing more lumber than the country

needs, operating without profit, and a desperate country behind him." Hardtner contended that a new tax system would encourage more sustainable forestry.[5]

While most timber companies preferred the severalty tax to property taxes, many resisted any tax as an affront to their property rights. As a result, it took over a decade for Louisiana to adopt a new severalty tax system. In the meantime, logging continued until the trees were gone.[6] While scientifically managed forestry gained ascendancy during the Progressive period, the slow-growing but fast-disappearing cypress forests remained out of the conservation circuit.

Hardtner's was not the only voice to direct attention to the despoliation of natural resources. In other regions, people began to notice the decline of fisheries, waterfowl, and game as a result of intensive drainage and leveeing; citizens recognized the unpleasant consequences of dumping garbage into the wetlands near their cities. While changing the land had always been a part of settling America, with the Industrial Revolution, change from natural abundance to impoverishment of the land occurred on such a sweeping scale that people couldn't fail to witness it. The new landscape surrounded and affected the lives of all Americans to some degree. While the orderly farmlands wrought from wetlands appealed to most citizens, others responded with regret, alarm, and outrage. These new perspectives were voiced not only by Romantics but also by Progressive activists, conservation reformers, and students of nature, science, and economics. Drawing upon experience, observation, and new scientific information, these people considered wetlands in a fundamentally fresh way; and through their work, they began to convey the sense that wetlands held important social, aesthetic, ecological, and utilitarian value.

A Voice from the Limberlost

Intensive wetland logging was not restricted to Louisiana. Baldcypress forests bordering coastal plain rivers from Virginia to Texas had been leveled. Logging operations had reached up all the major tributaries of the Mississippi to the Illinois River, cutting cypress and bottomland hardwood trees growing on the rivers' floodplains. Even the few remaining swamp woodlands of the Midwest were cut for lumber and then converted to cropland. Such was the situation where Gene Stratton Porter grew up, near the Limberlost Swamp in northwestern Indiana.

Influenced by the popular nature-study movement of the late nineteenth century and by seeing her beloved backyard swamp destroyed fragment by fragment, Porter wrote two novels featuring the Limberlost Swamp. *Freckles,* published in 1904, and *A Girl of the Limberlost,* published as a sequel in 1909, became two of the most successful of her twenty nonfiction and fiction works. All told, Porter's books sold over ten million copies, making her one of the best-selling women authors of the first half of the century.

Through these popular Limberlost books, general readers—and not just landscape aesthetes—came to know about the biological and moral virtues of swamps. In *A Girl of the Limberlost,* the main character, Elnora, overcomes a childhood of parental neglect under the tutelage of the nearby Limberlost Swamp. Learning about its natural history helps Elnora excel in science class. Collecting and selling biological specimens from the swamp helps her raise money for school. In writing about Elnora's adventures, Porter showed readers that animals, birds, and insects depend on swamps. But beyond moths and butterflies, she depicted Elnora and the other kind people who live near the swamp as possessing genuine moral character. They work hard, help neighbors, accept people as they are, and find joy in the simple pleasures of life. Their strong grounding in nature sets the Limberlost people apart from the book's city characters, who seem shallow, unknowledgeable, and obsessed with the unimportant. Echoing a popular contemporary theme, Porter attributed the integrity of the Limberlost people to their direct experience with the wild swamp frontier. By turning the Limberlost into the domain of a precocious child, Porter challenged the widespread and long-held understanding of wetlands as dangerous and unpleasant places.

Gene Stratton Porter drew heavily upon her own experiences in writing the Limberlost books. As a child, she had rambled out-of-doors and learned much about plants and animals from her father. Then in 1887, her husband built her a large cabin right at the edge of the Limberlost Swamp so she could pursue nature studies more easily. Porter was also an accomplished nature photographer. Her photos accompanied many of the articles she published in magazines such as *Recreation, Outing, Ladies' Home Journal,* and *McCall's.* As the Limberlost was incrementally cut over and drained for farming and oil wells during the first decade of the twentieth century, Porter had a harder time finding the birds, butterflies, and flowers she loved to photograph and collect. She eventually moved away from the deteriorating swamp—preserved as a powerful place only in the Limberlost books.[7]

Although Porter did not go so far as to make an explicit statement about conservation, her mainstream stories alluded to the biological and social problems of destroying the final bits of undisturbed nature. She portrayed the Limberlost as a last bastion of wildness. Without such places, she implied, there would no longer be a font of good character for Americans to draw on.[8]

The Limberlost books defended the oft-reviled swamplands, but their tone was elegiac. Porter did not call her readers to action but rather shared with them her sense of resignation that the beautiful and valuable would tragically be pushed aside to make way for the modern world.

The theme of the natural wild swamp as repository for qualities vital to humanity would be explored further by southern writers who witnessed the destruction of their own swamp forests. Beginning in the 1920s South Carolina's Archibald Rutledge wrote short essays describing the wildlife and celebrating the beauty of the swamps of his home state. While many of his stories focused on hunting adventures, Rutledge highlighted natural history and alluded to the social value of swamps that offered a place for fathers and sons to fish together.[9] Writing a little later, in the 1930s, William Faulkner used the destruction of wild swamps to symbolize and critique the erosion of traditional values by the modern industrialized world.[10] While not as commercially popular as Porter's Limberlost books, these authors' stories also presented readers with the new idea that people could gain moral virtue through experience with swamps—a stark jump from the view that had once aligned swamps with evil.

A Voice from the Fens

Though Frederick Law Olmsted made his reputation designing New York's Central Park, it was in Boston's Back Bay that the renowned landscape architect pioneered a new type of park that prompted people to reconsider the scenic qualities of wetlands.

To improve living conditions in the crowded metropolis and to keep pace with the park-planning fashion of the day, Boston leaders had decided to start their own park system and contracted with the well-respected Olmsted in 1878. Because the city was already choked with development, there were few parcels of land available for public use. The park commission proposed using the "full basin" of the Back Bay neighborhood.[11]

Since the very beginning of settlement on the narrow peninsula of Boston, people had filled in irregularities of the shoreline to create more

land for an ever growing population. While the embayment of tidal water
known as Back Bay had long been used as a sewer outlet and dump site, the
building of a dam and causeways in 1821 cut it off from the free circulation
of ocean water. As a result, the waters had become stagnant and fetid.[12]
Decades of unsanitary conditions compelled the legislature to authorize the
filling and selling of all soggy lands in the area. In 1857, contractors began
hauling gravel by railroad to dump in the mucky pit. Through the next two
decades, the Back Bay was transformed from contaminated marshes and
tidal flats into a fashionable neighborhood of spacious brownstones.[13] Still,
a small lagoon receiving flows of the polluted Stony Brook and Muddy
River, known as the full basin, remained near the new residential district.
As the populations of Boston and upstream Brookline swelled, the full
basin grew more and more foul. Outgoing tides carried much of the pollution—most notably raw sewage—to sea, but enough was left behind to bake
on the tidal flats and create a stench. Under such polluted conditions, the
once healthy salt marsh cordgrasses died off, and by the time park commissioners surveyed the estuary in 1877, no animal life was found.[14]

Presented with such abused and degraded terrain, Olmsted had to plan
not only for aesthetic appreciation and recreational use but for practical
sanitary purposes as well. Drawing upon his naturalistic style of landscape
design and what he called the "genius of the place," Olmsted envisioned a
park that would appear to be a natural marsh that the city had just grown
up around.[15] Surrounding the marsh, a host of shrubs and trees would grow
and blend into a more conventional landscape on the street level. Although
he recognized that the hundred-acre parcel could not be a typical park,
Olmsted sought to provide many aesthetic attributes while still attending to
the sanitary needs of the community.

Despite his own conviction about the "healthiness" of the natural marsh
design, Olmsted felt it necessary to justify the wetland park. The effect of
placing a marsh in the city, he explained, "would be novel, certainly, in labored urban grounds, and there may be a momentary question of its dignity
and appropriateness . . . but [it] is a direct development of the original conditions of the locality in adaptation to the needs of a dense community. So
regarded, it will be found to be, in the artistic sense of the word, natural,
and possibly to suggest a modest poetic sentiment more grateful to town-
weary minds than an elaborate and elegant garden-like work would have
yielded."[16] Although people did not usually appreciate the scenic qualities
of marshes, Olmsted sought to stretch their aesthetic sensibility.

The salt marsh theme committed Olmsted to an unprecedented planting program. To create the natural-looking marsh, he designed control gates that carefully limited the tidal fluctuation to one foot. With the small change in water level, he could include more varied vegetation than was found in natural salt marshes.[17] Still, the vegetation chosen for the new park would have to tolerate saltwater and salt spray. Olmsted thought that the beauty of a natural salt marsh lay in "the complete occupation of nearly level surfaces by a short fine grass." He consulted with horticulturists to learn about salt-tolerant grasses and the "taller, graceful moving reeds, rushes, and sedges, in which interest may lie in the variety and contrast of forms and tints."[18] Olmsted wrote about creating his salt marsh landscape as Martin J. Heade might have written about composing a salt marsh painting. He described adding "slashes of golden rods and asters" to the cordgrass just as a painter might describe adding brush strokes of color here and there.[19] Though his palette of vegetation was informed by biology, Olmsted's choices were largely aesthetic.

Foremost, with Olmsted's new plan, polluted and flood-prone streams would be diverted through subterranean conduits directly to the voluminous Charles River, where the contaminants would quickly dilute. As a result, tidal waters could adequately cleanse the full basin as it ebbed and flowed through estuarine channels.[20]

Crews began planting cordgrass both by seed and by sod in 1884. Much to Olmsted's dismay, the first grasses died, but after a second planting the following year, the marsh vegetation flourished. By the end of 1885, approximately two-thirds of the park had been dredged and filled, and contractors had finished the Beacon Street entrance. Within ten years, the newly renovated marsh looked as if it had always been there. To welcome Bostonians to the formerly undesirable space, Olmsted convinced the park commissioners to change the name of the park from simply the Back Bay to the Back Bay Fens, calling upon the British word *fen* to convey his unique aesthetic vision.[21] The Fens accomplished flood and pollution control and also served Olmsted's subtle social agenda of creating a natural refuge from the dirt and noise of urban Boston for people from all walks of life. The park physically presented Bostonians with a new and pleasant way to experience a salt marsh. With the Back Bay Fens, Olmsted also pioneered the nation's first marsh restoration project.

Olmsted was not alone in reappraising the aesthetic qualities of wetlands. In the face of despoliation, some writers followed the lead of earlier

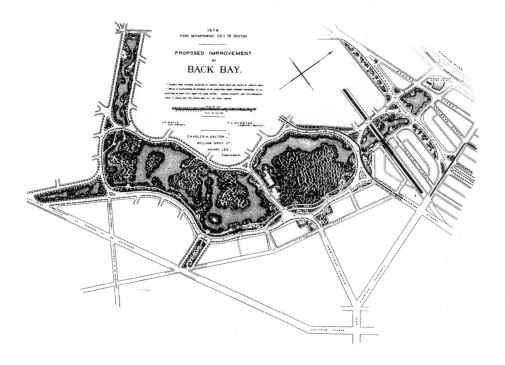

PROPOSED IMPROVEMENT OF BACK BAY, FEDRICK LAW OLMSTED, 1879.
By incorporating a tidal marsh into his plans for the Boston Back Bay Fens park,
F.L. Olmsted pioneered a new landscape aesthetic that recognized the natural
beauty of wetlands. This sketch was Olmsted's first published plan for fens. (Courtesy National Park Service, Frederick Law Olmsted National Historic Site)

Romantic thinkers by describing the beauty of the remaining natural wetlands around their towns and cities. In his book about landscapes, *Nature
for Its Own Sake* (1898), John C. Van Dyke extolled marshes: "How beautiful are they now garmented in the pale golden-greens of spring, the
emerald greens of summer, or the golds and browns of autumn!" Beyond
description, Van Dyke rejected the conventional understanding of wetlands. "Because they cannot be utilized to advantage," he wrote, "they have
been regarded with some contempt by mankind; and the preacher, the
orator, and the poet have always paralleled them with human stagnation or
vileness. But they do not deserve such odious comparisons." In a complete
turnaround from traditional aesthetic views of wetlands, Van Dyke
concluded that "there never was a simpler or a nobler landscape."[22]

In a 1916 article for *Harper's,* Richard Le Galliene pursued this theme further, considering what he regarded as the aesthetic paradox presented by the marshes. On one hand, he characterized them as "rude," "austere," "Dantesque," and "channeled with slime." Yet he also discovered a profound beauty in the marshes. "Here," he wrote, "is a beauty, spellbound, incredible, a miracle . . . which . . . leaves the senses in a dream."[23]

With their work, Olmsted, Van Dyke, and Le Galliene presented Americans with new ways to experience and see wetlands. While Olmsted's park design and the words of Van Dyke and Le Galliene did not represent mainstream views, they did resonate with the growing numbers of people repulsed by the ills of urban life. In the context of post-industrial America, wetlands gained a new sheen.

Alarum of the Sportsmen and Bird Lovers

Though landscape enthusiasts tended to think of them primarily as scenery, wetlands included not only moist land features but mollusks, crustaceans, insects, fish, birds, reptiles, and mammals as well. Integrally linked to the land by food chains and needs for shelter, these creatures were no less a part of wetlands than sedges, trees, mud, and water. As Americans reconsidered wetland landscapes through their reading, parks, and art, many became enchanted by the most visual and charismatic residents of the ecosystem. Birds, they realized, breathed life and animation into the natural world.

In the late 1800s, the popularity of nature study together with a resurgence in the science of ornithology sparked a fresh curiosity about birds. At the same time, a growing interest in recreational hunting directed notice to wild fowl. But more than anything, it was the latest fashion dictates from Europe that focused attention on birds. The style of adorning women's hats and clothing with feathers and wings had become so prevalent in the latter portion of the century that in many places it was more common to see feathers on hats than on wild birds. During a stroll through Manhattan in 1886, one ornithologist counted 542 birds—all stuffed and mounted whole atop women's gaudy hats. In that same year, the newly established American Ornithologists' Union estimated that five million North American birds were killed annually for "fashion."[24]

The millinery industry's demand for feathers wrought a new sort of havoc on wetlands. Even in remote areas, where the land and hydrology had not yet been tampered with, plume hunters stalked the most unique and colorful of wetland denizens. The noisy excitement of rookeries in southern swamps was replaced with a quiet pierced only by the flight of rifle shots. In 1870, an estimated 2.5 million wading birds nested in the south Florida Everglades; by the 1890s, this population had already taken a nosedive.[25] Big-city restaurants' demand for wild game also affected wetland bird populations, especially those in the marshes and swamps nearby. Market hunting, helped along by the advent of more efficient and inexpensive firearms and by the railroads with their associated urban markets, had decimated waterfowl and wading bird populations throughout the country.

Not only ornithologists noticed this decline; the growing contingent of sportsmen also found fewer birds to hunt. With the development of a larger middle-class population, more Americans had disposable income for leisure. The same advances in arms and transportation that boosted market hunting made hunting a more popular and accessible pastime. Even city dwellers could hunt ducks for sport by boarding special trains to nearby marshes at the Chesapeake, near San Francisco, or along New Jersey's Barnegat Bay. From Des Moines, hunters boarded the "Duck Special," which chugged northwest across wet prairies and through the towns of Mallard, Curlew, and Plover, stopping en route whenever a flock of birds appeared.[26] In these wetland places, the passion for recreational duck hunting was born.

The establishment of several new national periodicals devoted to sport hunting reflected growing interest. Articles frequently expressed the theme of regret, recounting with nostalgic sadness the abundant hunting opportunities of the past. But the popular weeklies contained more than old hunting stories. George Bird Grinnell, editor of the most influential journal, *Forest and Stream,* routinely encouraged sportsmen to practice proper technique and to become active in protecting their game. Unless sportsmen worked to conserve waterfowl, wading birds, and big game, he argued, there would be no sport left to enjoy. The journals created a sense of fraternity among sport hunters nationwide, which spurred the formation of sportsmen's clubs. During the winter of 1874–1875 nearly 100 sportsmen's organizations were founded, and by 1878, 308 had declared a commitment to proper sporting practices and conservation of game. Many of these clubs purchased marshes to provide habitat for ducks to feed and places for their members to hunt.[27]

But beyond fraternity, the journals provided a forum for important issues. Grinnell led the way with his acerbic editorials in *Forest and Stream* criticizing commercial hunting. While market hunting was profitable for

HuntingParty, Lee Bros., 1880.

Wetlands supported a seemingly inexhaustible bounty of waterfowl enjoyed by nineteenth-century hunters. Sportsmen boarded special hunting trains, like this one in Minnesota, that carried them from cities out into marshy realms of ducks and geese. As wetlands were drained and degraded by farming and industry, and as commercial hunting increased, the abundant flights of waterfowl diminished greatly. (Photograph by Lee Bros., reprinted by permission of Minnesota Historical Society)

the few, he argued, it destroyed the nation's natural wealth. Grinnell even appealed to the agrarian ethic in advising citizens to act on behalf of farmers whose crops were ravaged by the insects that songbirds had once controlled. In 1886, he beseeched his readers: "We desire to enlist in this work every one who is interested in our birds, and we urge all such to take hold and assist us."[28] Within one year, nearly thirty-nine thousand men, women, and children responded by signing pledges that they would not harm any bird. Grinnell called his new club the Audubon Society to honor the century's most-renowned bird lover. (Grinnell had been a grade-school student of Audubon's wife.) Membership grew so quickly that it could no longer be administered by the magazine, so Grinnell was compelled to set aside his nascent project.

The young bird-protection movement got another boost ten years later in the winter of 1896. Mrs. Augustus Hemenway of Boston, agitated by the gruesome reports of continued predation, personally contacted fashionable women and asked them to refrain from wearing bird plumes. Hemenway's efforts along with those of ornithologist William Brewster sprouted into the organization of the first state Audubon Society, in Massachusetts. By 1901, thirty-five states had groups dedicated to preventing the slaughter of birds; their memberships included ornithologists, sportsmen, and concerned citizens—many of them women interested in nature study. Other national organizations, such as the Boone and Crockett Club and the American Game Protective and Propagation Association—an advocacy arm of the growing firearms and ammunition industry—also joined the push for the protection of birds.[29]

State Audubon societies, local sportsmen's groups, and women's groups encouraged many states to pass laws prohibiting the sale of birds, but enforcement remained difficult. Some plumes were worth more than their weight in gold. Because the plume trade was so profitable to hunters and marketeers, they managed to find loopholes in the laws by transporting bird feathers and parts through states without laws or by transporting them in deceptively labeled barrels. Their ruses were often successful: who, for example, would consider checking a barrel marked "eels"?

The first major breakthrough for bird protection came when Iowa's Congressman John F. Lacey, an avid sportsman and Boone and Crockett Club member, introduced a bill prohibiting interstate traffic in birds and animals killed in violation of state laws. With the support of all the newly organized citizen groups, the Lacey Act passed in 1900 despite aggressive lobbying by the millinery industry. The act encouraged thirty-three states to adopt complementary conservation laws.[30]

The next breakthrough came with the presidency of Theodore Roosevelt, beginning in 1901. Because of his strong interest in conservation issues, Roosevelt knew that curtailing market hunting alone would not stem the decline of game populations. He recognized the additional need for safe sanctuaries where birds and animals could live and breed free from harm. By executive order, Roosevelt established the first national wildlife refuge to protect waterfowl in 1903 at Pelican Island in the Indian River along the east Florida coast. By 1909, he had established fifty-three refuges, including many wetlands such as the enormous Klamath and Tule marshes at the Oregon–California border, to ensure that waterfowl and wildlife resources could be conserved for future generations. Despite presidential enthusiasm, however, Congress failed to appropriate funds for managing the refuges, so the Audubon Societies pitched in by hiring wardens of their own to protect birds in the federal and state refuges.

Audubon wardens performed a dangerous job. Although most Americans supported the national mandate to conserve birds, attempts to enforce conservation laws were often unpopular with local residents who depended on the feather trade for income. These hostilities climaxed in 1905 when a plume hunter shot Audubon warden Guy Bradley near the Cuthbert rookery at the tip of Florida. Bradley's widely publicized murder galvanized even more public support for the protection of wild birds.[31]

Despite passage of the Lacey Act and the establishment of refuges, plume hunters still managed to find loopholes. They smuggled feathers and birds to Europe, where Americans of stature could still purchase hats with avian adornments. At ports of entry, fashionable American women sported their "aigrettes," or egret plumes, down the gangplanks of newly arrived ships.[32] Citizen groups, outraged by the continued depredations on birds, tried again to close the legal gaps by pushing for a federal law to protect all migratory birds.

In the fall of 1912, a promising bill was introduced in the House by John Weeks of Massachusetts and in the Senate by George McClean of Connecticut. To gain support for the bill, Audubon Society leader Gilbert Pearson showed members of Congress a persuasive film (likely the first conservation film ever) illustrating the brutal slaughter of wetland birds. He argued that only a federal law could protect birds that traveled back and forth between the states. But Missouri Senator James A. Reed was unswayed. "I really want to know," he queried, "why there should be any sympathy or sentiment about a long-legged, long-necked bird that lives in swamps, and eats tadpoles and fish and crawfish and things of that kind; why [should we] worry ourselves into a frenzy because some lady adorns her hat with one of its feathers, which appears to be the only use it has. . ."[33] Other opponents derided law enforcement efforts as "iniquitous and childish." Despite heavy lobbying from the millinery industry, and opposition on the basis of states' rights, the American love for birds carried the day, and the Weeks–McClean bill was successfully tacked as a rider onto an agricultural appropriation bill. Although President Taft had opposed the bill, in his haste to close down business and turn the White House over to Woodrow Wilson, he unwittingly signed the Migratory Bird Act into law on March 4, 1913 (the rider was buried in the twenty-eight-page statute).[34]

Because regulation of game had been traditionally considered within the realm of state purview, the Migratory Bird Act of 1913 was both conceptually and politically revolutionary. The law recognized for the first time that birds belonged to the nation as a whole and could be protected only when understood in terms of common stewardship rather than state ownership. Politically, the act superseded states and gave the federal government primary jurisdiction over migratory birds. Bird supporters knew that the constitutionality of the new law would be challenged, especially by states that lacked their own protective regulations.[35]

Conservationists tried to buttress the law quickly. Lobbying amidst the maze of World War I demands, they pushed for a treaty with Canada to encourage protection of birds that migrated across the border. When Wilson signed the Migratory Bird Treaty in 1916, the federal government assumed responsibility for the nation's migratory birds as part of its treaty obligations—forever eliminating the potentially thorny issue of constitutionality.[36] In addition to forbidding the detrimental practices of spring and night shooting, the treaty's enabling legislation prohibited outright the sale of game birds, outlawed particularly destructive firearms, and gave the secretary of agriculture the authority to further limit hunting seasons and impose bag limits.[37]

With the establishment of migratory bird laws and refuges, the federal government became the primary protector of waterfowl. Although the Migratory Bird Treaty was signed primarily to care for birds, it would later become a critical ingredient in the federal government's relationship with wetlands. As fragmentation and destruction of migratory bird habitat eclipsed market hunting pressures, the treaty obligations would hold the federal government responsible for safeguarding wetlands as well. It was through birds that American attention was first directed to protecting wetland refuges, and in later years it would be through birds that Americans would again discover the need to conserve more wetland habitat.

Women's Voices in South Florida

At the same time the Migratory Bird Treaty gave the federal government legal responsibility to safeguard birds, public debate and enthusiasm for conservation sufficiently riled up citizens to become more active in protecting natural areas. The women of south Florida were ready activists. As extended railroad routes spawned coastline development, civic organizations formed within new communities. In addition to an Audubon Society chapter started in 1900 in response to the depredations of market hunters, the state's Federation of Women's Clubs also enjoyed rapid growth in the first decade of the twentieth century. Most members were affluent women, the wives of the state's business and political leaders.

As the wetlands of south Florida became better known to property developers and prospective farmers, they also became better known to scientists and local amateur naturalists. A favorite spot was Paradise Key, a little upland island or "hammock" embedded in the ocean of Everglades sawgrass. Visitors were enthralled by a striking stand of royal palms that reigned over an understory of unique tropical plants and by the wading birds and alligators that thrived in the grassy sloughs surrounding the hammock.[38] Paradise Key remained undisturbed until the Model Land Company, a subsidiary of Henry Flagler's Florida East Coast Railroad, built a new road just past the hammock to holdings it planned to drain in the south Everglades.

Model Land Company head James Ingraham, like many business leaders of his day, belonged to local conservation groups and recognized that his company's new road threatened to open Paradise Key to citrus and sugar cultivation. When he discussed the dilemma with Mary Munroe of Miami, chair of the Florida Federation of Women's Clubs, she suggested a clever solution: that the land company donate Paradise Key to the Federation to be maintained as a public park. Munroe then proposed the idea to Federation member Mary Kenan Flagler, the wife of the railroad tycoon. The Flaglers were amenable to the donation, but a portion of land remained in state ownership, so political action would also be necessary.

Munroe enlisted the help of May Mann Jennings of Jacksonville, president of the Florida Federation, who took on the project wholeheartedly. No stranger to politics (her husband had been governor), Jennings invited Federation members to accompany her to Tallahassee to speak with state officials about the park proposal in December 1914. On behalf of the Federation, Governor Park Trammel presented the proposal to the trustees of the board of the Internal Improvement Fund (IIF), which approved the park summarily—subject to the consent of the legislature.[39]

May Mann Jennings then began to prepare for a legislative campaign, distributing pamphlets that emphasized the beauty and uniqueness of the proposed park. She urged six thousand Federation members to write to their legislators, and she organized talks around the state to drum up support. Former Governor Jennings drafted a bill calling for the state to donate 960 acres of the hammock and one thousand dollars for maintenance. Just before the legislature prepared to adjourn for two years, it passed the bill authorizing the transfer of lands for Royal Palm State Park. But lawmakers cut the appropriation out.[40]

Jennings was thrilled about the passage of her bill but troubled by the lack of money. "I am, of course, heartsick over the lack of funds to do immediate work," she wrote. "But I hope that we will find some way out of this difficulty."[41] The resourceful women did.

When the Model Land Company turned over its share of land, Mary Kenan Flagler came through with another land donation to endow the new park. Initially, the Federation planned to lease the endowment land for tomato farming, but lack of roads made that impractical. A new park committee of the Florida Federation of Women's Groups met in December 1915 to discuss ways to raise the sorely needed maintenance funds and then launched a statewide Mile-of-Dimes campaign. Club members distributed one-foot-long cardboard strips with slots for twelve dimes throughout the state. Although the committee hoped to collect over six thousand dollars with their catchy scheme, the dime-filled strips brought in less than one thousand dollars.[42]

Through these and other efforts, the Federation raised funds to hire amateur naturalist Charles Mosier as caretaker. In the spring of 1916, he and his family moved into a tent on the hammock and started making improvements. Work on the two-story lodge was begun, paths were cut, and picnic tables were built. Dade County road-building crews worked day and night improving the road to the park. In late November, nearly a thousand people traveled in a motorcade of 168 cars to attend the opening-day festivities at Royal Palm Hammock State Park.[43]

Yet even after the park opened, funding continued to be a problem. Occasionally, the federation managed to pry assistance from Dade County and from the state legislature. To raise money, the women's group also collected lodging fees and diked a portion of sawgrass prairie to build a nursery for growing palms, which they sold as souvenirs to park visitors. After years of lobbying the state legislature, May Mann Jennings finally succeeded in gaining a modest annual appropriation for maintenance in 1921.[44]

Not only did Royal Palm State Park represent a success for the citizen ac-

MEMBERS OF THE ROYAL PALM STATE PARK BOARD, CA. 1918.
In response to the industrialization that left few natural areas remaining, people began to see the natural values of wetlands as unique. These women of the Florida Federation of Women's Clubs spearheaded an effort to protect Royal Palm State Park, a tropical hammock in the heart of the Everglades that was threatened by the expansion of agriculture in the region. May Mann Jennings is standing in the second row, behind the woman in the dark dress. (Florida State Archives)

tivists, but it succeeded in directing public attention to the Everglades as a unique natural area for the first time. The Federation preserved the park primarily for its curiosity values; the landscape along with its plants and animals was an intriguing subject—especially for nature study. Articles appeared in scientific journals, and in 1927, thirty thousand visitors from around the country signed the remote park's register book.[45]

At the same time that Americans rooted for the success of drainage and farming efforts in the Everglades, they also began to celebrate the peerless natural aspects of the area. Even those individuals directly and indirectly involved with draining the Everglades—including James Ingraham, Henry Flagler, and even Mrs. Napoleon Bonaparte Broward—supported preserving Paradise Key.[46] By formally recognizing natural values, Royal Palm State Park would become a critical stepping stone for the preservation of natural wetlands throughout south Florida.

Voice of Scientists

Though the enforcement of new game-protective laws reduced depredations on waterfowl, populations continued to fall. The wetlands where birds had traditionally lived, bred, and fed had been cut over, farmed, and suburbanized. The areas that had provided food and cover for birds were now used by people for essentially the same purposes. Although the national refuges included some wetlands, these were a pittance compared to wetland habitat losses. While market hunting had long been regarded as the chief cause of waterfowl decline, after the turn of the century destruction of wetland habitat became the paramount concern.[47]

This trend of habitat loss was identified most clearly by scientists who had begun to study the unique plant and animal life of wetlands. Thanks to the national debates surrounding the decline of game, and to the conservation leadership provided by Teddy Roosevelt during the century's first decade, by 1920 every state had an administrative office responsible for stewarding wildlife and fisheries. The development of state and federal "bureaus" specializing in natural resources had created a new cadre of expert scientists who began to investigate the natural world. At first, these agencies focused on stocking fish and eliminating predators, which were at the time regarded as detrimental to game.[48]

However, this group of experts also began to witness and understand firsthand the consequences of unbridled drainage and development on natural systems. In California, drainage, levees, dredging, siltation, and municipal pollution had disrupted riparian wetlands and the Sacramento–San Joaquin Delta, where fish reproduced. As early as 1879, leading ichthyologist David Starr Jordan reported to the newly formed U.S. Fisheries Commission that San Francisco Bay did "not contain one-twentieth the number of fish that it did twenty years ago." The decline devastated commercial fishing. In 1852, a single fyke net had harvested 250 pounds of fish; by 1879, it took twenty nets to catch only 75 pounds of fish.[49] At the other end of the Central Valley, drainage had severely upset the hydrology of Tulare Lake. Although a commercial fishery had thrived through the early 1880s, the fish began to die off, and by 1900, they were gone.[50] From the perspective of the scientists, Californians were exchanging the wealth of the natural wetlands, in the form of fish and wildlife, for the agricultural wealth of the Central Valley.

Scientists at the Illinois Natural History Survey came to similar conclusions in light of their studies of the Illinois River and its bottomlands. By the turn of the century, they had determined that the productivity of the river's fishery was proportionate to the area of overflowed sloughs, bottomland lakes, and wetlands. Not only did these shallow backwaters provide sheltered areas for fish to feed and breed, but they supplied the food for the fishes of the river by producing plankton, which was swept into the river during floods. As the scientists learned more about the relationship between flooding of the river, the backwater slougths, and the plentiful fish, levee construction continued, and its harm to the fishery became evident. In 1910, biologist Stephen A. Forbes clearly warned: "Nothing can be more dangerous to the continued productiveness of these waters than a shutting of the river into its main channel and the drainage of the bottomland lakes for argricultural purposes."[51] But his words went unheeded.

In addition to the importance of wetlands for sustaining fisheries, with the rise of recreational hunting, the economic importance of wetlands as game-species habitat grew as well. Edward Goldman, biologist with the U.S. Biological Survey (USBS) noted that many wetlands—drained under the "erroneous impression" that property values would increase—would have been more valuable if maintained as shooting and fishing grounds.[52] In fact, many drained lands were less productive than expected and eventually fell into tax delinquency. According to E. W. Nelson, former chief of the Biological Survey, "One-sixth of the drained area of the United States is . . . definitely shown not only to have been worthless so far as developing valuable agricultural lands is concerned, but the work has been largely destructive in character, since a great part of it eliminated water areas which were productive in their natural condition. . . ."[53] Nelson urged immediate government acquisition of marshlands for habitat.

In the Mississippi River valley, USBS scientists and state conservation agencies recognized that widespread drainage created problems beyond the downstream flooding: shorebird, waterfowl, and furbearer populations declined, and mosquito infestations worsened in some areas.[54] Louisiana Department of Conservation Commissioner V. K. Irion issued an insightful statement in May of 1926 regarding drainage of wetlands: "We have come to realize that artificial drainage and reclamation of certain of our wet lands serves no utilitarian purpose, but on the contrary, is bringing about new conditions of existence which are inimical to the normal development of some of our most valuable natural resources."[55] In his statement, Irion referred to the loss of both recreational and commercial hunting and fishing opportunities—activities deeply engrained in Louisiana tradition—caused by conversion of marshes to farmland. The department published a series of cutting-edge bulletins in the late 1920s, authored by its fish biologist, Percy Viosca, Jr., calling attention to the enormous economic values lost along with the destruction of natural wetlands. Weighing costs and benefits, Viosca explained that the revenues from fresh- and saltwater fisheries, coupled with those from fur trapping and from other collecting, totaled over $20 million annually, or $3.00 for every acre of permanent wetland. He contended that converting more wetlands to farms would be "killing the goose that laid the golden egg," especially in light of the surplus of available farmland. Viosca suggested that a policy of conservation *equal* to that of agricultural development would be necessary to maintain the natural wealth of the state.[56] Viosca's expertise and authority in fish biology enabled him to observe and critique the largely unrecognized ecological and economic consequences of drainage. He was one of the first biologists to assign economic measure to natural wetland values.

USBS bird-banding studies also shed light on the importance of wetlands as waterfowl habitat. Biologist Frederick C. Lincoln organized the first national bird-banding program in 1920. Helpful duck hunters returned the tiny bands imprinted with identification numbers to the USBS for analysis. One humorous episode of the study occurred when the bird-band manufacturer transposed the "o" and the "i" in the abbreviated address on the band. Instead of "Biol. Surv. Wash. D.C.," the band read "Boil. Surv. Wash. D.C." According to Lincoln, this prompted many funny responses from banders and hunters, "one of whom was fearful that the legend would be misunderstood as cooking instructions, since the bands plainly stated: wash, boil, and serve."[57] Despite the band mix-up and a lack of funds, within the decade data revealed that waterfowl traveled along particular routes when they migrated, exhibiting year after year "a strong attachment for the ancestral flyways." Lincoln's data enabled him to map the four principal flyways: Pacific, Central, Mississippi, and Atlantic. But most important, Lincoln pointed out how vulnerable waterfowl were to extinction on a regional basis. If any one breeding ground, wintering ground, or important stopover habitat were destroyed, the waterfowl populations could be decimated. With the new concept of flyways, waterfowl biologists began to think of individual wetlands as connected to larger systems.[58]

In addition to government experts, scientists at independent institutions and universities contributed to the new scientific understanding of wetlands. John Kunkel Small, curator of the Bronx botanical gardens, had begun field studies in the ecologically sensitive Everglades in 1881. Fascination for the myriad subtropical species kept his interest and attention in the region for forty years. During those critical decades, he wit-

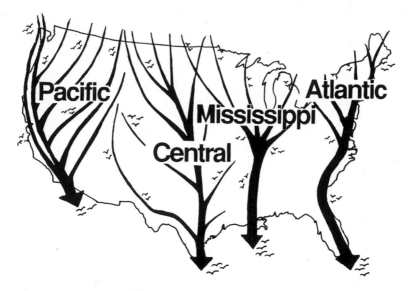

THE MIGRATORY FLYWAYS.
With his bird-banding studies in the 1920s, Frederick Lincoln determined that waterfowl migrated along four major flyways: Pacific, Central, Mississippi, and Atlantic. Destruction of important wetland habitat in one part of a route could have severe repercussions for many birds that used the flyway.

nessed the leveling and burning of cypress hammocks, drainage, and the subsequent subsidence and erosion of the fragile peat soils. In his 1929 book, *From Eden to Sahara: Florida's Tragedy*, Small warned that through "man's fast and furious" destruction of vegetation, the rich land would soon become a valueless desert.[59]

As scientists looked more closely, they began to piece together the causes and effects associated with the changing landscape. For the first time, they began to understand and clearly articulate the habitat functions that wetlands served.

Voices from the Accounting Columns and the Fields

Aside from the ecological consequences of converting wetlands to other purposes, there were economic results as well. Innovations that made drainage easier, coupled with the soaring demands of World War I, had encouraged farmers to bring more wetlands and other marginal lands into production. With increased production, farmers prospered and their standard of living rose, but they also assumed heavy debt reinvesting in new equipment. When demand collapsed after the war, so too did farm prices, prompting a devastating agricultural depression. Although agricultural reformers had long emphasized improved cultivation techniques to increase production, the new problem required a better understanding of economics, not just cultivation. As the nation had become more industrialized, farming had become increasingly commercial—dependent on national markets as well as local conditions. In a radical departure from the traditional view of farming as a highly individual endeavor, economists began to propose various controversial plans for limiting production in order to maintain prices. This was the genesis of the farm subsidy program.[60]

Some people recognized that, contrary to conventional wisdom, drainage actually hurt farmers because it put too much land into production, resulting in the newly apparent crop surpluses and low prices. With perceptive analysis that eluded lawmakers for the next fifty years, Professor William J. Berry of the Iowa State Normal College questioned whether his state or the country as a whole had yet received any real benefits from drainage. Although farmers could grow more corn on drained lands, it was far more than markets could absorb. "With the exception of the few wartime years," he wrote in the *Iowa Journal of History and Politics* in 1927, "drainage has merely contributed to a surplus that has so upset farming conditions as to threaten the very foundations of agriculture." Beyond its repercussions in the farm economy, Berry noted other problematic effects of drainage in Iowa. It had lowered groundwater tables and destroyed valuable migratory-bird breeding grounds. Berry went so far as to conclude that "it would have been better to have left the swamp lands in their original state," at least until the market demanded more crops.[61]

Berry was not alone. Hoover's secretary of agriculture, Arthur Mastick Hyde, also attributed the agricultural depression to the increased farming of submarginal lands, including drained areas. According to Hyde, even between 1925 and 1930, a period of alarmingly low farm prices, farmers brought 15 million acres of new land into production. Although each farmer acted to increase individual gain, the effect on the national market was, in fact, to lower profits. The only way out of the cycle was for farmers to organize voluntarily and reduce their outputs. And to lower production, they had to stop farming submarginal lands. Hyde advocated an end to homesteading laws that granted such lands to new settlers. Recognizing that marginal lands often possessed higher values for other "national uses" including "watershed protection, national forests, parks, and game preserves," Hyde instead encouraged government acquisition "to devote such lands to such uses as Nature intended."[62] Only after the dust bowl of the early 1930s would Americans accept the need for limits on production to protect the economic interests of society as a whole.[63]

New Perspectives

By 1930, in the wake of massive industrialization and urbanization, people began to see the effects of wetland destruction from many perspectives, and as a result they realized the need to reexamine long-standing attitudes toward wetlands.

On the basis of careful observation, scientists speculated that losses of wetland habitat had direct consequences in the decline of fish, waterfowl, and other game species and discovered new concepts such as flyways. Botanists and government agronomists recognized problems posed by the oxidation and erosion of peat soils exposed through clearing and drainage. During this period, people began also to understand more about the hydrological roles of wetlands. Farmers noticed that after drainage, they had to sink wells deeper to reach the water table. Foresters noted that forest cover in a watershed abated flooding. An awareness about services provided by wetlands grew as people saw the results of wetland loss firsthand. This new awareness—in light of habitat losses in particular—guided lawmakers to set aside some wetlands for their natural values as refuges. For the first time, scientists called attention to the damaging repercussions of changing the land.

From an economic perspective, people like Hardtner, Berry, and Hyde also recognized that completely consuming wetlands at a breakneck pace was not always the most profitable course. In the context of Progressive thinking, they realized that a better-informed use of wetlands would allow for more sustainable logging and agriculture over the long term. To bolster their economic arguments, these men drew upon scientific information about habitat and hydrology to suggest that the economic values of natural wetlands were worth consideration.

From a more emotional perspective, people like Gene Stratton Porter began to see beloved places, known through hunting and nature study, dried up and destroyed. Directing attention to the social effects of wetland losses, several writers reconsidered less tangible values of swamps and marshes. Frederick Law Olmsted responded to both the practical, sanitary needs of a city and the psychological needs of people stressed by a crowded urban environment by providing Boston with a new wetland park. The

Federation of Women's Clubs in south Florida also responded to the ills of urbanization by creating a protected island of nature. These wetland parks reflected a new alignment of art, science, and Progressive social policy.

With a better understanding of why and how wetlands are important, more people began to accept the possibility that there was good reason to preserve some of them. In response to the profound transformation wrought on the land by industrialization and urbanization, new voices had emerged to reconsider the values of wetlands. Some followed in the long line of Romantic wetland appreciators, reaching back to Thoreau, Heade, and Bartram; others simply recognized the wholesale destruction of utilitarian values associated with the natural landscapes. Although the dominant belief system continued to encourage drainage, the social, aesthetic, hydrologic, educational, and habitat values of wetlands were slowly coming to light.

NINE

The
Double Agenda

Men and nature must work hand in hand. The throwing
off balance of the resources of nature throws out of balance also the lives of men. . . . We seek to use our natural
resources not as a thing apart but as something that is in-
terwoven with industry, labor, finance, taxation, agriculture, homes, recreation, good citizenship. The results of
this interweaving will have a greater influence on the future American standard of living than all the rest of economics put together.
                    —Franklin D. Roosevelt, address to Congress, 1935 [1]

By the late 1920s, the American landscape was tired, abused, and broken.
Forests throughout the South, Midwest, and East had been completely cut
over, leaving loose soils to erode. Floods tore through the valleys, and hurricanes blasted the coasts. Then in the thirties, drought seared the nation's
heartland, turning a fertile breadbasket into an uninhabitable dust bowl.
Although these crises were commonly understood as natural disasters,
human manipulation and alteration of wetlands contributed heavily in
many places. Beyond the "natural" catastrophes, a slump in farm prices
through the 1920s, followed by the stock market crash of 1929 precipitated
the Great Depression, an unprecedented economic downturn that left one
out of four Americans unemployed.[2] While the federal role had grown
under the Progressive leadership of Theodore Roosevelt and Woodrow
Wilson, this onslaught of natural crises and economic upheaval compelled
the government to respond even more directly.

In south Florida, huge hurricanes in 1922 and 1924 caused extensive
flooding of crops—not because of pervasive rains—but because newly
drained peat soils around Lake Okeechobee had oxidized, dried, and subsided, as much as 4½ feet. When hurricane winds thrust water up against
the small dike along the lake's southern shore, the feeble structure collapsed, releasing a maelstrom of water that carried death or injury to four

thousand people and left many others without homes. The state down-
played the disaster to ensure that the steady stream of people moving to
Florida continued. The local drainage district patched the levee, and the
lake level was kept as low as possible to still maintain navigation. But four
years later, an even larger storm struck.[3]

The hurricane of 1928 devastated all of south Florida, including the
newly developed Atlantic Coast resort towns. By the early 1920s, auto-
battery manufacturer Carl Fisher from Indiana had provided the capital
necessary to transform a mangrove wetland island on the eastern edge of
the Everglades into a beach. Black workers had hacked away at the entangled mangrove roots while dredges pumped sand from the bottom of the
ocean to provide new land for Miami Beach's elegant hotels, golf courses,
and polo grounds. In Fort Lauderdale, developer Charles Green Rodes had
created high-value waterfront property out of cheap mangrove swamps by
"finger islanding." Rodes had dredged a series of canals at right angles to
the New River canal and then used the fill to make fingers of new land in
between. Each building lot faced a quiet residential street in the front and
enjoyed its own boat dock in the back. Rodes's development method inspired many other south Florida real estate developers to convert mangrove
islands into fancy resort communities. The powerful hurricane slammed
both Miami and Fort Lauderdale.[4]

But the farm communities around Lake Okeechobee were hardest hit.
Winds of 150 miles per hour pushed lake waters to breach the levee once
again. Floodwaters scoured the peat-soil farms and swept away buildings
and residents of the small town of Belle Glade. Nearly two thousand people
died—three-quarters of them black farm-workers.[5]

Beyond the tragic toll on human life, the flood dealt a sharp blow to ongoing drainage efforts. In heavy debt, the state-sponsored Everglades
Drainage District had to halt its reclamation operations, and landowners,
disgusted and broke, refused to pay drainage taxes amounting to $3 mil-
lion. Despite the district's accomplishments, the flood disaster proved too
great—especially given the region's small tax base—to repair the drainage
project. The state had spent $18 million—all to no avail.[6]

But the boom of the 1920s had divulged the promise of riches too sweet
for south Florida entrepreneurs and politicians to abandon. Like California
and Louisiana, Florida saw no choice but to request federal assistance with
flood control. In response, Congress appropriated funds for studies by the
U.S. Army Corps of Engineers. The Corps recommended building a thirty-

four-foot-high levee around the south shore of Lake Okeechobee and a smaller levee around the west and north sides. After heated congressional debate about the propriety of federal assistance for local flood control, in July of 1930 President Hoover signed a bill that directed the Corps of Engineers to tackle the Florida flood-control problem as part of its long-standing navigation responsibilities. The federal government would build and maintain the new levees; Florida would secure the necessary rights-of-way and contribute one-fifth of the costs.[7]

The state readily accepted this generous offer. The Everglades's short respite from drainage efforts ended when levee construction began in November. Eight years later, the Hoover Dike snaked for eighty-five miles around the shores of Lake Okeechobee. With the massive Corps levee, the federal government was finally drawn into having a direct stake in the Everglades. By 1942, the federal government had spent over $23 million on the construction and maintenance of the south Florida project.[8]

In 1927, flooding in the Mississippi River valley prompted new federal involvement in that region as well. When torrents of muddy water began to lap against the levees of the Mississippi, residents expected that the flood-control system planned and built by the federal Mississippi River Commission (MRC) would protect them. Corps engineers hoped that levees, still being fortified after previous flood damages, would encourage the river to carve a deeper channel to carry away floodwaters and provide ships with better passage. But the levees also prevented water from flowing into bottomland swamps along the river's edge that had long functioned to absorb and slow floodwaters. By constricting the river, the levees caused floods to rise to new heights. Furthermore, since more farms in the upper watershed had drained their soggy soils by the 1920s, more water than ever before spilled from plowed fields into the rivers that fed the Mississippi. It was these surplus waters from tributaries throughout the enormous watershed, coupled with rainwater, that overtopped levees and gushed into towns and farmlands of the lower valley in 1927. Driving 700,000 people from their homes, floodwaters covered 26,000 square miles.[9]

When citizens of the valley questioned the MRC's flood-control strategy, Army Corps Chief Edgar J. Jadwin conceded that the traditional levee-only flood-control plan was inadequate. Admitting that the river needed "more room," Jadwin developed a new plan for the Mississippi that included new floodways at the Atchafalaya and at Bonnet Carré to be opened during high flows to simulate the function of natural distributaries that the MRC had leveed off.[10] In the wake of the disaster, Congress readily adopted Jadwin's plan and assumed full costs with the Flood Control Act of 1928—a milestone for federal involvement in flood control.[11]

While Congress addressed flooding problems in the Mississippi Valley and in south Florida with the engineering expertise of the Corps of Engineers, yet another calamity beset the nation. Despite Migratory Bird Treaty regulations, waterfowl populations had continued to drop, and biologists realized that wetland drainage had left ducks and geese without safe places to live, breed, and feed.

Even the handful of federal refuges created by Teddy Roosevelt were vulnerable. During World War I, the Department of the Interior had caved in when local ranchers pushed to drain the waterfowl sanctuary at the margin of California's Lower Klamath Lake for rangeland. To the northeast, ranchers diverted water that had flowed into the Malheur Lake refuge despite opposition by the Oregon Audubon Society. Waterfowl that crowded into the few remaining sanctuaries became susceptible to predation and disease, such as avian cholera, which was likely introduced into wild duck populations by domestic chickens.[12]

Congress responded by reviving the project that Roosevelt had initiated twenty years earlier: a national system of refuges set aside for waterfowl. Bills introduced in 1921 and again in 1924 would have financed the bird refuges with one-dollar hunting-license fees and provided for public hunting grounds, but both were defeated by states' rights and antihunting interests. South Dakota Senator Peter Norbeck introduced a refuge bill again in 1928. This time Audubon Society and Women's Club members flooded Congress with letters and telegrams in support of the legislation. After much debate, senators stripped the license-dependent funding and public-hunting-grounds provision from the refuge bill before finally approving it. Minnesota Congressman August Andresen then introduced and gained House approval for the same bill. The stated purpose of the law was to meet obligations of the Migratory Bird Treaty with Canada by "lessening the dangers" that threatened migratory game birds, including "drainage and other causes."[13] Most significant, the Norbeck–Andresen Migratory Bird Conservation Act established the Migratory Bird Conservation Commission to carry out acquisition of important waterfowl habitat—chiefly wetlands.[14] With the passage of this bill, Congress formally recognized an unfavorable aspect of drainage for the first time. Although the Migratory Bird Conservation Act was a big step toward protecting wetlands for waterfowl, after lawmakers eliminated the hunting-license fee, they made no other provision for funding. As a result, the refuge program was left victim to the vicissitudes of congressional appropriations. And, as the depression mounted, Congress clenched purse strings still tighter.

Owing to the immense difficulties presented by all these catastrophes, the federal government dealt with each problem in remedial fashion, putting out brushfires here and there. Although planners tried to examine problems with an eye to the preventative and systemic, at times their solutions were reactive and narrow. As the federal government handled more and more national calamities during the next decades, the bureaucracy grew larger than ever before, making it increasingly difficult for the left hand to know what the right hand was doing. As a result, different offices developed policies appropriate to the distinct circumstances they took responsibility for—but counterproductive to the policies of other agencies. For example, policies designed by the Department of Agriculture to promote drainage counteracted policies designed by the Bureau of Biological Survey to protect waterfowl breeding areas and projects designed by the Army Corps of Engineers to prevent downstream floods. Even when conflicting goals of the agencies were recognized, change proved difficult. Nowhere was this bifurcation of policy more evident than in the nation's wetlands.

New Deals for Wetlands

When President Franklin Delano Roosevelt inherited leadership of the calamity-struck country in 1933, he had a powerful vision for how to set America back on its feet. Guided by a belief that government had a responsibility to ensure the general well-being of its citizens, Roosevelt set forth a new agenda to provide employment, stimulate the economy, and promote the wise use of resources.

To carry out his New Deal, Roosevelt set up a series of new agencies, including the Agricultural Adjustment Administration (AAA), the Soil Conservation Service (SCS), and the Civilian Conservation Corps (CCC), popularly known as the alphabet agencies because people referred to them by their abbreviated titles. In many cases, the alphabet agencies spelled trouble for wetlands.

Within the first one hundred days of the New Deal, Congress approved the Agricultural Adjustment Act of 1933 to counter rock-bottom farm prices. The law directed the newly established AAA to offer federal price supports for farm products and to limit production to keep supplies in better step with demand. Secretary of Agriculture Henry A. Wallace firmly believed that farmer participation was essential for the act's success, so he encouraged farmers to organize committees based on region and commodity specialization and to give suggestions about how best to run the new program.[15]

Billowing dust storms that darkened the skies above the plains called attention to another agricultural plight: the loss of topsoil. Hugh Bennett, a Department of Agriculture soil scientist, had recognized the connection between soil erosion and the loss of cultivable lands in the 1920s. Researching further, he discovered that 500 million tons of topsoil flowed to the ocean each year.[16] Bennett argued that this erosion accounted for losses of $400 billion in diminished farm productivity, without counting damages to fisheries and harbors caused by siltation. Erosion was exacerbated by the drought that began in 1930. Stiff prairie winds whisked parched, loose soils away from farms, turning the plains into a giant dust bowl.

In 1935, when dark clouds of dust literally blew into Washington, D.C., President Roosevelt appointed Bennett to solve the problem as head of the Soil Conservation Service (SCS). Bennett's new agency established thousands of demonstration projects to teach farmers how to lessen erosion by keeping soil anchored to the ground and water on the land. The SCS promoted contour farming, planting trees for shelter belts, retiring marginal lands, building gully plugs, and keeping legume crops in the soil during the winter. In 1937, the federal government required state and local cooperation as a condition of SCS assistance, which led to the creation of soil conservation districts. With a spirit of decentralized administration, the SCS message successfully spread.[17] By 1940, six million farmers had carried out soil conservation practices on 50 million acres of farmland with the technical assistance of the SCS.[18] Although the AAA's initial limits on production had acted as a disincentive to convert wetlands into marginal farmlands, rehabilitating farms meant revamping failed drainage in many areas. Through their mission of promoting "good" farm practices, the SCS engineers and soil scientists became increasingly involved in the drainage business.

Both the Soil Conservation Service and the USDA's Bureau of Agricultural Engineering (BAE) found assistance for their erosion-control and drainage-improvement projects from another alphabet program, the Civilian Conservation Corps, which set thousands of unemployed young men to work on conservation-oriented projects.[19] The CCC became most famous for planting one million trees on marginal cutover and erodible lands, but it had a hand in drainage as well.

In 1935, the BAE supervised forty-six CCC camps working to reconstruct and rehabilitate projects that had been set up under state drainage laws.[20] In Louisiana alone, eleven CCC camps renovated drainage networks that had fallen into disrepair during the depression. In some places, clogged ditches stopped up the flow of water, flooding farms and creating health problems. The CCC mostly disentangled and dredged these choked conduits. By 1939, the CCC drainage camps in Louisiana had cleared and reexcavated 18,400 miles of channels, built 4,300 water-control structures, and relaid 250 miles of drainage tiles.[21] In addition to labor supplied by the CCC, drainage districts received refinancing assistance from the Reconstruction Finance Corporation (RFC) so they could continue to operate during the depression without the threat of foreclosure.[22]

Working nationwide, the CCC repaired and rehabilitated agricultural drainage in Illinois, Indiana, Iowa, Kentucky, Louisiana, Maryland, Missouri, and Ohio. All told, thirty-eight CCC camps redrained more than 1.5 million acres in 1939.[23]

Beyond agricultural projects, New Deal agencies did other drainage work. In New Jersey and Delaware tidal marshes, CCC camps built, cleared, and maintained ditches to control mosquitoes and malaria. Dug in grids about 100 to 150 feet apart, the ditches rapidly removed water from the surface of the marsh, preventing the formation of shallow pools where mosquitoes bred. The CCC dug mosquito ditches for 248,000 acres in Delaware between 1933 and 1942. In Michigan, CCC camps and other federal relief agencies carried out mosquito drainage on 8 million acres—70 percent of the state's wetlands—by 1940.[24] Although ditching successfully eliminated mosquitoes, it inadvertently damaged many wetland ecosystems.

During FDR's second term, the Works Progress Administration (WPA) put thousands of laborers to work on public works projects including irrigation, flood control, and drainage, many of them designed to convert wetlands to more "productive" uses. In Oregon, WPA workers installed drainage tile in Columbia River bottomlands near Portland.[25] In Louisiana, WPA provided workers to the New Orleans Sewerage and Water Board. With supplied labor, the board was able to upgrade its drainage system by installing nine new pumps with the capacity to drain one billion gallons of water a day. WPA workers also laid more than sixty miles of drainage pipe in the city, opening many new areas for residential development. In conjunction with the work rehabilitating drainage districts, WPA workers manufactured the necessary concrete conduits and repaired and built new ditches throughout Louisiana, changing thousands of acres of wetlands into farmlands. Along the Atlantic Coast, the WPA also assisted with mosquito ditching, reconstructing 18,986 miles and digging 15,204 miles of new ditches by 1942.[26]

The WPA also provided labor for huge federal infrastructure projects. In Florida, for example, WPA workers upgraded the Intracoastal waterway and built part of the Hoover Dike around Lake Okeechobee. In California, WPA workers began construction of Shasta Dam on the Sacramento River in 1937. Part of the scheme to divert water for irrigation in the south Central Valley, Shasta permanently stopped the floods that had nourished 100,000 acres of riparian wetlands and replenished farmland soils. By reducing flooding in ancestral overflow channels, the dam and other water-control structures enabled farmers to convert riparian areas to farmland. By 1939, 85 percent of the Central Valley wetlands were gone.[27]

Congress also approved new laws designed to promote general welfare in the depression-ridden nation. Several of these laws incidentally encouraged wetland destruction. With the Sugar Act of 1934, for example, Congress allotted production quotas to buoy the price of sugar. Despite protective tariffs, world sugar prices had dropped to less than one-half cent per pound in 1932, making it difficult for cane farmers to stay afloat. The quotas limited the acreage that farmers could bring into production within regions. Sugar industry trade organizations then divided the apportionment among individual growers. Although the act initially limited production, within a few years, sugar prices were successfully boosted. And as the market subsequently expanded, vast wetland acreages in south Florida were drained and placed in production. Everglades sugar cane yields more than doubled, from 410,000 to 873,000 tons, between 1931 and 1941.[28]

With passage of the Flood Control Act of 1936, Congress extended the services of the Army Corps of Engineers to offer flood protection to communities nationwide, sparking the most significant round of dam and levee construction in the nation's history.[29] Hundreds of these structures permanently altered the hydrology and ecology of natural wetlands and opened up downstream floodplains for new agricultural and residential development.

THE DOUBLE AGENDA   175

Following the proactive stance of the federal government, some states began to assume greater responsibility for their own public works projects. Louisiana, for example, instituted a program in 1940 to enhance federal efforts to reinvigorate the hundreds of drainage districts that had fallen into onerous debt, disrepair, and bankruptcy. Recognizing that cooperation among landowners and planning were essential, the state Department of Public Works developed watershed-based drainage plans. Most local governments elected to join in the program and raised one-third of the funds needed to build new levees and ditches. In 1945, the state appropriated $5 million to implement new drainage plans and negotiated with the Corps of Engineers to provide better drain outlets in areas where levees had interrupted normal drainage.[30]

The state accomplished little beyond surveying and planning during World War II because dredging equipment and qualified operators were scarce. But afterwards, earthmoving began in earnest. In 1944, Louisiana Governor Sam Houston Jones heralded the program as a way to double the state's farm income and to bring in more farmers. "We have," he boasted, "the greatest undeveloped agricultural frontier in all America. . . ."[31] Thus, plans to drain 11 million acres in Louisiana went forward once again with an ethic of transforming swampland into cropland.[32] Little thought was given to the problem of overproduction or to the state Department of Conservation's concern for fish and game.

Although the economic downturn of the Great Depression reduced the capability of individual farmers, drainage districts, and investors to build massive drainage projects like those completed during the first decades of the century, the new involvement of the federal government and then state governments permitted the continued alteration, drainage, redrainage, and destruction of millions of acres of wetlands, causing severe damage to wildlife and fisheries. Beyond effecting significant changes in the landscape, the participation of the federal government with its expert agronomists and engineers provided new authority and support for drainage and conversion of wetlands to farms.

The Conservation Agenda

Grounded in principles of scientific planning, most New Deal projects focused on strengthening the economy and creating jobs as quickly as possible. Many make-work projects were born out of economic emergency. As a result, policies adopted by government agencies were at times contradictory. While many New Deal policies and projects directly harmed wetlands, others were intended to conserve them.

Despite the series of waterfowl protection laws passed by Congress prohibiting market hunting and providing nominal habitat, duck and geese populations continued to plummet. Little money had been appropriated for refuge acquisition under the Norbeck–Andresen Act of 1928. In addition, rail travel opened up regions for hunting that had been inaccessible. Driven to desperation, many hungry people shot birds for food during the depression without regard for bag limits. Widespread drainage projects had encroached upon areas inhabited by waterfowl, fish, and other animals. Most significant, the great drought of the 1930s parched the few remaining undrained wetlands. Areas in the northern prairie states that had formerly been important breeding grounds dried up, leaving ducks and geese with no place to rear new broods. Loose soils blew and drifted, leaving residents pining for their former wetlands.

By 1934, the continental waterfowl population had dropped to an all-time low of 27 million birds. The egret population was reduced to 150 birds, and whooping cranes numbered 14. Many conservationists predicted mass extinctions if nothing were done. The severity of the drought finally prompted concerned bureaucrats and citizens to seek solutions to the urgent problems of wetland fauna.

Franklin Roosevelt created a special Committee on Wildlife Restoration to study the possibilities for rehabilitating declining waterfowl populations. To this committee, he appointed Thomas Beck, a journalist who had long covered conservation issues; Jay N. Darling, a popular cartoonist who had been involved in wildlife conservation issues in his home state of Iowa; and preeminent wildlife biologist Aldo Leopold. Leopold had written the first wildlife management textbook and thereby influenced the first generation of wildlife biologists working in government agencies. After a thorough study of materials made available by the Bureau of Biological Survey, the committee urged the immediate allocation of $25 million to restore submarginal lands as wildlife refuges. As a long-term goal, Beck, Darling, and Leopold recommended setting aside 12.5 million acres as refuge lands.[33] Roosevelt promised $1 million of emergency funds to begin the project.

Shortly thereafter, FDR appointed Darling to head the Bureau of Biological Survey. In an era predating mass media, when there were few truly national celebrities, Darling enjoyed fame as a result of his cartoons syndicated in 130 papers. Under the pen name Ding, he had published clever

Why drain our lakes to make more farms when we are already suffering from overproduction? (1923).

Ding Darling made his national reputation as a cartoonist. Many Darling cartoons starkly criticized waterfowl management by depicting weeping, bandaged, emaciated ducks driven from their wetland homes by dredges, bulldozers, developers, and politicians. (Courtesy J.N. "Ding" Darling Foundation) cartoons criticizing waterfowl management since the turn of the century. Darling had followed conservation issues with great interest for many years. As a younger man, he had read George Bird Grinnell's books and articles and corresponded with Teddy Roosevelt and Gifford Pinchot. Darling's popularity, influence, eloquence, media savvy, and commitment to reform made him an ideal person to lead a new initiative to protect waterfowl. He put the poorly funded, poorly organized Bureau of Biological Survey into refreshing new order, hiring qualified wildlife managers. He made good use of his small but competent staff, focusing on enforcement of hunting regulations at first.[34]

Because there was little money available for refuge acquisition during the depression, Darling, even before becoming Biological Survey chief, had helped to gain congressional approval for the Migratory Bird Hunting Stamp Act of 1934, a creative law that authorized the sale of one-dollar stamps to all hunters to finance refuges. From his new position, Darling supervised the program and designed its first stamp, a brush-and-ink drawing of two mallards landing in a marsh pond. While the popular stamp program generated more money than ever before for refuges, even those revenues proved inadequate to purchase habitat needed by waterfowl.[35]

With scant funding lined up, Darling enlisted the aid of local conservation groups and hunting clubs to send suggestions for potential refuge sites. Then he began planning strings of refuges along the migration routes of each flyway and appointed dynamic fellow Iowan J. Clark Salyer to oversee the program. But Roosevelt and Congress stalled on providing promised moneys and even diverted duck stamp revenues to other purposes. When Darling reminded the president of the $1 million promised for waterfowl, Roosevelt laughed and handed him a scrap of paper with "IOU $1,000,000, FDR" scrawled on it.[36]

As Darling scrambled for money, South Dakota Senator Peter Norbeck came to the rescue. All the other senators knew that the beloved Norbeck suffered from terminal cancer. When he asked in his thick Scandinavian accent for a rider that appropriated the unexpended balance of the previous year's relief funds for waterfowl refuges, the proposal passed unanimously, on June 15, 1935, releasing $6 million for the refuge program. This appropriation together with the annual duck stamp moneys finally provided the funding for the Migratory Bird Conservation Act introduced by Norbeck six years prior. Darling later wrote that he doubted the other senators had understood a single word of Norbeck's proposal, but that if it had not been for his concern, "the whole Duck Restoration Program would have completely collapsed."[37]

Beyond the Norbeck appropriation and duck stamp revenues, Darling pieced together even more resources for waterfowl restoration by developing conservation initiatives that dovetailed with other federal programs. For example, he managed to acquire retired submarginal lands from the USDA for his refuge system. Because many of those marginal lands required revegetation and water sources in order to provide habitat for birds and animals, Darling and Salyer also recruited the help of the WPA and CCC to rehabilitate the new refuges. Thirty-eight CCC camps helped by building dikes and ditches to impound water for waterfowl in critical areas baked dry by the drought.[38]

The Souris Refuge in North Dakota was one of the first restoration projects carried out under Darling's tenure. Although once renowned as great duck hunting grounds, nearly all the marshes along the Souris River had been drained and then abandoned. When drought struck and dried up the surrounding potholes, ducks had no place to breed. CCC camps erected several dikes and water-control structures across the river to impound water and re-create shallow marshes. Then they set waterfowl food plants, fenced out livestock, and built a storage dam upstream to provide a steady water supply.[39] Refuge landscapes that to modern visitors appear highly manipulated were established during this time when aggressive management was necessary to make wholly devastated lands functional for waterfowl.

Darling and Salyer acquired many other wetlands in need of restoration, including Mattamuskeet Lake in North Carolina and Horicon Marsh in Wisconsin. In 1934, they purchased the rights to return water to Malheur Lake refuge, which had become an alkali bowl owing to diversions though ostensibly protected by executive order in 1908.[40] Beyond acquiring marginal lands for refuges, Darling and Salyer also protected areas of particular significance to migratory waterfowl, such as Aransas National Wildlife Refuge on the Texas coast—the sole place where whooping cranes still wintered.[41]

In order to garner income for continued management, Darling put many refuge lands to other uses such as grazing, haying, or trapping after their waterfowl-serving missions were met.[42] Through the drought, the refuge system functioned as a skeleton of wetland habitat, sustaining the minimum nourishment needs of the nation's waterfowl. Thereafter, the refuges continued to support waterfowl displaced by ongoing habitat losses.

Recognizing that successful waterfowl management depended on qualified biologists for the new refuges, Darling also established Cooperative
Wildlife Research Units at land-grant universities to educate a new generation of wildlife experts. To pay for the program, he imaginatively enlisted
the help of the firearms industry's American Wildlife Institute to augment
funding from the federal government.

Ding Darling resigned in 1935, but in the eighteen months that he held
office, he masterfully prevented the complete demise of continental waterfowl populations, elevated interest in conservation, and set in place institutions that would protect wetland habitat in the future. Darling remained active in conservation and founded the National Wildlife Federation the
following year to organize sportsmen's clubs nationwide into a more potent
political force.[43]

By the end of the decade, emergency funds had all been allocated,
leaving only duck stamp revenues for refuge acquisition—not nearly
enough to safeguard the habitat needed by waterfowl. At the second Annual
North American Wildlife Conference in March 1937, sponsored by the
American Wildlife Institute and Darling's newly created National Wildlife
Federation (NWF), participants remembered that a proposed excise tax to
fund refuges had failed in Congress a decade prior. In the political climate
of the New Deal, they thought such a tax might fare better. Carl Shoemaker, secretary of the NWF, diligently prepared a new bill, which provided for an 11 percent manufacturer's excise tax on sporting firearms and
ammunition. Revenues collected would be apportioned to states both to
conduct research and to acquire refuge lands on the basis of project merit.
State wildlife restoration proposals deemed "substantial in character and
design" would qualify for 75 percent federal funding. Conservation groups,
the Bureau of Biological Survey, state wildlife agencies, and the sporting
arms industry eagerly endorsed the bill.

With broad support secured, Shoemaker began to look for congressional
sponsors. Nevada Senator Key Pittman, chair of the Special Senate Committee on Conservation of Wildlife Resources, signed on early and thus encouraged many other senators to join him. Then Shoemaker approached
Virginia Congressman A. Willis Robertson. Robertson carefully scruti-
nized the bill and promised to introduce it in the House with one change: a
stipulation that states could not receive any federal funding if they diverted
their own game protection funds from hunting-license revenues to other

purposes, a common practice during those desperate financial times. In June 1937, Pittman and Robertson shepherded the bill through Congress, and President Roosevelt signed the Pittman–Robertson Federal Aid in Wildlife Restoration Act into law by that September. Within one year, forty-three out of forty-eight states became eligible for "P-R" funds by passing laws to prevent the diversion of hunting-license fees.

Darling's hand-picked successor, Ira Gabrielson, immediately appointed his assistant, Albert Day, to administer the new federal program. Utah's Department of Fish and Game implemented the first P-R project at the Weber River delta, where avian botulism had taken a chronic toll on waterfowl. With P-R funds, the state impounded river water as it entered the Great Salt Lake with a five-mile dike to provide more freshwater habitat.[44] Recognizing the role of beavers in preventing soil erosion and in creating wetland habitats, many states took advantage of P-R funding to restore these animals to their streams. During the first ten-year period of the excise tax, over $48 million was collected.

Yet despite successful projects, the P-R law did not live up to the grand expectations of its authors in its early years. Committing the same robbery of wildlife funds forbidden to states, Congress refused to appropriate full revenues from the excise tax. It was not until 1951 that Congress made P-R funds a permanent appropriation, and not until 1955 that it released the $13 million previously withheld. Eventually, the Federal Aid in Wildlife Restoration law hit its stride, heralded by one writer as "the most productive and far-reaching piece of wildlife legislation enacted in the U.S."[45] State dollars made the P-R funds go further and helped to acquire wetland habitat for waterfowl and other game animals. But, most significant, the availability of federal funding encouraged states to develop their own wildlife management expertise and programs. The requirement that proposals be approved also gave the federal Fish and Wildlife Service (successor of the Bureau of Biological Survey) considerable influence over the developing program.[46]

Beyond their financial support through the purchase of duck stamps and payment of the firearms and munitions excise taxes, sportsmen made further contributions to protecting waterfowl. Many duck hunting clubs acquired important wetlands as habitat and hunting grounds. Through the 1930s and 1940s, for example, Bakersfield, California, had over one hundred duck clubs, made especially famous by their Hollywood celebrity members, including Clark Gable.[47] Despite the clubs' habitat and federal refuge lands, hunters remained dissatisfied because duck populations continued to fall, severely limiting or even preempting hunting seasons.

In 1935, Joseph Palmer Knapp, a New York philanthropist and duck hunter, became intrigued by the idea of intensive game management and so started his own foundation, More Game Birds in America. The foundation started out with a survey of Canadian breeding grounds. The same pothole-dappled plains landscape of the northern U.S. prairie states stretched far into the Canadian provinces of Manitoba, Saskatchewan, and Alberta. And the same drainage and drought pressures that had desiccated the U.S. potholes had wrought havoc in Canadian breeding areas as well. The survey indicated that beyond creating refuges in the United States, restoring wetlands in Canada was essential to protecting continental duck populations. So in 1937 the More Game Birds foundation launched a new program, Ducks Unlimited, intended to triple duck production by rehabilitating wetlands in Canada's southern prairies. Early Ducks Unlimited (DU) leaders set about organizing and enlisting members in each state to raise funds for the necessary projects. In 1941, DU began a nationwide fund drive by distributing two thousand "Duk-A-Nikel" cans to hunting clubs. The colorful slotted cans featured a cartoon character named Jake-the-Drake, who demanded a nickel for every duck or goose bagged, as well as a cut of card game winnings. The cans brought in seven thousand dollars annually, but, most significant, they involved more hunters in supporting the Ducks Unlimited cause. The first DU project was the restoration of the 100,000-acre Big Grass Marsh in Manitoba, where employees built several small dams across the prairies to re-create shallow marshes that had been destroyed by drainage and drought. In 1939, DU biologists began the first large-scale, breeding-ground, bird-banding program in North America.

By 1943, Ducks Unlimited had accomplished 103 wetland restoration projects on more than a million acres and had institutionalized the commitment of duck hunters to protecting habitat.[48] Working beyond the parameters of the New Deal, efforts of American sportsmen in Canada directly aided the work of U.S. government biologists to maintain continental waterfowl populations.

Policies in Conflict

As federal biologists struggled to establish an adequate refuge system, they realized that New Deal development projects often thwarted the conservation policies they tried to implement. In particular, their work to prevent extinction of ducks and geese was undermined by federal construction agencies, such as the Corps of Engineers and the Bureau of Reclamation, that destroyed wetland habitat with their levees and dams.

Congress attempted to reconcile these conflicts by passing the Fish and Wildlife Coordination Act in 1934. To encourage the consideration of wildlife needs in public works planning, the act directed government construction agencies to consult with federal and state fish and game agencies to minimize loss of wildlife habitat caused by federal water projects.[49] Although the language of the act was revolutionary, it was not mandatory; rather, it was offered in the "spirit of cooperation."[50] As a result, this potentially powerful legislation was never taken seriously. Although amendments in 1946 and 1958 strengthened the law by requiring consultation and mitigation for habitat loss, federal construction agencies still reserved discretion in making final decisions.[51] The law's most positive result was that the fledgling refuge system received several units of flooded marshland at the edges of newly constructed reservoirs to compensate in part for riparian wetlands drowned under the impoundments and for those left high and dry downstream from the new dams.

While the Fish and Wildlife Coordination Act addressed the habitat destruction caused by the construction agencies, it did nothing to temper the drainage activities of the agricultural agencies. Early on, USBS biologists working to protect waterfowl had recognized that USDA drainage programs worked at odds with their own attempts to preserve habitat through leasing and purchasing wetlands. To resolve this conflict, a 1938 memorandum directed USDA agencies to send their drainage plans to the chief of the Bureau of Biological Survey for consultation. Although the memorandum officially cautioned against initiating drainage projects that might harm or destroy important wildlife habitat, the admonishment lacked teeth and allowed for wide interpretation in the field.[52] Then in 1944, Congress allotted $2 million specifically for SCS drainage and irrigation work in the Midwest, Southeast, and Mississippi Valley.[53]

When questions arose about the propriety of the SCS promoting drainage, memoranda were sent to field staff in 1941 and then again in 1946 to clarify that both drainage and irrigation were to be considered "technical conservation practices." The memos asserted that the SCS had full authority to assist farmers in carrying out these practices as part of their farm conservation plans.[54] These plans typically focused on reducing soil erosion, but in some locales retiring erodible lands depended on draining wetlands for new cultivation. In other places, basic drainage was simply

December
1947

SOIL CONSERVATION

OFFICIAL ORGAN OF THE SOIL CONSERVATION SERVICE

D STATES DEPARTMENT OF AGRICULTURE, WASHINGTON, D. C.

THE OFFICIAL ORGAN OF THE SOIL CONSERVATION SERVICE, MAGAZINE COVER.
With the New Deal, the federal government entered the drainage business. In the
decades that followed, the Soil Conservation Service (SCS) encouraged farmers to
drain their lands by offering technical assistance with tiling and ditching as shown on
the cover of this 1947 SCS magazine.

deemed necessary for good farming, so SCS helped to plan lateral ditches. Beyond offering technical assistance, the USDA provided funding for drainage with its Agricultural Conservation Program (ACP). In Arkansas, for example, farmers took advantage of the organizational opportunities afforded by the soil conservation districts, SCS expertise, and ACP money to launch large-scale drainage operations.[55]

Although these federal farm programs started in the mid 1930s with the New Deal, they did not reach full swing until drought and depression conditions subsided and World War II ended. With farm prices and demand for agricultural products up during and after the war, ACP drainage assistance peaked in 1947.[56]

The effects of the indiscriminate drainage encouraged by the government did not go unnoticed by conservationists. In the late thirties, the National Association of Audubon Societies published a thirty-page booklet documenting for the first time the ecological values of wetlands and criticizing government policies of mosquito ditching and agricultural drainage. Entitled *Thirst on the Land,* the booklet, authored by William Vogt, described how ditching altered the ecology of marshes to the detriment of fish and birds. According to the booklet, USBS studies had already revealed that within six months, ditched marshes contained only half the animal life of nonditched marshes. Vogt also criticized agricultural policies, contending that wetland drainage worsened the effects of the drought. The booklet encouraged Audubon chapters and other citizen groups to organize against drainage.[57]

While conservationists were angry about sweeping agricultural drainage, farmers were furious about ducks. The seasonally inundated Central Valley had since time immemorial provided ideal wintering conditions for ducks and geese. Although drought had decimated waterfowl populations, rainy years coupled with the absence of hunting pressure during World War II spurred a comeback. There were finally more waterfowl, but because of increased farm development, there was no longer sufficient wetland habitat to sustain them. When birds arrived in winter months, they found irrigated fields of barley and rice in place of the natural foods that had thrived in riparian wetlands. Ducks and geese quickly learned to make do with the cereal grains, especially rice, though it didn't fully meet their nutritional requirements. In the winter of 1943–1944, widgeons devoured 40 acres of commercial head lettuce. Because eelgrass in the coastal bays had died off, brants ate pea and barley crops instead. Farms expanding into the remaining Central Valley wetlands met with intense depredation by ducks and geese.

Irritated by heavy losses, farmers complained that federal waterfowl protection programs compounded their crop predation problems. In response, Congress passed the Lea Act in 1948 to fund federal purchase of nearby wildlife management areas, where food could be grown to entice waterfowl away from farmers' fields. Tule Lake and Klamath Lake near the California–Oregon border would provide adequate feed to hold up the waterfowl flocks until crops in California ripened for harvest.[58] Moreover, Congress required California to match the federal refuge lands by starting its own refuge system, so the state acquired nearly 7,000 acres in four separate management areas: Colusa, Sutter, Merced, and Salton Sea.[59] As people rapidly converted natural habitat into human developments and farms, refuges became ever more critical to waterfowl and wildlife. The Lea Act refuge lands coupled with intensive management, including the herding of ducks by airplane, controlled crop predation problems to some degree, but the small amount of wetland acreage protected was a pittance given the habitat needs of Pacific Flyway waterfowl.[60]

In the same way that water formed a commons component of wetlands, so too did flights of waterfowl. As destruction of wetlands produced effects that rippled throughout watersheds—such as increased flooding or salt-water intrusion—it also had effects that reverberated up and down flyways. If habitat in one part of a flyway was ruined, then all duck and geese populations that relied on the route would be affected. To protect the common value of the nation's waterfowl, government involvement was essential to safeguard refuge lands and to restrict overhunting. Federal and state refuges also protected farmers from the public nuisance of crop predation by baiting the displaced birds away from cultivated fields; only with such help could farmers reap the benefits of their private land. In order to preserve waterfowl and citizens' rights to hunt and to enjoy birds on their properties, but also to protect the investments of farmers on their properties, the commonage of wetland resources had to be acknowledged. Although the government responded to specific problems, a more holistic vision of the interconnection of wetland ecosystems was yet to be understood.

Return to the Everglades

Perhaps no place better illustrates how varying government policies created a tug-of-war over wetlands than the Everglades. At the same time that the

Army Corps of Engineers stopped the flow of water with Hoover Dike, that Congress set sugar quotas encouraging conversion of more sawgrass wetlands, and that the Reconstruction Finance Corporation bailed out the Everglades Drainage District, wetland enthusiasts picked up where May Mann Jennings had left off and began to promote the natural merits of the Everglades as a potential national park.

Despite the passage of laws banning market hunting and the preservation of Royal Palm State Park, bird populations in the Everglades continued to fall. It became evident that, as elsewhere, the primary threat was loss of habitat to agriculture and development. Although drainage in south Florida had proceeded in a piecemeal manner, it wholly changed the area's ecology. Incised by deep ditches, the sawgrass marshes dried out and became prone to fires that raged through the grasslands, consuming peat soils and leaving nothing but bare limestone bedrock. Without sufficient food and water, flocks of exotic tropical birds no longer returned to their roosts and rookeries in the Everglades.

The establishment of Royal Palm State Park in 1916 had directed attention to the biological values of the Everglades, and in 1923, National Park Service director Stephen B. Mather had recommended that the area be considered for the national park system. Mather's recommendation went nowhere until Ernest Coe, a Coconut Grove landscape architect, stepped forward to champion the idea. Impressed by the unique natural beauty of south Florida, Coe gained the backing of the Florida congressional delegation and then formed the Tropic Everglades National Park Association in 1928 to organize local support for a park. The following year, the state legislature created the Tropic Everglades National Park Commission to advance the cause.[61]

A first breakthrough came when Congress authorized a Park Service study of the area. In 1930, Mather's successor, Horace Albright, led a group of experts, along with Florida Congresswoman Ruth Bryan Owen, to determine if parts of the Everglades merited national park status. The Tropical Everglades Park Association and the Federation of Women's Clubs provided tours and briefing papers on the natural values of the area. After the investigation, Albright recommended creation of a national park, and Representative Owen eagerly introduced legislation in the House. The bill failed but was reintroduced by Owen and by Senator Fletcher in 1932. Congress again voted it down.

Coe's association stepped up its publicity campaign at the national level.

ERNEST COE.

Beginning in the 1920s, citizen activist Ernest Coe tirelessly worked for decades to make the Everglades into the nation's first wetland national park. The park was finally dedicated in 1947. (Historical Museum of Southern Florida)

Stories appeared in *National Geographic* and *Science* and routinely made their way into the *New York Times*. One article written by Marjory Stoneman Douglas for the *Miami Herald* included quotes from dozens of experts expressing support for the park.[62] The National Parks Association hired landscape architect Frederick Law Olmsted, Jr., son of the renowned designer of Central Park and the Back Bay Fens, to study the park proposal. After a tour of the park by boat and blimp, he too submitted a favorable report. Secretary of the Interior Ray Lyman Wilbur also made an Everglades trip and recommended national park status. Despite the lack of congressional interest, the state of Florida began to purchase lands for the future national park.

The following year, an amended bill passed the Senate with the backing of both Florida senators, but the House bill was debated acrimoniously, with partisan politics determining battle lines. Northern representatives suggested that since their states had developed park systems on their own, Florida should do the same. Others thought that Congress should be concerned with the depression—not with swamp parks. New Jersey Representative Frederick Lehlbach (R) attacked the proposal: "This bill is to create a snake swamp park on perfectly worthless land . . . so the fact that it would not cost the Government anything for the initial acquisition of this worthless swamp is the height of irony."[63] The word "worthless" and the phrase "alligator and snake swamp park" were used frequently by Republican opponents, drawing upon the traditional understanding of swamps as useless and terrifying lands. Descriptions of alligators and forty-pound snakes that "infested" the Everglades continually crept into the spicy discourse. As if words alone were not adequate proof, landowners opposing the park brought a fat snake to the House hearings and released it on a table as evidence. To diffuse the effect of the grandstanding, Representative Ruth Owen bravely grabbed the snake—though she'd never done such a thing before—wrapped it around her neck, and declared, "That's how afraid we are of snakes in the Everglades."[64]

Opponents argued that the Everglades lacked the stunning scenery of the Rocky Mountains or Yosemite and would degrade the standards of the park system. But advocates challenged that the unique biological values of the Everglades more than made up for its plain scenery. Park promoters focused their arguments on the birds and fish in danger of extinction. Supporters listed the numerous government agencies, conservation organizations, and prominent scientists that favored the bill. Three times, the Senate passed the Everglades National Park bill, but each time the House defeated it.[65]

Despite a Republican filibuster, the bill finally passed the House, 222 to 145, on May 24, 1934—only because representatives tacked on an amendment that blocked appropriations for five years. The Senate concurred, passing the Everglades National Park Act the next day, and President Roosevelt signed it five days later. Despite the congressional and executive authorization to create the national park, the struggle to protect the Everglades was just beginning.

Roosevelt earmarked all remaining federal lands within the designated two-thousand-square-mile Everglades area for possible inclusion in the park, but the ball fell to Florida to acquire privately owned parcels. Pockets of opposition opened up in the southwestern part of the peninsula, which retained a frontier flavor in great contrast to the cosmopolitan, park-supporting east coast. Striking in his six-foot stature, white seersucker suit, and snowy hair, Ernest Coe tirelessly attended meetings and answered angry questions to gain local favor.[66] Despite legislative interest, Governor Fred Cone remained lukewarm and refused to make available eighty-seven thousand dollars already appropriated for title searches. Further complications arose in 1939, when oil discovered within the park's proposed boundaries catapulted land prices upward and diminished local support for the park. Fearing damage to the park from oil drilling, Secretary of the Interior Harold Ickes refused to accept any lands without full mineral rights. Orchid merchants, game hunters, oil prospectors, and real estate developers all lobbied against state efforts to acquire lands. Gubernatorial opposition together with depression economics, oil speculation, and then World War II kept the park on the backburner for a decade.[67]

Journalist John O'Reilly called attention to the ongoing degradation of the Everglades owing to the numerous delays in a series of articles run by both the *Miami Herald* and the *New York Herald Tribune* in 1939. According to O'Reilly, drainage continued within the designated park area, drying sawgrass, causing destructive fires, and forcing "the wholesale migration of birds and animals from a habitat which has been their home since before history."[68] Land acquisition progressed too slowly to safeguard the park lands. By 1941, Florida had turned over only a few isolated tracts to the secretary of the interior.

In 1944, to keep the park plan moving forward, outgoing Governor Spessard Holland and Governor-elect Millard Caldwell proposed to reserve mineral rights to original landowners for a five-year period and to compromise with a smaller park that excluded the most controversial drilling areas.[69] They drew up a new boundary, shaving off 20 percent of the area originally slated for the park, including Big Cypress, lands north of the Tamiami Trail, and Florida Bay frontage. With these provisions and positive newspaper publicity supplied by *Miami Herald* editor John Pennekamp, Florida was able to continue purchasing lands. The state's Everglades National Park Commission, together with civic groups including the state Chamber of Commerce, the National Association of Audubon Societies, and the Florida Parent-Teachers Association, worked hard to raise the needed funds. The Federation of Women's Clubs deeded Royal Palm State Park to the state for the national park. Ernest Coe took on the challenging job of working with private inholdings for the state commission. To speed land acquisition, the commission eventually negotiated a deal to enlist the federal government's power of eminent domain.

In March 1947, the state of Florida deeded 850,000 acres to the National Park Service and then three months later gave the Department of the Interior $2 million to complete the necessary condemnations and acquisitions. Ironically, 3 million acres of land in the Everglades National Park area had been granted to Florida by the federal government's Swamp Land Acts one hundred years prior. At the formal dedication on December 6, 1947, a crowd of park supporters, including May Mann Jennings—leader of the first generation of Everglades advocates—gathered to celebrate. Thirteen years after it was first authorized by Franklin D. Roosevelt, President Harry Truman officially opened the new national park. "In this park," he announced, "we shall protect hundreds of all kinds of wildlife which might otherwise soon be extinct."[70] The national park preserved roughly 10 to 15 percent of the original Everglades.[71]

The opening of Everglades National Park was the culmination of a tremendous citizens' effort. Their successful, two-decades-long national publicity campaign explained to Americans for the first time the reasons for protecting the ecological values of wetlands. Even though people did not use the word *wetland* just yet, the controversy surrounding this national park issue stimulated a new consideration of the wetlandscape.

To celebrate the occasion and introduce the new park to citizens throughout the nation, the Postal Service issued a green and white Everglades commemorative stamp depicting a white heron.[72] In that same year, Marjory Stoneman Douglas's landmark book, *The Everglades: River of*

Grass, was published and began its enduring career of teaching Americans about their unusual park.[73] The Everglades would become a significant focal point and barometer for the condition of wetlands nationwide.

Although the land of the Everglades was officially protected with national park status, the water upon which it depended was not. At the same time supporters struggled to establish Everglades National Park, the Army Corps of Engineers was girding Lake Okeechobee with levees. With the completion of the mammoth dike in 1942, vital water that had flowed for centuries into the sawgrass meadows of the Everglades stopped. When the freshwater ceased flowing southward through the Everglades, saltwater began to seep in from the coast. In 1942 and 1943, saltwater invaded coastal wetlands at a rate of 235 feet per year, increasing to 800 feet during the dry year of 1944.[74] Intruding saltwater killed the plants adapted to freshwater living and irreparably damaged the area's ecology and hydrology. Even during drought, drainage canals conveyed water from Lake Okeechobee to the sea, carrying with it the potential to recharge the fast-dropping water table. Intruding saltwater also began to contaminate the Biscayne Aquifer, threatening the water supply of Florida's east coast cities.

Engineers of the Everglades Drainage District had recommended deepening existing canals to maintain drainage in agricultural areas but halting construction of new canals to conserve soil, water, and wildlife. During a series of hurricanes in 1947, however, the deepened drainage canals hastened the flow of floodwaters toward the cities of coastal Florida, causing $59 million in damages. South Florida again appealed for federal assistance. The year after President Truman dedicated the Everglades National Park to protect "all kinds of wildlife," he signed into law a new flood-control project that included the construction of an enormous perimeter levee to the east of the Everglades to protect the urban Miami and Fort Lauderdale areas. In addition to retaining floodwaters, the new levees featured three conservation areas to store water for use in times of drought and to help replenish the aquifer. Construction of the one-hundred-mile perimeter levee began in 1950.[75] Reflecting the change in water policy focus, the state legislature replaced the Everglades Drainage District with the Central and South Florida Flood Control District. The new levee projects would further block the natural flow of water into the Everglades.

Not only did public works agencies fail to understand the hydrology of the area for their drainage and flood-control purposes, but park planners also misunderstood the Everglades's need for a natural, sheetlike water supply. Moreover, no government agencies recognized the consequences of their own projects on other agencies' projects. The result of these divergent policies would be decades of conflict and wetland degradation.

Leaving behind its traditional laissez-faire approach, during the course of the New Deal the federal government took an active role in promoting both wetland drainage and conservation. Without federal assistance, many wetlands would have remained only partially drained or entirely undrained, and natural flood regimes of undammed rivers would have continued to nourish millions of wetland acres. Yet without federal assistance, continental waterfowl populations might have dropped irreversibly, and there would be fewer refuges, fewer wildlife biologists, and no Everglades National Park. By lending its authority to both drainage and conservation, the federal government legitimized both contradictory policies. This dichotomy of opinion not only became entrenched in government institutions but also reinforced the primary attitudes Americans held about wetlands. While to some, wetlands were wastelands, to others, wetlands held intrinsic and critical value.

TEN

In the Path of the Boom

He has long since become convinced that marshland development is well worth the cost in time and money. Here is why: he paid $800 each for 180 acres in 1949. He has spent $1,500 an acre to improve it. And today the land is valued at $12,000 an acre.

—*House and Home* magazine (1958)[1]

As members of a presumably rational and enlightened society, do we need to let the destruction of our wetland values continue as long as someone feels able personally to profit thereby?

—Paul L. Errington, *Of Men and Marshes* (1957)[2]

Gearing up for World War II finally pulled the nation out of its depression doldrums. With all sectors of society, industry, and government contributing to the titan effort, full employment returned, innovation abounded, and the faltering economy accelerated into a propitious machine. With all energy directed toward the war, most projects to drain and alter wetlands were quieted. But not for long. The war's most significant legacy for wetlands was the booming era of prosperity, confidence, and optimism that followed.

As the country welcomed home its soldiers, there were suddenly demands for more housing, more food, more appliances, more energy, more cars, more roads, and more fun. The economy flourished as many families enjoyed new wealth. Within ten years, vast suburban housing tracts sprang up to meet the needs of the growing population, and millions of automobiles traveled the ribbons of new highway that crisscrossed the country. Amid the bustle, formidable political, institutional, and financial incentives to destroy wetlands emerged, but few Americans grasped the import of the changing landscape. New demands of the affluent population reverberated in wetlands everywhere, but nowhere was the clamor so striking as in our farmlands.

On the Farm

Day County, South Dakota, lay within the glaciated pothole region of the northern plains. Thousands of bowls of glimmering water of shapes and sizes irresistibly inviting to ducks nestled into the undulant landscape. In the spring of 1948, a cacophony of bluewings, gadwalls, shovellers, widgeons, redheads, and other ducks courted in the county's sedge-edged potholes. But by autumn of the same year, many of the potholes had disappeared. Instead, drainage ditches connected the low spots where water had once accumulated.

Drainage had swept the northern prairies during the first decades of the century, but the dust bowl thirties made farmers question the practice. In fact, most stopped for a while. After the hard times of drought and depression ended, prairie farmers welcomed the high post-war prices. To increase production and profits, they began draining wetlands again. But high farm prices weren't the only motivation. The federal government, well established through local conservation districts during the New Deal, offered technical assistance and subsidies for drainage, which directly encouraged farmers to transform even marginal areas into croplands.

In Day County, for example, the USDA Extension Service mailed bulletins to 450 local farmers, promoting the merits of draining potholes and explaining how to sign up for the Soil Conservation Service's free drainage-engineering assistance. Until 1950, when large earthmoving machinery became more readily available, the SCS even provided farmers with war-surplus bulldozers and draglines to excavate ditches.[3] Beyond considering drainage a fundamental "conservation" practice, SCS agents regarded drainage as a way of bringing farmers into their network to learn about other soil conservation practices. By helping farmers to drain their lands, SCS agents developed good rapport with local people and firmly established their advisory role. With the bargaining chip of drainage aid, SCS agents could press farmers to draw up farm conservation plans to reduce erosion.

Even more enticing than SCS technical assistance, the USDA's Production and Marketing Agency (PMA) offered to share the costs of on-farm drainage projects. The PMA paid farmers eight cents for every cubic yard of ditch dug and seventy-five cents for every thousand square feet of waterway planted in grass—a subsidy amounting to 60 percent of the total

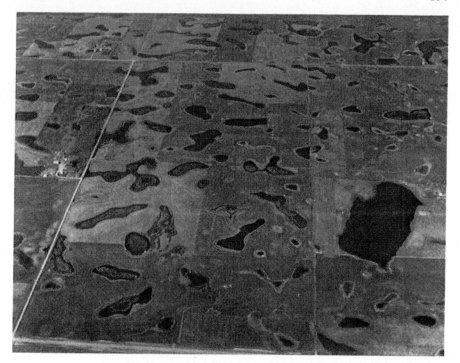

PRAIRIE POTHOLES IN NORTH DAKOTA.
Millions of prairie potholes dappled North Dakota, South Dakota, Minnesota, and
Iowa, providing breeding grounds for the continent's waterfowl. Drainage of these
important habitat areas has had dire consequences for waterfowl throughout North
America, especially in times of drought. (Courtesy North Dakota State Game and
Fish Department)

costs of drainage. In Day County, the PMA paid farmers $17,285 in 1948
for digging forty-three miles of ditches.[4] Coupled with price supports available for surplus wheat, the federal drainage subsidies effectively removed
the risk of investing in the marginal wetlands. The government even provided insured loans for drainage, further cushioning the risks associated
with farming waterlogged lands.[5] With the sanction of the federal government and the approval of local farmers and contractors, drainage proceeded as a mission unifying communities with a patriotic, agrarian zeal to
make their lands as productive as possible in the hungry post-war world.

The drainage that occurred in Day County was typical of farm practices
throughout the pothole region. SCS records for six counties in northeastern South Dakota documented 16,376 potholes drained with federal
assistance in 1947. All told, the PMA funded drainage on over 1.1 million
acres in South Dakota, North Dakota, and Minnesota that year.[6] Along

with the technical and financial assistance given to thousands of individual farmers, the USDA agents aggressively disseminated the message that drainage was not only a good conservation practice but also an industrious and smart way to improve croplands. By draining lands, farmers could jump on the wave of prosperity that carried the rest of the nation. This agreeable message restored the eroded traditional identity of the farmer as a patriotic, intelligent steward of the land who created the very basis of the nation's wealth and could rise to the challenge of feeding an ever-growing population. The message also revived the traditional drive to make wetlands into useful and uniform farmlands.

If one considered only the limited scope of short-term agriculture, drainage made perfect sense. It opened up fertile lands and successfully increased yields and profits for individuals. But farmers and farmlands exist amid larger landscapes and time frames. At the same time the SCS encouraged farmers to drain new potholes, the Fish and Wildlife Service was spending duck stamp money to restore potholes needed for waterfowl survival.

In the April 1949 issue of *Field and Stream,* journalist Clay Schoenfeld called national attention to these contradictory federal policies in his article "Good-By Pot-Holes." "No wonder duck hunters are now objecting," he wrote, "when they see part of their tax dollar being spent to drain the very type of habitat that is costing money to develop elsewhere."[7]

Schoenfeld directed his article to the magazine's growing readership of hunters. Many returned soldiers enjoyed their new prosperity and leisure time hunting ducks and geese. In fact, the number of waterfowl hunters jumped from 9.8 million to 12 million after the war, and many were interested in conservation. Ducks Unlimited alone had 40,000 members in 1947. Hunter indignation gave the Fish and Wildlife Service backing needed to push for research funds and better consideration of wildlife in federal projects.[8]

While biologists had long suspected that drainage destroyed waterfowl breeding areas, there was little scientific evidence to document the extent of the damage. Better information was needed to convince farmers and government agricultural agencies about the critical values of potholes. The Schoenfeld article prompted the Fish and Wildlife Service to investigate more seriously the effects of pothole drainage on waterfowl breeding areas.[9]

The preliminary results of the studies were astounding. In Minnesota, 16 percent of the potholes had been drained between 1945 and 1950—accounting for the loss of one-third of the state's waterfowl breeding area in only five years. Outraged duck hunters pressed the state legislature to adopt the Minnesota Wetland Purchase Program in 1951, which provided state funds to buy important pothole breeding areas otherwise slated for drainage.[10] The following year, the state Association of Soil Conservation Districts concurred with the hunters' sentiments and voted to withhold drainage assistance to farmers until the Department of Conservation had a crack at purchasing lands for wildlife. Even the *Minneapolis Tribune* lambasted ill-conceived drainage projects with incriminating headlines like "Sibley County Drainage Project Ignores Wildlife" and "Kandiyohi Project Perils Wildlife."[11] Despite public support, Minnesota's pioneering wetland acquisition program was not large enough to outweigh the effects of high farm prices and federal assistance programs.

By 1954, in response to growing criticism from conservationists, the Agricultural Conservation Program Service (ACPS, successor of the PMA) issued new regulations that required its staff to consider the effects of drainage on wildlife habitat when planning projects. Furthermore, the agency would share costs of draining preexisting farmland only—not unfarmed potholes. The new regulations proved inadequate. Farm surpluses the following year prompted even more stringent ACPS rules that precluded cost-sharing for all projects bringing any additional lands into production.[12] But pothole drainage continued.

Some drainage was subsidized by state governments, which—lacking the waterfowl expertise of the federal agencies—made no effort to curb habitat damage. North Dakota, for example, appropriated $810,000 from 1943 to 1957 to promote drainage in the state. SCS engineers often helped to plan the state-assisted projects.[13]

Most federally assisted pothole drainage resulted from confusion about what constituted important waterfowl habitat. Despite the official word that potholes should not be drained with federal money, local agents made a distinction between potholes and "nuisance" areas. Most agents and farmers understood that the deep pools ringed by cattails and bulrushes served waterfowl needs and left them alone. But they did not recognize value in the shallow depressions that held water only temporarily in the spring and required annoying detours for the new larger plows. Such areas were routinely scheduled for drainage.[14] Ducks, however, made no such distinction and, in fact, specifically depended on the smaller, shallow pools for springtime breeding.

Furthermore, federally assisted programs often encouraged drainage beyond that called for in farm conservation plans. Once a large drainage outlet was constructed with SCS help, farmers could more easily build additional lateral ditches on their own. Once a dragline was on the premises, farmers could easily use it for unplanned extra projects. Often soil excavated from ditches was heaped into "nuisance" areas. But not all the earthmoving was necessary. Many farmers freely admitted that they wouldn't have drained their potholes if the bulk of the job hadn't been paid for by the government.[15] The ACPS routinely funded drainage projects that might not otherwise have been built.

While official USDA policy required agents to consider the effects of drainage on wildlife, many regarded the provision as discretionary. Most soil conservationists preferred efficient, well-planned drainage to poorly executed drainage and to the farming of erodible soils. By working closely with farmers, they could secure what they felt were the best soil conservation practices. Their training and the singularity of their agency's mission made this priority incontrovertible. Before they could change gears, soil conservationists needed more clear-cut scientific evidence and specific guidance about what marshes and potholes were important to waterfowl.[16]

Federally assisted drainage in the northern prairie states generated the most criticism because of the region's importance for waterfowl breeding, but the USDA encouraged drainage in other regions as well. From California to Maryland, from Louisiana to Illinois, the SCS provided technical help to cooperating soil conservation districts and drainage districts.[17] Research at agricultural experiment stations in Indiana, the Everglades, North Carolina, and Louisiana determined the best drainage and cultivation techniques for a wide variety of poorly drained soils so that extension agents could advise farmers.[18] With the spread of electricity to rural locales, SCS agents recommended pump drainage for the wettest areas. By 1950, use of electrical pumps had increased markedly; they served 315,000 acres in Illinois, 293,000 acres in Florida, 172,000 acres in Louisiana, and 149,000 acres in Missouri and Iowa.[19] In the Mississippi Valley, the SCS worked in conjunction with the Army Corps of Engineers to reactivate the infrastructures of many local drainage districts. Reluctant to stray from its navigational orientation, the Corps focused primarily on building major drainage outlets along rivers, enabling drainage districts, farmers, and the SCS to collaborate on more extensive on-farm drainage works. The Corps's Mississippi River and Tributaries project spent over $92 million on major drainage improvements through 1958, resulting in the conversion of over 2.2 million acres of wooded wetlands to crop production.[20]

Congress further enlarged the SCS's capacity to assist with drainage nationwide by enacting the Federal Watershed Protection and Flood Prevention Act of 1954, well known as PL-566. This law authorized USDA agencies to work with state and local governments through a new Small Watershed Program ostensibly to reduce large floods by damming streams high in watersheds. Years of erosion caused by poor farming practices had left many streams choked with sediment, so the SCS program also took responsibility for channelizing waterways to carry away floodwaters more effectively. Since the channelized streams could also carry drain waters, many drainage projects fell under the rubric of the Small Watershed Program. In fact, over one-fifth of its projects included drainage.[21] Because drainage figured so prominently, the Fish and Wildlife Service and the SCS adopted a Memorandum of Understanding to incorporate federal or state wildlife agency recommendations into watershed plans.[22] Ultimately, however, decisions hinged on the concerns and wishes of local soil conservation districts. Although PL-566 projects were not specifically intended to drain wetlands important for waterfowl and other wildlife, local landowners routinely drained their wetlands into the federally constructed channels. As with all USDA wetland policies, implementation of the wildlife memorandum and the successful conservation of wetlands depended on the attitudes of local farmers.[23]

By 1955, the USDA could boast that 103 million acres of land nationwide—an area larger than Ohio, Indiana, and Illinois combined—had been organized into state, county, and district drainage systems and that $900 million had been spent on ditches, outlets, levees, and pumps. In fact, despite mushrooming automobile use, more miles of public drainage ditch than highway threaded the country. During one four-year period in the early 1950s, the USDA spent eighty-three times as much money to convert 256,000 acres of waterfowl habitat into farms as the Fish and Wildlife Service spent from duck stamp funds to safeguard only 3,462 wetland acres in the same three states. The agencies within the USDA had contributed in large measure to the success of the nation's drainage enterprises and to the demise of the nation's wetlands.[24]

The Landmark Inventory

In the wake of wetlands destruction caused by ongoing agricultural drainage, flood-control improvements, explosive suburban growth, and a general dearth of understanding, the Fish and Wildlife Service initiated a landmark survey to document the distribution, quality, and extent of the nation's wetlands. Although the federal government had sponsored surveys that included wetlands in the past, the primary intention had been to identify potential farmland. The new Fish and Wildlife Inventory focused exclusively on wildlife values, especially on ducks and geese.

Financed with duck stamp moneys, the Office of River Basin Studies began collecting data for the inventory in the early 1950s. Their goal was to create an inventory as comprehensive as time and limited resources would allow. First, a committee of biologists established a scheme for classifying the various types of wetlands.[25] Then, using aerial photographs, USGS maps, USDA surveys, charts of the U.S. Coast and Geodetic Survey, and even county highway maps, they identified and classified the locations of significant and large wetlands in the forty-eight states. Finally, state fish and game departments made field observations to assess the relative importance of those remaining wetlands to waterfowl.

In 1956, the Fish and Wildlife Service published *Wetlands of the United States,* authored by Samuel P. Shaw and C. Gordon Fredine, to explain the results of the inventory. Judiciously comparing their data to past surveys, the authors estimated that 45 million acres of native wetlands had been lost to other uses. Acknowledging that the most prevalent contemporary sentiment would have all wet areas drained and filled for development, the report encouraged government agencies, especially the Corps of Engineers and the Agricultural Conservation Program Service, to consider instead the important values of remaining wetlands to wildlife. "Never before in the Nation's history," the authors declared, "has it been so necessary to plan for the setting aside of land and water areas to serve the future needs of fish and wildlife."[26] Only through planning and cooperation, the report recommended, could waterfowl populations be maintained to meet the country's growing recreation demands. Within the Fish and Wildlife Service and in the other agencies that frequently referred to it, the influential report became known as Circular 39. Beyond clearly articulating wetland values, Circular 39 laid out a specific taxonomy of twenty wetland types and documented the acreage of each type remaining. It also recorded the acreage of wetlands of high, moderate, low, and negligible value on a state-by-state basis. Out of nearly 75 million wetland acres surveyed, Circular 39 identified more than 22 million acres of high and moderate value to waterfowl.

Although it was completed with crude methods by modern standards, and later wildlife biologists would recognize the limits of its waterfowl focus, this first wetlands inventory established a baseline and mustered many states to keep closer track of their wetlands. Moreover, Circular 39 gave Fish and Wildlife Service personnel a readable public document—a new tool to push for protection of dwindling waterfowl habitat in the pothole region and nationwide.[27]

The Challenge to Farm Drainage

In August 1958, Congress responded to the well-documented loss of wetland waterfowl habitat by approving a Wetlands Easement Program funded by duck stamp money, to protect important privately owned waterfowl breeding areas.[28] In order to better balance farm and wildlife needs in the prairie states, the Fish and Wildlife Service also suggested changes in USDA regulations. Although SCS and ACPS administrators declined to adopt those specific recommendations, they did issue a new memo to state soil conservationists in Minnesota and the Dakotas outlining criteria for providing drainage assistance. Once again they affirmed that federal funds should "not be used to assist in draining lands for the purpose of developing new farms nor for the primary purpose of bringing new land into agricultural production."[29] Aside from concerns for waterfowl habitat, the additional drained lands, along with new pesticides and larger tractors, contributed to sizable crop surpluses, for which the government still provided support payments.[30]

Despite the clear intention of the official memorandum from agency heads, drainage continued. County Agricultural Stabilization and Conservation committees made up of local citizens interpreted guidelines to give local farmers the most benefits. Ironically, the decentralized structure of the federal agricultural agencies, which had worked so well to motivate and commit self-determined farmers to soil conservation practices during the depression, backfired when the agencies imposed guidelines and subsidy restrictions from the top down. The generation of farmers that grew up receiving farm subsidies in exchange for conservation practices, including drainage, came to believe that they were *entitled* to such benefits. Even limitations on technical assistance were regarded as an affront. Only in areas where individual USDA agents took a strong stand on the official guidelines was the destruction of waterfowl habitat kept in check. Furthermore, dry conditions in the late 1950s enabled farmers to establish crop histories in formerly wet areas and then qualify for drainage assistance. According to its 1960 annual report, the ACPS helped 2,886 Minnesota farms to permanently drain 141,908 acres with open ditches and 26,747 acres with tile drainage.[31]

As unrestrained drainage continued, one duck hunter and wildlife biologist addressed the conflict in more poetic terms. In his book *Of Men and Marshes,* published in 1957, Paul Errington, a professor of wildlife management in Iowa's Cooperative Wildlife Unit program, expressed the values of pothole marshes not just in abstractions about waterfowl populations and acreages, but in a personal manner. He recounted childhood memories of unfathomable duck flights over his family's South Dakota farm. He explained how the pothole landscape had enriched his life by providing opportunities to hunt and to observe the details of marsh life. He encouraged his fellow prairie residents to reconsider the value of their own experiences in the potholes as he had and to recognize the intrinsic values of the land. "I believe that marshes could add greatly to human enjoyment if more people really knew them," he wrote.[32] Errington's book described marshes through the seasons and offered advice about exploring natural history. The nationally sold book explained the contradictory policies of the federal agencies to people unfamiliar with the significance of the pothole region.

While literature helped to form public opinion, scientific information, especially the inventory, proved invaluable for influencing policy. Recognizing the authority of such data, the Fish and Wildlife Service continued to monitor how agricultural drainage destroyed pothole habitat. In their study of ninety-three counties in Minnesota, North Dakota, and South Dakota, researchers found that over forty thousand waterfowl habitat areas had been drained with USDA technical and financial assistance between 1954 and 1958. Despite the Department of Agriculture's claims of discouraging wetland drainage, the Fish and Wildlife Service proved conclusively that potholes were indeed still being drained. The agency's 1961 report recommended that the USDA cut all assistance for drainage in the prairie states immediately.[33]

With the urgent situation in the pothole region clearly illumined, Congress approved the Drainage Referral Act in 1962 at the urging of Representative Henry Reuss (D-WI). The law prohibited the Department of Agriculture from helping farmers in Minnesota, South Dakota, and North Dakota to drain marshes if the Department of the Interior determined that wildlife was at risk. Similar to Minnesota's early wetland acquisition law, the act also delayed drainage assistance until the Bureau of Sport Fisheries and Wildlife (BSFW) or state fish and game departments had an opportunity to protect the wetland through either acquisition or easement. (The name of the Fish and Wildlife Service was changed to the BSFW from 1956 to 1974; then it was changed back.) The federal agencies worked coopera-tively to implement the new law. In the 1963 Agricultural Appropriations Act, Congress extended the new policy beyond the prairies and prohibited the use of federal funds for cost-sharing and technical assistance to drain in-land freshwater marshes anywhere.[34]

Beyond protecting wetlands from impending drainage, Congress also authorized the Wetlands Loan Act in 1961 to fund the acquisition of fast-disappearing habitat nationwide. Ding Darling's Biological Survey had set the goal of reserving 12.5 million acres of waterfowl habitat through federal and state administration. But twenty years later, in 1956, the goal had been only 40 percent realized.[35] Because the revenues generated from duck stamp sales had been improperly diverted and didn't keep pace with rising land values and ongoing conversions, the Wetlands Loan Act enabled the BSFW to draw upon the anticipated revenues of future duck stamp sales to expedite the purchase of 2.5 million acres deemed critical for waterfowl. Congress authorized an appropriation of up to $105 million to be spent over a seven-year period to purchase necessary habitat.[36]

Although the new federal laws and the associated Small Wetland Acqui-sition Program had only limited funding, they nonetheless represented a healthy stride toward making wetland conservation a national priority. While ducks had long depended on wetlands for their survival, now the ta-bles were turned. Wetlands depended on ducks—or at least American ap-preciation of ducks—for their very existence.

Off the Farm

The post-war prosperity that propelled farms to expand into wetlands also spurred other development in wetlands. Along the Atlantic seaboard, cities grew quickly, raising land values and making formerly worthless wetlands in the shadows of their skyscrapers attractive to businesses and industries. Cities wanting to build airports found that the only nearby large open spaces were wetlands. Almost all metropolitan airports, including those of Philadelphia, Washington, D.C., Boston, New York, Portland, Seattle, Salt Lake City, and Los Angeles were built in wetlands during this period with federal funding.[37]

Wetlands that remained within the range of commuters also fell under siege. Eleven million new homes, mostly of the rambler or split-level design, were constructed in the suburbs between 1947 and 1957.[38] Along with the houses came lawns and buzzing power mowers, swing sets and baby-boom children, garages, cars, and curving roads. Supermarkets and shopping centers with large parking lots formed the functional centers of the new suburbia. Wetlands often provided the space needed for the new developments. The urban sprawl of New York City, for example, spread onto the eastern third of Long Island, an area highly endowed with tidal wetlands. A 1959 survey of Long Island wetlands by the New York State Conservation Department and the Bureau of Sport Fisheries and Wildlife (a spin-off of the first wetland inventory) revealed that 12.5 percent of valuable wetland habitat areas had been destroyed between 1954 and 1959. The trend was projected to continue with no end in sight.[39]

Inexpensive wetlands offered good economic value for those seeking real estate near high-priced cities and coastal areas. For this reason, a 1958 article in *Home and House* magazine encouraged home builders to "take a look at marshland" and showcased "outstanding subdivisions" replacing marshland in Connecticut, New York, New Jersey, Ohio, and Florida.[40] Hit hard by residential growth, wetlands were also filled to create beaches and dredged to make marinas to meet the recreation demands of the growing population.[41] Construction disturbed wetlands not only by destroying habitat but also by introducing large amounts of suspended solids into the aquatic environment, which increased turbidity and siltation to the detriment of aquatic life. Construction also altered natural drainage patterns, permanently changing the hydrological regimes that wetlands depended on.[42]

In this era of booming technology, two innovations in particular made wetlands more inhabitable for people: pesticides and air-conditioning. Born as a by-product of World War II, pesticides replaced marsh ditching as the primary method of insect control. Public health officials and resort communities seized the new "miracle" chemicals and immediately targeted nuisance insects that bred in wetlands. While ditching had already reduced food for fish and birds by changing the vegetation and invertebrate communities of 90 percent of Atlantic tidewater marshes from Maine to Virginia, pesticides had far more damaging effects.[43] In 1955, for example, 2,000 acres of marsh on Florida's east coast were treated with the pesticide dieldrin to destroy sandfly larvae, but the poison also killed nearly 1.8 million fish. Crustaceans that ate the dead fish then died as well. The pesticides did not readily break down; instead, they accumulated in soil, water, and animal tissues and were passed up the food chain to consumers on top. As coastal communities nationwide applied large amounts of pesticides in wet-lands to combat annoying insects, these rich aquatic ecosystems became bi-ologically barren. Although fish kills were not subtle, few people under-stood the full consequences of pesticide use at the time.[44] Troubling mosquitoes were gone, and that was what mattered. Pesticides made it more pleasant for people to reside in otherwise insect-ridden wetland re-gions—especially the South.

Inexpensive household air-conditioning also made living in the South at-tractive. In 1951 cheap, efficient window units hit the market, enabling newcomers to control their indoor climate and making sultry southern sum-mers tolerable for hundreds of thousands of people. By 1955, one out of ten homes in the South had an air conditioner.[45] The availability of industrial air-conditioning made it possible for manufacturers to open up plants in the region as well. The pleasant winter climate coupled with job opportunities compelled many vacationers to stay for good. As more people migrated south, that predominantly wetland region became more industrialized and urban. By 1958, the South's industrial and manufacturing workforce ex-ceeded its agricultural workforce for the first time.[46] To accommodate the growing population and its housing, employment, and recreation needs, many wetlands were drained and filled.

New demands for energy also affected wetlands. Power plants con-structed in tidal zones nationwide discharged warm waters that changed the ecology of nearby coastal wetlands. Dams built for hydroelectric power changed the flood regime of rivers, thus altering the hydrology of riparian wetlands.[47]

One of the greatest demands for energy came with the automobile, the centerpiece of new prosperity in America. Cars enabled commuters to work in the city and yet live on little patches of suburban countryside. In the decade from 1947 to 1957, twenty-five million new cars came onto Amer-ican roads, and each one of them guzzled gasoline.[48] Along the gulf coast, oil exploration intensified as demand for petroleum grew. Since the first oil well drilled into coastal Louisiana in 1901, thousands of miles of canals had been punched into the thick golden swath of gulf marshlands, damaging much of the rich habitat. Commercial fishermen contended that the dyna-mite blasts used to open areas for exploratory drilling killed oysters and shrimp.[49] The canals also changed the ecology of marshes by allowing salt-water to penetrate and intrude into freshwater areas. Furthermore, leaked

or spilled oil polluted waters that shrimp, fish, birds, and other animals depended on. These were no small concerns, given that the gulf coast supported one of the largest commercial fisheries in the nation.[50]

The explosion of automobile use also sparked a boom in new road and
highway construction, which transformed still more wetlands nationwide.
Between 1947 and 1957 alone, the nation invested $28 billion in new
roads and highways.[51] Congress furthered the cause in 1956 when it authorized the construction of forty-one thousand miles of road with the
Interstate Highway Act. To finance this grand construction project,
Congress created a fund generated from federal gasoline taxes. With the
nondivertible source of money securely in place, road building and maintenance could continue unencumbered, indefinitely. Little consideration
was given to the environmental impacts of the new roads.[52] Because remaining wetlands afforded undeveloped, flat, open space, construction
crews built roads through many wetlands. Interstate 10 most notably
crossed the Atchafalaya River swamp in Louisiana with the help of a sev-
enteen-mile bridge. Constructing roads through wetlands usually altered
their hydrology and opened up formerly inaccessible areas to new development. Not only newly roaded wetlands were affected. Because many
paving materials were quarried from coastal areas and rivers, wetlands in
those places were altered as well.[53]

Ambivalent Attitudes

As Americans spread out and enjoyed their new prosperity, they profoundly
changed the landscape around them, and wetlands lay on the front line of
change. The belief that nature must yield in the face of American progress
prevailed. Reflecting that belief, the political winds of the fifties ushered the
boom along with little interest or patience for conservation.

Into the post–New Deal vacuum of conservation leadership, President
Eisenhower had appointed former Oregon governor Douglas McKay as
secretary of the interior. The wealthy auto dealer, known as "Chevrolet"
McKay by his critics, had made substantial campaign contributions but
had little experience in natural resource issues. Although waterfowl and
wetlands had long benefited from the expertise and aid of the Department
of the Interior's Fish and Wildlife Service, McKay changed that.

Rather than follow the established custom of promoting personnel from
within the agency, McKay fired or forced the resignation of agency leaders
and career biologists, then appointed unqualified staff or left positions un-

filled. When Congress trimmed appropriations for the Fish and Wildlife Service in 1954, McKay diverted $36 million of duck stamp moneys for general operating expenses—in direct contradiction to the law. Morale within the agency sank. The Fish and Wildlife Service had long taken pride in its apolitical, scientific orientation, but the new "politicized" leadership undermined its ability to function.

McKay even took a swipe at the integrity of the wildlife refuges. Since the refuge system began fifty years earlier, oil and gas interests had unsuccessfully pressured the Department of the Interior for access. In just three years, McKay issued sixty-four drilling permits, including many in refuges along the fragile gulf coast, the only marsh habitat expressly protected for wildlife in the region. In this giveaway atmosphere, the military also requested use of refuge lands for bombing ranges and bases. Even Aransas Refuge, the sole wintering grounds of the nearly extinct whooping crane, was threatened. Bitter public and congressional opposition swelled and finally blocked the military encroachment. McKay resigned soon after.[54] Although optimism for booming growth crowded out most concern for conservation, when presented with a clear choice, Americans still wanted to protect their birds.

In his pivotal book *The Affluent Society* (1958), preeminent economist John Kenneth Galbraith pieced together some of the disparate themes of the post-war era. While by all counts the nation was advancing fabulously with an increased gross national product, increased personal income, and increased retail sales, Galbraith questioned whether these measures truly reflected progress. At the same time Americans enjoyed their new cars and their plastic gadgets, air and water—the fundaments of life—became dirtier. Such questioning struck a chord with many people and would become a hallmark of the decade that followed.[55]

While the fifties might best be remembered for crew cuts, Formica, ranch houses, and early rock and roll, another auspicious event marked the decade. The new word, *wetland*, slipped into American vocabulary. The appearance of a new word usually signals to the historian that something is afoot. In this case, the word *wetland* marked a significant valuation of a varied collection of landscapes—all crucial to fish, wildlife, and waterfowl and all threatened by the din of an effervescent and overflowing culture. In place of words that had carried traditional meanings and oftentimes misconceptions—*swamp* and *bog,* for example—*wetlands* conveyed positive symbolic value born from trustworthy modern scientific expertise. *Wetland* most notably entered the language in the preparation of the first wetlands inventory and its accompanying report, Circular 39. By identifying their increasing scarcity and clearly articulating their importance, Circular 39 formally conferred value upon wetlands. But, most significant, the report affixed a new label to the landscapes. Following the lead of the Fish and Wildlife Service, other agencies and waterfowl advocates began to refer to "wetlands." The linguistic step furthered a long process of institutional acceptance and valuation within society in general, though it also underscored the long-held understanding of these ecosystems as land. Within a decade, "wetlands" made the leap into *Webster's Dictionary* and so into the mainstream realm of the definable.[56] With a word, an inventory, a taxonomy, and legislation to prevent federal drainage assistance, wetlands had taken a big step toward becoming a valued part of our landscape.

Although awareness of wetland values began to grow, the trend of permanent destruction continued. In the mid 1950s, an estimated 108.1 million acres of wetlands remained in the lower forty-eight states out of an original 221 million acres.[57] Although biologists and hunters began to better understand the problems associated with wetlands loss, their knowledge did not translate into popular appreciation of wetland values or into protection for wetlands just yet. Acre by acre, wetlands were still converted to housing tracts, marinas, and farms. Although the Fish and Wildlife inventory of 1954 had given a glimpse of the wetland landscape and losses from a national perspective, it offered no broad vision for how to proceed. Americans still blindly hoped and expected that we could have all of our growth and our wetlands too. There was a loosely held notion that publicly owned wetlands could be managed to protect wildlife so that adjacent private lands could be fully exploited for maximum private gain. No one even considered the possibility of regulating new development in privately owned wetlands. But as the affluent population continued to grow and encroach upon more and more wetlands, it would become evident that public acquisition could never keep pace as the sole means to protect necessary wetland habitat values.

The consequences of widespread wetland destruction soon appeared in marshes and swamps skirting towns and cities everywhere, prompting dismayed citizens to learn more and to search for ways to protect wetlands in their communities. With a growing understanding of wetland values, there was hope for the 108 million acres that remained.

ELEVEN

Citizens and Lawmakers Enlist in the Wetlands Cause

A town is saved, not more by the righteous men in it than by the woods and swamps that surround it. . .
—Henry David Thoreau, quoted by
Secretary of the Interior Stewart Udall in speech to Great
Swamp of New Jersey Committee, November 27, 1962 [1]

Walking across her marsh-edged property in Duxbury, Massachusetts, in the summer of 1957, Olga Owen Huckins came upon a horrid sight: bodies of dozens of poisoned birds. "Their bills were gaping open," she wrote to her friend Rachel Carson, "and their splayed claws were drawn up to their breasts in agony."[2] Huckins linked the macabre scene to the town's aerial spraying of nearby wetlands with DDT to eradicate mosquitoes. Trained as a biologist, Carson tried to learn more about the pesticide, only to realize that no critical research on its effects existed—even though the chemicals were sprayed indiscriminately. "The more I learned about the use of pesticides," she later recalled, "the more appalled I became. . . . I discovered that everything which meant the most to me as a naturalist was being threatened."[3] Shocked and outraged, Carson turned her expertise to the monumental problem. In 1962, her findings were published in *Silent Spring*. The frightening book chronicled the repercussions of pesticides in the environment and on public health. Raising the possibility that business and government did not adequately protect citizens from dangerous poisons, *Silent Spring* inspired citizens nationwide to demand environmental quality. Although the chemical corporations did their best to discredit Carson, her work had touched a sensitive nerve, and the irrefutable evidence of dead birds and fish continued to mount in communities everywhere DDT was used. While Carson's book certainly remains the best-known response of outrage, there were many other noble citizen reactions to the ruin of the natural world by unbridled development and industry.

Throughout the 1960s, headlines carried more and more disheartening news of toxic rivers, oil-coated bays, and fish killed by pesticides. Since the post-war boom, wetlands had been subjected to tremendous pressures by urban and industrial growth, by pollution, by expanding agriculture, and by large federal water projects constructed for flood control, water storage, drainage, and navigation. While post-war prosperity unleashed many ills onto the land, it also enabled a generation to become better educated and more involved in civic affairs. When threats of dirty water and unsightly development edged into suburbs, citizens responded. As these isolated threats multiplied, grassroots environmental activism spread across the map and became an all-out movement of people pushing their governments to accept new responsibilities to safeguard citizens against rampant urbanization, industry, and pollution. Because wetlands remained the only apparent vestige of the natural world in many places, they became a significant cause for local activism. In many cases, aesthetically oriented citizens led the charge because they preferred their town's peaceful marshes to sprawling shopping plazas. In other cases, scientists took the lead discovering and documenting important ecological and economic values of wetlands. The new scientific information moved still more citizens to action. Whatever the root, an awareness of wetland values began to penetrate the consciousness of the nation. Like seeds in a fertile field after spring rain, concern for wetlands sprouted everywhere, and citizens working to protect their local wetlands became a vital part of the new environmental movement.

Save the Bay

Late in 1960, an illustration printed in *The Oakland Tribune* caught Catherine Kerr's eye. A schematic map showed that San Francisco Bay would be only a narrow channel in the year 2020. According to the Army Corps of Engineers, all shallow areas would be filled if development continued at its astounding rate—swallowing over 2,000 acres of marsh and bay per year. While most readers simply accepted the map as the inevitable consequence of a promising future, Kerr recognized a threat to the natural marshes she could see from her home in the East Bay hills. Little by little, the wetlands would be paved under a conventional landscape of condominiums, parking lots, and shopping centers. That which was naturally unique about the bay area would be silently squandered in the name of progress and profit.

BAY or RIVER ?

SAN FRANCISCO BAY IN THE YEAR 2020 (1960).
When Catherine Kerr saw this drawing in her local newspaper, she realized that the natural marshes surrounding San Francisco Bay would be filled and paved over with development. In 1963, Kerr founded the Save San Francisco Bay Association, which then pushed for a state planning and permitting program to safeguard the natural values of this important wetland ecosystem. (Courtesy *The Oakland Tribune*)

Married to the president of the University of California, Catherine was well connected to the academic community. She discussed the troubling article with friends Sylvia McLaughlin and Esther Gulick, also faculty wives. Looking out the window at the magnificent view of the bay, splendidly skirted by golden marshes, they decided that they had to do something.

The women began by learning all they could about the bay: Who owned the waterfront property? What had developers planned? Gulick then enlisted the help of a retired Harvard economist to evaluate some of the most ambitious urbanization proposals. Kerr convinced the university to fund a study, which confirmed without a doubt that in the absence of regional planning, the bay was doomed. It had already shrunk from 780 to 550 square miles through diking and filling for housing, office buildings, marinas, and runways. Kerr, McLaughlin, and Gulick talked about the problem with everyone they knew, and concerned friends and colleagues offered information, mailing lists, and money. The women founded the Save the San Francisco Bay Association, and by the summer of 1965, membership had reached nearly nine thousand.[4]

The group's initial efforts to influence planning on a local level were thwarted by the Association of Bay Area Governments. Cities and counties owned half the bay's shallow waters and wetlands, and they intended to earn revenues by filling and developing. For them, destruction of the bay was a real estate venture. "The city of Berkeley was planning to fill more than 2,000 acres," Sylvia McLaughlin later recalled. "It was the dream of the city manager. . . . I remember the headline in the *Berkeley Gazette,* 'Double the Size of Berkeley.'" Another plan, reminiscent of earlier centuries, would cut the top off of San Bruno Mountain to create new land offshore. According to Kerr, "They didn't want to have anything to do with regulating their fill, because it was all potential development."[5]

Blocked on the local level, the women took their case to the state legislature, where they found an advocate in Assemblyman Nicholas Petris. In both 1963 and 1964, Petris introduced legislation to halt the filling of the bay while a special committee could study the problem. Both times the bill failed owing to heavy lobbying by cities and development interests. A breakthrough came when San Francisco's powerful state senator Eugene McAteer put his clout behind the bay cause. By the end of 1964, the legislature passed a bill to create the San Francisco Bay Conservation Study Commission.

Given four months and a budget of $75,000, the eight-person commission chaired by McAteer began work on a preliminary plan for the bay.

At twelve public hearings, commission members, including Petris, heard comments from developers, park planners, biologists, water-quality experts, engineers, airport officials, and other interested citizens.

The lively hearings attracted the attention of the press and the public. Reporter Harold Gilliam wrote articles about the bay in the *San Francisco Chronicle*. Popular disc jockey Don Sherwood told thousands of listeners about the bay issue and urged them to write to their legislators. The Save the San Francisco Bay Association also sponsored write-in campaigns that deluged the state legislature with mail condemning the rampant filling. Many people sent sacks of sand with notes that lyrically admonished: "You'll wonder where the water went—if you fill the bay with sediment."[6]

The study commission finally recommended that the legislature create a new Bay Conservation and Development Commission (BCDC) to prepare a long-term plan for the bay and its shoreline over the course of four years. In the meantime, the McAteer commission would hold authority to grant or deny permits for all bay filling. McAteer sponsored the bill in the Senate, and Petris sponsored it in the House. With strong citizen support pitted against big-moneyed development interests, controversy raged, but the McAteer–Petris Act finally passed in 1965.

The BCDC began work on a long-term plan right away and ultimately recommended regulation of filling on a permanent basis. After a replay of rancorous debate in the legislature, bay supporters prevailed, and with minor modifications, the commission was directed to carry out its plan. Within the first year, the rate of fill dropped to 75 acres; the next year it dropped to 25.[7] In the case of the San Francisco Bay, local citizens pushed state government to protect wetlands through both a regional planning and a regulatory process. But even with the BCDC in place, as Catherine Kerr astutely realized, "The bay is never really saved . . . it's always in the process of being saved."[8] The Save the San Francisco Bay Association remained organized and kept watch over the new commission.[9]

Citizens, Science, and Regulatory Approaches

It is no surprise that the grassroots movement to protect wetlands emerged in coastal towns and cities such as Berkeley. With the bulk of the U.S. population living within fifty miles of the shoreline, coastal wetlands were hard hit by development pressure. Construction activities accounted for 90 percent of wetland losses attributed to human activities, with the greatest decreases in California, Florida, Louisiana, New Jersey, and Texas.[10] Furthermore, as scientific evidence began to link marshes with the rich

offshore harvests of fish and shellfish, coastal towns dependent on commercial fishing became concerned about wetland destruction. With vast
tidal marshes along the populous Atlantic Coast, it was there that many pioneering efforts to preserve wetlands began.

The first voices of public outcry against destroying coastal marshes
came from citizens concerned about the changing character of their communities. They liked the open space and aesthetic values provided by undeveloped marshlands. Graceful wetland grasses were traditional elements
of their communities' landscapes that created identity. The drive-ins,
marinas, and industrial complexes that took the place of wetlands threatened to turn their towns into homogenous commercial strips.

Citizens of Westport, Connecticut, faced the tidal wave of wetland development head-on when they learned in 1956 that the salt marsh at nearby
Sherwood Island State Park would be used to stockpile 3.5 million cubic
yards of gravel hydraulically dredged from the bottom of Long Island
Sound. Most of the gravel would be used to construct the new Connecticut
Thruway, and the salt marsh was slated to become a huge parking lot for
beach visitors. Local citizens' groups—including sportsmen's clubs, garden
clubs, and Audubon chapters—formed a statewide conservation group,
Connecticut Conservationists, to organize a protest.

With no precedent for preserving marshes on the law books, the group
tried a backdoor strategy. They challenged the legality of state officials
selling materials from the bottom of Long Island Sound without legislative
or public oversight. Attorneys for the highway contractor, the dredging
company, and the state, however, managed to obtain an easy dismissal because the conservationists could not show that they would suffer any unique
financial damage that was "not shared by all the citizens of the state."
Gaining standing in court would remain an obstacle for activists until environmental laws specifically provided for public involvement.

With the case lost, the Sherwood Island marsh was filled by dredge spoils
soon after. Only twenty square miles of tidal marsh were left along the
Connecticut shore, so the group pushed for legislation to regulate future
dredging. As a result of their efforts, the legislature passed Public Act 554,
which gave the state Water Resources Commission the authority to grant or
deny dredging applications in order to safeguard wildlife habitat, improve
navigation, and prevent shoreline erosion. The act also provided for public
hearings on all applications to give people a stake in the future of their
towns' wetlands.

In the fall of 1957, the law met its first test. A New York sand and gravel company applied for a permit to begin an enormous dredging operation that included plans to turn an 80-acre salt marsh tract into a large marina. Because the project would have firmly established gravel mining off the Connecticut coast, and furthermore destroyed the last significant marsh on the western end of the shoreline, the Water Resources Commission denied the permit in a resounding victory for the Connecticut Conservationists. Citizen activists had successfully pushed the state to ratify a law that could protect threatened coastal marshes.[11] Here and in a number of north-eastern states, interest in protecting coastal marshes sprang first from residents' aesthetic attachments to the traditional shoreline landscapes and from concern for maintaining the special character of small communities in the face of rapid change.

In addition to the aesthetic and open-space values of wetlands, scientists began to offer ecological reasons for keeping coastal marshes in their natural state. While government biologists had studied and established the habitat value of wetlands for waterfowl, some university scientists began to study wetlands with a different tack. After World War II, wetland science reached a new plateau through an unexpected venue. The Atomic Energy Commission provided funding for ecologists to study the effects of radiation on the environment, and this infusion of dollars pushed the science of ecology in new directions—in particular, to refine the concept of "ecosystems."[12] It was University of Georgia ecologist Eugene Odum who engineered a link between ecosystem studies and coastal wetlands.

The coast of Georgia remained fringed with a nearly ten-mile-wide strip of tidal marsh nestled behind a series of barrier islands, including Sapelo Island. Hearing about exotic birds there, Odum and his colleagues gained permission to visit. The island's wealthy owner, Richard Reynolds, received the scientists in his southern mansion and explained that he wanted to keep Sapelo preserved. When he asked if the university might have a use for the island, the biologists suggested that the natural salt marshes and estuaries made Sapelo an ideal spot for research. Reynolds set up a special foundation to support a university marine institute, which then began to recruit top-notch ecological researchers.[13]

With Reynolds's generosity, Sapelo Island became the birthplace of modern salt marsh ecosystem research.[14] According to Odum, initial studies were broadly based. "We just said, 'Here's the marsh—study it!'" Scientists soon realized that the visually monotonous marsh landscape was ecologically complex. In 1958, they hosted the first Sapelo Island conference to present information and new questions generated by the first round of inquiry. Early studies dealt with microbial productivity and hydrology. By studying nutrient cycling, ecologists discovered that salt marshes could combine solar and tidal power and thus produce more organic material than any other type of ecosystem in the country. A typical wheat field produced 1.5 tons of dry organic matter per acre annually, but a Georgia tidal marsh produced 10 tons of the same![15] Although the high productivity was not evident in fruits or grains that could be harvested, Sapelo Island ecologists identified the concept of outwelling. Organic detritus, created when marsh plants died and fragmented, was transported outward by the tides and provided nutrients for juvenile fish and shellfish in nearby marine waters. The ecologists also reaffirmed that marshes served as nursery grounds for many fish. Through their productivity and habitat value, marshes translated directly into the rich commercial harvest of seafood along Georgia's coast.[16]

As the timely work of the Sapelo Island scientists became widely known, conservationists up and down the Atlantic Coast began to understand the ecological necessity of the remaining salt marshes. Soon activists started to use ecological evidence to bolster their arguments for protecting these wetlands. Eugene Odum, in particular, did not shy away from the role that science could have in influencing public policy. His numerous articles in both scientific journals and magazines popularized the research at Sapelo and clearly revealed that the full value of wetlands had not been appreciated.[17] Economic markets recognized conventional property values but failed to recognize the common benefits provided by wetlands. These nonmarket values included not only sustaining waterfowl and fish but also maintaining water quality and buffering the coast from storms. As a single parcel of property, a salt marsh might appear to have limited economic worth; but understood as a vital part of larger ecosystems such as ocean fisheries and flyways, that same marsh had great value. Odum pioneered methods of assigning price tags to the nonmarket values of wetlands and thereby helped to convince policy makers of the economic importance of wetlands.[18]

Ecologists at Sapelo and elsewhere showed that one of the most economically compelling reasons to protect wetlands lay in the connection between tidal marshes and ocean fisheries. One study of the coast near Palm Beach found a direct correlation between drastic declines in fish populations and the widespread bulkheading of mangrove wetlands during the 1950s. Within ten years of extensive coastal wetland alteration, for example, the annual commercial landing of spotted sea trout dropped from

336,936 fish to only 857. Similar correlations were noted with shrimp in Boca Ciega Bay on Florida's west coast.[19] These trends had direct consequences for the livelihoods of the nation's ninety thousand commercial fishermen and for anyone who ate seafood.[20] The increasing evidence linking wetlands and fisheries was not lost on academe. At a fisheries convention in 1957, Assistant Secretary for Fish and Wildlife Ross Leffler had warned, "The diking, draining, dredging, filling, spraying and polluting of our river basin and estuarine waters is readying the ink for the death warrants of the young of the menhaden, shad, salmon, rockfish, striped bass, shrimp, crabs, oysters, croakers, flounders, and so many other important fish and shellfish."[21] In the 1960s, several studies confirmed that approximately two-thirds of the major commercial fisheries depended on estuaries and tidal marshes for nursery and spawning grounds.[22]

Savvy state governments also noted the new ecological findings and began their own research. A two-year study of marine resources conducted by the state of Massachusetts revealed that most commercial and recreational fisheries in the state depended on coastal marshes for nursery grounds and for nutrients. Given the importance of the state's fishing industry, the legislature in 1963 gave its Department of Natural Resources (DNR) the authority to grant and deny permissions for any alteration of private or state-owned wetlands that might threaten marine resources.

The authority of the new law was soon challenged when the owners of a 49-acre tidal marsh near the town of Wareham announced plans to build a marina and yacht club. Materials dredged to construct the ship canal and yacht basin would be used to fill the marsh and create land for the clubhouse. As required by law, the owners sought approval from the state DNR. After careful study, the department approved the dredging aspect of the project but prohibited placing fill on the salt marsh. The DNR justified its decision on the basis of "protecting marine fisheries and maintaining the ecological components of this estuarine complex." Because filling the marsh was an essential aspect of the yacht club plan, the owners appealed the decision in court in what became known as the Squaw's Hole case. On March 9, 1964, Superior Court Judge Horace Cahill upheld the DNR's finding and explained that private citizens acquire property "with the tacit understanding that it shall not be used to the detriment of the public."[23] With this significant decision, the common, public value of wetlands, even privately owned wetlands, was formally acknowledged.

In 1965, the state broadened its wetland policy by tacking on an amendment that included public health, wildlife, and flood control as criteria for preserving wetlands. The state legislature also established protective orders (essentially state-level zoning) to permanently protect 45,000 acres of the most highly valued coastal wetlands before building projects were initiated. Finally, an additional amendment enabled property owners who felt deprived by restrictions placed on their lands to go to court for compensation. Under its power of eminent domain, the state could then buy the valuable marshland. Because few landowners objected to the goal of conserving wetlands, there were few court cases. By the end of 1970, Massachusetts had preserved 46 percent of its top-priority wetlands with this law.[24]

Interest in protecting marshes grew as information about wetland ecosystems and their newly understood values became more widespread. Botanist William Niering wrote the first popular book about marshes, *The Life of the Marsh,* published in 1966. With striking photographs and diagrams, the volume delivered a gentle conservation message and showed how marshes functioned. Sapelo Island ecologist John Teal and his wife, Mildred, also wrote a popular marsh paperback, *Life and Death of the Salt Marsh,* first published in 1969. (By 1991, this durable title had been reprinted seventeen times, spreading understanding of wetlands to tens of thousands of readers.) Beyond explaining the fascinating adaptations of salt marsh plants and animals, the Teals' book described the effects of human pollution and development on the fragile landscapes and offered convincing arguments for salt marsh conservation. In addition to these books, articles about wetlands appeared in national magazines such as *Life* and in increasingly popular nature magazines. Television programs such as the *Wild Kingdom* also stirred people's interest and awareness of the environment in general.[25]

The media became an important vehicle for informing people about specific issues and shaping public opinion. For example, in Georgia when Kerr-McGee proposed to lease state-owned estuaries to mine phosphate, Governor Lester Maddox appointed a blue-ribbon committee, including prominent University of Georgia ecologists to evaluate possible consequences of the mining. The committee decidedly recommended against the project, stressing the values of the salt marshes, the threat to the state's fisheries, and the marginal economic benefits accorded by the phosphate mine (ore would be shipped to Oklahoma for processing). Maddox readily concurred. To safeguard against future threats, the committee recommended long-term protection for all of the state's coastal marshes and then pushed for ratification of the Georgia Marshlands Protection Act. Passed in 1970, the act gave the state Department of Natural Resources the authority to issue or deny permits for altering coastal marsh areas. During the campaign to enact this law, salt marshes regularly made the Sunday magazine of the newspapers in Atlanta. The articles, based on cutting-edge research at the University of Georgia's Sapelo Island marine research institute, helped to develop public opinion in favor of marsh protection. Consequently, support for coastal wetlands protection was strong among both lawmakers and citizens.[26]

While data linking wetlands to the productivity of fisheries had prompted several state-level conservation efforts, scientists began to discover other wetland functions. Research revealed that water flowing out of the modest Tinicum Marsh near Philadelphia, for example, was much cleaner than the polluted water flowing in.[27] Although the marshes had once stretched to 5,700 acres along the north bank of the Delaware River, the rapid growth of the city along with its airport and industries had swallowed all but 200 acres. In 1969, Philadelphia owned and administered 145 acres near the eastern end of the marsh as a wildlife preserve, but the rest of the wetland was endangered by a proposed landfill and the route of Interstate 95. Citizens working to protect the marsh used the water-quality research to strengthen their case for securing much of the remaining marsh as a national wildlife refuge. Tinicum became a refuge in 1972.[28]

In many urban areas, garbage and pollution posed dire threats to wetlands. Because of their low land values and topography, wetlands had routinely been used by cities as dumps. Nowhere was this practice more pronounced than in remnant marshes around the densely populated New York–Newark metropolitan area. Only four miles from Manhattan, the Hackensack Meadows suffocated under the heavy burden of intense urbanization. More than one-third of New Jersey's refuse was dumped into the Meadowlands, where it became a source of toxins when rainwater leached through the toppling mounds. In addition to garbage, nearby towns flushed poorly treated sewage from thirteen plants into the river that fed the marshes. Coke plants, oil and chemical companies, and printing-ink manufacturers dumped heavy metals and organic pollutants as well. In the degraded marshes, a monoculture of giant reed crowded out more varied native vegetation. Where the expansive 31,000-acre salt marshes at the mouth of the Hackensack River had inspired the paintings of Martin J. Heade only one hundred years before, toxic garbage heaps stood instead. The story of Hackensack Meadows exemplified the plight of many urban estuarine marshes.

Aside from clear public health concerns, the Meadows posed economic problems as well. Located just across the river from the nation's business center, the remaining wetlands had the potential to be high-value real estate if they were not so choked with pollutants. As one report stated, "No one would pay $100,000 for a Hackensack condominium if the stink from the river meant closed windows four seasons out of the year."[29] In addition, haphazard zoning and difficult development conditions accorded by the soggy terrain had conspired to make the area an industrial wasteland. Few new businesses would consider locating in the area without the prospect of an improved environment.

To turn the situation around, the New Jersey state legislature tried a new approach in 1968; it created a regional authority, the Hackensack Meadowlands Development Commission (HMDC). Directed to deal with the garbage, the growth, the economy, and the environment, the HMDC was given the authority to grant or deny permits for construction and pollution and to allocate property taxes in the fourteen communities within the thirty-two-square-mile district. The premise of the HMDC project was that a healthy environment would be essential to economic growth. This made intensive cleanup and management worthwhile investments. In its entrepreneurial endeavor, the HMDC planned to capitalize on the unique natural feature of the Meadowlands—its remaining marshes—by integrating restored wetlands into plans for development. The master plan included zoning prescriptions that preserved one-third of the district as open space—much of it marsh—and other portions as "highly developed" and "residential areas." The plan acknowledged that wetlands could offer the community aesthetic and recreational values as well as wildlife habitat. Furthermore, the district plan included high-tech solutions to the ever-growing garbage problem. Trash was compacted into refrigerator-sized blocks and used as fill in wetlands slated for development. A park, tennis courts, riding stables, a racetrack, and a new stadium for the New York Giants were all planned for the new trash-bale landscape. In addition to zoning, by 1971, HMDC had placed limits on the amounts and types of pollutants that could be discharged. Within the decade, fish and birds began to return to the recovering Hackensack estuary wetlands.[30]

By the early 1970s, through both citizen activism and state concern, many Atlantic states had adopted specific coastal wetlands protection laws. Rhode Island (1967), Connecticut (1969), New Hampshire (1967), Maine (1967), Georgia (1970), New Jersey (1970), Maryland (1970), and Delaware (1970) all enacted coastal wetland protective legislation in response to development pressures on their shorelines. The strongest laws gave states the authority to grant and deny permits. Weaker laws simply put moratoria on the sale of state-owned marshlands. In states where specific legislation did not come until later, natural resources departments purchased wetlands to preserve as wildlife sanctuaries and for open space. New York, for example, provided loans to local Long Island governments for purchase and conservation of wetlands, and New Jersey used 1964 Green Acres bond money to purchase large areas of salt marsh. Virginia, which instituted its Wetlands Act in 1972, placed primary responsibility for coastal wetland protection with local governments. Although they protected tidal marshes with varying degrees of success, the collection of state laws and policies that evolved by the early 1970s made it clear that conserving coastal wetlands had indeed become a priority.[31]

Airport Wars

Concern spread inland from the coasts as development encroached upon freshwater wetlands as well. New jet aircraft technology required hundreds of larger airports, many slated for wetlands. The proposed jetports generated unrelenting controversy. Citizens staved off plans for new airports in the Great Swamp of New Jersey near Morristown and in the Great Dismal Swamp near Norfolk, Virginia. There, the Nature Conservancy negotiated the donation of 50,000 acres from the Union Camp Corporation in 1973. Valued at $12.6 million, the land ranked as one of the largest single corporate gifts in history. In both areas, conservation groups acquired the sensitive wetlands and then donated them to the Department of the Interior as national wildlife refuges.[32] Many more wetlands, however, became runways, hangars, and air terminals. The most significant airport war of all took place further south.

Spilling out along the coast and west into the Everglades, Miami had grown from a resort town to a full-fledged city. In line with this growth, in 1967 Dade and Collier counties began planning a new airport, big enough to handle the increasing jumbo-jet traffic. The search committee decided on a site forty-five miles west of Miami, straddling the county line. No nearer site was feasible, they claimed, because so much land in the region was already under the jurisdiction of Everglades National Park and the South Florida Flood Control District (FCD). Although officials of the National Park Service, the FCD, and the state Game and Freshwater Fish Commission raised no serious objections when the Dade County Port Authority released its plans, Florida's citizen conservationists immediately recognized unacceptable problems at this site only six miles from Everglades National

Park. Beyond the obvious threat of noise and air pollution to wildlife and visitors, the commercial and industrial area that would grow up around the airport threatened to ruin one of the park's primary water sources by disrupting and contaminating its flow. Nevertheless, the Port Authority proceeded quickly, acquiring the sensitive land and breaking ground for its concrete runway.

Robert Padrick, chairman of the FCD's governing board, voiced one of the first protests. Upon learning that Interstate 75 would be extended from Tampa through the new jetport to Miami, he realized that the road would block the park's water supply. Padrick sent letters to more than a hundred conservationists urging them to organize against the jetport and road. Everglades author Marjory Stoneman Douglas formed a local group, Friends of the Everglades, to fight for the park. An article in the National Parks and Conservation Association magazine alerted park enthusiasts around the country to the new Everglades threat. Because the jetport posed a risk to a national park and involved the Federal Aviation Administration (FAA), local activists garnered support from national environmental groups such as the Audubon Society. Once again, a spotlight illumined the plight of the Everglades, but this time, a more receptive and environmentally aware audience was watching. By spring of 1969, representatives from twenty-one conservation groups together with the United Auto Workers and the United Steel Workers organized an Everglades Coalition and appealed to the U.S. secretary of transportation to withdraw federal support and money from the jetport.[33]

Through the summer, supporters and opponents of the proposal jockeyed. The Port Authority director dismissed environmentalists as "butterfly chasers" and told them, "A new city is going to rise up in the middle of Florida. . . whether you like it or not."[34] A local FAA manager disregarded the detrimental effects to the Everglades, claiming that "nobody [would] be close enough to complain—except possibly, alligators."[35] But from as far away as Wisconsin, senator Gaylord Nelson (D) spoke for the Everglades: "Either we stop the jetport at the present site, or we publicly admit that we are going to destroy the Park."[36] In mid September, The U.S. Geological Survey released a condemnatory study conducted by well-respected hydrologist Luna Leopold (son of the renowned biologist Aldo Leopold). In his critical report, Leopold warned that the jetport would "lead to land drainage and development for agriculture, industry, housing, transportation, and services in the Big Cypress Swamp which will inexorably destroy the South Florida ecosystem and thus Everglades National Park."[37] The report proved influential.

In its wake, Florida governor Claude Kirk (R) finally came out against the project, and his aide Nathaniel Reed persuaded President Nixon's secretary of the interior, Walter Hickel, to press for relocation. On January 15, 1970, representatives from the Departments of Interior and Transportation, the state of Florida, the Dade Port Authority, and Dade County signed a formal agreement recognizing the need for a new regional airport at an alternate site. Attorney Daniel Paul, who had been advising the National Audubon Society, called the agreement a "complete victory" for Everglades supporters. Furthermore, concern generated for the Big Cypress area during the jetport fight led to protection for that area in the early 1970s.[38]

By effectively organizing, conservationists managed to orchestrate a national constituency for the Everglades and garnered the necessary support of the Nixon administration. One of the first significant victories of the young environmental movement, the high-profile jetport fight drew more national attention to the Everglades and to wetlands than ever before.

Kingdom in the Swamps

While environmentalists worked to contain the effects of development in the Miami area, another growth burst overwhelmed the interior wetlands of central Florida. Amid scrubby flats and swamp forests near Orlando, construction of the $300 million Walt Disney World neared completion. In the early 1960s, the Disney Company had secretly purchased 27,400 acres, an area twice the size of Manhattan. Disney planners then changed the natural landscape to emphasize the best and eliminate what they regarded as the worst aspects of the swampy terrain. Workers built 140 miles of canals and sixteen water structures to maintain a water table high enough to support the luxuriant tropical vegetation but not high enough to cause flooding. A lake made brown by natural tannins was drained, dredged, leveed, and then refilled so that visitors could swim in clear water. In Disneyland style, all canals, ditches, and water-control structures were carefully tucked away so that the pleasing landscape appeared natural. Last, the planners permanently set aside more than 7,500 acres as a natural buffer to insulate the theme park from outside development. Although Disney planners addressed a number of environmental concerns on their own lands, they did not anticipate the growth that would unfold around their Magic Kingdom fiefdom.[39]

Soon after Disney World opened in 1971, new hotels, gas stations, stores, restaurants, and roads sprang up outside the buffer to meet visitors' demands. A growing population of employees also required housing and services. Many of the surrounding lakes and swamp jungles were made into residential developments and shopping centers. Between 1967 and 1974, entrepreneurs purchased more than 75,000 acres between Orlando and the nearby Green Swamp for development. The land boom transformed Orlando from a sleepy citrus orchard town to a sprawling city.

The Green Swamp was the most significant wetland threatened by Orlando's explosive growth. It played a vital role in recharging the Florida Aquifer—an underground body of water that supplied 2.4 million people, including city dwellers, ranchers, manufacturers, and farmers. Before the boom, phosphate mines, citrus groves, and processing plants had consumed increasing amounts of water, causing the water table to drop. Now using millions of gallons each day, Disney World and surrounding developments further siphoned the Florida Aquifer for water slides, milk shakes, and manicured lawns. Between 1966 and 1973, the surface of the aquifer declined by eight feet.[40]

With three major developments on the docket for the Green Swamp, state planners became alarmed. Because the swamp was so critical to the state's water supply and so imminently threatened by new construction, the state Bureau of Land and Water Management recommended that 323,000 acres of swamp be designated as an area of critical concern. While Florida had no official mechanism for protecting inland wetlands per se, the strategy of special designation sidestepped the politicking that usually went hand in hand with legislating new policies. Lawmakers didn't have to worry about the repercussions of regulating all wetlands in the state; just the Green Swamp would be protected for its necessary water supply functions.

When the planners' recommendation came before the Florida cabinet, landowners disputed the issue. Having purchased their parcels with the expectation of profits, developers argued that protecting the aquifer would unfairly hamper their businesses. After listening to five hours of testimony, the governor and three cabinet members approved of the designation, while three others opposed it. In July of 1974, the governor designated the Green Swamp as an area of critical state concern, but skyrocketing growth continued to affect countless other wetlands throughout Florida.[41]

In the same era, several northeastern states, also stressed by urbanization, approved broader laws to protect inland wetlands. Recognizing the instrumental role that freshwater marshes played in safeguarding municipal water supplies, Massachusetts passed an Inland Wetlands Act in 1968.[42] Concern for these wetlands arose mostly in coastal states, where the need for protecting tidal wetlands was already well accepted.

New Attitudes Ascending

When astronauts first transmitted striking photographs of the blue marble of earth isolated in space, the image underscored the need to steward limited resources. Already, hosts of active citizen groups were keenly aware of the scarcity within their own backyards. As a new environmental ethic spread across America, people in hundreds of communities came to appreciate the aesthetic and ecological values of wetlands. Citizens seeking to maintain the character of their towns prompted local governments and several states to adopt conservation policies for wetlands. Between 1965 and 1977, local governments alone created more than one thousand wetland protection programs.[43] In some cases, citizen groups purchased sensitive places directly to safeguard them from development.

The growing scientific evidence that linked wetlands to fisheries and to water purification played an even larger role in compelling states to act. Coastal states sampled a full range of strategies, including direct regulation through permitting, state planning, land acquisition, special designation, fostering local zoning, and the creation of regional authorities. The state agencies and local councils officially directed to steward wetlands became aware of problems with pollution and development. Citizen groups and states even enlisted the help of the national government in some instances to block federally funded projects such as airports and to create refuges.

With protective local and state laws in place, citizen groups began to call upon the courts to ensure enforcement. Even in the absence of specific environmental laws, activists began to find recourse in the courts. After several fish kills in Long Island's Suffolk County, the Brookhaven Town Natural Resources Committee brought a class-action suit to stop the use of DDT in local marshes and lakes in 1966. Made up of scientists from the state university and the nearby Brookhaven national lab, plus attorney Victor Yannacone, the group drew upon detailed scientific testimony to convince the judge that pesticides destroyed natural aquatic systems. Yannacone asserted that all citizens of the county had a right to a clean environment and demonstrated that the local mosquito commission had been ill informed about the detrimental effects of DDT.

In response to the group's impressive and exhaustive evidence, the court issued a temporary injunction to block further spraying. That the court

accepted citizen-group standing and provided relief—even temporary relief—for an environmental problem was a breakthrough. With the discovery
of this successful combination of science and law, the Brookhaven group
went on to form the Environmental Defense Fund (EDF) in 1967.[44]

EDF became one of a new generation of environmental groups that pursued legal action on the public's behalf. Although conservation groups had
long protected waterfowl and parks through lobbying, public education,
and refuge acquisition, the new groups focused on building a body of case
law to clearly establish citizen rights to a clean environment. Both EDF and
the Natural Resources Defense Council (NRDC), which formed in 1970,
began their vanguard work with staffs of young attorneys and scientists. Initially funded by the Ford Foundation, both the EDF and NRDC expanded
the influence of conservation groups by bringing informed lawsuits against
polluters and others who refused to comply with environmental laws.[45]
Pioneering the strategy of litigation, these new groups paved the way for all
conservation groups—local, state, and national—to cope more effectively
with modern environmental crises. As local, state, and eventually federal
governments passed more environmental laws, litigation would become a
critical enforcement tool.

Through the decade of the 1960s, what had begun as local concern
in many different places grew into a broader movement of wetlands
conservation as many Americans discovered more about the connections
between their lives and these lands. Grassroots activists started to organize
on a wider scale. Several state-level conservation groups formed, and the
memberships and staffs of national environmental advocacy organizations
swelled. Relying on new scientific information, the citizen groups pushed
for stronger laws and took legal action to ensure enforcement. Again and
again, citizen activists in their communities dealt with broad choices facing
the society at large: to embrace boundless growth with all its side effects or
to protect remaining natural values before they were lost. In a most visceral
and physical way, it became evident that saving towns from pollution and
runaway development truly did depend, as Henry Thoreau had once
predicted, on saving the surrounding marshes and swamps.

While many states adopted laws to protect their wetlands, many more
did not. And many of the most destructive threats to wetlands were still
posed by federal agencies. By the mid 1970s, an estimated 105.9 million
acres of wetlands remained.[46] Only action on the national level would
protect these important lands from destruction.

TWELVE

Federal Bulldozers and Draglines

Getting the Corps of Engineers . . . to change . . . is like
burning a pile of damp newspapers. It's a slow process in
which you have to continually ventilate the field.

—Gilbert White [1]

The Yukon River threaded the remote wilds of Alaska much like the Mississippi wound through the heart of America's central lowlands in the 1500s. Ungirded by levees, unhindered by dams, the river was free to overspill its banks into a vast tangle of wet sloughs. In these rich wetlands, warmed by the unceasing summer sun, countless flocks of ducks and geese gathered annually to breed. Wolves, moose, and caribou abounded in this watery domain.

Even these distant wetlands of interior Alaska did not escape the ambitious dreams of development that marked the decades of the 1950s and 1960s. The U.S. Army Corps of Engineers proposed to plug the enormous Yukon with a 530-foot dam that would crank out five thousand megawatts of electricity and form the world's largest reservoir—a body of water the size of Lake Erie. Because Alaska's economy, tied tightly to military operations, had collapsed in the 1950s, state politicians eyed the $3 billion Rampart Dam as their economic development salvation. Promoters hoped that the electricity-thirsty aluminum industry could be lured northward. Regarding the wetlands of the Yukon Flats as wastelands, one Alaska senator's staff member explained that "it would be difficult to find an equivalent area with so little to be lost through flooding." He supported this assertion with the evidence that "not more than ten flush toilets" could be found in the proposed reservoir zone. [2]

But many people disagreed with that evaluation. Just upstream of the proposed dam site, the grand river meandered regally for 180 miles in enormous bends and sloughs through the boggy Yukon Flats. Aside from the wildlife that inhabited these sloughs, the flats were connected to other

229

continental wetland ecosystems by the Pacific and Central flyways. Altogether 1.5 million ducks migrated south from the flats—more than the annual production of all other federal, state, and private wildlife refuges combined in 1964. Millions of acres of valuable breeding grounds would be
flooded. Furthermore, the dam and reservoir threatened to block the continent's longest salmon runs and to flood native hunting grounds, inciting
angry opposition from native Athapascan Indians, whose livelihoods depended on fishing and trapping.

In keeping with the Fish and Wildlife Coordination Act, the Corps accepted comments from the Bureau of Sport Fisheries and Wildlife, which
vehemently opposed the project. "Nowhere in the history of water development in North America," the agency's biologists warned, "have the fish and
wildlife losses anticipated to result from a single project been so over-
whelming."[3] Despite the grave criticism, plans for the dam proceeded with
full steam.

While citizen groups had prompted many local governments and states
to protect wetlands from damaging development through the 1960s, the
national government was slower to react. Despite new scientific information about wetlands and a revolution in the way that many Americans understood environmental values, the federal construction agencies still rode
the post–World War II wave of boundless growth. Although the Corps and
the Soil Conservation Service began to hire biologists and sociologists to
address growing environmental concerns, most projects under construction in the 1960s had been congressionally authorized and fully planned in
the decade before. With deteriorating water quality, destruction of habitat,
and loss of recreational opportunities becoming more evident in the wake
of the federal projects, conservation groups raised opposition. But they
found few ways to change or even to comment effectively on the stacks of
federal dam, ditch, and drain proposals. Confronting a monolith of government intransigence, conservationists dug in for political battle in the far
north.

Beyond finding fault with the project's damage to habitat, conservationists in the lower forty-eight criticized Rampart for creating thirty times more
electricity than the state could use, while costing more than any dam in history. In 1963, fifteen conservation groups pooled funds to sponsor an independent scientific study and then mounted a national campaign against the
project. In the Audubon Society magazine, A. Starker Leopold and Justin

Leonard alerted members that the dam "would negate 30 years of endeavor in waterfowl preservation."[4] An article in *Field and Stream* similarly warned hunters that Rampart would be a "catastrophe of major proportions."[5]

Despite such strong opposition to the Corps project, it was only when Alaskan political interests turned toward the new trans-Alaska pipeline and the Corps identified a better dam site near the coast that the boondoggle Rampart was abandoned, leaving Yukon Flats to the birds.[6] Although economic circumstances eventually reprieved the Yukon Flats, the Rampart Dam controversy forced the Corps to reckon with the growing environmental movement and its concern for wetlands. Never before had a Corps project been so fiercely contested on environmental grounds. Though the Rampart fight prompted conservation groups to organize nationally, it did little to change the Corps.

Hindered by the inertia of its massive bureaucracy, the federal government could not respond readily to new ideas. A conveyor belt of Corps dam, flood-control, and navigation projects continually threatened significant riparian wetlands, and the Department of Agriculture's drainage and flood-control programs still wrought havoc in the marshes and swamps of farm regions. The bulldozers of the federal construction agencies stuck firmly in their inherited ruts.

Wetlands Need Water: The Everglades Saga Continues

While the Yukon Flats survived, other wetlands met a different fate. In south Florida, work on the Corps's Central-Southern Florida Flood Control Plan—authorized after the devastating 1947 hurricane to contain Lake Okeechobee overflows—was well underway. By 1965, with $174 million spent, the Corps had completed many of the key elements of the project and turned over operation of the complicated plumbing system to the South Florida Flood Control District. With all its canals, levees, dams, spillways, and pumping stations, the FCD was supposed to deliver water necessary for the Everglades. From its inception, however, conservationists had accused the district of favoring agricultural interests at the expense of urban consumers and wildlife. On top of this, a ban on Cuban sugar imports following the Bay of Pigs confrontation opened up the previously restricted domestic market. Between 1961 and 1964, the sugar industry built eight new sugar mills and brought 170,000 acres of undeveloped swampland into cane production in the Everglades.[7] When drought struck Florida

in the early sixties, more users than ever before depended on Lake Okeechobee's overtaxed water supply.

The Corps had designed its project largely with floods—not droughts—
in mind. Construction of the perimeter levee and two cross-Florida highways had already severely disrupted the hydrology of the Everglades. The
natural flow regime, formerly a wide sheet of water seeping steadily and
evenly southward from Lake Okeechobee through the sawgrass glades, was
replaced with four culverts, which allowed some water to flow into the park
under the roads. Furthermore, the levees around Lake Okeechobee funneled excess waters—roughly 715 billion gallons a year—into the St. Lucie
Canal and the Caloosahatchee River for high-speed trips to the sea.[8] Other
valuable lake water was directed into three leveed conservation areas, where
much of it evaporated. Despite these formidable, engineered obstacles to
natural water flow, rainfall kept the Everglades wet enough to support much
of the tropical vegetation and animal life. But when drought struck, the
Everglades was entirely dependent on the FCD for its water, and, not surprisingly, the national park ended up at the bottom of the water delivery list.
In 1961 southern Florida received only half its average rainfall, and the first
months of 1962 brought hardly any rain at all. Water flow remained dan-
gerously low for several years.[9]

The Everglades dried up. Millions of fish in the Shark River slough died.
The popular Anhinga Trail, where visitors had enjoyed viewing alligators
and tropical birds from boardwalks, overlooked a cracked and dusty mud
hole. Intrusions of saltwater threatened the ecosystem with irreparable
damage. When the FCD announced that the trickle of water flowing into
the park would be cut off completely to hold back more water for potential
irrigation and municipal needs, Governor Claude Kirk drew the line. He
secured an agreement from the district that at least one hundred cubic feet
per second (cfs)—still just a pittance—would continue to flow into the
Everglades park. Only this scant water supply along with emergency water
holes dug by the National Park Service sustained populations of birds and
alligators, already stricken by poaching and habitat losses elsewhere.[10]

Aside from advocating the needs of the area's wildlife, the National Park
Service along with the Audubon Society and other conservation groups defended the Everglades on economic grounds. The park had become a prime
tourist attraction, drawing 800,000 visitors in 1964. Unlike scenery-
oriented parks, the crown feature here was wildlife. Without water, the birds
and animals would vanish, leaving little for tourists to enjoy. Furthermore,

the commercial fishing industry in Florida Bay depended on a healthy Everglades as nursery grounds for shrimp and fish. To maintain both ecological and economic values, the Park Service and conservation groups requested that Congress guarantee an allotment of water for the park.

Although the Corps of Engineers had long since turned responsibility for its project to the FCD, Congress, in response to Interior Department protests, directed the Corps to reexamine the water needs of south Florida.[11] But this time—for the first time ever—their job was to deliver water to *protect* wetlands.

The Everglades could not wait for the completion of lengthy studies, so in 1965 the Corps proposed an interim project for getting more water to the park. The next spring, Miami Congressman Dante Fascell (D) garnered the first $1.5 million appropriation for the new project. In the meantime, the FCD promised a minimal water supply of 140 cfs—the amount flowing in a medium-sized creek—provided that Lake Okeechobee did not sink below the navigational "safety level." The following year, their promise was tested when the searing drought dried Lake Okeechobee to within one-tenth of an inch above the critical 12.5-foot level.[12]

Publicized by magazines and television programs, the plight of the Everglades gained national attention through the drought and engendered outrage. Responding to public support for Everglades protection, the Corps in 1967 unveiled its new allocation proposal, which could provide up to 315,000 acre-feet of water for the park each year—the minimum quantity biologists considered necessary (an average flow of 432 cfs).[13]

With all parties showing willingness to cooperate, Congress authorized the new $70 million Corps plan in 1968. By the time the project gained approval, rains returned, and the quenched Everglades began to heal from wounds of desiccation. But supporters knew that future droughts were inevitable. In 1970, Senators Gaylord Nelson (D-WI) and Edmund Muskie (D-ME) successfully pushed for a stipulation that guaranteed the park would receive at least 16.5 percent of all water deliveries during dry spells.[14] With plans in place to provide water to the park, the Corps of Engineers embarked upon a new path of using their engineering expertise to protect and restore the environment. But the complexity of the ecosystem's hydrological regime would be far more difficult to simulate and sustain than anyone imagined.

Although the park's water supply looked secure on paper, another component of the Corps's Central-Southern Florida Flood Control Plan continued to ravage less glamorous wetlands of the Kissimmee River floodplain north and upstream of the Everglades. Construction of the $31 million Kissimmee portion of the project had begun in the early sixties. While drought quieted the natural world, a noisy battery of Corps draglines dredged the Kissimmee. To carry floodwaters more quickly off the land, the Corps channelized the entire river, which had naturally meandered in wide loops for one hundred miles through extensive marshlands from its source just south of Orlando to Lake Okeechobee. The project cut the length of the Kissimmee almost in half and transformed graceful twists and bends into a ruler-straight ditch. Although the Bureau of Sport Fisheries and Wildlife, the Florida Game and Fresh Water Fish Commission, and local conservation groups opposed channelization on ecological grounds, the dredging continued. In 1971, the Corps finished replacing the Kissimmee River with Canal 38.[15]

Even by the time the Corps had completed its engineering marvel, signs of unacceptable environmental deterioration became evident. Waterfowl populations declined by 90 percent, and six species of fish vanished from the river. Most significant, in its natural, wetland-bordered state, the Kissimmee had provided a free water-purifying system that supplied clean water to Lake Okeechobee. But now channelization had drained 31,000 acres—more than three-quarters of the former marshland—and dredge-spoil heaps damaged thousands more acres. In their place, trampling herds of cattle grazing on the newly reclaimed lands dropped fecal wastes that fouled runoff. Storm water from the booming upstream Orlando area also polluted the water. Like a pipeline, Canal 38 whisked all these contaminants straight to Lake Okeechobee. Burdened by the new organic waste load, the lake became eutrophic, choked by algae that threatened not only an excellent fishery but also the water supply of all south Florida. University of Florida microbiologist John V. Betz described the tragedy: "What was intended to help answer the coming water needs in south Florida has instead brought them to a crisis by forging a short circuit from the bathrooms and streets of central Florida to the major drinking-water reservoir of south Florida."[16]

By this time the Corps had turned operation of Canal 38 over to the FCD. The district tried to reduce eutrophication by building a temporary dam and reflooding some of the marshes, but the problem proved too large to tackle without outside help. In 1973, the Florida legislature appropriated

$1 million to assemble a team of experts and set up a Special Project to Prevent the Eutrophication of Lake Okeechobee. By 1975, the scientists released portions of their startling report.[17]

Beyond the Kissimmee, the Everglades Agricultural Area (EAA), where enormous levees enclosed 700,000 acres of farmland just south of the lake, also turned out to be a significant source of contamination. Sugar and vegetable growers drew heavily on the waters of Lake Okeechobee for irrigation but then returned large quantities (about 480,000 acre-feet per year) to the lake through backpumping. The used water was crammed full of pesticides and saturated with nitrogen and phosphorus from the oxidized peat soils. When the legislature's panel recommended putting an end to backpumping, EAA growers—long the beneficiaries of public drainage works—suddenly faced the shocking prospect of dealing with their own polluted wastes.[18]

Avoiding the larger and more volatile regional water issues exposed by the report, the 1976 session of the Florida legislature instead focused its attention on a comparatively simple proposal pushed by Johnny Jones of the Florida Wildlife Federation: a bill to restore the Kissimmee River. The idea of repairing environmental damage on such a grand scale was entirely new. Despite the diverse interests involved, the unprecedented and unlikely bill passed unanimously. However, when the legislature approved a plan to fill 60 percent of the canal and restore two-thirds of the marshes in 1977, local ranchers objected. They had grown accustomed to grazing on wetlands that had been drained by the federal channelization project. Because restoration would reflood these marshes, ranchers demanded compensation. Yet much of the drained land had been formerly "submerged" and owned by the state, and buying out the federally reclaimed lands would cost a fortune. With uncertainty about who owned what, restoration plans stalled out.[19]

Stuck in legal and technical quagmires, the state turned to Congress to fund another Corps of Engineers study. With the state mandate of restoring the Kissimmee coming almost immediately after the channelization was finished, Congress and the Corps were taught a hard lesson about the environmental consequences of altering wetlands. South Florida's water-control structures contained floods, but they also destroyed habitat, degraded water, and threatened to undermine drinking supplies. By failing to consider the full effects of its projects, the Corps had engineered a whole suite of new problems.

THE KISSIMMEE RIVER NORTH FROM LAKE OKEECHOBEE, FLORIDA, BEFORE
CHANNELIZATION.

As part of the South Florida Flood Control Project, the Corps of Engineers dredged
the meandering Kissimmee River into a ruler-straight ditch. By the time the project
was complete in 1971, the disastrous environmental side effects of the project became evident. Aside from the decline of birds and fish, the canalized river hastened
the flow of pollutants to Lake Okeechobee and threatened the quality of south
Florida's water supply. (Courtesy Corps of Engineers, Jacksonville District)

THE KISSIMMEE RIVER NORTH FROM LAKE OKEECHOBEE, FLORIDA, AFTER CHANNELIZATION.

Reconsidering Atchafalaya

Across the gulf in southern Louisiana, the Atchafalaya was another grand wetland altered by Corps flood-control work. As part of the strategy initially developed under its 1928 Mississippi River Tributary Plan, the agency had built water-control structures and levees and dredged the main channel of the Atchafalaya River as a floodway. A major distributary of the Mississippi, the Atchafalaya diverted a large portion of that enormous river's flows from a point north of Baton Rouge, through swamp forests, to the Gulf of Mexico—145 miles in all. Although most of the ancient cypress had been removed from the basin by the 1920s, new hardwoods and some young cypress had grown up once again. A large portion of the Atchafalaya was a great 800,000-acre river swamp, which provided essential habitat to fish and wildlife and attracted hunters, anglers, photographers, and boaters.

By the early 1960s, it became clear to Corps engineers that the Atchafalaya channel did not function properly as a floodway. The containment levees continuously subsided into the swampy terrain, and silt choked the lower stretch of the river, raising the level of its bed and necessitating larger and larger levees. In 1963, the Corps proposed a new plan to funnel the turbid water more quickly downstream before it could drop its silt. To do this, the engineers would block off side sloughs and dredge a 60-mile-long, 100,000-square-foot channel (area of cross section). According to Corps historian Martin Reuss, "The Corps was unprepared for the controversy its proposals generated."[20]

Sportsmen worried that closing side channels and dumping dredge spoils would threaten their fish and wildlife quarry by preventing overflows from rejuvenating bottomland swamp habitat. Commercial fishermen feared that dredging could endanger their livelihoods by blocking access and destroying the productivity of favorite fishing sites. With ninety species of fish, crabs, and shrimp, the basin hosted a substantial fishery. In particular, the swamp annually produced twenty-three million pounds of Louisianans' favorite delicacy—crawfish—known locally as mudbugs. A growing state conservation movement also had reservations about the new dredging project. The basin remained one of the largest chunks of natural habitat in the region, supporting three hundred species of birds and numerous fishes and mammals, including black bears, fox, and mink. The Greater Atchafalaya Basin Council, established in 1963 by the Lafayette Chamber of Commerce, wanted to create an Atchafalaya National Recreation Area to attract more tourists.[21] Petroleum companies were concerned

ATCHAFALAYA RIVER SWAMP, LOUISIANA.
Controversy erupted when the Corps of Engineers dredged the Atchafalaya for flood control in the 1960s and early 1970s. By becoming involved in the Corps's work of preparing an environmental impact statement as required by NEPA, citizens influenced the final plan for the swamp. (Photo by Tim Palmer)

that closing channels would impair their shipping access to well sites. On the other hand, landowners within the floodway and citizens of the downstream towns favored the best flood control possible.

The Louisiana state government wanted the Corps to develop a plan that provided effective flood control without damaging the swamp's commercial and recreational values, but state wildlife officials remained skeptical of the federal agency's ecological sensitivity. In 1963 the opening of another dredged Corps canal, the Mississippi River–Gulf Outlet, had delivered unanticipated consequences, including saltwater intrusion that killed 6,400 acres of cypress and caused significant declines in fisheries and furbearer populations.[22] So the state issued resolutions specifically urging the Corps to consult with the federal and state fish and wildlife agencies to ensure that damage was minimized. But despite careful recommendations by the wildlife agencies, the New Orleans Corps District sent its General Design Memorandum to the chief of engineers for approval without integrating *any* fish and wildlife considerations. With flood control as its paramount responsibility, the Corps began work in earnest.

Frustrated fish and wildlife agencies and sportsmen stepped up agitation against the project, and in response to growing angry sentiment, the Corps conceded some changes. It agreed to construct dikes to contain dredge spoils at many locations and reconsidered the possibility of leaving some side channels open. But for the most part, construction of the 100,000-square-foot channel continued as planned. By the fall of 1967, levees on both sides of the basin had been upgraded, dredging had enlarged forty-one miles of the main channel, and associated natural erosion had substantially enlarged the uppermost fifty-five miles of river. Only lack of funds in the Vietnam War–drained treasury finally stopped the dredging in 1968.[23]

Shortly thereafter, Congress approved the National Environmental Policy Act (NEPA) in 1969, finally giving citizens a way to influence damaging federal projects administratively. The new law required all agencies to evaluate the environmental impacts of their projects along with impacts of alternative plans in an environmental impact statement (EIS) before work began. States, wildlife agencies, and citizen groups could then offer their expertise and input ahead of time.

The idea behind NEPA was to consider ecological consequences ahead of time to prevent blunders like the Kissimmee channelization. But many projects had been authorized the decade before with little heed for environmental effects. Such was the case in the Atchafalaya (initially authorized in 1928!). Not until 1971, when the National Wildlife Federation pressed the Corps to prepare an EIS before it resumed dredging work, did the army engineers fully consider the environmental repercussions of their Atchafalaya dredging plan.

Beleaguered by NEPA litigation on at least a dozen of its projects, the Corps was receptive to the NWF's out-of-court approach and its offer of assistance. To prepare the EIS, the Corps set up a collaborative steering committee with representatives from federal and state environmental and public works agencies. As one of the first large environmental impact statements ever prepared, and certainly the first to be prepared by a multi-interested committee, participants broke new ground with their attempt to develop a consensus document.

Although everyone tried to work together, participants had fundamentally different visions for the Atchafalaya. Engineers, who had collected data for decades, had a precise understanding of flood threats and could articulate specific goals. Natural scientists needed more information about habitat values and spoke about environmental quality in general terms.

Despite skepticism and differences, a preliminary draft of the EIS was completed in 1974.[24]

Already well acquainted with the potential for opposition, the New Orleans Corps District decided to elicit public comments early on to save time and money later. At a packed meeting in Lafayette, Corps and state officials presented their draft EIS. Much to the disappointment of sportsmen and conservationists, the statement failed to consider alternatives and instead focused almost entirely on completing and maintaining the original massive channel. But the large turnout of citizens impressed district engineer Colonel E. R. Heiberg III, who left the meeting convinced that the EIS and the flood-control plan must better account for fish and wildlife needs.

At Heiberg's urging, the steering committee considered a wider scope of alternatives, including acquisition of land and easements within the floodway. The Corps's highest leadership in Washington, D.C., wanted to address the concerns of sportsmen and conservationists with a progressive document, yet creating such an EIS was difficult for rank-and-file engineers who worked on the local level and often disagreed with the new environmental values. Responding to the fears of state public works officials and landowners, regional Corps officials wanted to start dredging as quickly as possible to fulfill the agency's traditional flood-control responsibilities. When the Corps presented a new draft EIS in February 1976, it was riddled with many of the same deficiencies as the first.

Getting nowhere with the steering committee approach, the Fish and Wildlife Service (FWS) decided to propose its own alternate plan, which used natural swamp habitat as floodway. This required the acquisition of 443,000 acres of privately owned land to establish the Atchafalaya Fish Wildlife and Multi-Use Area—all at about one-tenth the cost of the 100,000-foot channel project. Although several engineers thought the proposal had merit, the Corps declined to endorse it officially. But the real surprise came when environmental groups opposed the plan. They feared that the specter of federal land condemnation would unhinge landowners and jeopardize all habitat protection efforts in the basin.

They were right. The release of the FWS plan in October 1978 provoked bitter controversy. Billboards around the state denounced the federal government; debates raged on television and radio talk shows; landowners published a pamphlet portraying the FWS plan as an attack on private-property rights; bumper stickers warned "Stop Federal Land Grabs."[25]

While antigovernment rhetoric flared, National Wildlife Federation attorney Oliver Houck and landowner attorney Newman Trowbridge initiated private meetings to find common ground. After consulting with the Corps, in 1981 Houck and Trowbridge finally presented their proposal, which featured the outright sale of 46,000 acres from private landowners to the state to be used for wildlife management and floodway purposes. State purchase was critical to the landowners not only because of antifederal sentiment but also because Louisiana law enabled sellers to retain mineral rights to their land for ten years after the sale.

At the same time, the Corps released a third-draft EIS that included environmentally sensitive features, such as sediment-control structures, water-management units, and greenbelts along some of the levees. With all parties amenable to the plan brokered by Houck, Trowbridge, and the Corps, it was highlighted as the option of choice in the final EIS, published in 1982.

What began in 1971 as a proposal to dredge a mammoth channel was scaled back by the work of wildlife agencies and, more significant, by the work of citizens. With its EIS requirement, NEPA opened the door for citizens to voice opinions about the federal flood-control project. Although millions of dollars had been spent and dredging plans had been drawn up, the EIS process compelled the Corps to redesign its project to reflect new environmental values. In the end, both conservationists and landowners wielded considerable influence over the final shape of the Corps's work in the Atchafalaya.[26] Here and elsewhere, NEPA enabled citizen groups to influence many projects that would otherwise have damaged important wetlands.

Saving Wetlands and Money

Though NEPA required the Corps to consider wetland values in its planning, those values often seemed at odds with Corps goals. Usually a balance had to be struck between preserving wetland habitat for fish and wildlife and providing flood control for communities, and typically flood control carried more weight. But while working in Massachusetts, the engineers made an important discovery about how wetlands actually served their flood-control aims.

Flowing eighty miles before emptying into Boston Harbor, the Charles River posed a flood threat to the metropolitan area. When the Corps began developing a plan for the Charles in 1967, it recommended replacing an antiquated dam across the river's mouth to reduce urban flooding. But in the course of their studies, engineers came up with a different strategy for dealing with floods on the middle and upper reaches.

Examining the hydrological data assembled during previous floods, Corps engineers spotted an anomaly. While waters raged in the bottom end of the basin, there were few signs of flooding in the upper and middle sections of river. Engineers wondered if the thousands of acres of natural wetlands still scattered throughout the watershed played a part. In the middle of their 1968 study, a major storm brought another flood of record and with it a timely opportunity to study the matter firsthand. Engineers watching in the upper and middle basin were astounded by the slow-moving nature of the flood crest. They could literally get a night's sleep and still find the crest only slightly downstream the next morning. In contrast, engineers in the lower portion of the basin, where former wetlands were impenetrably crusted in concrete and asphalt, saw the flood crest in a matter of hours. When floodwaters in the lower part of the watershed subsided, waters from the upper basin were slowly and safely released. Engineers estimated that the wetlands in the upper Charles watershed held more than 50,000 acre-feet of water during the flood—the same amount of water held by the average New England flood-control reservoir. Witnessing this natural process, engineers realized that they could build no structure that controlled floods more efficiently than the 20,000 acres of wetlands that remained in the watershed.[27]

Although the Corps had historically considered only projects that involved building dams, dikes, or other water-control structures, the engineers now recommended capitalizing on the attributes of the natural wetland landscape. Though many Charles River basin wetlands remained undeveloped in 1968, sprawling suburbs would soon swallow up the critical natural landscapes. Many towns near Boston had lost more than half their wetlands since 1950.[28] In 1971, the Corps announced its Natural Valley Storage Project to acquire 8,500 acres of wetlands for flood control.

A 1972 report explained the new strategy: "Nature has already provided the least-cost solution to future flooding in the form of extensive wetlands. . . . Rather than attempt to improve on this natural protection mechanism, it is both prudent and economical to leave the hydrologic regime established over the millennia undisturbed. . . ."[29] Natural wetlands best complemented the new dam at the mouth of the Charles River to provide flood control to the valley.

The subtle and compelling logic of Natural Valley Storage made good sense. Its predicted price tag, $7.3 million, was one-fourth the cost of building another dam. It required no condemnation of homes and no relocation of families as large reservoirs did. In fact, it did little to alter the character of the communities in the watershed. Massachusetts already owned 20 percent of the wetlands needed for the project. Privately owned wetlands and flowage easements would be purchased outright at fair market value. Massachusetts's prior experiences with wetland protective legislation laid the foundation for widespread acceptance of Natural Valley Storage. Because the Corps worked carefully with a Citizen Advisory Committee, the project had strong local support. From all fronts, the nonstructural, wetland flood-control project received accolades.

Only Nixon's Office of Management and Budget dragged its heels on funding, so Massachusetts Senator Edward Kennedy sought a special appropriation in Congress. Increasingly besieged with pleas for flood-damage relief, senators were intrigued by the nonstructural flood-control plan. With the whole Massachusetts delegation behind the proposal, Congress authorized the project as part of the Water Resources Development Act of 1974, which thereafter required the Corps to consider nonstructural alternatives for all flood-control projects. Because the Corps would purchase only a portion of wetlands in the basin, however, Congress required a commitment from the state to enforce its Inland Wetlands Act (1968) and floodplain zoning more stringently. If unpurchased wetlands in the basin were developed, the Natural Valley Storage Project would not work as planned. Most local communities cooperated readily by adopting local zoning laws to protect their wetlands. The Corps began land and easement acquisition in 1977 and completed the project in six years.[30]

By redesigning old projects to account for environmental problems as in south Florida, preparing environmental impact statements as in the Atchafalaya, and developing its Natural Valley Storage Plan, the Corps of Engineers gained a greater understanding about the hydrology, habitat values, and water-filtering and storage capacities of wetlands. This new knowledge would be helpful in planning new projects and critical as the Corps became even more deeply embroiled in wetland regulatory issues through the 1970s and 1980s.

The Channelizing Trials of the Soil Conservation Service

The USDA's Soil Conservation Service was not left out of the growing environmental concern of the late sixties and early seventies. In line with its

original mission of promoting soil conservation, the organization had educated farmers about how to decrease erosion. But since the dirty thirties,
the agency's focus had changed. With the mandate of the Federal
Watershed Protection and Flood Prevention Act of 1954 (PL-566), the
SCS began its Small Watershed Program and undertook more drainage
and engineering projects. What had started earlier as a service of natural
scientists and agronomists, over the course of fifteen years became an
agency of engineers.[31] Even SCS administrator Kenneth Grant noted the
change: "In the eyes of some, a conservation agency that used to be on the
side of the angels . . . has suddenly grown horns and a tail."[32] Tight reins
on federal spending had confined the channelization program to SCS
drawing boards, but when more funding became available during the
Kennedy administration, bulldozers went to work and the program flourished.[33] Channelizing many streams in the late 1960s, the SCS began to
draw criticism from biologists for failing to consider effects of its work on
wildlife habitat. Called "stream improvement" by the SCS, channelizing
meant straightening and deepening water courses by dredging sediment
and removing snags and vegetation to provide a clear conduit for flushing
off floodwaters. While channelization obviously affected rivers and
streams, it severely altered the hydrology of associated riparian and pothole
wetlands as well.

Criticism spiraled into national controversy when the Mississippi Game
and Fish Commission adopted a resolution denouncing channelization in
May 1969. Then fish and game agencies of several other southeastern states
followed suit. With 70 percent of projects with drainage and channelization
components slated for the Southeast, the state resolutions raised serious
questions.[34]

The Georgia fish and game agency condemned the $10.9 million chan-
nelization project planned for the Alcovy River, a tupelo gum river swamp
located less than twenty-five miles from Atlanta.[35] Farmers who owned
property along the banks had complained that the river's occasional
flooding kept them from cultivating some of their land, so the SCS proposed to straighten and deepen seventy-three miles of the river and its tributaries. While the state fish and game agency objected to habitat loss,
Georgia Representative (R) Ben Blackburn discovered that 43 percent of
farmers along the Alcovy, whose lands would be cleared at federal expense,
were already receiving USDA payments not to plant existing cleared and
drained lands.[36] Blackburn launched a campaign against the channelization

by authoring an article in the December 1969 issue of *Field and Stream.*
State and local conservation groups joined in opposing the project.

A series of well-publicized studies also lambasted the Alcovy proposal.
In one, Georgia State University ecologist Charles Wharton determined
that undisturbed, the Alcovy River was worth over $7 million annually
when nonmarket values, such as aquifer recharge, water purification, sustainable logging, and fisheries were taken into account. The river swamp
produced thirteen hundred pounds of fish per acre. Wharton also called attention to the rare animals that found strongholds in the swamp, including
ivory-billed woodpeckers, cougars, and wolves.[37] A second study conducted by economists at George Washington University refuted SCS claims
that $1.40 of benefits would accrue for every $1.00 spent. Uncovering serious cost omissions and grossly inflated benefits, the study revealed that
the project's benefits would amount to less than $.45 per dollar spent.[38] Be-
cause Congress required small watershed projects to produce benefits at
least commensurate with costs, the reports caused delays and changes to
original plans.

Amid growing discord, long-time wetland champion Representative
Henry Reuss (D-WI) called for his Subcommittee on Conservation and
Natural Resources to hold oversight hearings on channelization in June of
1971. As part of the subcommittee's investigation, Reuss and other committee members toured a nearby SCS project in Maryland to see firsthand
what channelization looked like.

Where a slow river had long meandered through the wooded Gilbert
Swamp in southern Maryland, only a shallow watercourse bordered by
bulldozed and barren banks remained. The visual impact of the denuded
stream banks was indictment enough, but a biologist explained further that
perch and herring, which had once thrived in the swamp stream, would no
longer return. According to the Maryland State Planning Department,
SCS channelization had already destroyed more of the state's inland wetlands than all other causes combined, having eliminated 11,960 out of
23,717 acres of wetlands lost between 1942 and 1968. The Gilbert Swamp
drainage project alone had destroyed 4 percent of Maryland's swamps.[39]
Reuss immediately realized that only twenty-four more such projects would
mean the annihilation of all the state's interior wetlands.

When a local watershed association chairman explained that the newly
converted lands enabled farmers like himself to make a better living by
growing corn, soybeans, and tobacco, Reuss pointedly questioned the
ethics of the government developing more lands for tobacco at the same

time it banned cigarette advertising on television. Then he turned to the SCS engineer and demanded: "Do you think it is economical for the federal government to pay farmers *not* to grow corn and on the other hand pay for canalization so that farmers can *grow* corn?"[40] Reuss returned to Congress with new resolve to place a year's moratorium on channelization until a more thorough review of ecological and economic effects could be undertaken.[41]

The Reuss subcommittee hearings provided an opportunity for supporters and opponents of channelization to air a broad array of opinions, experience, and information. As of 1971, SCS had spent an estimated $90 million channelizing six thousand miles of waterways; one thousand projects were in the works; and another two thousand applications awaited their rubber stamps.[42] Through a series of amendments to the original PL-566 legislation, most of the small watershed projects had incorporated public components such as recreational facilities and water-supply reservoirs. Proponents claimed that the Small Watershed Program represented democracy at its finest: local soil and water conservation districts decided on projects they needed for flood control and other purposes, and then the SCS simply furnished technical expertise and helped to line up federal funding. Vice President of the National Association of Conservation Districts (NACD) George Bagley praised the grassroots aspect of the SCS program and made the zealous claim that in his community PL-566 "made it possible for the people to have shoes to wear, schools to go to, and churches in which to worship."[43] The SCS's Small Watershed Program proudly took credit for building forty-nine public water supply reservoirs, for preventing $142 million of flood damages, and for providing over fifty thousand new jobs. SCS Assistant Deputy Administrator Eugene Buie declared that "American agriculture couldn't survive without it."[44] Resting on its dust-bowl-era conservation laurels, the SCS further claimed that its projects always took fish and wildlife concerns into account and oftentimes even enhanced habitat.[45]

Conservationists countered that projects were not actually initiated by small communities, but that the NACD—backed by local development and construction interests—proposed projects to get the ball rolling. They contended that the SCS routinely exaggerated benefit estimates for recreation and flood control but underestimated lost recreational opportunities, lost flood-control benefits, and lost fish and wildlife habitat. Only through this fiscal sleight of hand could the destructive projects be approved and funded. Following ecological principles rather than engineering

REPRESENTATIVE HENRY REUSS.
Wisconsin Representative Henry Reuss championed wetland conservation efforts first in the pothole states by successfully pushing to cut federal funding for pothole drainage in the early 1960s and then by pushing for a nationwide moratorium on channelization as practiced by the Soil Conservation Service in 1971. (Library of Congress, Prints & Photographs Division, *U.S. News & World Report* Magazine Collection)

ones, conservationists preferred the more complex biological systems embodied by natural swamps and rivers to the SCS "improved" streams.

Bureau of Sport Fisheries and Wildlife studies backed up the conservationists' contentions. In testimony to the House oversight committee, Assistant Secretary of the Interior for Fish, Wildlife, and Parks Nathaniel P. Reed explained that reports compiled from Montana, Missouri, Florida, North Carolina, and Mississippi revealed that channelization reduced local populations of fish, vegetation, and ducks by 80 to 99 percent. Reed contended that if the SCS completed all 1,119 watershed projects planned for southern states, up to 300,000 acres of forested habitat—much of it bottomland hardwood forest—would be lost. "Stream channel alteration under the banner of 'improvement,'" he warned, "is undoubtedly one of the most destructive water management practices." In the ultimate insult to the SCS, Reed called the agency's program "the aquatic version of the dust-bowl disaster."[46]

Regardless of wildlife issues, fiscal conservatives began to recognize the sheer inefficiency of the Small Watershed Program. Its drainage and channelization work ran not only counter to BSFW attempts to stem wetlands destruction but also counter to other USDA subsidy programs, which paid $3 million annually to keep land that produced surplus crops out of production. From the standpoint of some local communities and landowners, channelization provided economic benefits, but from a national perspective, the Small Watershed Program converted wildlife habitat into unneeded cropland and barren riparian zones—all as a costly burden to the taxpayers. In an age of modern corporate farming, some Congress members asked, Did agriculture still need federal funds to keep water off private land?[47]

Despite Reuss's resolve and unanimous support from environmental groups, the generally favorable reputation of the SCS, along with Nixon administration backing and pressure from the nation's more than three thousand conservation districts, meant a sound defeat for the one-year moratorium on channelization.

With the failure of the Reuss amendment, environmentalists began to take issue with what they saw as the SCS's loose compliance with the newly enacted National Environmental Policy Act. For the numerous projects planned and approved before 1969, the SCS had stridently declined to write environmental impact statements—even if ground wouldn't be broken for several years. In response to mounting criticism, the agency devised its own system of evaluating the effects of its projects. SCS administrator Kenneth Grant issued a memorandum to conservation districts directing that all ongoing projects be rated on a one-to-three scale, with the third category representing particularly high environmental disturbance. The evaluations were then to be discussed with BSFW biologists. Although the SCS rating system did highlight the worst projects, the BSFW contended that "three" ratings were given too rarely and that evaluations were superficial. Furthermore, the SCS routinely built three-rated projects.[48]

Using the new strategy of litigation, conservation groups pushed the SCS to follow the NEPA requirements. In 1971, five local and national groups filed a suit against the SCS to halt the channelization of sixty-six miles of North Carolina's Chicod Creek until the agency completed an EIS. Since the project had been approved in 1966, the SCS deemed the impact statement unnecessary. Yet environmental groups were convinced that the project's costs far exceeded its benefits. After issuing a temporary restraining order that stopped channelization, a federal district judge agreed with the conservationists and required the agency to complete an EIS. With such a legal precedent set, the potential for lawsuits holding up hundreds of projects became evident, so SCS administrator Grant directed the agency to complete environmental impact statements for all projects that used fiscal year 1973 funds or that had ratings of two or three.[49] At the same time, the Natural Resources Defense Council launched a nationwide campaign to involve citizens in policing SCS activities.[50]

The SCS completed its Chicod Creek EIS in 1972, but the court deemed the hasty job unacceptable. Over the course of six years of evaluation, research, and compromise, a settlement was finally reached in 1977. Channelization began in 1978 but with many modifications designed to reduce impacts, such as excavating from one side only, building sediment traps, and stopping construction for the four months when herring spawned.[51] Through diligent participation in the EIS process, citizen activists did not stop channelization of Chicod Creek but did lessen the damages and push the SCS to acknowledge the ecological effects of its projects.

Environmental impact statements brought the consequences of other SCS channelization projects more clearly to light as well. The Starkweather Project, for example, had been planned for two large watersheds in the pothole region of northeastern North Dakota in 1967. All told, the area harbored over 50,000 acres of ecologically significant prairie potholes. As many as 40,000 of those acres would be damaged by channelization, and the project would likely spawn additional private drainage.[52] Because

Starkweather would eliminate waterfowl habitat, the BSFW pushed the SCS to lessen the project's impacts. The two agencies agreed that 85 percent of the permanent wetlands could be preserved, but local agricultural interests exerted political pressure. One water management district demanded that the North Dakota congressional delegates reprimand the regional director of the BSFW.[53] Finally in 1971, Governor Guy strongarmed the agency by refusing to approve any federal purchases of habitat under the Small Wetland Acquisition Program until it approved a plan to drain most of the Starkweather wetlands. The BSFW buckled and relaxed its mitigation requirements by improperly crediting refuge lands acquired with national duck stamp moneys to compensate for habitat that would be destroyed by the vast drainage project.

Aside from its disruption of wildlife, Starkweather had questionable economic worth. All ninety-one farms the project would benefit grew surplus wheat. In 1971, the U.S. government had paid farmers more than $2.75 billion to idle 37 million acres of cropland. Even during the agricultural boom of 1972, 62 million acres lay fallow.[54] At a time when the government paid farmers both to retire cropland and for their surplus crops, the idea of subsidizing the conversion of wetlands to create even more farmland seemed fiscally irresponsible.

Furthermore, the drainage of the potholes funneled water off the land more quickly, heightening flood dangers downstream. Bob Scheer, president of the North Dakota Wildlife Federation, astutely recognized in Starkweather the skewing of the original intent of PL-566: "Congress really passed this small watershed law to stop floods where they begin, to hold the water on the land. But instead we seem to be using the law to get the water off faster."[55] Like many small watershed projects, Starkweather passed flood problems off to people living downstream.

Only when the SCS completed an EIS were the intolerable effects of the Starkweather Watershed Project illumined. The critical comments made by fish and wildlife agencies and conservation organizations gained broad exposure in congressional oversight hearings. With opposition growing, the USDA finally withdrew its support for Starkweather in 1973.[56]

Although it had proved impossible to stop damages caused by the Small Watershed Program with a congressional moratorium, preparing environmental impact statements prompted the SCS to consider the consequences of its projects, just as it had helped the Corps..

NEPA remained the wetland conservationists' most powerful tool for opposing and influencing SCS channelization projects through the 1970s.

President Jimmy Carter built upon this important law when he issued the first Executive Order on Wetlands (E.O. 11990) in 1977, a milestone in conservation as the highest administrative action ever taken to protect wetlands. President Carter directed all federal agencies "to avoid to the extent possible the long and short term adverse impacts associated with the destruction or modification of wetlands. . . . "[57] Overall, the landmark order institutionalized an awareness of wetland values among all federal agencies. In accordance with the directive, in 1978 the USDA eliminated cost-sharing for wetland drainage and officially limited the technical drainage expertise SCS engineers could furnish. In 1979, the Fish and Wildlife Service also helped the SCS to write new guidelines for "channel modification," and in 1982, the SCS finally issued a formal policy to implement the Executive Order.

Despite changes in policy, SCS-fostered drainage continued in the field. Although engineers could no longer offer assistance for draining wetlands per se, they could still help farmers to drain existing cropland more thoroughly. Moreover, the USDA still offered cost-sharing and technical assistance for soil conservation practices such as land leveling and terracing that often changed natural hydrology and incidentally drained wetlands. In many places, SCS agents disregarded the newly developed guidelines altogether and perpetuated the status quo.[58] The broad latitude given to agents carrying out the new policy undermined national efforts to protect wetlands nestled amid agricultural lands.

Although attitudes and policies concerning wetlands were changing in the national arena, government agencies did not readily change their ways to reflect the new values. However, with its environmental impact statement requirement, NEPA gave citizen groups and states a strong tool to influence federal projects that damaged wetlands and ultimately forced the Army Corps of Engineers, the Soil Conservation Service, and even the Congress into a grand-scale education about the environment. By deliberately weighing the long-term effects of their projects, the federal agencies learned they could no longer disregard the values of wetlands.

Yet despite growing recognition of wetland values within the agencies, federally sanctioned wetland destruction continued, impelled by an insidious momentum to keep on draining, dredging, damming, and developing and inspired by traditional attitudes that still held wetlands to be wastelands. To change this deep-rooted inertia, the nation needed more tools for reform.

THIRTEEN

With New Tools in Hand

It has been said that every Congressman has become an ecologist overnight, though few could have defined the word a year ago.

—Philip Wylie, *New York Times* (1970)[1]

At the same time that citizen activists urged the Corps of Engineers and the Soil Conservation Service to quiet their bulldozers, the U.S. Congress also greened up. In addition to the National Environmental Policy Act, law-makers passed several other laws that promoted wetlands conservation in the early 1970s, including the Federal Water Pollution Control Act of 1972 (commonly known as the Clean Water Act), the Coastal Zone Management Act, the Flood Disaster Protection Act, and the Endangered Species Act. In the past, the federal government had restricted its wetland conservation efforts to encouraging cooperation between construction and wildlife agencies, limiting financial aid for drainage, and purchasing wetlands for habitat. The new federal laws relied on a variety of strategies, such as planning and incentives, but most notably included a new approach: direct regulation. As the loss of wetlands became more grave and political support to protect them grew, Congress responded with stronger national laws.

These laws, together with new information and professional scientists and environmental specialists hired in both state and federal governments, enabled wetlands conservation to blossom. Because thorough enforcement of the new laws proved nearly impossible for the understaffed and, in some cases, uncommitted federal agencies, litigation became an increasingly common way to tackle environmental problems. In fact, the very structure of our nation's environmental protection program came to rely on the legal action of watchdog citizen groups pushing agencies to enforce regulations properly. Nowhere was this influence more evident than in the implementation of the Clean Water Act.

The Epic of 404

Within the broad legislation of the Clean Water Act, Section 404 became the provision that most explicitly governed wetlands. Although Congress gave the new Environmental Protection Agency authority to supervise most aspects of the law, it reserved Section 404 for the Army Corps of Engineers. While it may seem puzzling that Congress gave the bulldozing Corps the primary responsibility to oversee the nation's wetlands, the rationale in part stems from the Corps's long-standing history of regulating discharges in the nation's rivers.

In addition to building dams and levees, the Corps of Engineers had overseen navigational routes for seventy years. With the authority of the Rivers and Harbors Act of 1899, the Corps used a permit system to regulate dredging, filling, construction, and dumping that could block barge and boat traffic. Although the Corps had traditionally restricted its purview to navigation, when environmental quality became a priority in the 1960s, some engineers were receptive to considering such concerns in their permitting process.

This receptivity became official policy in 1967 when the secretaries of the army and the interior signed a Memorandum of Agreement that gave the Fish and Wildlife Service an opportunity to review proposed dredge and fill permits. Recognizing the importance of public support to its work, the Corps's regulatory branch also instituted its own review procedure to evaluate effects on "fish and wildlife, conservation, pollution, aesthetics, ecology, and the general public interest."[2] By conducting "public interest reviews," the Corps could better incorporate recommendations from natural resource agencies, environmentalists, and other citizens.

The Corps's new intentions were soon tested when two developers in Florida's Boca Ciega Bay planned to dredge and fill eleven acres of their tidal wetland property to build a commercial trailer park. Such projects had been commonplace. After gaining necessary state and local permits, the developers, Alfred Zabel and David Russell, sought the necessary Corps dredge and fill permits. At the same time, about seven hundred citizens, several state agencies, and the Fish and Wildlife Service wrote letters to the Corps opposing the trailer park project. Relying on recent scientific studies, they argued that dredging and filling the tidal wetlands would destroy a valuable fishery. As a result, in 1967 the Corps's district engineer, Colonel R. P. Tabb, decided that though trailer park construction would not affect navigation, siltation caused by dredging and filling would severely harm the bay's marine life. Acting in the public interest, Tabb denied the permit. Although the developers sued the Corps and initially won their case, the U.S. Court of Appeals for the Fifth Circuit reversed the first ruling and affirmed that the Corps had complete authority to refuse the permit on environmental grounds. The court cited the Fish and Wildlife Coordination Act and buttressed its decision by applying the intention of NEPA retroactively to the case. Both laws, according to the court, required federal agencies to consider "a government-wide policy of environmental conservation."[3] Thus the case *Zabel v. Tabb* established a precedent that the Corps could use its age-old discharge permitting authority to help protect water quality and wetlands.

While the Corps of Engineers tested this new role, the quality of the nation's waters had deteriorated to an inadmissible state. Blazing with chemical fires, the Cuyahoga River made the headlines in 1969, and more and more signs warned swimmers away from public beaches. Egregious water quality could no longer be ignored. Although several states had tried to cope with pollution, their efforts were frustrated by the lack of controls in neighboring states. Water pollution moves, of course, like water—without respect for political boundary lines. In this context of state failure, Congress and the Nixon administration began to view the Corps's existing Rivers and Harbors Act permit program as a ready federal vehicle to control all sorts of water pollution. As the issue reached its zenith, Maine's Senator Edmund Muskie championed strong national standards and regulations to protect waterways from pollution. Having seen the rivers and fisheries of his state spoiled unmercifully by industries, Muskie pushed the Federal Water Pollution Control Act of 1972 through Congress—even after a veto by President Richard Nixon, who thought the law cost too much.[4]

Rather than rely on the existing Corps permit program, the new law vested authority for regulating water quality with the new Environmental Protection Agency (EPA). But after considering a series of amendments, Congress decided that the Corps should retain its traditional jurisdiction over dredge and fill of waterways for navigation.[5]

This particular aspect of the legislation, Section 404, was interpreted in very different—in fact, diametrically opposed—ways. Most Corps engineers, along with the development and dredging industries, regarded Section 404 as an exemption from EPA's new authority over water quality. Because the Corps routinely dredged to maintain the navigability of waterways, it made sense to old-guard engineers that this work be freed from EPA oversight. Furthermore, developers and dredgers preferred to continue working with the Corps rather than the EPA when they needed permits for land development or filling near or in waterways.

Robert Losch, an attorney who worked on drafting Section 404 in 1972, later reflected, "At the time, there was no idea at all about wetlands, they weren't even discussed." Losch, who had represented, among others, the National Association of Dredging Contractors, recalled that he and other supporters of Section 404 had only two intentions in mind: "To see to it that the Corps of Engineers retained permit authority for dredging rather than have it go over to EPA, and to provide for the regulation of open-water disposal of dredged materials, including the designation of special confined, or diked, disposal areas."[6] Victor V. Vesey, assistant secretary of the army for civil works, similarly explained, "Section 404 was intended as a 'carve out' to keep alive the dredge permit program being run by the Corps under Section 10 of the Rivers and Harbors Act of 1899."[7] Although Congress directed the EPA to provide guidelines for issuing permits and gave it the authority to veto Corps decisions, the new agency had a very small staff to oversee rapidly increasing responsibilities. To the dredging and development establishments and the Corps, Section 404 seemed to be a deliberate loophole that allowed dredging and filling along navigable rivers to proceed as usual.[8]

But those sitting across the table understood Section 404 in an entirely different manner. Although dredge spoils had long been considered just dirt, scientists had recently discovered that they often contained toxic pollutants, such as lead, arsenic, and DDT. Even more important, scientists had learned that dumping spoils physically smothered and destroyed critical aquatic and wetland ecosystems.[9] As a result, the EPA and environmental groups saw Section 404 as a way for the Corps of Engineers to use its proven talents to protect water quality and wetlands from indiscriminate spoil dumping. By the early 1970s, it became clearer to scientists that wetlands played integral roles both in the hydrologic cycle and in maintaining water quality. Protecting rivers from pollution depended on a broad definition of waterways; otherwise, pollutants discharged into unregulated portions of a hydrological system would quickly contaminate the regulated areas. On the floor of the House just prior to the vote that approved the Clean Water Act, Congressman John Dingell (D-MI) clarified that the broad definition encompassed "all water bodies, including mainstreams and their tributaries, for water quality purposes. No longer are the old narrow definitions of navigability, as determined by the Corps of Engineers," he declared, "going to govern matters covered by this bill." As such, environmentalists believed that Congress intended "navigable waters" in the Clean Water Act to be interpreted in the broadest manner possible and to include small streams, riparian and tidal wetlands, and all water bodies hydrologically connected to traditionally navigable waterways.[10]

Although environmental groups remained suspicious about giving the Corps what they saw as a formidable role in protecting the nation's wetlands—Senator Muskie once referred to it as putting a fox in charge of a chicken coop—many conservation leaders respected the Corps's technical and scientific expertise and its reputation for carrying out tasks expeditiously.[11] Furthermore, because Congress gave the Corps and the EPA shared responsibilities with Section 404, and made the Fish and Wildlife Service and the National Marine Fisheries Service consultants, the Corps could take advantage of new ecological expertise that it hadn't used much before. Through a brief editorial in its magazine, the National Audubon Society advised its members to support the new program: "We must, in short, become an influential part of the constituency of the U.S. Army Corps of Engineers if we expect the Corps to serve our broader interests. In the past, only developers, inland waterway promoters, and other business interests comprised this constituency."[12] But what seemed like a new opportunity for cooperation between conservationists and the Corps soon backfired.

While the EPA, the Department of the Interior, and environmental groups believed that any attempt to control pollution in the nation's waters would have to control pollution in the nation's wetlands, the Corps saw wetlands differently. In line with their long-standing constituents, Corps engineers regarded wetlands as potentially developable land, despite their clearly wet nature. That any private lands, even private potential lands to be created by filling, could be regulated by federal laws seemed an unjust and erroneous reach to old-guard engineers.

Despite the Corps's readiness to regulate on environmental grounds in the *Zabel v. Tabb* case and its willingness to comply with NEPA regulations on numerous structural projects, it responded to Section 404 responsibilities with a more traditional attitude.[13] Objecting to broadened jurisdiction, the Corps relied on the ambiguity of the law to avoid doing anything new. When the agency finally released regulations in April 1974, it became clear that initial skepticism about the Corps's commitment to wetlands had been on target: the regulations applied only to the narrowly defined navigable waterways that the Corps had always overseen.

Indignant environmental groups filed a lawsuit. Contending that the regulations violated the intention of the Clean Water Act, the National Resources Defense Council and the National Wildlife Federation demanded the Corps take its new responsibilities seriously and promulgate regulations accordingly. In the landmark case, *NRDC v. Callaway*, Judge Aubrey Robinson decided in favor of the environmental groups. Robinson explained that Congress had clearly asserted that the "navigable waters" referred to in Section 404 of the Clean Water Act meant *all* the waters of the United States, including territorial seas, rivers, and adjacent wetlands—in sum, all bodies of water having an influence on interstate commerce as defined by the Commerce Clause of the Constitution—not just the traditionally defined navigable waterways. Judge Robinson ruled that the engineers had acted "unlawfully and in derogation of their responsibilities under Section 404" and advised the agency to revise and expand its regulations. The lawsuit prodded the Corps to consult with the EPA and prepare more appropriate rules.[14]

Although the Corps complied with Judge Robinson's ruling, most agency leaders disagreed with the decision. They regarded extending their jurisdiction to all U.S. waters as a mistaken expansion of federal land-use control. More important, the new regulatory role mandated by the court ran against the grain of the Corps culture, against what most engineers believed the Corps's very purpose to be: the promotion of economic development. Expanding the agency's regulatory role turned the respected engineers into "police," who would have to dampen down the projects they had always supported enthusiastically. The Corps leadership prepared an appeal to contest Robinson's order, but the Department of Justice advised them against filing it. Frustrated by a lack of guidance from the Ford administration on how to proceed, Corps officials realized that their only recourse would be political.[15]

The Corps delayed its implementation of Section 404 by publishing four alternative sets of regulations for public comment on May 6, 1975. To ignite public outrage at its broadened jurisdiction, General Kenneth McIntyre, who was responsible for implementing the 404 program, decided to issue an inflammatory press release along with the regulatory alternatives. McIntyre and his staff reasoned that if the public better understood the implications of a broader Section 404, they would support the weakest regulations. To accomplish his goal, McIntyre directed the Public Affairs Office to develop the news release. The final draft contained many exaggerations specifically designed to produce an angry public response. For example, it cautioned that "Federal permits may be required by the rancher who wants to enlarge his stock pond, or the farmer who wants to deepen an irrigation ditch or plow a field, or the mountaineer who wants to protect his land against stream erosion." The release then warned that "millions of people may be presently violating the law" and that they would be subject to fines of up to $25,000 a day, plus a year of imprisonment, and would be required to remove any fill materials they had placed without a permit.[16] Just as McIntyre had planned, newspapers across the country picked up the incendiary press release.

In its report, the *New York Times* depicted the regulatory alternatives as a brash attempt by the Corps to expand its jurisdiction. Similar stories across the nation unleashed a flood of public opposition to the Corps's extreme regulations, including intense criticism from forest and agriculture interests. Even Secretary of Agriculture Earl Butz railed against the Corps's new authorities in letters to congressional leaders warning against injecting "the federal presence in land use control and planning."[17] A USDA news release further fueled public fears by declaring the Corps's regulations to be "like the legendary Hydra—you cut off one head and two grow back in its place."[18]

But flames burned in the other direction as well. The press release incited harsh criticism from national environmental groups, who aptly recognized it as a deliberate attempt to stir opposition to the Corps's new court-ordered regulatory role. The NRDC issued its own dispatch to illuminate the Corps's true intentions. "With the outrageous threat that they are going to strictly police the plowing of fields and construction of farm ponds across the nation," the letter warned, "Corps officials are attempting to incite an uninformed backlash from citizens to help the Corps escape the environmental responsibilities Congress has given it."[19] Environmental groups demanded that the Corps call off its scare campaign and clarify the matter for the public. The NRDC began its own massive public information campaign. What had once looked like a promising chance for cooperation between conservationists and the Corps of Engineers dissolved. According to Corps regulatory specialist William Hedeman, when the press release hit the newsstands, "the relationship between the Corps and the environmental groups hit its all-time low."[20]

Beyond criticism from environmentalists, the Corps's antics were criticized by Congress and EPA Administrator Russell Train as well, prompting Assistant Secretary of the Army for Civil Works Victor Vesey to apologize for the "unfortunate" and "misleading" press release.[21]

After reviewing the numerous public comments and consulting with the EPA, the Corps issued revised regulations in July of 1975. This time around, the highest agency officials participated directly to ensure close cooperation between the Corps and the EPA. When Chief of Engineers Lieutenant General William Gribble heard reports of reluctance to adopt the new regulations among field personnel, he sent a memorandum to division engineers requesting "continued personal effort to assure that members of the Corps avoid being drawn into discussions which may lead to misunderstanding or the impression that we do not support our own regulations."[22] Though the Corps's Section 404 responsibilities were rooted in its age-old Rivers and Harbors Act authority, through political process and judicial interpretation, its wetland-protective role evolved.

According to historian Jeffrey K. Stine, who has thoroughly researched this episode, watchdog environmental groups played a critical role in finally compelling the Corps of Engineers to accept its part in regulating wetlands. After adopting the 1975 regulations, the Corps approached its Section 404 responsibilities with greater resolve.[23] However, adopting regulations and enforcing them are two different matters.

To the Test

The real litmus test of the Corps's commitment to Section 404 came when the Deltona Corporation requested a permit to develop a new resort community in the mangrove swamps of the 8,000-acre Marco Island, just off the southwest coast of Florida. Deltona, one of Florida's largest and most well-respected land-development firms, had planned to create thousands of waterfront lots by dredging and filling the mangroves into finger canals. Such dredge-and-fill development had become common in the coastal areas of Florida, Texas, New Jersey, New York, and California.[24] Deltona first started transforming mangrove swamps into a resort—with the necessary Corps-approved dredge-and-fill permit—in the Marco River area in 1964. Five years later, the Corps had reluctantly issued a permit for the next phase of development over objections of the Fish and Wildlife Service. Because attitudes toward wetlands were changing in the political arena, Corps officials dutifully warned Deltona that issuance of the first two

MAKING FINGER CANALS AT MARCO ISLAND, FLORIDA.
The Corps of Engineers commitment to protecting wetlands as sanctioned by Section 404 the Clean Water Act was tested at Marco Island. In the 1960s, Deltona Corporation had dredged and filled mangrove swamps to develop finger canal resort homes on Marco Island. But by the early 1970s, scientists had learned about the role of mangroves as nursery grounds for fish and shrimp, and wetland-protective laws had come into effect. The Corps ultimately decided that more dredging and filling at Marco Island would be detrimental and declined to issue a permit. (Courtesy Corps of Engineers, Jacksonville District)

permits could not guarantee future approval. Deltona, however, continued to sell lots in the unpermitted portions of the development and actually began to dredge and fill Collier Bay.

When Corps engineers discovered the unpermitted work in 1971, they issued a stop order. Deltona soon applied for the necessary state permits to develop its final 2,200 acres of Marco Island wetlands, and then in March of 1973 the company applied for the necessary federal permits to dredge and fill the Collier Bay, Barfield Bay, and Big Key areas of the island. Without securing the permits, Deltona had already sold 70 percent of the lots in the unpermitted areas—most were still mangrove clumps.

As Corps officials had thought possible, attitudes toward wetlands did sharply change after Deltona applied for its initial permits. In the intervening decade, the Corps had adopted its public interest review; scientists had documented the importance of mangroves to fishing productivity; citizen awareness about wetland values had grown; and Congress had passed NEPA and given the Corps new regulatory responsibilities with Section 404 of the Clean Water Act.[25]

With a name well suited to the difficult task ahead, Colonel Donald Wisdom, the Jacksonville district engineer, held the job of considering Deltona's permit request. Determined to make a fair decision, Wisdom visited the site and attended public hearings. He reviewed technical reports prepared by his staff, lengthy documents submitted by Deltona, reports of construction unions and the Department of Labor, and recommendations against granting the permits filed by the Fish and Wildlife Service, the EPA, the National Marine Fisheries Service, and environmental organizations. After evaluating the mountain of information, Wisdom decided to issue a permit for the work already begun at Collier Bay, but to deny the other permits, which he believed ran counter to the public interest. In October 1975, when Wisdom sent his recommendation to the South Atlantic division engineer, it was overturned. Because Deltona stood to lose millions of dollars, the division engineer thought that not granting the permits would be tantamount to taking private property. The division engineer sent his decision to the Office of the Chief Engineer in Washington, D.C., where the mammoth controversy surrounding the regulatory jurisdiction of the Corps stormed.[26]

In Washington, it became evident that the Deltona permit decision was not just about the mangrove swamps of Marco Island. The decision would more significantly reveal just how committed the Corps of Engineers was to its new Section 404 responsibilities and to protecting water and wetland quality nationwide. The chief of engineers, Lieutenant General William C. Gribble, would have to resolve the critical policy question.

The decision was not an easy one. Gribble's personal disposition reflected the Corps of Engineers' culture; he simply detested the idea of telling a developer not to build. Gribble assigned two top-level staff members to help work on the case. They prepared arguments both for and against granting the permits. Gribble devoured all the information presented to him, including detailed technical reports and a voluminous environmental impact statement. Finally, based on the Corps's responsibilities for protecting national public interest, Gribble announced his final verdict on April 15, 1976: He agreed with Colonel Wisdom's initial decision.[27]

The Corps received accolades from environmental groups, the EPA, and the president's Council on Environmental Quality. CEQ Chairman Russell Peterson commended Gribble's judgment: "The wetlands of this nation . . . were served well by this difficult and well-reasoned decision. . . ."[28] But developers were stunned. Deltona's president Frank Mackle summed up the attitude: "I still can't get over it. The Corps—they've been like us. They're engineers, our kind of people."[29] Deltona appealed, but the court held up the Corps decision. Deltona was partially compensated by exchanging mangrove parcels on Marco Island with less sensitive lands located elsewhere.[30]

Gribble's decision, upheld by the court, sent a resounding message through the hallways of Corps offices nationwide that the new 404 regulations would be applied with more than lip service. Made in the face of prodevelopment political pressures, the Deltona permit decision gave the Corps greater credibility by diminishing its long-held reputation as a pliable bedfellow of development interests.[31]

The controversies surrounding both the *NRDC v. Callaway* case and the Marco Island decision sparked enormous debate in Congress in 1975 and 1976. Should Section 404 apply only to navigational waters or to all waters of the United States, including wetlands? One bill passed by the House would have completely eliminated the Corps's new jurisdiction, but another in the Senate kept the Corps's authority over wetlands intact. Since 1972, the science of hydrology had advanced considerably and better substantiated the aqueous connections between rivers, wetlands, and aquifers. Moreover, owing to educational efforts by scientists, concerned federal agencies, and environmental groups, lawmakers better understood the reasons for protecting wetlands.[32] Eventually, Congress agreed on a set of amendments to reauthorize the Clean Water Act. They replaced the term "navigable waters" with "waters of the United States" and then defined those waters to include "adjacent wetlands" and "isolated wetlands lakes . . . prairie potholes, and other waters . . . the degradation of which could affect interstate commerce."[33] President Jimmy Carter signed the new law in December 1977. Most significant, these amendments confirmed that the Corps's jurisdiction over the nation's waters specifically included wetlands.[34]

While the new legislation clarified the Corps's legal responsibility for wetlands, it nonetheless watered down some provisions that had been included in the 1972 law. In response to the scare generated by the Corps's disingenuous press release, for example, congressional amendments included explicit exemptions for "normal farming, silviculture, and ranching activities."[35] Furthermore, Congress approved a streamlined "general" permitting program developed by the Corps regulatory staff to deal with its new workload.[36] Critics, however, identified general permits as yet another way for the Corps to avoid taking on its full regulatory responsibilities. The 1977 amendments also exempted all federal projects, which were subject to NEPA requirements, and enabled states with approved water-quality programs to assume authority for Section 404 permitting.[37]

Despite the clarification of congressional intent to protect wetlands in the 1977 Clean Water Act amendments, the EPA and the Corps continued to lock horns over the unresolved details of Section 404 jurisdiction. As a result, the law was poorly enforced, and wetlands continued to be filled. Between 1977 and 1980, of 76,000 dredge-and-fill permit applications, many received general permits, and the Corps denied only 960—less than 1.3 percent.[38] In an effort to untangle conflicting interpretations, the secretary of the army formally requested the attorney general's opinion about which agency had the final authority to interpret the scope of jurisdiction under Section 404. In September 1979, Attorney General Benjamin Civiletti concluded that the EPA had the ultimate authority over all jurisdictional questions pertaining to the Clean Water Act. The following year, emboldened by Civiletti's opinion, the EPA revised its permitting guidelines to include a specific presumption against altering wetlands for developments that could just as easily be built elsewhere. Then after restructuring and enlarging its regulatory staff, the agency geared up to assume a more stringent enforcement posture, making it clear that EPA guidelines were not advisory but mandatory.[39] Although the Corps would still handle the day-to-day work of approving and denying permits, they were unequivocally bound to do so under EPA oversight. Nearly eight years after enactment of the Clean Water

Act, the regulations and jurisdictions were finally hashed out, and the protection of wetlands was clearly affirmed as a national priority. But this clarity would not last long.

Along the Rivers and Seashores

Though Section 404 of the Clean Water Act purportedly protected wetlands from damage by dredge-and-fill operations, even with the broadest interpretation of jurisdiction, a large portion of the nation's wetlands fell outside the Corps's authority. Construction of flood-control dams through the 1960s and 1970s had encouraged extensive homebuilding on downstream floodplains. Because dams increased the value of undeveloped floodplains, landowners and developers pressed the federal government to build more. In fact, much of the justification for building dams was safeguarding floodplains for speculative development.[40] Although low-lying lands along rivers shared many characteristics and functions of wetlands, such as absorbing floodwaters, maintaining water quality, and providing critical habitat, they were generally saturated at lower frequencies than wetlands and so did not readily meet the technical criteria for protection under the Clean Water Act. Yet many true wetlands lay embedded within these important riparian zones.

It was not so much concern for ecological values, but rather concern for the federal pocketbook that directed the attention of lawmakers to floodplains. Despite $12 billion in public expenditures for flood-control projects built by both the Corps and the SCS, annual losses from floods had increased to an estimated $1 billion in 1958, to $2 billion in 1972, and then to a staggering $3.8 billion in 1973.[41] As more and more structures encroached upon floodplains, more and more flood damage occurred, and more and more demands for disaster relief besieged the treasury. In the course of this dangerous and costly cycle, the water-retaining qualities of floodplain wetlands were entombed under fill and concrete, worsening the effects of floods.

In 1968, Congress had tried to plug the endless drain on federal funds by creating a federal flood insurance program to provide subsidized insurance for people who already owned homes built on floodplains, but only on the condition that local governments institute zoning to prevent further floodplain development. The voluntary program found few takers. Four years later, when Hurricane Agnes struck the eastern seaboard, only a handful of communities had obtained federal insurance. Still more relief requests deluged Washington, and Congress once again used tax dollars to bail out private landowners who had chosen to risk building on floodplains.[42]

To make the incentive for floodplain zoning stronger, in 1973 Congress banned the federal insurance of mortgages in all communities that did not sign up for its floodplain insurance program. Because all banks required such insurance, realtors, bankers, and developers pressured local governments to adopt floodplain zoning. Although thousands of towns and cities participated in the program to some degree, the effectiveness of the regulations remained questionable—especially where there were strong development pressures. Inadequate funding made it impossible for the Federal Insurance Administration to map the hazard zones in a timely manner. Furthermore, the Federal Emergency Management Agency (FEMA) did not have the staff to provide technical assistance, let alone to enforce regulations. As a result, some communities incorrectly administered their floodplain ordinances.[43] In other cases, towns adopted floodplain zoning policies on paper but readily issued exemptions. For example, in 1981, the federal government filed suit against several land developers in St. Bernard and Jefferson parishes (the equivalent of counties) in Louisiana, demanding over $93 million compensation for insurance moneys paid out to property owners for flood damages in 1978 and 1980. The developers had failed to meet requirements for substantial improvements to existing structures and for new construction. Moreover, the parishes had approved new construction in flood-prone areas where drainage systems were known to be inadequate.[44] With a lack of proper maps, technical support, enforcement, and oversight, the federal flood insurance program afforded little new protection for riparian wetlands except in places where conscientious planners fully understood the repercussions of reckless floodplain development.

Although the insurance program's sensible economic incentives pushed many local governments to develop zoning ordinances, in Washington, D.C., the powerful developers' and home builders' lobby pushed FEMA to dilute its general guidelines for building in floodplain areas.[45] As a result, structures could be approved if they were "flood-proofed"—built, for example, on stilts, fill, or behind protective levees. Many critics contended that these guidelines actually encouraged more floodplain development than they prevented. Furthermore, the federally subsidized insurance enabled people who lost their homes in flood disasters to rebuild on the same flood-prone lots. While the local zoning encouraged by the federal flood insurance program extended protection to many riparian wetlands in floodways, it barely restrained rampant floodplain development. By the late 1970s, an estimated 3.5 to 5.5 million acres of floodplain land had been developed, including more than six thousand towns with populations over twenty-five hundred.[46] Because federal policies were oriented exclusively toward minimizing flood damages and not toward preserving the natural functions of floodplain wetlands, still many more wetland-damaging structures were built on floodplains.[47]

Development pressures struck coastal areas even harder, gobbling up seashores and wetlands in their wake. By 1964, one-quarter of the nation's salt marshes had been destroyed.[48] Wetland and shoreline losses generated new concern for the coasts. In particular, citizens began to worry about diminishing access to beaches. A 1962 study by the Outdoor Recreation Resources Review Commission reported that of the twenty-one thousand miles of recreational shorelines of the Great Lakes and the oceans, only 5 to 7 percent were in public ownership and dedicated to recreational use. Furthermore, the new residential areas that swallowed up beachfronts were also vulnerable to extreme damage from dangerous hurricanes and tropical storms. The cost of disaster relief required to repair those unsafe developments was often shouldered by taxpayers. Widespread interest in beach access and in reducing costly, unsafe development prompted more serious consideration of coastal planning.[49]

Coastal planning also intrigued those who wished to exploit ocean resources more rigorously. In 1966, with the Marine Resources Act, Congress authorized the Stratton Commission to investigate the untapped and unknown potential of ocean and coastal resources. Foremost, the commission recommended better joint management by state and federal governments to encourage proper planning and to stimulate more use.[50]

Beyond recreation and resource development, the ecological studies that had pushed states to consider their coastal wetland resources more carefully finally encouraged Congress to launch its own study of the nation's estuaries. More propitious in name than in fact, the National Estuarine Protection Act of 1968 directed the Fish and Wildlife Service to survey the nation's estuaries and to devise a plan to protect and restore important ecological and economic values of those areas.[51] In 1969, a massive oil spill off the coast of Santa Barbara, California, called further attention to ecological threats facing shorelines.

These varied recreation, development, and conservation interests spurred the introduction of dozens of coastal-planning bills in Congress, some prodevelopment, some favoring environmental protection. In 1972, Congress finally approved a law that fell somewhere in between: the Coastal Zone Management Act (CZMA).[52]

A landmark planning law, the CZMA offered federal funding for states to design coastal management plans that balanced competing shoreline interests. State plans were supposed to protect natural resources, to discourage development in hazard-prone areas, to provide more access to beaches and the ocean, and to increase cooperation among the government agencies overseeing coastal resources. Once a plan gained approval from the national Office of Coastal Zone Management in the new National Oceanic and Atmospheric Administration (NOAA), the state had full authority to implement it.[53] Although protection of natural resources was one of its primary objectives, the law had no particular environmental prescriptions. Instead, the CZMA operated on the presumption that proper planning would allow states to consider both conservation and development and decide on the best balance.

The coastal zone management plans that resulted were a mixed bag for wetlands. In at least eight states, legislatures enacted new wetlands legislation and regulations in response to CZMA requirements. The CZMA also promoted improved enforcement of the existing state wetland laws and spawned new state agencies devoted to coastal issues. But in many other states, the coastal zone management plans were strident blueprints for development that offered little wetland protection.[54] In the state of Washington, for example, the first estuary management plan for Grays Harbor, touted primarily by the Port of Grays Harbor, proposed filling extensive mudflat and wetland portions of the bay to create a new industrial park.[55] Yet, even where planning showed little attention to wetland conservation, the CZMA procedures opened up new doors for citizen involvement. In the case of the Grays Harbor plan, the Fish and Wildlife Service and local citizen groups protested and eventually managed to protect 400 acres of wetlands in the Bowerman Basin area.[56] Although the CZMA articulated distinct federal concern for protecting estuaries, in many locales heed for natural resources receded like the tides. Many states viewed the law primarily as a neutral planning and procedural directive.[57]

Endangered Species Need Wetlands

Construction of homes, shopping centers, and roads had torn apart riparian and coastal lands, displacing wildlife at an unprecedented pace. In some places, habitat loss was so extreme that species were pushed to the brink of extinction. To counter this problem, Congress passed the Endangered Species Act (ESA) in 1973. Although prior federal laws had identified "endangered" species, protected them on federal lands, and banned their sale in international markets, these steps had not stemmed the destruction of habitat or the decline of species. In January 1973, Representative John Dingell, (D-MI), with the support of the Nixon administration, introduced a new version of the law that more specifically addressed habitat loss. Under the proposed law, the Fish and Wildlife Service and the Marine Fisheries Service would develop recovery plans for endangered species designed to identify and safeguard critical habitat. In addition, the law directed federal agencies to make sure their own work did not harm endangered species or destroy necessary habitat. The popular bill passed the House by a vote of 390 to 12, and the Senate unanimously passed a similar bill.[58] When he signed the act in December 1973, President Richard Nixon agreed, "Nothing is more priceless . . . than the rich array of animal life with which our country has been blessed. . . ."[59]

One of the first endangered species helped by endangered species laws was the American alligator, threatened primarily by overhunting for its attractive hide. Listed under the first incarnation of the ESA in 1967, the elimination of hunting was all that the alligator needed to repopulate its swampy range. By the mid 1980s, more than a million alligators inhabited wetlands in the Southeast, and limited hunting had resumed.[60] For most species, however, the path to recovery proved more rocky because human developments had permanently encroached on critical habitat.

For example, intense development of marshes in the San Francisco Bay had fragmented habitat essential for the salt marsh harvest mouse and the California clapper rail. With its recovery plans for these species, the FWS identified critical wetlands to be protected through federal management or outright purchase. Over the course of many years, the FWS, the National Audubon Society, the state Department of Fish and Game, and other local organizations worked to acquire suitable tracts of marsh habitat for protection. But in the meantime, other important habitat was lost.[61]

In another case, the FWS in 1983 listed two species of endangered fish endemic only to Ash Meadows, a desert wetland straddling the Nevada–California border. Much of the critical habitat area was privately owned and slated for a residential complex. Although the ESA listing did not specifically preclude the development, it would have required the landowner to modify his plans in order to protect the fish. But the regulatory approach was not necessary; instead, the FWS, with the help of The Nature Conservancy, purchased the land outright for a national wildlife refuge.[62]

In addition to developing recovery plans and acquiring habitat, the FWS advised federal agencies on how to avoid disrupting the habitat of endangered species in their project plans.[63] The FWS, for example, advised the Federal Aviation Administration in 1978 to realign a runway at its jetport near Miami to protect the only remaining 160 Everglades kites.[64] Also in the Southeast, fluctuating water levels caused by the U.S. Department of Energy's Savannah River nuclear power plant rendered existing habitat unusable. The FWS advised the department to enhance alternate wood stork habitat when the bird was listed as endangered in 1984.[65] Although protections of this type occurred, of about fifty thousand federal projects undertaken between 1976 and 1986 with endangered species implications, only 1 percent were found to have a serious impact on a species, and even most of those proceeded with minor changes.[66]

As an additional benefit to wetlands, the ESA influenced the Corps of Engineers' decisions to grant permits for dredging and filling under Section 404 of the Clean Water Act. If a permit applicant's wetland hosted an endangered species, the Corps required that project plans be altered to accommodate the species' habitat needs. But regardless of regulations and constraints, loopholes routinely enabled development to occur. In the San Francisco Bay, for example, some developers plowed land to remove wetland indicator plants so the Corps would grant their permits.[67]

As with other laws, environmentalists soon found they had to litigate to compel government agencies to follow the habitat provisions of the ESA. In 1975, for example, the National Wildlife Federation sued to stop the construction of a highway interchange on Interstate 10 near Jackson, Mississippi, because it threatened critical roosting grounds of the last forty Mississippi sandhill cranes. Although the NWF lost, a favorable decision in appeals court prevented the most harmful aspects of construction.[68]

Despite its successes, the ESA could not keep up with ongoing losses of habitat. Before long, scientists would find that half of all animals and a third of all plants listed as endangered depended on wetlands.[69] As such, wetlands served an essential public role in protecting biodiversity—the genetic storehouse provided by the wealth of different species adapted to a variety of habitats. So many species were imperiled that, rather than focus on individual species, the only way to preserve the commons of biodiversity would be to protect larger blocks of habitat, including wetlands.

With NEPA, the Clean Water Act, the Endangered Species Act, and other environmental laws of the early 1970s, the focus of wetland protection moved from the realm of citizen activism to the desks of government scientists and managers. Responding to public needs, the professions of wetland science and wetland management grew. By 1977, the first large wetlands conference, the National Wetlands Symposium, drew together seven hundred people, including scientists, managers, and policy analysts. In 1980, the Society of Wetlands Scientists formed. And in 1983, Jon Kusler founded the Association of State Wetland Managers to provide a better nationwide forum for communication among those who worked on wetlands issues at the state level.[70] With mandates to protect wetlands in place, these managers and specialists struggled with limited staffs and budgets to reverse centuries-old trends of wetland destruction. The pressure to protect wetlands grew, but in the sharpened public forum of land use and public responsibility, the seeds of a vehement backlash were sown.

The National Wetlands Inventory

Working to meet obligations of the long-standing international migratory bird treaties, the Fish and Wildlife Service had continued to protect waterfowl habitat through its Small Wetland Acquisition Program and its refuges. But in the early 1970s, broad habitat losses compelled the agency to take a fresh look at the state of wetlands. In 1974, the FWS instituted a new survey to assess sweeping changes in all the wetlandscape. The idea for the inventory had come from within the ranks of the service's field biologists; they recognized firsthand the need for newer information than could be found in the twenty-year-old Shaw and Fredine Circular 39. (See chapter 10.)

The project of the National Wetlands Inventory (NWI) fell onto the shoulders of John Montanari, a geologist who had inventoried wetlands for several states. From the outset, Montanari sought input from government agencies and interest groups about their needs for wetland information. Larry Jahn of the Wildlife Management Institute, for example, recommended developing maps to show the specific locations of wetlands. But before any inventory or mapping work could begin, a method for classifying wetlands had to be agreed upon. Fish and Wildlife Service and SCS personnel had a strong attachment to the familiar Shaw and Fredine classification system, but Montanari and other scientists realized that it was too general and led to inconsistent application in the field. A new system was needed.

Montanari joined with Lew Cowardin and thirteen other wetlands experts from around the country to hash out the specifics of a new classification scheme. On Superbowl Sunday in 1975, instead of indulging in the game, the scientists sequestered themselves at a research center in Slidell, Mississippi. Excited by the challenging task at hand, they shared slides of wetlands from Alaska to Florida and scrawled pages of notes on yellow legal pads. After a week of collective brainstorming, they emerged with an outline, and Cowardin together with Virginia Carter and Frank Golet volunteered to write a draft report. While the old Shaw and Fredine system had simply identified twenty different wetland types, the new system worked more like a taxonomic key, classifying landscapes by significant ecological traits to make identification more accurate.[71] Despite the cooperative effort, the draft wetland classification system was sharply criticized by state agencies and some old-guard FWS staff at first. What Montanari had expected to develop in six months ended up taking several years, but extensive field testing and input from many different people ultimately made the resulting scheme unimpeachable.

With the foundation of a classification system, the real work of inventorying could begin. In 1976, Montanari hired his first staff member, Bill Wilen, and moved the NWI office to St. Petersburg, Florida, where field testing and training could occur year round. To speed up the grand-scale project, they cleverly planned to convert the latest military point-to-point targeting device into a digital analytical stereoplotter. This tool could accurately capture the boundaries of wetlands in digital format, which could then be converted to maps directly. But the effort took years and thousands of lines of computer code. While technicalities were sorted out, Montanari and Wilen began the inventory with classical cartographic techniques in 1979. Their national office supplied aerial photographs for interpretation to coordinators hired for each region. Wilen later reflected, "When the NWI staff drew the first wetland boundary on the first wetland map, they changed wetlands from a concept to a reality."[72] The maps made the location of wetlands truly tangible for the first time.

Because Montanari had invited other agencies that worked with wetlands, including the SCS, the Corps, the U.S. Geologic Survey, and the EPA, to participate in the planning process, the NWI maps could be used by everyone. When scientists first started the inventory, few federal laws governed wetlands, but by the time the project was up and running, there were many regulations. According to Wilen, who succeeded Montanari as the NWI project leader, one of the most important decisions made early in the planning process was to avoid "tying a value system to the classification system." Because of this, the system could continue to be useful despite changes in regulations and in the ways society valued wetlands.[73] Although Montanari initially intended to produce only 450 coarse-scale maps, it became evident that more detailed wetland maps would be useful in the new regulatory context. In 1981, the inventory staff decided on a new 1:24,000 scale (1 inch = 2,000 feet), requiring a daunting fifty-seven thousand maps. While the maps did not identify the regulatory boundaries of individual wetlands (field delineators identify this line on the ground), they could be used during the early planning phase of most wetland-related projects. In this way, the maps could eliminate confusion for those seeking to develop lands that might be subject to regulation (though the maps had nothing to do with regulations or regulatory definitions per se). Eventually, the NWI would produce inexpensive, readily available blueline maps.[74]

While NWI staff struggled with the technical details of digital mapping, Congress became impatient and wanted to see results. The resource agencies and conservationists also anxiously awaited inventory information, as they were confronted with the Reagan administration's hostility toward wetland regulations. When the NWI finally completed a statistical survey of aerial photographs and determined the losses and gains of wetlands since 1953, Secretary of the Interior James Watt personally brought the astounding findings to Congress in 1982. Our country had lost *54 percent of its wetlands*. Between the mid 1950s and the mid 1970s alone, 458,000 acres of wetlands—an area half the size of Rhode Island—had been whittled away *each year.* Agriculture accounted for 87 percent of those losses.[75]

Recognizing the import of this data, regional coordinator Ralph Tiner saw an opportunity to make the NWI's technical work more useful in the policy arena. To explain the significance of the survey to lawmakers and the general public, he wrote *Wetlands of the United States: Current Status and Recent Trends,* published in 1984.[76] With this easy-to-read, straightforward, illustrated report, the NWI made a big splash.

According to John Montanari, "All of a sudden people had a number they could hang their hats on."[77] The report generated tremendous interest in wetlands and was cited in magazines, journals, and newspapers again and again. The report influenced all wetland policies forged by Congress throughout the decade in much the same way that the 1956 inventory had encouraged passage of state wetland laws and the important Drainage

Referral Act in the 1960s. The new National Wetlands Inventory created a sense of urgency regarding the loss of wetlands, only this time on a broader scale because the scope of wetland protective efforts had grown.

A New Height of Concern

As government agencies began to implement the Clean Water Act, the Coastal Zone Management Act, the Floodplain Insurance Program, the Endangered Species Act, and carry out the National Wetlands Inventory, the number of people working with wetlands grew to a strong and increasingly effective cast. With the new federal laws, the focus of wetlands conservation moved into the realm of national policy and politics.

Reflecting scientific information and a growing ecological ethic, the federal laws articulated a new vision for preserving environmental quality in America. By protecting wetlands from pollution and development, the laws strived to help local communities benefit from cleaner water, fewer floods, less storm damage, open space, and more abundant fish and wildlife.

While the federal laws sought to safeguard wetland values for the benefit of all Americans, they restricted the activities of people who had planned to fill and develop wetlands. Most had purchased swamps and marshes with the belief that they could convert them into more lucrative property, but new laws now stood in their way. Resentment and anger began to fester among those who disliked regulations and who disagreed with the aim of wetlands protection.

By virtue of their very nature, wetlands once again challenged traditional concepts of property. Because the "wet" part of wetlands offered public benefits, the government had become involved to protect common values. Yet the "land" part had traditionally accorded owners the right to do what they wanted. Sooner or later Americans would have to address the apparent conflict between safeguarding environmental quality for society at large and preserving landowners' rights. The wetlands were part land and part water, part private and part public. The future of this enigmatic physical and cultural landscape lay in the delicately shifting balance of public opinion and in the stark exposure of raw political power.

FOURTEEN

The Reagan Agenda Challenges Wetland Gains

Up to now those of us who are concerned with the environment have enjoyed a honeymoon period. It has been . . . relatively easy to generate public support and Congressional support for the goals that we have written into law. Now we are getting into a crunch period, and it is going to be difficult to avoid the pressures of those who would throw away much of what has been accomplished.
—Senator Edmund Muskie[1]

Economic jargon aside, the matter is basic—private, unregulated ownership of wetlands insures their destruction.
—Keith Harmon and Chester McConnell[2]

During the early 1980s drought spread across much of the country, and at the same time the election of Ronald Reagan brought a dramatic change of climate for environmental reform. And wetlands, vulnerable to the sway of administrative policy, lay on the front line of assault.

Voted in to quell an inflationary economy, Reagan regarded his election in 1980 as a mandate to govern by accounting column. "Reaganomics" dictated that "budget was policy," but this tenet applied primarily when it furthered the administration's political agenda. Defense spending soared, and the federal deficit climbed steeper than it ever had, while social and environmental programs were cut in the name of fiscal austerity. In response to industry complaints about federal regulation, President Reagan established a Task Force on Regulatory Reform to dismantle regulations, including those designed to implement hard-won environmental legislation of the prior decade. Because regulations were costly and nettlesome to business, protecting wetlands suddenly became an unaffordable policy, despite the growing knowledge of their values. Interior Secretary James Watt explained the administration's strategy as follows: "We will use the budget

system [as] the excuse to make major policy decisions."[3] Watt's Department of the Interior did just that.

Despite the alarming reports of the National Wetlands Inventory and
other studies documenting the degraded condition of the national wildlife
refuges—often critical wetland habitat—the Department of the Interior decided to expand economic uses of the refuges. In a bluntly worded directive
sent to regional managers in 1982, the deputy director of the Fish and
Wildlife Service explained the new policy: "We believe that there is potential to expand economic uses in such areas as grazing, haying, farming,
timber harvesting, trapping, oil and gas extraction, small hydroelectric generation, concessions, commercial hunting and fishing guides, guided interpretive tours, and commercial fishing. We believe if you use innovation and
creativity and, if necessary, a redirection of effort, these as well as other uses
can be expanded."[4] Although environmentalists warned that many of the
proposed uses were incompatible with the primary function of the refuges
as habitat for waterfowl and wildlife, an administrative report in 1983 identified the potential economic gains to be made: "Assuming that the private
sector would capitalize fully on the economic opportunity identified in this
report, up to $2.1 million more in refuge revenues could be generated in the
future."[5] Despite the poor conditions of the wildlife refuge system, the administration sought to squeeze every ounce of revenue from the existing
lands. Following in the footsteps of "Chevrolet" McKay, Watt also opened
1 million acres of refuge lands to oil and gas drilling, claiming that multiple
use did not detract from proper stewardship.[6] Moreover, though Congress
appropriated $27.2 million from the Land and Water Conservation Fund
(obtained from oil and gas leases on the outer continental shelf) for purchase of wildlife refuge lands in fiscal year 1983, Watt requested only $1.6
million for that year and none for 1984.[7] He believed that existing refuge
lands should be better managed before the government purchased more.[8]
Although Watt's reasoning sounded like common sense, it ignored the fundamental fact that wetland habitat was disappearing left and right. The only
way to preserve wetland refuges for the future was to secure as many as possible, as soon as possible.

Watt was not the only Reagan appointee who posed a threat to wetlands.
Although Attorney General Civiletti's 1979 opinion had pushed the EPA to
gear up for stronger Section 404 enforcement with a greener Corps of
Engineers, Reagan's EPA administrator, Ann Gorsuch, in line with other
appointees, adhered to the belief that regulations impeded economic

growth—even though the primary mission of her agency was regulation. Career bureaucrats hunkered down and tried to do their jobs, creating as little turbulence as possible, but agency morale fell to an all-time low. Even though the EPA had just been given enormous new responsibilities for hazardous waste cleanup by Congress, its budget and staff were gutted. Within two years of taking office, Reagan cut the EPA budget by $400 million and its staff by 1,462 people. Between 1981 and 1983, funding for EPA's water-quality programs was slashed by more than 40 percent. Staffing for wetlands protection was chopped, and the remaining skeleton crew was split between two crippled offices.[9]

At the same time, the man appointed to oversee the Corps's civil works program, William R. Gianelli, put the shearing of the Corps's Section 404 jurisdiction at the top of his docket.[10] Gianelli assisted the President's Task Force on Regulatory Reform by heading up a committee to analyze ways to make it easier for developers to get the 404 permits they needed. "Almost daily," he said, "we hear of some sort of horror story about the 404 program."[11] The American Petroleum Institute had ranked Section 404 as one of the most burdensome regulatory programs.

The Corps enthusiastically embraced the Reagan administration's regulatory relief agenda. Given their long-held ambivalence toward regulation, the dwindling old-guard engineers regarded the Task Force's reforms as a way of trimming their giant, distasteful task down to size.[12] In its May 1982 report, the Task Force directed the Corps to take steps to reduce uncertainty and delay in permitting, to give states more authority, to eliminate multilevel review, and to clarify the scope of the 404 program. In response to the report, the Corps began to supply more "general" permits to approve projects more quickly without individual scrutiny.[13] In the same year, the Corps entered a Memorandum of Agreement with the Gorsuch EPA, the Fish and Wildlife Service, and the National Marine Fisheries Service (NMFS) to speed the processing of permits by cutting the opportunity for administrative appeals and by reducing mitigation requirements. Including these agencies with wetlands expertise had been part of the Corps review process since before NEPA, but now environmentalists feared that the new memorandum would cut fish and wildlife agencies out of the picture. With its regulatory cuts and its memorandum, Gianelli's Corps rejected the fact that Section 404 was a wetlands protection program.[14]

In May 1983, the Corps proposed even more dramatic reductions in its regulations by cutting mention of the EPA 404 (b)(1) permitting guidelines altogether and by reversing the rule against filling wetlands if other suitable locations for development existed. Instead, the Corps's new regulations stated that "a permit will be granted unless its issuance is found to be contrary to the public interest." After knifing the EPA guidelines, the Corps argued to make them solely advisory and not binding.[15] In addition to regulatory changes, environmental laws were further diluted by budget cuts. By 1984, the expenditures for environmental protection fell to 1.2 percent of the federal budget, 0.3 percent less than expenditures in 1970—before the passage of most environmental laws.[16]

But the administrative momentum to destroy the Section 404 program ran into heavy roadblocks. At the EPA, a scandalous knot of mismanagement, missing funds, and conflicts of interest came untied in early 1983, compelling the embarrassed Reagan administration to replace EPA leader Ann Gorsuch with William Ruckelshaus.[17] Ruckelshaus, who had served as the very first administrator of EPA under President Nixon, brought with him not only firsthand experience but also a strong vision of his agency's mission. Although he agreed with the Reaganites' contention that regulations needed reform, he held fast to the original goals of the environmental laws and insisted on changing only the means of achieving them. Ruckelshaus identified the 404 program as a priority and stood his agency's ground against proposed changes in the guidelines and their status. Ruckelshaus reclaimed a portion of the EPA's lost funding, reassembled the wetlands staff into one office, and encouraged the agency to take more aggressive regulatory stands.

As the Reagan administration cut environmental programs, widespread public support for environmental protection resurged. Though President Reagan enjoyed high popularity ratings, a 1983 *Newsweek* poll found that 47 percent of Americans disapproved of his environmental policies. A Harris poll found that 83 percent of all Americans believed that it was "very important" to preserve the nation's remaining wetlands.[18] Reflecting these environmental values, the membership of national environmental groups skyrocketed in 1981 and 1982; Sierra Club's membership alone rose by 44 percent in only twelve months. Those organizations played an important role in blocking efforts to dismantle wetlands laws and regulations.[19] Using legislative tools won in the early seventies, the environmental groups began to litigate to press both the EPA and the Corps of Engineers to enforce Section 404 and other important laws. In this climate of intense conflict, a series of significant lawsuits in the 1980s hammered out little by little the wetlands protection parameters of the Clean Water Act.

For example, the Avoyelles Sportsmen's League contended that Louisiana's bottomland forests were wetlands, and so converting them to soybean fields should be subject to the permitting process required by Section 404. In 1983, the Fifth Circuit Court of Appeals concurred. Because turning natural forested swamps into farms went beyond "normal farming practices" and clearly involved redepositing soils, the court determined that bottomland conversion fell under the jurisdiction of Corps wetland regulations.[20]

When the Corps relaxed wetlands requirements by expanding its "general permit" program in the early 1980s, sixteen environmental groups filed suit to block the change in *National Wildlife Federation v. John O. Marsh* (as secretary of the army, Marsh was ultimately responsible for the Corps). Since 1977, when the general permit program began, the Corps had issued general permits (not requiring individual review) only for isolated wetlands up to 10 acres. Because the Corps's new policy eliminated this 10-acre limit, the groups contended that vast acreages of wetlands would be removed from the protection of individual permitting procedures. In February 1984, the involved parties reached a settlement in which, among other things, the Corps agreed to adhere to the mandatory nature of the EPA 404(b)(1) guidelines, to maintain the rule against filling wetlands if other suitable locations for development existed, and to reinstate the 10-acre requirement for general permits.[21]

In 1985, the Supreme Court heard its first wetlands case, *United States v. Riverside Bayview Homes*. The Corps had denied a permit to a developer who wanted to fill in marshes near Lake St. Clair in Michigan to build a housing complex. When the developer first appealed the decision, a lower court, narrowly defining wetlands only as frequently flooded areas, found the Corps's permit denial an unconstitutional taking of property. The Supreme Court, however, unanimously reversed the lower court's decision and clearly reaffirmed the Corps's ecologically based wetlands definition and permit decision.[22]

Then in the Sweedens Swamp case, the Ruckelshaus EPA vetoed a Corps permit issued for building a shopping mall in a forty-nine-acre red maple swamp in Attleboro, Massachusetts, in 1986. The developer had considered purchasing a site less endowed with wetlands but then decided on Sweedens Swamp instead. Although the Corps's permit stipulated that the developer mitigate for the losses by creating new wetlands elsewhere, the EPA felt that the proper sequencing required by its guidelines was not followed, because another suitable site had been available. Moreover, the conversion of the Sweedens Swamp to a shopping mall would result in too great a loss of wildlife habitat. Although the developer aggressively sought to overturn the decision, three different circuit courts upheld the EPA determination.[23] In general, the courts strongly backed the regulatory authority of the federal agencies and interpreted exemptions judiciously, as, they believed, Congress intended. In these cases and others, the courts tempered the environmental effects of the Reagan administration's antiregulatory agenda.

Even with strong court backing, new EPA leadership, and more public support, the 404 program continued to flounder owing to lack of funding and tensions with a Corps of Engineers that still fundamentally rejected its role of regulating wetlands. Under the leadership of William Gianelli and his successor, Robert Dawson, wetland protection remained shackled.

In Congress, several prominent senators had tried to block Dawson's appointment as assistant secretary of the army for civil works. When confirmation hearings began in the Armed Services Committee, Senator John Chafee (R-RI), chair of the Environmental Pollution Subcommittee, convened special hearings to investigate charges that the Corps 404 program was improperly administered. Dawson, in his capacity as acting secretary, had overseen the 404 program for over a year. Several national environmental groups opposed the Reagan appointment, contending that Dawson had shown "hostility to protection of wetlands under section 404." In his testimony before the subcommittee, Dawson explained his belief that "Congress did not design Section 404 to be a wetlands protection mechanism."[24] Despite 1977 amendments, questions about the original intent of Section 404 continued to hamper the law.

Senator Robert Stafford (R-VT) brought the findings of the subcommittee to the Armed Services Committee overseeing the confirmation. Stafford advised his colleagues that Dawson had administered the 404 program "in a manner that ignored the environmental impacts of development on our nation's wetlands." He urged the committee to "stress to Mr. Dawson in the clearest possible way the need to implement section 404 of the Clean Water Act the way it was written by Congress, not the way Mr. Dawson wishes Congress had written it."[25] When Stafford's impassioned testimony failed to influence the committee, a bipartisan group of ten senators, including Stafford and Chafee, placed a hold on the nomination. In a letter to Majority Leader Bob Dole, they expressed concerns that Dawson's confirmation would "mean the end of the federal government's regulatory role in the conservation of wetlands." Already, they believed that Dawson's administration of the 404 program had "effectively dismantled the governmental component of the most important regulatory program the federal government has to curb the loss of the nation's fast-disappearing wetlands."[26]

In response, Dawson supporters argued that he was a "strong and articulate advocate of the Reagan administration's policy" and urged rapid confirmation. When the vote to confirm Dawson came to the Senate floor, Senators Chafee and Stafford stood fast in their opposition. "I do not question Mr. Dawson's character or integrity," Senator Chafee declaimed, "but at a time when our wetland resources are seriously threatened, it is just plain wrong to confirm a nominee who is unwilling to uphold the law and who has instead worked actively to subvert it or passively preside over its subversion by his subordinates."[27] These strong words fell on the seemingly deaf ears of a large block of Reagan supporters.

Although Stafford and Chafee ultimately failed to block Dawson's confirmation as assistant secretary, their delaying tactics effectively pressured the Corps to renegotiate the controversial Memorandum of Agreement of 1982 and restore consulting roles for the EPA and fish and wildlife agencies at the field level. Still, wetland advocates questioned whether the new agreement meant much since the assistant secretary reserved the right to deny appeals from the EPA, the Fish and Wildlife Service, and the National Marine Fisheries Service.[28]

The administration's lax posture toward 404 enforcement had opened the door once again in Congress to consider the extent of the Corps's authority. Several bills emerged that would pare its jurisdiction solely to traditionally navigable waterways, though environmentalists warned that such amendments would unravel protection for millions of acres of wetlands.[29] In light of the National Wetlands Inventory's alarming findings that 54 percent of wetlands in the continental United States had been lost, Senator Chafee, in his role as chair of the Environmental Pollution Subcommittee, stood hard against threats to undo Section 404. But in the meantime, the program remained essentially toothless.

Although development interests complained loudly about excessive 404 regulation, a series of reports by the Office of Technology Assessment (OTA) in 1984 and the General Accounting Office (GAO) in 1988 revealed that the 404 program far more frequently *provided* than prevented permits and wetlands destructive activities.[30] For example, in Louisiana, the Corps issued permits to 99.36 percent of all applicants between 1980 and 1986.[31] The Corps routinely ignored violation reports and, in the districts studied, actually issued permits over the objection of other federal agencies more than one-third of the time.[32] In addition, the Corps frequently awarded after-the-fact permits to violators. In the sensitive Everglades area, loosely given, after-the-fact permits led other landowners to argue that they too had the right to develop wetlands to the extent of the preceding projects. In 1985 alone, the Corps approved 191 permits affecting at least 3,000 acres in the Everglades. The large-scale absence of enforcement functioned to condone further infringements. The GAO report found that the Corps accepted at face value whatever the applicant wrote about the necessity of the project and the lack of alternative sites. Furthermore, the Corps rarely verified compliance with permits or put effort into detecting unpermitted activities in wetlands. Although it was difficult to assess Section 404's success because the Corps didn't keep track of wetland acreage saved by permit denials or project modifications, the OTA report estimated that the program reduced the amount of wetland loss proposed in original permit applications by half.[33]

The Corps justified its poor enforcement record with the claim that it "traditionally viewed seeking voluntary compliance rather than punitive legal action as 'good government.'" The Corps also professed that it had more work than it could handle.[34] Yet a leaked internal memo dated June 18, 1985, revealed more specific intentions. "The regulatory program has a long-established policy and understanding," it advised Corps staff, "that 'when in doubt err in favor of the applicant,' not in favor of the environment."[35] These policies directly countered public opinion. According to a 1985 poll, 85 percent of all Americans favored strict enforcement of the Clean Water Act *and* its wetland protection requirements.[36]

Beyond poor enforcement, the GAO and OTA reports elucidated that the program could never even dent the problem of wetlands destruction because it sought to regulate only a small portion of activities. With draining, diversion, excavation, land clearing, channelizing, flooding, and normal farm activities all exempt from regulation, about 80 percent of the nation's wetland losses were not even covered by Section 404.[37]

While historical baggage, an understaffed regulatory division, and administrative directives kept the Corps in the developers' camp, an acute lack of staffing crippled EPA effectiveness. By 1988, the EPA had used its veto authority to press for Corps compliance only five times in sixteen years.[38] With inadequate funding, staffing, and administrative support, the Section 404 program blundered through the 1980s, protecting only a handful of wetlands from development yet drawing more and more attention to the conflict between conserving wetlands and maintaining private land rights.

The Principle of Cost-Accountability

While Section 404's poor enforcement record was reprehensible, wetland conservationists held tight to the program. If only there were more funding and a more cooperative administration, they thought, surely the bugs in the system could be worked out. With strong opposition from the Reagan administration and a development-oriented majority in the Republican Senate, opening the law up for a careful overhaul could risk losing all. This hostile alignment of political planets forced environmentalists into a defensive stance—holding what ground they could against assault. But they also started to ask what could pass muster in the existing political and budgetary climate. They began to identify how application of the principle of cost-accountability could benefit the environment. Cutting federal programs that destroyed wetlands fit the bill.

Subsidized development of coastal areas was the first target, with the passage of the Coastal Barriers Resources Act (CBRA) in 1982. Recognizing that barrier islands and wetlands nestled behind them protected coastal communities against storm flood damage, CBRA sought to eliminate all federal expenditures, including funding for bridges, roads, and other infrastructure, that promoted development and growth in nearly half a million acres of specifically designated barrier island areas.[39] Most significant was the innovative strategy CBRA used to accomplish its mission. At the same time the act averted enormous disaster damages and eliminated wasteful spending, it protected the natural values of the coastal barrier islands. Tying conservation goals to fiscal cuts would become an increasingly compelling strategy as budgetary constraints and needs for environmental protection grew.

Environmentalists also joined budget trimmers in pushing for cost-sharing provisions of the 1986 Water Resources Development Act (WRDA). Although the law authorized 270 new and potentially wetland-damaging Corps of Engineers projects, it also permanently decommissioned 300 planned but unnecessary projects that had never been built. Most significant, the WRDA changed federal cost-sharing requirements to make local beneficiaries shoulder a larger percentage of costs for Corps projects. If local people had to pay more, lawmakers reasoned, only the most needed projects would be built. The new cost-sharing ratio was designed to eliminate pork-barrel schemes, by which the government dealt out millions of tax dollars for plans with only limited worth.[40] Pork-barrel dams and canals had destroyed many wetlands over the course of the past thirty years.

Furthermore, the WRDA envisioned a new environmental mission for the Corps by requiring the agency to emphasize fish and wildlife conservation in its construction plans. In particular, the act featured a well-articulated mitigation procedure that required the Corps to submit plans for mitigation of lost habitat ahead of time as part of project proposals. In the past, the Corps had offered to replace wildlife values only as an afterthought if funding allowed. Under new provisions of the WRDA, mitigation would proceed concurrently with a project, and the costs would be shared with local beneficiaries just like all other project costs. Although the act established a fund of $30 million annually to redress past damages, such as the Kissimmee River channelization, Congress never appropriated the money.[41] While the Corps dragged its feet on enforcing regulations, it proved more open to accepting environmental considerations in its engineering projects. Changes authorized with the WRDA reflected both environmental and budgetary concerns. Through the late 1970s and early 1980s, fiscal cuts edged into the traditionally well-padded Corps public works construction budget, and in 1983 funds for operation and maintenance exceeded the budget for new building and construction for the first time in the agency's two-hundred-year history.[42]

In addition to the CBRA and the WRDA, perhaps the most important laws passed by Congress in the spirit of cost-accountability during the mideighties were the 1985 Farm Bill, which eliminated subsidies for farmers who converted wetlands to farmlands, and the Tax Reform Act of 1986, which removed several key tax incentives that promoted wetland conversion (these laws will be covered in chapter 15).

While budgetary constraints inspired much of the legislation of the 1980s, a growing antiregulatory sentiment fueled criticism of existing wetlands programs. While holding off assaults on the Clean Water Act, Senator Chafee put the wetlands issue up front by encouraging his Senate colleagues to consider more proactive legislation.[43] In addition to the wetland losses revealed by the National Wetlands Inventory, in 1983 the National Marine Fisheries Service estimated that the national fishery loss due to estuarine destruction from 1954 through 1978 was $208 million annually.[44]

SENATOR JOHN CHAFEE.
Through the 1980s and early 1990s, Rhode Island Senator John Chafee (R) has fended off numerous assaults on the Clean Water Act and led bipartisan efforts to conserve wetlands.

With impressive evidence about the economic and ecological values of wetlands mounting and the simultaneous news of sweeping losses, Chafee emphasized that timely action was critical.[45]

In 1983, Chafee introduced the Reagan administration's proposed wetlands legislation, the Protect Our Wetlands and Duck Resources Act (POWDR), which would identify "environmentally significant" wetlands and place them within a special POWDR system. In those areas, federally funded development would be prohibited. The act would also authorize matching grants to states from the Land and Water Conservation Fund for wetlands acquisition and conservation. But POWDR had enormous loopholes and a gamut of critics from realtors to fish and wildlife advocates, who derided it as "mostly puff."[46]

The same year, a more popular bipartisan bill, the Emergency Wetlands Resources Act (EWRA), was also introduced by Senator Chafee in the Senate and by Congressman Edwin Forsythe (R-NJ) in the House. The word "emergency" drew attention to the astonishing rate of wetland losses and the urgency with which they needed to be faced, but Congress didn't finally approve the law until November 1986. By focusing on government acquisition of wetlands, the act responded to antiregulatory sentiment. Paying landowners for their wetlands sidestepped the sticky issue of whether regulation constituted the taking of private property. The act pieced together several means for buying up wetlands, including a two-year extension on the Wetlands Loan Act, which allowed the Fish and Wildlife Service to borrow $200 million against the revenues of future duck stamp sales in order to speed up the purchase of important habitat. The act also provided more income for the Migratory Bird Conservation Fund by allowing the collection of entrance fees at certain national wildlife refuges, by raising the price of duck stamps, and by putting an excise tax on imported weapons and ammunition—a tax estimated to draw $10 million each year. The act also encouraged states to purchase wetlands by offering Land and Water Conservation Fund money for that purpose. In addition, the EWRA directed the secretary of the interior to make a list of wetlands in the greatest need of protection, which could then be used by federal and state governments as well as private groups interested in buying and preserving wetland habitat.[47]

Beyond promoting wetland purchase, the EWRA required the National Wetlands Inventory to speed its mapping, especially of coastal and riparian zones and of the prairie pothole region. Both the priority listing and the mapping would give developers a better idea in advance of which wetlands to avoid. The act also charged the NWI with producing "Status and Trend" reports every ten years. Finally, the act directed the Department of the Interior to prepare a report that identified all federal programs and policies that induced unwanted wetland degradation and loss. Congress members hoped that wetlands might someday benefit from the same strategy of efficiency used to stop subsidized development with CBRA.

With the EWRA, Congress explicitly recognized the need for action and provided money for acquiring critical wetlands. The act envisioned protecting wetlands with a patchwork of complementary efforts including the 404 regulatory program, a system of federally owned and protected wetlands, a strong base of information, and robust state and private-sector involvement. Though the law started many balls rolling in the right direction, most provisions merely restored ground lost through the administrative rampage of the early Reagan years.

In the same autumn that Congress approved both the WRDA and the EWRA, the Senate also ratified the Ramsar Convention, an international agreement first adopted in Ramsar, Iran, in 1971 to encourage conservation of wetlands around the world. Participants were obliged to promote wetlands conservation in their planning and policies and to designate at least one "wetland of international importance." In November of 1986, President Reagan signed the convention and designated four national wildlife refuges as Ramsar sites: Izembek Lagoon in Alaska, Forsythe in New Jersey, Okefenokee in Georgia, and Ash Meadows in Nevada. Eventually, several more wetland sites would be designated. Although largely a symbolic program in this country, U.S. participation in the Ramsar Convention fit in well with the tenor of the times. Without spending money or imposing regulations, the Reagan administration could demonstrate environmental concern, an issue that had become something of an Achilles' heel for the Republicans under his leadership. Most important, the Ramsar Convention elevated awareness about wetland values and helped to create a greater sense of pride in wetlands, which fostered greater interest in their conservation at home and abroad.[48]

Waterfowl Lead the Way

While Congress wrangled over details of wetlands protection, and federal agencies struggled to accomplish their mammoth regulatory jobs with bantam budgets, waterfowl populations continued to crash. Extensive urbanization of breeding, migratory, and winter habitats simply left no place for ducks, geese, and swans to carry on. Although more than 3.5 million acres of waterfowl habitat had been preserved with duck stamp money since the 1930s, severe drought once again reduced duck populations to the lowest numbers since that time. With the mandate of the Migratory Waterfowl Treaty of 1916, the Fish and Wildlife Service knew that something more had to be done on a continental scale, yet with the lack of administrative support and with antifederal sentiment raging in the areas most critical to the birds, a new approach was needed.

Because waterfowl traveled such great distances, migratory bird management had long demanded the cooperation of experts all along the birds' seasonal routes. In the early 1950s, the Fish and Wildlife Service and states had established a system of Flyways Councils to coordinate conservation studies and efforts. While the American councils wrote plans that identified habitat needs and desired waterfowl populations, the Canadian Wildlife Service developed similar plans with the provinces. From those ground-level planning efforts, the idea for a larger, umbrella waterfowl plan coalesced during the drought of the 1980s. Realizing that waterfowl habitat needs were too big for the governments alone to handle, Fish and Wildlife Service waterfowl biologist and administrator Harvey Nelson and his Canadian counterpart James Patterson had the idea of involving communities along the flyways in the process.[49]

According to Nelson, it took two years of administrative work to forge a grand plan that accommodated habitat needs, political needs, and financial limitations. On May 4, 1986, Secretary of the Interior Donald Hodel and Canadian Environment Minister Thomas McMillan signed the North American Waterfowl Management Plan (NAWMP). With those signatures, the two nations embarked upon the largest-scale landscape planning process in the world.[50] With Nelson and Patterson as its first directors, the NAWMP set goals for a waterfowl breeding population of sixty-two million birds and a fall flight of one hundred million, the average numbers during the 1970–1979 period. Rather than regulate hunting, the plan recognized habitat destruction as the primary cause of waterfowl decline and set forth acreage goals for protection, restoration, and management.

The NAWMP was a classic Reagan-era environmental policy: it purported ambitious goals but had little government funding. Instead, responsibility for implementing the plan fell to the private sector. Hodel clearly explained that the plan was "not a commitment by either signatory government to expend funds beyond its borders or to bear the total cost or responsibility for its execution; rather, it is a challenge to all those who enjoy and benefit from waterfowl to contribute their share toward its attainment."[51] Unlike the earlier treaties, this agreement was not binding, but it did allow expenditure of U.S. funds in Canada. Because the Treasury purse strings were held tight when it came to conservation, planners set the initial project budget at a modest $1.5 billion to protect, restore, and enhance 6 million acres. Plan supporters were afraid to ask for anything more, though this amount equaled only one month's subsidy payments to farmers.[52] Most of the moneys would have to come from private organizations and corporations. Ducks Unlimited committed to raising $300 million for the project, Dow Chemical donated $3 million, and Phillips Petroleum contributed $600,000 for the plan.

Despite its small budget, the project got off to a good but slow start. According to David Smith, a Fish and Wildlife Service staff member who worked to implement the NAWMP, "The plan was a good alternative in the eighties to regulation. It was proactive, not reactive."[53] Given the contentious antifederal sentiment in many areas critical for waterfowl, the NAWMP offered a solution. The plan's backbone was its joint ventures—coalitions of people, known as cooperators, who lived and worked along the flyways and who were willing to act together to secure waterfowl habitat. Joint ventures included state governments, local governments, local offices of the Fish and Wildlife Service, sportsmen's clubs, conservation organizations, businesses, and individuals. By pulling together to accomplish common goals, the joint ventures had more success than all entities working separately and could better work with private landowners. Because private landowners held 74 percent of wetlands in the lower forty-eight, their cooperation was crucial to any meaningful wetlands and waterfowl protection plan. Within the first few years, the joint ventures organized and took stock of their resources. They soon realized that more work on the ground was needed.

In 1989, the program got a boost when Congress approved the North American Wetlands Conservation Act of 1989. Sponsored by Senator George Mitchell (D-ME), the law made $15 million available annually for matching funds, from appropriations and from interest on the Pittman–Robertson account (see chapter 9). This new funding source breathed vitality into a NAWMP program that was geared up and ready to take off; the funding also prompted lawmakers to consider more seriously the protection of habitat in Canada and Mexico. In its first two years, that act provided $49 million, matched by $93 million from non-U.S. government sources in the United States, Canada, and Mexico. These moneys brought more than 600,000 wetland acres in all three countries into the NAWMP system. Mexico joined the NAWMP agreement in 1994 as a full partner.[54]

One particularly successful Atlantic Coast joint-venture project area emerged in South Carolina's Ashepoo, Combahee, and Edisto rivers' estuary—collectively known as the ACE Basin. There the NAWMP catalyzed the efforts and energies of many parties interested in wetlands, waterfowl, and wildlife protection in the region. According to Nature

Conservancy project director Mike Prevost, "All of the participating organizations and people were interested in the area, even before the North
American Plan, but with the plan, a lightbulb clicked on: 'We should work
together.'"[55] A national wildlife refuge unit, together with state wildlife
management areas, and a national estuarine research reserve formed the
initial land base for the project. The Nature Conservancy and Ducks
Unlimited began working with conservation easements on private lands,
and then landowners became involved by donating easements and lands
outright, or by agreeing to manage their lands for waterfowl. The ACE
Basin Task Force picked up so much momentum that it far exceeded the
expectations of the initial project plan. As a result, over 100,000 acres were
ultimately preserved as waterfowl and wildlife habitat, and many more
acres were managed to maintain the health of the ecosystem. For example,
Westvāco, a large timber company in the basin, agreed to practice conservation management on its ACE Basin lands.[56]

Of the eight joint-venture areas initially set up, three met their habitat
protection goals within the plan's first five years.[57] Despite the promising
numbers of acres, not all essential areas were protected. In many places,
such as the ACE Basin, enthusiasm created unexpected opportunities to
protect more, but less significant, habitat. Yet some of the most critical joint
ventures, particularly those in the prairie potholes and along the Pacific
Coast, lagged behind. And even in the most successful regions, wetlands
losses continued.

The North American Waterfowl Management Plan, together with the
priority wetlands list developed by the Department of the Interior in accordance with the Emergency Wetlands Resources Act, helped to galvanize the
support of private organizations for waterfowl and wetlands. During a period when few public funds were available, private foundations, such as the
Richard King Mellon Foundation, and conservation groups, such as the
Nature Conservancy and Ducks Unlimited, contributed heartily, purchasing the most critical wetland habitats for long-term protection.

A Matter of Balance

Although the Reagan administration tried to block environmental regulation with staffing and budget cuts through the 1980s, wetland conservation
was an idea whose time had come. Congress made new laws that both protected wetlands and reflected budgetary concerns. Section 404 survived
legislative hurdles and a pocket veto to emerge in 1987 with stronger penal-

ties for violators.[58] While the ineffective regulatory program allowed many wetlands to be destroyed, wetland acquisition initiatives safeguarded new acreages, and the rate of losses slowed. Nonetheless, in the absence of conservation leadership from Congress and the White House, between the mid 1970s and the mid 1980s, 2.6 million more acres of wetlands disappeared, and the average loss of wetlands was still an alarming 290,000 acres each year. By the mid 1980s, 103.3 million acres of wetlands remained.[59]

The Reagan administration's laissez-faire consignment of environmental values to the marketplace pushed environmental issues into a strongly partisan light. Although wetland supporters had long come from both the Democratic and Republican parties, the new crop of Reagan Republicans saw wetlands primarily from the antiregulatory perspective of business. They focused on the difficulties created by the regulations and were disinclined to recognize wetland services, such as the cost savings of flood-damage reduction and the economic underpinning of wetlands to the fishing industry. Deregulation, under the new Republican agenda, would leave wetlands to the fate of a free market insensitive to their public values.

Some spoke of the Reagan administration's environmental policies as the swing of a pendulum. As if the oscillations of a pendulum would ultimately track the truest course, they suggested that the environmental laws of the 1960s and 1970s needed to be balanced with more attention to property rights, business needs, and costs. The metaphor addressed political ideology in principle, but when applied, it failed to account for the fact that over half the nation's wetlands had already been lost and that even at our protective best, 290,000 acres of a finite resource continued to be destroyed year after year. If "balance" was truly sought, it would take a much deeper swing in the direction of conservation to offset the dominant vision of converting wetlands that had guided centuries of land use in America.

FIFTEEN

Making and Breaking the Farm Connection

> Our intent is not to create hardship by saying, "Mr. Farmer, you can't farm something that you have been farming over time," but on the other side, it is to say that no new wetlands can be brought into production, either. They are sacred, so to speak. I think we can make farmers understand that; that is where we want to be.
>
> —Milton J. Hertz, *Agricultural Stabilization and Conservation Service*, 1988[1]

Although many Americans began to understand the values of wetlands during the 1960s and 1970s, destruction continued at full bore. While development and pollution played their parts, agriculture accounted for a whopping 87 percent of wetland losses through the mid 1970s.[2] While appreciation of wetland values grew, particularly in coastal states, most farmers did not embrace the change of values. In farm communities, demands of the global market overshadowed newfound public concern for wetlands.

The blitz surged when the Russian wheat crop failed in 1969, and then widespread drought conditions devastated much of the world harvest, creating a sudden and ravenous demand for commodity crops such as soybeans and wheat. American farmers rushed to meet the new call for food. Production increased 6 percent each year from 1970 to 1973. By 1974, the prices of corn and soybeans had doubled, and the price of wheat had tripled.[3]

Lured by skyrocketing prices, farmers not only brought existing croplands into full production, but between 1972 and 1982 they also expanded into previously uncultivated wetlands and other marginal lands, 60 million acres in all.[4] Tax write-offs for clearing and improving new land added further incentive to convert wetlands into farms.[5] Innovations such as plastic tubing and larger land-clearing machines made drainage easier.

293

At the same time that farmland acreage expanded, the number of farms and farmers shrank. In the 1930s, there had been 6.3 million farms, and farmers accounted for 21 percent of the national labor force; but by 1980, there were 2.4 million farms, and farmers accounted for only 2.8 percent of the workforce.[6] Family farms were bought up by large corporations, which had the capital necessary to bring sizable acreages of marginal land into production. In many areas, board rooms replaced grange halls as the meeting places of the modern agricultural community. As prices rose, opportunities for profit overwhelmed concern for wetlands. Regions that fell most vulnerably to the giant four-wheel-drive tractors were the prairie potholes and the bottomland forests of the Southeast.

Potholes to Wheat, Forests to Soybeans, Boom to Bust

In the rolling pothole country, chronic overproduction problems had stalled wetland conversion, but that changed with the high farm prices. In 1973, Secretary of Agriculture Earl Butz urged farmers to meet the needs of a hungry world. "For the first time in many years the American farmer is free to produce as much as he can," Butz exclaimed.[7] The USDA's push for production was based on the belief that foreign demand would grow over the long term and eventually eliminate the need for price supports and production controls. The Bureau of Reclamation's Garrison Diversion Project in North Dakota epitomized the vigorous expansion of agricultural production that Butz espoused.

The proposed diversion would sluice water via massive canals from the reservoir behind Garrison Dam on the Missouri River across miles of pothole-pocked prairie to irrigate fields already producing dryland crops such as wheat, barley, and oats. To irrigate only 250,000 acres of alfalfa and corn, Garrison's canals and other infrastructure would take 220,000 acres out of production. Carrying water through the heart of pothole country, the project would damage 73,000 acres of pothole wetlands and 70,000 additional acres on twelve national wildlife refuges, including one intended as mitigation for the original Garrison Dam. At a cost exceeding $1 billion, U.S. taxpayers would provide irrigation benefits to fewer than one thousand farms—a million dollars per farm. Garrison proponents used high demand to justify the project's bad arithmetic, but the huge benefits to North Dakota farmers undoubtedly accounted for the congressional delegation's support. Wisconsin Senator William Proxmire (D) derided the project as "sheer, unadulterated pork."[8] Environmental groups also opposed Garrison Diversion, and in 1977, a National Audubon Society lawsuit delayed construction.[9] Despite misgivings in Congress and among conservationists about the federally funded boondoggle, the potholes were not reprieved.

Although national environmental policies, such as NEPA and President Carter's Executive Order, had tempered the role of the Soil Conservation Service in draining wetlands, those policies had little effect with farm commodity prices so high. Elevated prices made marginal lands worth farming even without federal assistance. With huge new tractors and wide farm machines that excelled in plowing straight, efficient strips, it became inconvenient to steer around small potholes. Acres of virgin, pothole-dappled prairie sod were plowed under.

The push for production threatened even long-established soil conservation measures. According to Butz, reports from the northern plains states told of farmers "plowing up grassed waterways . . . steep slopes . . . and tearing out windbreaks that took many years to establish."[10] Reports to Congress made by the comptroller general in 1977 and 1983 called attention to erosion problems that were worsening despite a forty-year history of federal soil conservation efforts.[11]

Although many environmentalists had criticized the USDA for promoting drainage, one retired soil conservation engineer from Minnesota recalled that when the SCS stopped helping farmers plan their drainage, even more ecological damage resulted. Well-trained soil conservationists could consider wetland values in their drainage plans and produce orderly drainage, but when farmers driven by high prices were left to figure out the technical aspects of drainage themselves, they made a mess of the land. Often, they illegally drained their wetlands and croplands into highway ditches.[12]

With little understanding of the consequences, farmers drained more and more potholes. In Minnesota alone, nearly 17 percent of the state's wetlands inventoried in 1974 were drained by 1980.[13] Not only did pothole drainage shrink habitat, it made flooding more frequent and problematic. In McLeod County, Minnesota, for example, ten farmers petitioned for ditch improvements in 1979 because their lands flooded after farmers in the upper watershed drained more wetlands; upstream farmers refused to pay their share of the costs.[14] Extensive drainage in the Devil's Lake, Red River of the North, and James River watersheds of North Dakota passed off

flooding to downstream areas as well.[15] Of 134 million acres with severe
flood problems in the lower forty-eight states, 92.8 million acres were farmlands, many of which were drained wetlands or lands where the drain water
was sent.[16]

In North Dakota, motives for draining potholes ran even deeper than potential profits. Fueled by conservationists' blocking of the Starkweather
Project (see chapter 12) and then the Garrison Diversion, many people,
particularly farmers, developed an antiwetland attitude. The U.S. Fish and
Wildlife Service, with its mandate to safeguard the nation's waterfowl,
became the prime target of angry sentiment. A series of North Dakota governors (Guy, Link, and Olsen) badmouthed and then outlawed the Fish
and Wildlife Service's Small Wetland Acquisition Program, which had used
duck stamp money to purchase a million acres of wetland waterfowl habitat
from willing owners.[17] Draining wetlands became a way to assert individual
liberty and local control. Simply put, any good North Dakotan drained
wetlands. The pervasive antifederal grudge kept farmers doing what they
wanted to do with their land despite effects on downstream neighbors and
on waterfowl. Many northern prairie grasslands with duck-filled pothole
swales became monoculture wheat fields.

In the Southeast, a soybean boom enticed farmers to turn hardwood bottomland forests into fields. Wetland forests that had slowly grown up after
the turn-of-the-century cutover were once again razed by landowners who
stood to gain doubly by selling the timber and then draining the land to cultivate soybeans. The high fertility of the swamp soil almost guaranteed successful crops, and high farm prices ensured a hefty return on investments.
Federal income tax deductions for the costs of clearing new lands also lowered the price of wetland conversion. One study showed that 1978 tax provisions reduced the cost of clearing bottomlands in east Arkansas by 30 percent. Furthermore, federal crop insurance and the promise of disaster
payments removed much of the risk inherent in farming the floodplains of
the voluminous Mississippi. Most significant, drainage projects and flood-
control projects built by the SCS and the Corps of Engineers made it possible for farmers to bring wetlands of the Delta region into production.[18]

High farm prices along with all of the federal incentives and safety nets
propelled an enormous transformation of the Delta landscape. Between
1965 and 1978, soybean acreage increased by 65 percent, most of it fin-

gering into bottomland hardwood forests.[19] In Arkansas, 90 percent of the bottomland hardwood forests was cleared for soybean production. Across the river in western Mississippi, an original expanse of 4 million bottomland acres that had been cut to 1.2 million acres by 1970 was reduced yet another 60 percent between 1970 and 1976, leaving fewer than 500,000 acres.[20] According to the U.S. Fish and Wildlife Service, 165,000 acres of bottomlands were cleared each year in the lower Mississippi River valley in the late 1970s.[21] The immense floodplain that had remained as a restored habitat to wood ducks, woodpeckers, red wolves, panthers, and black bears and as the primary wintering grounds of North America's waterfowl was fragmented into scattered tracts.[22] As SCS administrator Kenneth Grant explained, "The loss . . . is regrettable but understandable from the landowner's point of view. Instead of $4–8 per acre annual return from timber production, landowners can net $40 per acre for soybeans."[23]

Not only the hardwood swamps of the Mississippi Delta fell under the soybean spell, but forests and pocosins of the Carolina coastal plains were cleared as well. Although moderate soil fertility had prevented the coastal plain from becoming highly developed for agriculture in the past, elevated farm prices made the use of expensive fertilizers feasible. In 1974 alone, large corporate farms, including First Colony Farms, American Cyanamid, and John Hancock Mutual Insurance Company, purchased more than 41,000 acres of forested wetlands on the Albemarle-Pamlico Peninsula with the intention of growing soybeans, winter wheat, corn, and sorghum and making pastures and feedlots. Between 1973 and 1983, North Carolina lost 1.2 million acres of wetlands, the highest loss among all southeastern states. By 1978, the soybean boom had pushed the total number of wetland acres drained for farmland in the South to 36.7 million acres.[24]

Inflated prices didn't last long. By the early 1980s, the price of soybeans plunged. The percentage drop in farm values between 1981 and 1986 was greater than for any other five-year period since the Civil War.[25] With the boom over, more farmlands than ever before produced surplus crops. Farmers who had taken out enormous loans to purchase enormous farm equipment were heavily in debt and had little income. They faced two choices: to continue draining and planting as much land as possible to pay debts, or to reduce their acreage and receive payments offered by the Department of Agriculture in an effort to maintain prices without stockpiling monstrous surpluses. Through its Payment-in-Kind (PIK) program, the USDA compensated farmers who took land out of production with commodities equivalent to what they would have grown.

In the uncertain economy, the security of federal price and income supports became crucial to rural communities—especially in pothole country. In 1983, farmers in North Dakota led the nation in the percentage of farmers participating in the PIK subsidy program and in the number of acres of wheat land idled.[26]

Although low prices and land idling slowed the rate of wetland conversion overall, federal support programs actually worsened the plight of the remaining potholes. Many farmers who had set aside up to 30 percent of their land under the federal PIK program spent spare time draining wetlands to cultivate tax benefits and to increase the acreage they would be paid not to plant.[27] Other farmers drained wetlands to increase their output of surplus crops and their income of price-support payments. Such support payments made lending institutions willing to finance still more wetland conversion. The combination of guaranteed income, inactive equipment, and idle land resulted in higher-than-average pothole drainage in 1983.[28] Wetlands were being plowed up simply to reap federal largesse. By including the federal treasury in the farmers' decision-making loop, the USDA unintentionally subsidized poor stewardship. Furthermore, rules made by the SCS to implement President Carter's Executive Order protecting wetlands were watered down in 1982 by the Reagan administration's regulatory-relief agenda.[29]

With the bitter channelization controversy of the early 1970s, growing awareness of pesticide dangers, and information that farm conversion accounted for the majority of wetland losses, people had begun to make the connection between agriculture, USDA policies, and environmental consequences. Furthermore, states working to meet Clean Water Act standards identified erosion from marginal farmlands as the prime culprit in degrading water quality.

As farm commodity program costs soared to $17.7 billion in fiscal year 1985, public opinion about agriculture started to change. Large urban constituencies plugging for their own programs increasingly criticized the giant subsidies given to the small farm population. Although in the past, agriculture had been recognized as a unique industry with particular needs for government aid, in the early 1980s many Congress members thought that farms receiving federal assistance—many of them corporate farms—should be required to at least meet environmental standards.[30] Recognizing the

connections between agriculture and the environment, national environmental groups began to take a more active role in agricultural policy.

Swampbuster

Congress began deliberations over the 1985 Farm Bill with strong concern
for soil, wetlands, water quality, and especially the high cost of farm programs. Linking farm programs with conservation programs became a popular strategy because both environmental and fiscal problems could be
tackled at once.[31]

A plan to eliminate subsidies for farmers who plowed up new sod came
directly from the Great Plains, where sodbusting caused dust to pile up on
downwind farms. Irritated leeward farmers, with the help of Senator
William L. Armstrong (R-CO), pushed to suspend USDA income support
and disaster payments for farmers who busted new sod. In addition to this
"sodbuster" provision, Congress adopted the Conservation Reserve Program, known commonly as CRP, to retire the most highly erodible lands
from production for ten years. Despite controversial details, both conservation provisions enjoyed broad support.[32]

In discussions about tying conservation measures to eligibility for farm
subsidies, environmentalists realized that wetlands might benefit from a
similar approach. The USDA and the Department of the Interior had long
talked about protecting wetlands in agricultural areas. In 1970, the USDA
water bank program—though scarcely funded—began to pay farmers to
conserve valuable wetlands and buffer zones on their properties for ten-
year periods.[33] The Fish and Wildlife Service had also purchased some
wetlands and wetland easements in the prime waterfowl-breeding pothole
country with their Small Wetland Acquisition Program. But the talk had
gone only so far, and wetlands, especially potholes, continued to disappear.
Because price and income supports provided incentives to farm greater
acreages than the market alone would demand, farm subsidies encouraged
farmers to convert wetlands that might otherwise be left alone.[34] With
farmlands in surplus and wetlands in short supply, subsidized drainage no
longer made sense as a national policy. To environmental groups, it seemed
that a wetland version of Sodbuster could act as a disincentive for drainage,
reduce flooding, and also save the federal government from paying extra
crop subsidies.

The concept of a "swampbuster" provision bounced around conservation circles before it was formally introduced in the House Agriculture

Committee hearing in April of 1985. From the outset, Swampbuster had the support of national environmental groups and conservation-oriented farm groups, such as the National Association of Conservation Districts. This conservation coalition soon found congressional supporters in Representatives Howard Wolpe (D-MI) and Tom Daschle (D-SD) and Senators Robert Kasten (R-WI) and Ed Zorinsky (D-NE). Both the House and Senate Agricultural Committees developed Swampbuster provisions in the bills they drafted.[35] Committee members carefully considered the bill's description of wetlands and ultimately chose a definition based on soil, hydrology, and vegetation similar to that used by the Corps of Engineers in regulations for Section 404. The bill denied swampbusting farmers their commodity price supports, disaster payments, Farm and Home Administration loans, and crop insurance.[36] Because the Swampbuster provision was based on reasoning similar to the well-accepted Sodbuster, it sailed through Congress with little debate. Conservationists were pleased with its inclusion, but several farm groups were shocked when the provision passed. Some reported that Swampbuster was intended to be a bargaining chip, but no bargaining ever took place.[37]

Given the larger context—that protection of wetlands was a national priority, that agricultural conversions posed the greatest threat to wetlands, and that shaving enormous subsidies was a fiscal goal—Swampbuster fit the Farm Bill well. USDA price-support programs had long worked at cross purposes with conservation programs. Not only did the Farm Bill finally rectify these policy contradictions, but it also married economic benefits with environmental benefits. President Reagan signed the Food Security Act (FSA) into law on December 23, 1985—a date well remembered by farmers. Drainage projects started before this date were grandfathered, but those commenced afterwards were subject to Swampbuster. The strong conservation compliance measures approved in the FSA were testament to the more active participation of national environmental groups in the legislation.[38]

In the course of considering Swampbuster, Senators David Boren (D-OK) and Charles Grassley (R-IA) called attention to antiquated stipulations in the federal tax code that also encouraged wetlands drainage. Left over from a time when Congress sought to encourage development, deductions for land clearing and improvement threatened bottomland forests in particular. The following year, the senators introduced a bill to remove these harmful deductions. Passed as part of the Tax Reform Act of 1986, the Boren–Grassley provision finally updated the outmoded view of wet-lands long perpetuated by the tax code.[39] With both tax reform and Swampbuster in place, environmentalists were optimistic that wetland losses owing to agriculture might finally be curbed.

The Soil Conservation Service and Fish and Wildlife Service staffs drew up guidelines and sent the first notices announcing Sodbuster, CRP, and Swampbuster to state and county SCS offices in March of 1986. Within the ranks of the nearly seven thousand SCS field staff, resistance to the new provisions, especially Swampbuster, bristled. Beyond a general worry about the increased workload, most SCS field staff had little knowledge of wet-lands. Furthermore, rather than act as soil conservation advisors as they had always done, Swampbuster required that SCS agents do something akin to policing. They would have to determine what was and what was not wetland. What was the fine line between maintaining old drains and im-proving them? Did drainage begin before or after December 23, 1985? SCS agents would have to report suspected Swampbuster violations to Agricul-tural Stabilization and Conservation (ASC) committees—groups of local farmers—that made the ultimate decision regarding loss of eligibility for Agricultural Stabilization and Conservation Service subsidies. In small farm communities where everyone knew everyone and there was only one coffee shop to go to in the morning, the pressure not to enforce the provi-sion was tremendous. Although Congress directed the SCS and the ASCS to implement Swampbuster jointly, it was no surprise that few violations were reported by SCS, and even fewer farmers were denied their subsidies by the ASCS and other agencies.[40]

The difficulties of enforcement aside, communities in pothole country regarded Swampbuster as a heavy blow. After federal agricultural policies that had encouraged vigorous drainage and production for decades, Swampbuster clearly indicated that the tide had turned. Though farmers were at complete liberty to ignore the Swampbuster provision and do what-ever they wished with their land, if they drained wetlands and planted crops on them, they could lose all their federal subsidy payments for that crop year and as long as they continued to plant on the converted wetlands. In North Dakota, where 90 percent of farmers relied on USDA commodity programs, people had come to regard their income and price-support pay-ments as entitlements and saw any change in the status quo as a threat.[41]

Beyond solely monetary concerns, the issue was cultural. For decades upon decades, when the long, harsh winters finally broke, cabin-fevered farmers had come out into their fields and drained nuisance low spots and potholes that they'd had on their "to-do" list all winter. In line with values held dear by most people, they worked hard to improve their land to grow more food. How could such deeply engrained customs and values change overnight? Moreover, past wounds were reopened in 1986 when a compromise agreement scaled back the Garrison Diversion Project in what many farmers regarded as a victory for the same interest groups that had pushed for Swampbuster.[42]

As Vernon Fahy, secretary of the state water commission, explained, North Dakotans thought it unfair that wildlife groups expected their state *not* to develop in order to satisfy the nation's wildlife needs when other states, such as Iowa, had already drained all of their potholes. Why should North Dakotans be stuck with the waterfowl bill? he charged.[43] State Game and Fish Department director Dale Hennegar concurred that farmers would not simply preserve wetlands "out of the goodness of their hearts." "If [a wetland is] of value to us the way it is," he continued, "we need to put a price on it—and that's going to cost bucks."[44] The fact that federal programs designed to compensate farmers for not converting wetlands (the very "bucks" Hennegar suggested) had been outlawed by three state governors was eclipsed by strong antifederal sentiment and a local imperative to drain. Furthermore, the basis of the new wetlands programs was simply to quit *subsidizing* farmers for eliminating wetlands.

By 1986, the North Dakota legislature responded to Swampbuster with its own "no net loss" law, which required farmers to obtain permits for drainage projects affecting watersheds greater than 80 acres. Although proponents hoped that the state law would help to conserve wetlands by quelling antifederal sentiment, it was poorly implemented. Again responsibility for enforcement fell to local farm communities, in this case, county water boards that purposefully avoided taking action. In one instance, a local water board dismissed aerial photographic evidence of violations collected by Fish and Wildlife Service staff to avoid censuring a local farmer.[45] The state law was a classic case of maintaining appearances for outsiders to show that North Dakota could attend to its own problems without federal involvement. Although the law did little to protect wetlands, critics had a harder time rebuking a state with a no net loss law. Both the state wetland law and the federal Swampbuster provision were disregarded as farmers ferreted out loopholes. With the help of friendly ASC committees, most people who wanted to drain a wetland could choose from over a dozen exemptions to Swampbuster guidelines.[46]

Lack of enforcement enraged national environmental groups. Some saw the whole program as a sham. Even within the purview of the law, farmers could grow crops in wetlands as long as they didn't drain them, though the practice diminished wetland soil fertility and introduced pesticides into the potholes. Furthermore, farmers who converted wetlands did not lose their subsidy *until* they planted a commodity crop in the area. Because local ASC committees failed to enforce Swampbuster, pothole drainage continued as it had in the past. In fact, fair autumn weather encouraged farmers to pick up the pace in 1987. That year, drainage rates in North Dakota and Minnesota were the highest in the decade, and North Dakota farmers still received $700 million of subsidies.[47] In 1988, USDA records revealed that only two farmers nationwide had been denied subsidies though hundreds of drainage violations were reported.[48]

In the pothole states alone, Fish and Wildlife Service staff reported hundreds of suspected violations to ASC committees; but typically the committees declined to enforce the law and told farmers only that they had been reported, further perpetuating antagonism and accomplishing nothing to protect wetlands. The ineffectual Fish and Wildlife Service became reluctant to step in.[49] Instead, the National Wildlife Federation, which had set up shop in Bismarck in 1982, took on a watchdog role for Swampbuster enforcement and started public education programs to inform Dakotans about the unique values of their wetlands. Sidestepping the contentious Swampbuster altogether, Ducks Unlimited helped farmers interested in conservation to restore wetlands and manage surrounding uplands to provide the cover needed by waterfowl. Many of these restored wetlands fell in crucial areas targeted by the North American Waterfowl Management Plan (see chapter 14).[50]

Though environmentalists were dissatisfied with enforcement of Swampbuster, and the farm community disliked restrictions on their subsidies, Congress made only minor adjustments to the provision when the Farm Bill came up for reauthorization in 1990. Environmentalists pushed to cut subsidies as soon as wetlands were drained—not later, when crops were planted. The agricultural community pushed for graduated penalties to protect farmers who didn't fully understand the law. Congress also added a Wetlands Reserve Program (WRP), similar to the CRP, to retire wetlands from crop production. These new provisions of the Food, Agriculture, Conservation and Trade Act of 1990 (FACTA) passed without difficulty, owing to an agreement between the agricultural and environmental lobbies. More than sixteen environmental groups endorsed other enormous farm subsidies, and the agricultural lobby agreed not to touch the conservation compliance provisions.[51] FACTA also amended PL-566 (see chapters 10 and 12) to reflect modern knowledge by including wetland and floodplain easements for water quality, flood control, and habitat among advised watershed protection practices.[52]

Despite the farm community's initial contempt for Swampbuster and the lack of enforcement, proponents thought the disincentive still worked—especially given the situation prior to its enactment. They thought that USDA staff in the field who already knew the land could best cooperate with local people. Because Swampbuster acted as a disincentive rather than as a regulation, it was more palatable to farmers than a permit program like Section 404. In conjunction with the CRP and WRP, Swampbuster made both potholes and surrounding cover available for waterfowl breeding. Most significant, with Swampbuster, the message of wetlands conservation started to sink in. According to USDA analysis, wetland conversions on agricultural lands nationwide slowed to less than 30,000 acres per year between 1987 and 1991, down from 51,000 acres per year between 1982 and 1987.[53]

Environmentalist critics contended that the slowing reflected a whole host of factors, including low wheat prices, and that the most feasibly drained wetlands had already been altered. Furthermore, they pointed to a 1988 USDA study that revealed how Swampbuster neglected two-thirds of wetlands most vulnerable to conversion because the law did not work in areas where crops were ineligible for commodity programs and where farmers did not rely on government support payments. For example, an exemption for artificial wetlands excluded crops planted in the highly manipulated Central Valley wetlands from Swampbuster. In the Everglades, Swampbuster had limited effect because sugar processors, not the growers, benefited from price-support programs.[54]

Even in places where Swampbuster should deter farmers from drainage, weak enforcement hampered the law. By 1991, for example, the ASCS granted "good faith" exemptions to 556 farmers who had been cited by the SCS for draining wetlands in violation of Swampbuster. The National

Wildlife Federation, along with local conservation groups and private landowners, brought suit against the ASCS for granting such exemptions to farmers who drained eighteen prairie potholes in Minnesota's Yellow Medicine River watershed. Ruling that the farmers should restore the potholes or lose their subsidy payments, the circuit court of appeals created a precedent that environmentalists hoped would pressure ASC committees to enforce the stipulations more stringently.[55] But in a 1993 USDA audit in Nelson County, North Dakota, investigators found that ASC committees still provided improper exemptions from Swampbuster in eleven out of thirty randomly selected cases.[56] The decentralized structure of the agricultural agencies, which had made them so successful during the 1930s, undermined the USDA's ability to implement federal laws.

Other statistics began to reveal more clearly the degree of enforcement problems. In 1993, USDA auditors sampled nineteen farmers in Cavalier County, North Dakota; Monroe County, Missouri; and Duplin County, North Carolina, and discovered that between 1987 and 1990, six farmers collected nearly $1.2 million in benefits that should have been denied.[57] Farmers routinely provided faulty information about their compliance with Swampbuster so they could continue collecting subsidies. Overall, only 544 farms lost benefits between 1986 and 1992. Although the penalized farmers initially lost a total of nearly $12 million, the ASCS ultimately restored 48 percent of the benefits; so most farms ended up losing less than $3,000 each. Moreover, a drawn-out appeals process enabled farmers to shop courts for favorable rulings.[58] Yet when Congress reauthorized the Farm Bill in 1996, Swampbuster and the WRP remained intact with only minor changes.[59]

With the conservation compliance provisions of the 1985, 1990, and 1996 farm bills, Congress finally recognized the connection between federal agricultural policies, subsidies, and wetland losses, but breaking that long-standing connection proved difficult. As one veteran Fish and Wildlife Service staff member suggested, "Of course it's slow going, but it's like turning an aircraft carrier around. It's on the way."[60]

Blood of the Ecosystem

Aside from physically transforming wetlands into farmland through drainage, agriculture also degraded wetlands by diverting vital water sources and polluting them with chemicals and sediment. In many cases, federal policies and structures originally designed to promote intensive farming worsened water quality and threatened the very blood of wetland ecosystems.

In the mid 1980s, problems of polluted runoff came to a grotesque apogee at Kesterson National Wildlife Refuge in California's Central Valley. Because nearly 95 percent of Central Valley wetlands had been converted to farmlands, the few remaining wetlands—mostly federal, state, and private wildlife areas—provided crucial habitat for feeding, resting, and wintering to Pacific Flyway waterfowl.[61]

Although a refuge in name, Kesterson was actually a wetland formed at the terminus of the San Luis agricultural drain, a conduit of the federal Bureau of Reclamation's Central Valley Project. Hundreds of miles of CVP canals, pipelines, aqueducts, and ditches diverted the flood of Sierra Nevada snowmelt waters, which had once nourished the valley's wetlands, into orchards and fields. Diversions and groundwater withdrawals depleted the Sacramento and San Joaquin rivers by up to 70 and 90 percent, respectively, of their natural spring runoff. After farms used water for irrigation, only the leftovers drained via ditch into wetland refuges. In the San Joaquin Valley, for example, less than 1 percent of CVP water, mostly wastewater, flowed into wildlife areas. Refuges typically received only 7 to 8 percent of the water they needed to retain their wetlands functions.[62]

In 1983, when Kesterson biologists found hundreds of birds dead, and still more hatchlings with missing eyes, beaks, and wings, they realized that water flowing into the refuge was toxic. Necropsies revealed that tissues of dead and deformed birds had high levels of the heavy metal selenium. At the same time, drought struck, and California's wintering duck population plummeted from 7 million to 2 million birds between 1980 and 1985.[63]

Restrained by the explicitly anticonservation policies of the Reagan administration, the federal agencies responsible for the refuge were reluctant to investigate the matter thoroughly, but *Sacramento Bee* reporter Tom Harris pursued the selenium mystery. He learned that the repeated plowing and irrigating of intensive agriculture made selenium, arsenic, and boron leach from Central Valley soils into the drain water, where along with pesticide residues and salts, it accumulated in drainage sinks, such as Kesterson. With minimal clean water flowing into the refuge, the toxicity of the wastewater was highly concentrated. Although farms had irrigated for decades, the amount of selenium finally reached an extreme level—with devastating effect. Although 1,200 acres of shallow ponds and wetland vegetation made

Kesterson still look like a safe haven to waterfowl flying overhead, in reality it was a death trap. Harris's articles in the *Sacramento Bee,* accompanied by heartbreaking photographs of malformed ducklings, pressured the federal agencies to begin their own belated studies. In the meantime, refuge staff shot noisy guns to keep ducks from landing in the poisoned wetland.[64]

Downditch of Kesterson, agricultural diversions also had an effect. Without sufficient freshwater flows to fend off the salty arm of San Francisco Bay, salinity levels in the Sacramento–San Joaquin Delta increased five to fifteen times, stressing vegetation and animal life specially adapted to the brackish ecosystem and allowing for the invasion of harmful exotic species. Without freshwater circulations, toxicity of other contaminants also increased. Furthermore, the operation of dams and irrigation infrastructures eliminated the migration and spawning habitat of salmon, striped bass, and shad. By 1987, the number of striped bass declined to one-tenth its 1970 level, and the delta smelt population was nearly annihilated. As a once bountiful estuarine fishery crashed, commercial fisheries suffered economic losses of over $3 billion for the decades spanning the 1960s through the 1980s.[65]

With the decline of the ecosystem aggravated by severe drought, support to protect the Sacramento–San Joaquin Delta and its endangered species mounted. More than thirty citizen groups joined in a new coalition, Share the Water, and demanded delivery of more clean CVP water to the head of the estuary. Central Valley farms, which were using most of the water, had little incentive to use less because they irrigated with water furnished far below cost by federal water projects. Besides receiving heavily subsidized CVP water, these corporate farms netted federal price-support payments for surplus crops they grew on roughly 1.2 million acres. In 1986, $379 million in crop-support payments went to federally irrigated farms, and California had the largest proportion of land planted in surplus crops. Such "double-dipping" in both water and crop-support subsidies came under intense criticism and eventually prompted fiscal conservatives to join the call for reform. Delta advocates also found support in the state's metropolitan areas, which wanted to use CVP water in times of drought.[66]

In 1992, efforts of California environmental advocates finally paid off when Senator Bill Bradley (D-NJ) and Congressman George Miller (D-CA) successfully pushed the Central Valley Project Improvement Act (CVPIA) through Congress. In addition to setting water-quality standards, the law dedicated 800,000 acre-feet of water each year from the Central

Valley Project largely for fisheries and 426,000 acre-feet to guarantee a water supply for publicly owned wetland refuges. (An acre-foot is the amount of water needed to cover an acre of land in water one foot deep.) The law also reformed water pricing and established user fees both to reduce subsidies and to pay for costs of environmental protection and restoration. The shutdown and cleanup of Kesterson alone had cost tens of millions of federal dollars.[67] Despite tremendous opposition from agricultural interests and the governor of California, President George Bush signed the CVPIA in October 1992.[68] Although the law addressed the water needs of publicly owned wetlands, three-quarters of the remaining Central Valley wetlands were still in private ownership.[69]

California was not the only state with water flow and quality problems, and Kesterson was not the only wetland refuge that received agricultural drain water. A 1986 U.S. Fish and Wildlife Service report identified toxic contamination as a problem in eighty-four refuges nationwide.[70] Just on the other side of the Sierra Nevada, the Carson River was heavily tapped for desert irrigation before it finally meandered into Carson Sink. Prior to diversions, the sink had brimmed with lush marshes, providing a true desert oasis for migratory waterfowl and shorebirds. Since 1947, a small marsh area protected as the Stillwater National Wildlife Refuge had held fast despite diversions. Like Kesterson, Stillwater sat at the bottom of its watershed and at the end of the water list. During the drought years of the late eighties, the refuge received only the dregs of agricultural wastewater. As flow into the refuge waned, the desert encroached upon the dying wetland like a vulture circling closer and closer. With less than 5,000 acres of marsh remaining in 1987, refuge staff found fifteen hundred birds and seven million fish dead and realized that selenium had poisoned their water as well. Collecting dead birds became a daily task—a grisly scene for a "refuge."

With no support available within the Fish and Wildlife Service, the refuge manager sought assistance from The Nature Conservancy (TNC), which took on the challenge of purchasing water rights in the rural Nevada community to assure a better supply for the refuge. By successfully purchasing marginal desert farmlands and their water rights from willing sellers, TNC was at once able to retire selenium-producing soils (preventing further contamination) and to supply the refuge with water. Purchasing water rights to protect a wetland was a revolutionary strategy for conservation advocates. Despite years of drought, the small amounts of clean water trickling into the marshes helped to maintain the ancient ecosystem.[71] By 1990, the plight of Stillwater had aroused enough citizen concern that Nevada voters approved a bond issue providing between $5 million and $9 million to protect the wetlands of the Carson Sink. Nevada Senator Harry Reid (D) then pushed for the Truckee–Carson Settlement Act, which required the secretary of the interior to acquire the water rights needed to sustain Stillwater.[72]

There and throughout the West, water-flow and water-quality problems threatened wetlands. Located mostly along verdant corridors bordering rivers, western wetlands provided especially critical habitat for birds and wildlife in otherwise arid terrain. Yet diversion of water for farms and cities often sucked rivers and nearby wetlands dry.[73] In Colorado's San Luis Valley, decades of groundwater-tapping irrigation lowered the water table, leaving the valley with few of its wetlands. Though wetlands comprised less than 5 percent of the state's land, 90 percent of wildlife species relied on them for habitat.[74] Along Utah's Green River, polluted farm runoff contaminated wetlands and the habitat of threatened endangered fishes, such as razorback suckers and Colorado squawfish.[75] All told, 90 to 95 percent of western riparian wetlands had been degraded or destroyed since Euro-American settlement.[76]

Farther east, in Nebraska, heavy diversions from the Platte River changed the character of riparian wetlands that Central Flyway waterfowl—including the endangered whooping crane—depended on.[77] Overpumping of groundwater by center-pivot irrigation in Kansas also dried up Cheyenne Bottoms, another critical stopover spot for birds.[78] Instead of finding their plentiful, age-old wetland sanctuaries glimmering with water, migratory waterfowl found a landscape marked by enormous disks of crops and sun-baked dirt.

Troubled Waters in the East

The insufficient water-flow and water-quality problems that plagued wetlands west of the hundredth meridian occurred in the East as well. On North Carolina's coastal plain, where swamp forests and pocosins had been converted to farmlands in the 1970s, polluted runoff diminished water quality in Albemarle and Pamlico sounds.[79] Over 90 percent of the state's commercial fishery depended on healthy estuaries, but areas affected by runoff produced fewer shrimp, crabs, fish, and oysters. Although wetlands generally filter pollutants, these were overtaxed with more than they could assimilate. Elevated nutrient loads on the Chowan River caused algal blooms that sickened the fish in Albemarle Sound. In 1976, one-half of the total commercial catch had to be discarded because of red-sore disease lesions.[80]

Farther north, the grand Chesapeake Bay received polluted runoff from a vast 64,000-square-mile watershed stretching from the headwaters of the Susquehanna in New York state to the headwaters of Virginia's James River. Although cities and suburbs within the bay's intensely populated watershed created much of the pollution, agriculture constituted the primary source of nitrogen, phosphorus, and sediment. Within the Chesapeake watershed, farmers worked roughly 10 million acres and applied nearly 700 million pounds of commercial fertilizer each year. Manure from dairy, pig, and poultry farms also contributed nutrients. Funneled down dozens of rivers, all these nutrients and sediment ended up in the shallow bay, where they nourished algal blooms that depleted oxygen. As a result, meadows of aquatic vegetation, such as eelgrass, celery, and widgeon grass, died. Shoreline marshes that had provided nurseries for fish, crustaceans, and birds were degraded as well. With these important wetlands went the habitat for fish and waterfowl that had formed the foundation of the bay's natural wealth. After Hurricane Agnes unleashed floods of still more pollutants and silt into the Chesapeake in 1972, the bay's water quality and productivity finally crashed. Throughout the rest of the decade, commercial harvests of American shad declined by 95 percent in the Maryland portion of the bay, and herring catches declined by 95 percent all across the bay. Plunging populations of oysters, striped bass, and white perch punctuated the demise of one of the nation's richest commercial fisheries and left bay shore communities stranded without their livelihoods.[81]

Yet at the time, the connections between upstream activities and the health of the bay were not entirely clear. In 1967, concerned citizens had formed the Chesapeake Bay Foundation to begin pushing for bay cleanup, but because the large watershed spread across four states, unanswered scientific questions created political inertia. In response to worsening water-quality problems, the U.S. Congress, prompted by Maryland Senator Charles Mathias (R), directed the EPA to do an intensive study of the Chesapeake. After seven years, forty-five exhaustive technical reports showed conclusively that the bay's water quality had degraded as a result of changing land uses, urban growth, wetland drainage, increased fertilizer use, and other pollution throughout the enormous watershed. Beyond specifically identifying many sources of pollution, the study found that water quality was better near areas with intact, high-quality wetlands. Most significant, the study warned that without strong measures to halt degradation, the Chesapeake's ecological downslide would accelerate.[82]

In response to the alarming EPA study, governors from Virginia, Pennsylvania, and Maryland, along with the mayor of the District of Columbia and the administrator of the EPA, met in 1983 and signed a pathbreaking agreement to improve water quality and to restore the Chesapeake's valuable aquatic life.[83] Each state agreed to take action by upgrading treatment plants, tightening sewage treatment regulations, and encouraging farm practices that minimized runoff. Maryland Governor Harry Hughes made the greatest commitment, promising a one-year, $39 million expenditure for cleanup, restoration, monitoring, and education. Hughes also pushed his state legislature to approve the Chesapeake Bay Critical Area Law in 1984 to limit further land development in sensitive wetland habitat around the bay.[84] The three-state Chesapeake Bay Agreement created a new forum for coordinating regional efforts and for the first time made a public commitment to halting decline and restoring the bay. The Chesapeake Bay Foundation, which had grown to twenty-three thousand members by 1985, closely watched implementation of the agreement, which was updated in 1987 with the goal of reducing unwanted nutrients by 40 percent before the year 2000. Finally, by the early 1990s, positive results could be seen. Striped bass began to rebound, and aquatic vegetation returned to the Chesapeake.[85]

Farming the Everglades

Despite the efforts of lawmakers, environmentalists, engineers, and biologists, poor water quality and inadequate flows still plagued the Everglades. For decades, farms, growing cities, and flood-control conduits had diverted water that once flowed naturally from Lake Okeechobee into the sawgrass wetland. As a result, the remnant marsh collected water from only 32 percent of its watershed and had shrunk to 48 percent of its original size. In 1900, Twenty-seventh Street marked the boundary between Miami and the marsh; eighty years later, 180 city blocks had encroached upon the glades.[86]

Although agreements forged in the early 1970s guaranteed flows for Everglades National Park, water releases occurred before biologists understood the ecological effects of timing. Too much water dumped into the park at the wrong time inadvertently disrupted the wetland as much as

droughts of the past had. For example, wood storks breed only when dropping water levels restrict fish to small pools, where the birds catch by touch
reflex rather than by sight.[87] Excess water undermined this fishing technique and left birds unable to feed their young. The stork population
dropped by 75 percent from 1967 to 1982. The poorly planned water
regime endangered more than just wood storks. Biologists estimated that
the number of wading birds in the Everglades had declined by 90 percent
since the turn of the century.[88] According to Nathaniel Reed, former assistant secretary of the interior for fish and wildlife, the park was "on the brink
of death."[89]

Although a subsequent release plan based on rainfall better simulated
the natural timing of water flow, the amount and the way it moved—in conduits rather than by sheet flow—remained problematic. Because the water-
delivery infrastructure —fourteen hundred miles of canals, levees, ditches,
and pumping stations—was built primarily to serve agriculture and flood-
control needs, water could be readily diverted to farms or storage areas but
less easily delivered to meet ecological needs. Redesigning the plumbing to
get water to the park was essential, but not just any water would do.

As in other regions where agriculture dominated, water in the Everglades
was severely polluted. The Florida legislature had recommended the
restoration of the Kissimmee River in 1976, but through the 1980s, the
waterway languished as a series of dammed pools beside stranded oxbow
lakes, which still fed waste into Lake Okeechobee.[90]

Moreover, wastewater still flowed from the Everglades Agricultural Area
(EAA), where huge corporate farms devoted over 400,000 acres of former
sawgrass marsh to growing sugar cane. The crop was worth hundreds of
millions of dollars, but had many environmental side-effects.[91] Much of the
year, seven giant pumping stations drained four major channels to keep the
water table low enough for the cane. But during dry times, crops demanded
heavy irrigation, consuming much of the region's surface water. Cane also
required large amounts of pesticides, and intensive farming damaged peaty
soils, which oxidized and blew away when harrowed up and exposed to
drying air. As a result, the surface of the EAA fields dropped approximately
an inch a year. Furthermore, microbial activity in the cultivated soils released excess phosphorus and nitrogen, which was absorbed by irrigation
water streaming through fields. For years, sugar growers returned this irrigation wastewater—filled with sediment, toxic pesticide residues, and over
222 tons of nutrients each year—to Lake Okeechobee.

When the lake's eutrophication problems caused an uproar in the mid 1970s, the state had directed the South Florida Water Management District (SFWMD, successor of the South Florida Flood Control District) to come up with a new place to dispose of EAA wastewaters by 1983. Sugar growers eventually agreed to a plan that shunted their polluted runoff into the nearby water conservation areas, including one managed by the Fish and Wildlife Service as the Arthur R. Marshall Loxahatchee National Wildlife Refuge. Environmentalists countered that the growers should dispose of wastewater on their own land instead of on public land.

Long-time Everglades activist Marjory Stoneman Douglas, at the wise age of ninety-three, summed up the litany of subsidies reaped by the sugar growers: "They hardly pay for the water; taxpayers paid for the project and private property owners in the towns pay for most of the upkeep. . . . They use up our land, they pollute our waters, they get a taxpayers' subsidy in price supports, and now they want us to pay for cleaning up the water. . . !"[92] The largest subsidy came in the form of long-standing import quotas that kept the price for domestic sugar at about twice the world-market price, high enough to encourage the conversion of more Everglades into sugar fields.

Despite opposition, wastewater flowed into Loxahatchee, and problems soon appeared. Cattails began to take over, clogging ponds used by water birds. At the fundamental microscopic level, blue-green algae displaced periphyton, the micro-organic base of the sawgrass ecosystem's food chain. Algal blooms also depleted oxygen, suffocating a rich icthyologic fauna. In addition, researchers found deadly mercury accumulated in fish tissues. Because the polluted conservation area supplied water for Everglades National Park, park officials and environmentalists became alarmed when they noticed similar changes within park boundaries.[93]

In addition to problems directly associated with eutrophication, changes in the park's water quality and flood regime made it possible for exotic tree species to colonize significant acreages, displacing the native species of vegetation that mammals, birds, reptiles, and fish had evolved to depend on. Paperbark, for example, had been first introduced from Australia at the turn of the century by developers who thought the thirsty trees would dry up the land. By the mid 1980s, they had infested more than half a million acres.[94] Furthermore, freshwater flowing from Lake Okeechobee through the glades had long maintained the salinity balance of Florida Bay, an estuarine complex that supported 85 percent of south Florida's offshore fishery.

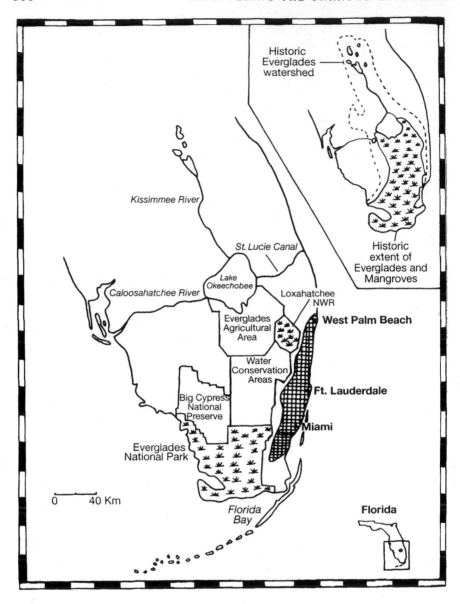

THE EVERGLADES.

With over 2 million acre-feet of freshwater diverted instead to the gulf and the Atlantic directly from the lake, the salinity of Florida Bay increased acutely.[95] Water that did make it to the bay carried excess nutrients, which caused algal blooms that depleted oxygen, blocked light, and killed thousands of acres of sea grass.[96] Shrimp populations, dependent on the grass beds for nurseries, took a nosedive. During the 1980s, the commercial shrimp catch dropped from ten million pounds to three million pounds. Stocks of snook, sea trout, redfish, and spiny lobsters also declined dramatically, leading Everglades National Park to close its waters to commercial fishing.[97]

In 1983, the Everglades received a boost of political support when Governor Bob Graham launched a Save Our Everglades campaign. The ambitious program set out to make the wetland look and function as it had in 1900. "In the process of draining the Everglades," Graham lamented, "the developers reduced a natural work of art into a thing pedestrian and mundane."[98] Beyond his rhetoric of turning back the clock, Graham appointed more environmentally conscious members to the board of the SFWMD. The water management district together with the Florida Department of Agriculture sponsored a program to buy out dairy farms that polluted Lake Okeechobee. The Everglades Coalition, a group of twenty-eight local and national organizations that had rallied to oppose the jetport in the early seventies, reconvened in 1984 to support the governor's cause. In response, the Army Corps of Engineers initiated studies about how to reintroduce the needed sheet flow of water back into the Everglades. Eventually, the U.S. Congress backed the state's Save Our Everglades plan by authorizing acquisition of 107,600 acres to expand the park.[99] Despite the many successes of the state's Everglades campaign, it completely sidestepped the modern issue of pollution created by the sugar industry.

Not until 1989 was the issue of water quality addressed head-on. The U.S. attorney for the Southern District of Florida, Dexter Lehtinen, filed suit against the state, demanding that the Florida Department of Environmental Regulation (DER) enforce its water-quality laws to protect Loxahatchee Refuge and Everglades National Park. Instead of fighting the lawsuit, Governor Lawton Chiles "surrendered," and the state legislature engineered the Marjory Stoneman Douglas Everglades Protection Act in 1991, which financed the construction of special facilities to treat wastewater from the EAA and directed the SFWMD to implement a new pollution-control plan for the Everglades. With the state law passed, DER director Carol Browner was able to negotiate the final agreement of the federal lawsuit, which required farms to control their runoff, allowed the SFWMD to use 35,000 acres within the EAA for water treatment, and set nutrient-level goals for 1997 and 2002.[100] However, Mrs. Douglas and other environmentalists were not pleased by the act named in her honor. Instead of stopping pollution, it allowed the contamination to continue into the future and let the sugar growers off the hook for cleanup costs. The environmentalists' perspective was shared by a growing urban population, which disliked the prospect of paying to clean up after a sugar industry that threatened to pollute its drinking water. Nor did sugar growers agree with the plan that regulated their wastewater; they filed more than a dozen lawsuits against the state.[101]

In the Everglades, as in the Chesapeake, the Central Valley, and the pothole country of the northern plains, destruction and degradation of wetlands through drainage, diversions, and pollution posed numerous public costs. These costs revealed again and again that each wetland was not simply a plot of land bounded by firm property lines, but a nexus of land and water, connected to larger hydrologic cycles and offering many public values. In south Florida, habitat of several unique species was fragmented, and an important fishery collapsed. The destruction of wetlands ruined a natural water purification system and threatened the recharge of an important aquifer that supplied drinking water for four million people. In many other places as well, wetland destruction led to flooding, pollution, and the demise of commercial and sport fisheries, wildlife, waterfowl, and endangered species. The losses to society were not only ecological, but threatening to public health and damaging to economies. For example, costs for drinking-water treatment rose, and jobs dependent on clean water declined. All those costs were passed on to local communities and taxpayers, while those individuals and corporations that exploited wetlands continued to reap profits.

Although the agricultural boom of the 1970s provided a boost for the nation's economy and offered many farms the opportunity for profit, it left many wetlands drained and degraded in its wake. Like the agricultural boom of the 1920s, the profits were short lived, but the degradation of the land and its consequences persisted.

However, in this era of corporate agriculture, subsidized surpluses, and fiscal austerity, lawmakers finally recognized the connection between farm policy and the decline of wetlands. Through the 1980s, Congress, together with states and private conservation groups, took important steps to eliminate outdated policies and practices that threatened wetlands nationwide. But making the new policies work proved to be a formidable challenge, requiring not only a change of attitude among the general public and in the agricultural community, but also aggressive support from the highest levels of government.

SIXTEEN

A Contentious Era for Wetlands

These silent marshes are as valuable as a Van Gogh, as precious as the Hope Diamond. . . . [They must] no longer play the victim in the national version of the Texas chain-saw massacre.

—New Jersey Governor Thomas Kean,
Chairman of the National Wetlands Policy Forum[1]

While Congress made efforts to curb agricultural destruction of wetlands during the Reagan years, deep budget cuts and politically appointed agency heads scuttled enforcement of the Clean Water Act, so wetlands continued to be carved up for development. By 1987, rather than cooperating with EPA and following its 404(b)(1) guidelines as the Clean Water Act directed, the Army Corps of Engineers had loosened up on regulation and was using its own wetland delineation manual and mitigation procedures. The EPA clung to its manual and criteria for mitigation but had few resources to counter Corps decisions. Because the agencies used different measures to enforce the same law, those who were regulated complained about confusion. While environmentalists chided the Corps and developers who wanted to loosen wetland laws, industry and development interests criticized the EPA and environmentalists for wanting to regulate them out of business.

In this contentious atmosphere, EPA administrator Lee Thomas decided to break the deadlock and move forward with wetland policy. With the help of the Conservation Foundation, Thomas convened a National Wetlands Policy Forum so various interest organizations and agencies could meet face to face and resolve quarrelsome issues. Chaired by New Jersey Governor Thomas Kean (R), a group of twenty individuals representing divergent interests met continually for a year and a half to hammer out a national wetlands policy that all parties could agree on.[2] The forum's final report, published in autumn of 1988, reflected a consensus on all recommendations;

only the representative from the National Association of Homebuilders withdrew support at the last moment.

Because of the consensus process, the just-before-elections timing of the report's release, and the support of influential Republican conservationists, presidential candidate George Bush readily adopted the forum's recommendations as part of his platform.[3] It seemed to be a prefab job guaranteed to please everyone and a way to green up Bush's poor environmental record.

On June 6, 1989, President Bush announced his policy at a Ducks Unlimited symposium. "It's time to stand the history of wetlands destruction on its head," he declared. "From this year forward, anyone who tries to drain the swamp is going to be up to his ears in alligators. . . ." Bush then asked the audience to consider what future generations would think: "It could be that they will report the loss of many millions of acres more of wetlands. The extinction of species. The disappearance of wilderness and wildlife. Or . . . they could report that, sometime around 1989, things began to change. . . . And that, in that year, the seeds of a new policy about our valuable wetlands were sown—a policy summed up in three simple words: 'no net loss.'"[4] With those words, Bush unleashed the pent-up energies of the federal agencies that had been in need of a clear mandate to cooperate and take action.

The U.S. Fish and Wildlife Service, under the leadership of forum participant John Turner, quickly published a booklet, *Meeting the President's Challenge,* encouraging all staff to step up their wetland conservation efforts. For the first time in years, the EPA and the Army Corps of Engineers, under the guidance of William Reilly and Robert Page, respectively, began to work together. Within a year, they came to a new agreement concerning mitigation. Scientists from federal agencies involved with wetlands, including the Corps, EPA, Fish and Wildlife Service, and SCS, also met for the first time to develop a single delineation manual that all agencies could use to determine what lands were officially wetlands.[5] Using recommendations from the forum as a blueprint, President Bush pushed wetlands protection on a fast track, and under his leadership, federal agencies began to enforce regulations more aggressively. Once again, money became available for wetland habitat acquisition, and the Fish and Wildlife Service wetland budget rose 220 percent in four years. Within the EPA and the Corps, staff held high expectations that the 404 program could finally become effective.[6]

The adoption of an explicit no-net-loss policy marked a clear landmark in the country's thinking about wetlands. With no other landscape type had we counted our remaining stock and decided it should be saved up. Although citizens had slowly come to learn about wetland values over the course of twenty years, that the president seized upon their protection as a part of his policy platform conferred particular value on the landscape. In stark contrast to the swampland giveaway 130 years before, the Bush administration clearly advocated special protection for wetlands. The president undoubtedly believed that the majority of Americans would support the conservation of this underdog landscape. While his hunch was correct, powerful people disagreed.

With the establishment of the new mitigation agreement, the Corps and the EPA had decided that they would indeed require "sequencing" for mitigation of wetland projects. Avoiding wetland destruction would be the first consideration, and then, only if no alternatives could be found, would a project be approved with mitigation to compensate for losses. This requirement had been agreed upon by forum participants and was considerably flexible, even including a provision for off-site mitigation designed to allay worries of the Alaska oil and gas industry. But now, that industry reneged and led a charge against the agencies' agreement. Over the course of several months, the oil and gas industry needled broader opposition to federal wetlands regulation, including the farm, real estate, development, and property-rights lobbies, as well as Congress members, two Cabinet secretaries, and the White House chief of staff. The long hours of discussion and careful compromise forged by forum members quickly eroded. The fragile consensus dissolved, and hopeful progress came to a standstill once again.[7]

Into this hostile political arena, the Bush administration released its new interagency federal wetlands delineation manual. Because the manual outlined the specific criteria that government officials would use in the field to determine what was and what was not a wetland, the technical document had direct consequences for all who wanted to develop wetlands. The issuance of what was dubbed the "1989 manual" was like pouring gas on wildfire. Basing their wetlands delineation criteria on Fish and Wildlife Service studies, the interagency scientists had used the best available information, but their new definition included more areas than had previously been considered wetland by the Corps. Although Section 404 of the Clean Water Act had long recognized a categorical exemption for agriculture, the new delineation manual included farmed wetlands. Mark Maslyn of the Farm Bureau explained the farmers' perspective: "Suddenly, people were getting nabbed and being told that a soybean field their dad had worked for 50 years was a wetland and they'd need a permit."[8] This may have been true if the landowner wanted to develop the property into a shopping mall, but not if it was to remain a soybean field.

Piqued by the broadened regulations, the Farm Bureau organized a national campaign to abolish the new manual, charging that it extended regulation to 60 million acres of "prior-converted" croplands (wetlands fully drained and converted to crops before December 23, 1985, when Swampbuster took effect). The Farm Bureau then joined with the disgruntled oil and gas industry and formed the disingenuously named National Wetlands Coalition (NWC) to counter conservation efforts. Members of the industrial lobbying group had given more than $2 million to the Reagan and Bush election campaigns and expected to cash in on their investments.[9] Fueling the rhetoric of the NWC, vice president Dan Quayle labeled the 1989 manual as "one of the largest land grabs in modern times."[10]

Provoked by such assertions, private-property rights advocates soon entered the fray, declaring that federal wetlands regulations devalued private lands and therefore constituted illegal "taking" of property by the government. At the heart of the issue, the right of property owners to do what they wanted with their land was pitted against the obligation of the government to prevent uses of property that harmed neighbors or the environment.[11]

Escalating the conflict further, writers for the *Wall Street Journal* and *Newsweek* vilified federal regulators for imprisoning a Pennsylvania mechanic who allegedly didn't know he was filling a wetland while doing "routine" cleanup of his garage's yard. Emphasizing the severity of the punishment, articles characterized the incident as "an atrocious misuse" of federal clean water regulations. Although court hearings later revealed that the mechanic had clearly known about the wetland status of the land, had negotiated a lower price for that reason, had planned to expand onto it anyway, and had failed to heed several federal cease-and-desist orders before finally being sent to jail, he became a martyr and hero to those who opposed regulations.[12]

As the controversy grew, environmentalists claimed that property rights advocates exaggerated the purview of the manual. For example, Louisiana Representative Jimmy Hayes (D, later R-LA) told an apocryphal story about a grandmother fined by the Corps for planting roses in her front yard. Even the scattering of seeds, they claimed, was absurdly construed as fill in the parade of misinformation.[13]

Angry letters of protest poured into the offices of the Corps, the EPA, and the White House. In attempt to quell the unrest and confusion, the agencies jointly issued a question-and-answer paper directed to farmers, but the attack had already developed a venomous life of its own. Fearing that the whole wetlands regulatory program might be lost, the Corps quickly issued a guidance letter to its district offices specifically exempting prior-converted cropped wetlands from Section 404 jurisdiction. The EPA made no protest.

But environmentalists criticized the agencies for blatantly disregarding the conclusions of their scientists and caving in to paranoia. According to the National Wildlife Federation, exempting wetlands that had been cropped yet still retained wetland qualities released 60 million acres for development. "What you're talking about," Jan Goldman-Carter of the NWF explained, "is selling out a farm to turn it into a K-mart or housing project."[14] But the Corps's retreat on prior-converted croplands failed to placate the farm-and-developer-backed NWC.

Responding to political pressure, the Bush administration pushed the autonomous interagency committee of federal scientists to dilute its manual further. To speed matters along, the White House, the Office of Management and Budget, and the Vice President's Council on Competitiveness became directly involved. In an unprecedented manner, politicians replaced scientists at the technical drawing board, and what had begun as a collaborative effort of wetland experts was taken over by White House officials who had little knowledge of the issues. In fact, they had to be given a special wetlands glossary at their decisive meeting.[15]

On August 14, 1991, the Bush administration released its new manual featuring a narrower definition of wetlands. "I think we are going to have no net loss," President Bush explained, "but we're not going to screech this country to a halt and throw everybody out of work in the process."[16]

The new manual drew fire from scientists, environmentalists, state governments, and others interested in wetlands protection. While the 1989 manual lacked political support, the 1991 manual lacked scientific grounding. Within five months, more than eighty thousand formal comments, almost all of them highly critical, deluged the EPA.[17] Critics charged that the administration's new definition of wetlands ignored seasonal variations, had no basis in ecological understanding, and catered to business interests—shifting the burden of proof entirely to the government. According to the National Wildlife Federation, 20 to 40 million acres of wetlands could fall through holes in the administration's manual. In Wisconsin alone, between 3.2 and 4.2 million acres—60 to 80 percent of wetlands identified by the

1989 manual—would not be considered wetlands. Even large portions of Everglades National Park would no longer be considered wetlands.[18] Fish and Wildlife Service director John Turner directed teams of wetland specialists to apply the proposed definition to hundreds of sites across the country and reported that "the lost acreage in many wetland categories was devastating."[19]

Representing a groundswell of opposition from the scientific community, a panel of experts called on President Bush to send the manual to the National Academy of Sciences (NAS) for unbiased review. "So flawed is the administration's new manual, so incomprehensible is the manner in which it is written and so indefensible is the science on which it is based," observed Mark Brinson of the Society of Wetlands Scientists, that important gains in water quality would be reversed, flood potential would increase, and wildlife would be disrupted if it were used.[20]

Though other wetlands acquisition initiatives flourished under Bush's tenure, pundits accused the president of reneging on his promise of no net loss. Conservationists accused Bush of buckling under political pressure from the oil and gas, agribusiness, and development industries. Jay Hair, president of the NWF, said, "Protecting wetlands by redefining them out of existence is like ending homelessness by redefining a home as a cardboard box."[21] His metaphor was particularly apt since wildlife depend on wetlands as habitat—or homes. The avalanche of objections was effective: the poorly conceived 1991 manual was never proposed for final adoption.

Although national leaders had hoped that the forum would break the divisive deadlock and find an effective and agreeable strategy for protecting wetlands, the consensual, bipartisan political process that had embraced a federal no-net-loss policy was derailed by raw political power. The outcome was deeply entrenched stalemate.

Mitigation: Solution or Illusion?

While the details of defining wetlands sparked the most controversy in the late 1980s, it was mitigation that had first ignited the conflagration. Though mitigation had been part of federal policy for fifty years, scientific evidence about wetland values finally began to raise questions about its efficacy.

The concept of mitigation had first started with the Fish and Wildlife Coordination Act as an attempt to compensate for waterfowl habitat drowned under the reservoirs of federal dams constructed during the 1940s and 1950s. Then in 1969 with NEPA, Congress strengthened requirements by directing federal agencies to avoid and minimize environmental impacts, or to "mitigate" for them by providing "substitute" resources.[22]

At the same time, as part of its multimillion dollar Dredged Material Research Program, the Corps of Engineers experimented with creating new marshes from its dredge spoils as an alternative to the detrimental practice of dumping spoils on existing wetlands. Engineers found they could grade spoil piles and plant them with cordgrass and pickleweed to look like natural marshes. Given the apparent success of these experiments, the Corps felt confident it could make new wetlands to compensate for wetlands destroyed in building projects.[23]

NEPA's mitigation requirements applied not only to federal construction but to federally permitted projects, including those governed by Section 404 of the Clean Water Act. As the Corps issued more and more Section 404 permits, mitigation became more commonplace. When Reagan's regulatory relief agenda pushed the Corps to speed its processing of permits, consulting agencies felt they had no alternative but to recommend mitigation. At least then there would be some environmental benefit gained in exchange for destructive wetland filling.[24]

Developers soon learned that it was far easier to plan for mitigation than to dispute it. In fact, large companies realized that they could avoid permit hassles if they "banked" mitigation credits ahead of time. In 1984, for example, Louisiana's Tenneco Company started one of the first mitigation banks. In Terrebonne Parish, in an area where saltwater intrusion and subsidence threatened large areas of freshwater marsh, the oil and gas company invested over $20 million constructing levees and water-control structures to maintain the marshes. Under terms of a special agreement with several government agencies, the company pledged to spend $3 million annually over a twenty-five-year period to enhance fish and wildlife habitat in a protected marsh area. In return, Tenneco received 8.5 million habitat units, which could be redeemed to compensate for dredging canals through other marshes for access to drilling sites.[25] Public agencies, such as state departments of transportation, also pioneered mitigation banks. Any time they needed to build an exit ramp through a wetland, they could simply draw upon credits in the bank.

Even without setting up a bank, developers could compensate for damages on a project-by-project basis. By 1986, the Corps estimated that it had required mitigation, including project redesign, for more than 50 percent of the Section 404 individual permits (as opposed to "general" permits) it issued; that totaled roughly eighty-eight hundred cases that year.[26] Several states followed suit, adopting mitigation as part of their wetland policies.

Mitigation seemed to be the way to have it all. Developers could destroy marshes to build new condominium complexes, and ducks and environmentalists could be content with newly built or restored wetlands. Moreover, government agencies avoided accusations that they deprived landowners from using private land. To the Corps, mitigation sidestepped contention and made up for damages.

But the EPA was not so pleased. The agency believed that mitigation should be used only as a last-ditch effort if a project was water dependent and there was no other suitable place to locate it. As one EPA regional administrator explained, "In the past, if you had a project with wetland implications, you moved the project. Under this interpretation, you move the wetlands. In my view, nature has a rather remarkable track record in creating wetlands, and developers do not."[27] The two agencies butted heads over this issue through the 1980s.

In the meantime, scientists had begun to question the very basis of mitigation. Could wetlands and all their functions actually be created? Since the days of the Fish and Wildlife Coordination Act, people had come to understand many more values and functions of these landscapes. Though diked ponds might have sufficed as compensation in the past, scientists now knew that wetlands served many more complex functions than providing landing strips for ducks. There needed to be suitable soil and hydrology, proper vegetation, and a whole chain of species from invertebrates on up. Beyond habitat, how could the flood-retention qualities of a wetland be remade? Even more complicated still, how could a created wetland be engineered to contribute to aquifer recharge? Few of these questions had ever been addressed though mitigation had been fully adopted through administrative practice. It was as if the country had been driving around in a car arguing about what direction to go and in the meantime drove far down a wrong street. Now, it was going to be very hard to turn around.

When scientists looked more closely at mitigation, they found abysmal results. In many projects where 404 permits had been issued contingent upon mitigation, the work was simply never done. In other cases, developers mitigated for only a small portion of the promised acreage. Because the Corps had meager enforcement capabilities, developers knew that undone mitigation work would likely go undetected. Even where developers mitigated in good faith, they often failed.[28] Although researchers had some moderate success at re-creating simple salt marsh ecosystems where the tides took over as architect, most attempts at inland wetlands, especially those built quickly by developers, flopped. Oftentimes, the whole purpose of mitigation was lost in the shuffle of paperwork and bulldozing. For example, tiny wetlands might be created in a sea of concrete; and as builders developed surrounding uplands, additional runoff severely degraded the mitigation wetlands. At the Tenneco bank, critics contended, the system of dikes and ongoing dredging hastened the decline of wetlands outside the protected area.[29]

Now more intimately familiar with the details and workings of wetlands, scientists realized that the existing characteristics and capacities of most wetlands resulted from thousands of years of gradual seasoning. As wetland expert Frank Golet explained, "Wetlands simply cannot be moved around the landscape like so many chessmen without seriously disrupting their natural functions and degrading their values."[30] Other scientists warned that natural wetlands were being replaced incrementally by artificial substitutes whose long-term survival and value were questionable.[31] Because there were so many uncertainties, trading functioning natural wetlands for created ones was like trading in real money for Monopoly money—gambling the future on odds that engineers could make wetlands as well as nature does.

In response to the increasing use of mitigation and to growing questions about its actual success, the EPA issued a report in 1989 on the scientific grounding of wetland restoration and creation. After surveying all existing studies, the report's authors concluded that though it might be possible to re-create some floodwater storage, it would be exceedingly difficult to re-create groundwater recharge. Though created wetlands could likely offer some habitat values, they could not prevent the loss of biodiversity. Ultimately, it would be impossible to duplicate all of the functions of a natural wetland.[32]

Though mitigation offered the most politically expedient way out of the bind of wetland regulation, it could no longer be regarded as a panacea for wetland losses. In light of this information and the Bush administration's initial no-net-loss policy, the Corps agreed for the first time to adopt EPA guidelines to allow mitigation only if there were no alternatives to destroying wetlands. It was this 1990 agreement that scared members of the industrial National Wetlands Coalition, who feared that the Corps might actually begin to regulate seriously.

Despite NWC opposition and the subsequent manual controversy, the

1990 EPA–Corps agreement survived, officially allowing mitigation only as a last resort. In the absence of proper enforcement, however, many Corps offices continued to prescribe mitigation as a palliative for their wetland woes.

Private Property and Wetland Commons

While the Bush White House jockeyed to find a tenable wetlands policy, the National Wetlands Coalition and property-rights advocates took their discontent to the Capitol. There, the complex issues of wetlands regulation and private property emerged in stark black and white. In the ensuing discourse of anecdote and hyperbole, the very principle of environmental protection was equated with the derogation of private-property rights. With the Clean Water Act up for reauthorization, partisan debate raged in Congress as representatives introduced round after round of wetland and property-rights legislation through the early 1990s.

Antiwetland sentiment first picked up steam in the House, where a coalition of southern members backed the deceptively titled Comprehensive Wetlands Management and Conservation Act of 1991, sponsored by Louisiana representative and real-estate developer Jimmy Hayes. Touted as a law to "protect" landowners from wetlands regulations, the Hayes bill featured an even narrower wetland definition than the 1991 manual did, protecting only those wetlands deemed most ecologically valuable, or "class A." It would also create more exemptions and eliminate EPA's veto authority.[33]

Most significant, the bill included a provision that required the federal government to pay landowners for not developing class A wetlands. If the government failed to purchase the property within a given time, the owner would be free to drain, fill, and develop those most critical wetlands without restraint. Arbitrarily, the bill stipulated that no more than 20 percent of wetlands in any county could be graded class A.

Other representatives raised practical concerns about the compensation provision: If the federal government had to pay people not to fill wetlands, would it then have to pay people to follow all laws? For example, would a county have to pay a company not to set up its factory in a zoned residential area if it had purchased land there? And the costs of compensation would be colossal. The Congressional Budget Office estimated that the Hayes bill could cost taxpayers up to $45 million. After it failed in 1991, Hayes reintroduced his bill in 1992 with 174 cosponsors.[34]

Environmentalists warned that the bill would instantly disqualify more than 50 percent of the nation's wetlands from protection. Countering the stories of property-rights advocates, they pointed at understaffed Corps of Engineers and EPA offices that rarely enforced the Section 404 permitting program. In San Francisco Bay, for example, citizen activists identified numerous cases of unpermitted wetlands filling, including forty cease-and-desist orders ignored by developers, for which no action was taken.[35] In the Florida Keys, the Corps readily issued 404 permits despite the ecological fragility of the area. According to Vero Beach Fish and Wildlife Service supervisor David Ferrell, the Corps was "not denying anything, even when everybody and their dog [were] recommending denial."[36]

But despite environmentalists' claims that the Corps readily issued permits allowing development in wetlands, much of the dialogue in Congress remained focused on how regulations unjustly prevented ordinary citizens from developing wetlands they owned. Three-quarters of the remaining wetlands in the lower forty-eight states were privately owned. In many cases, the wetlands offered public values but did not generate any particular gain for the landowner. Property-rights advocates argued that if the private wetland property truly afforded public services, then taxpayers should pay for them. While debate over Section 404 had long centered on wetlands, property-rights activists in 1992 shifted the discourse from wetland protection to property-rights protection. Those who opposed wetland regulations traded in the black hats they had worn as unconcerned developers and readily donned white hats as property-rights champions.[37]

Louisiana Representative Billy Tauzin (D-LA, later R), expressed the concerns of the property-rights advocates. "Those who treasure our constitution and our form of democratic government," he explained, "fear that our system of private property will be discarded in the name of protecting the environment."[38] The grassroots Fairness to Land Owners Committee (FLOC) also testified in defense of all the "moms and pops" harassed by what they called the federal government's "draconian permitting and enforcement program."[39] The property-rights advocates charged that wetland regulations violated the takings clause of the Constitution that specifically precluded the government from "taking" private property for public use without compensation.

Wetland supporters argued that the court system was already in place to decide when property owners deserved compensation for their lands. Government taking of property had rarely been an issue for two hundred years, ever since high-handed plundering by the Revolutionary Army had first prompted lawmakers to add the takings clause to the Bill of Rights in 1791. The original intent of the clause—"nor shall private property be taken for public use without just compensation"—was to prevent soldiers from stealing chickens and pigs from farmers during wartime. Not until a twentieth-century lawsuit, when a coal-mining company argued that regulations to prevent land subsidence and damage to surface structures infringed upon its mineral rights, did federal courts even consider that regulations could result in "takings." In that 1922 case, Supreme Court Justice Oliver Wendell Holmes reasoned that, while owners might lose through restrictions placed on their property, they gained from restrictions placed on neighboring properties. Moreover, Holmes recognized that "government could hardly go on" if it had to pay for every regulation that lowered property values.[40]

Even then, the issue of regulatory takings rarely came up until the post–World War II boom in population and technology created circumstances that demanded more regulations for public health and environmental quality. Still, takings cases pertaining to wetlands regulations were few, and Holmes's seminal words influenced rulings by both liberal and conservative courts, which tended to compensate owners only when regulations wholly wiped out the value of property. In only a handful of cases had courts decided that government wetland regulations actually took away the value of property.[41]

Most courts decided that owners held property with an implied obligation not to use it in ways that harmed the public. According to the courts, if a regulation prevented a public harm, then it clearly did not constitute a taking. Often, however, wetland regulations did not prevent direct injury to others but rather provided public goods such as pure water. Could the elimination of public benefits preserved by regulations be construed as a public harm? The law was less clear on this matter.

Environmental Defense Fund attorney James Tripp tried to turn the property issue around by calling attention to the ways that wetlands *destruction* diminished property rights. "When we are talking about property," he warned, "it is not only the property of the person who owns the wetland, but the property and economic rights of millions of small business owners . . . [and] fishermen . . . whose well-being we have to take into account."[42]

Underscoring the complexity of the issue, Tripp rhetorically questioned: "Should Congress care more about the property rights of the agribusiness that would drain a bottomland hardwood swamp and turn it into a soybean field, or more about the property rights of the farm downstream that would be flooded as a result? Should Congress care more about the property of the vacation home developer who would turn a wetland into a condominium on the eastern shore of Maryland, or more about the investments of oyster fishermen who have seen their jobs disintegrate at the hands of excess phosphorus that results from wetland loss?"[43] While the Hayes bill addressed the rights of wetland owners head-on, it ironically did so at the expense of other property owners.

For this reason, environmentalists tended to regard the apparently grassroots property-rights coalition as a new front for the antiregulatory agenda of interests that had fought wetland conservation all along. Even though the regulations lacked effectiveness, environmentalists feared that opening them to scrutiny under such inimical circumstances would result in too many compromises, eliminating what little protection there was for remaining wetlands. While environmentalists seemed unwilling to concede that regulations were unduly burdensome, the property-rights groups seemed unwilling to acknowledge the importance of conserving wetlands.

Regarding wetlands solely as property, the private-rights discourse omitted fundamental information offered by science. Because water linked wetlands to aquifers, rivers, and ocean fisheries, these landscapes provided public values that traditional conceptions of property didn't sufficiently address. This wetland commons was shared by all Americans, though most wetland parcels were privately owned.

Although the lens of science shed light on wetlands as complex ecological systems of land *and* water beginning in the 1960s, centuries of legal practice had reinforced the understanding of wetlands as land. Under the traditional view, wetland regulations impaired the rights of landowners and businesses; but according to the newer ecological view, wetland regulations sought to balance the rights of landowners, businesses, communities, and future generations. As the debate over policy intensified, these two views of wetlands clashed. To resolve the enigma of the wetland commons, there would need to be a more accurate way of integrating wetlands' public values into the existing property scheme or a wholly new way of thinking about wetlands.

While Congress considered the Hayes bill and other property-rights bills, no momentous wetland laws passed in 1992 or 1993. Congress did, however, direct the National Academy of Sciences to study and come up with a new wetlands definition to resolve contentious technical issues raised by the 1991 manual fiasco and the proposed legislation.[44]

The 104th Congress

While the antienvironmental policies of the Reagan administration had first placed ecological concerns in a partisan light, the polarization of environmental issues reached new heights with the election of the 104th Congress in 1994, and the contention surrounding wetlands became even more divisive. A very conservative Republican majority entered the House of Representatives in January 1995 with a specific ten-point agenda, the "Contract with America," which included a private-property-rights plank. On the very first day, representatives introduced four "private-property protection" bills.[45] The bill that later passed the House targeted environmental protection by requiring the federal government to compensate landowners if their property was devalued by 20 percent or more as a result of the Clean Water Act, the Endangered Species Act, or Swampbuster. As applied to Swampbuster, the bill implied that even receiving federal subsidies was a property right.

The House also passed amendments to the Clean Water Act drafted by Bud Shuster (R-PA). Most galling to environmentalists was that representatives pointedly refused to wait and consider the results of the National Academy of Science study that Congress had commissioned two years earlier. Just one week after the study finally became available, the House passed what environmental groups called the Polluters' Bill of Rights.

Not surprisingly, the House legislation contradicted NAS recommendations. It resurrected the Hayes bill's extremely narrow wetland definition, which, according to a multiagency evaluation would eliminate protection for 73 to 76 million acres of wetlands (71 percent of all remaining wetlands in the lower forty-eight states).[46] The bill also contained many loopholes. For example, it established that wetlands "delineation shall be conducted during the growing season *unless otherwise requested by the applicant.*"[47] Such language would allow farmers to request the SCS to identify wetlands on their property in late summer when seasonal wetlands dried up, opening the door for drainage of prairie potholes. Representative Norm Mineta who tried to delay the vote for consideration of the NAS report, argued, "We should not simply ignore the science . . . available to us. . . ."[48]

Both the Bush administration's wetland manual makeover and the 104th Congress's neglect of the NAS report represented a fundamental change in the place of science in public policy. Thirty years before, when scientists had first begun to understand the vital importance of wetlands, policy makers, especially at the state level, eagerly kept apprised of the newest information to make laws accordingly. Lawmakers held a respect for the expertise of scientists, and scientists saw an important role they could play in the rapidly changing society. By the 1990s, however, when scientific information did not correspond with political goals, it was discarded and, worse, discredited. Scientists grew reluctant to enter the bitter, quarrelsome political arena where the integrity of their profession was attacked. The preface of the National Academy of Science report, for example, clearly indicated that the committee of scientists did not intend to make decisions about "the degree of rigor with which wetlands should be protected" but rather left those "matters for resolution through law and administrative policy."[49]

But the congressional domain of law and policy was particularly hostile to wetlands in 1994. The chief of the Army Corps of Engineers, Michael Davis, criticized the Shuster bill as a "meat cleaver approach when the precision of a scalpel" was needed.[50] When President Clinton promised to veto the bill, Representative Shuster warned that if the president declined to sign some version of the law, there would "not be one dime for federal clean water programs for the 1996 fiscal year."[51]

Though Shuster's bill never made it out of Congress, the House carried out its threat, passing an appropriations bill that reduced the EPA budget by 34 percent and weakened the agency's ability to regulate wetlands.[52] Former EPA administrator William Ruckelshaus derided the House for refusing to give the agency funds needed to carry out its mandated duties. Already, he argued, the agency had only the resources to do less than 10 percent of what former Congresses had charged it to do. "That is a little like cheering the launch of an airplane bound from New York to Los Angeles while only giving it the gas to reach Chicago, and then decrying the crash as further evidence of pilot ineptitude," Ruckelshaus said.[53] Congress tried repeatedly to inject into budget bills riders that would substantially scale back wetland protection, without discussion. Although those extreme provisions never made it past the president's desk because of intense, partisan budget gridlock, funding for the National Wetlands Inventory project was ultimately slashed by 50 percent—a cut that some saw as strategically mandated ignorance.[54]

On another front, House members considered legislation that would roll back key conservation elements of the Central Valley Project Improvement Act, including provisions that ensured water for California's wetland refuges and fisheries. Implementation of the CVPIA, signed by President Bush in 1992, was also targeted by the Appropriations Committee.[55]

Wetland regulations became a lightning rod for the most recurrent question in American history—What was the proper role of the federal government? Unlike conflicts in the past, the environmental nature of the wetland controversy added a new dimension of protecting the public interest. But the underlying source of debate may have had little to do with political ideology: Between 1990 and 1995, $25.4 million in contributions were given to political candidates by political action committees (PACs) associated with lobbying efforts for weaker wetlands protection laws. When Maryland Representative Wayne Gilchrist (R) offered an amendment to remove the most damaging antiwetland provisions from the Shuster bill, it was defeated 247 to 180. Members who voted against Gilchrist's amendment had received antiwetlands PAC contributions exceeding $4.1 million in the 1994 and 1996 election cycles, or roughly $16,768 per vote.[56]

While Congress wrangled over the controversial wetlands regulations, the Clinton administration worked on wetlands policy administratively. During the previous session of Congress, seven senators had asked the president to take a lead in resolving the vexing issue. Clinton created a White House wetlands working group composed of wetlands experts from nine agencies to hear testimony from a wide variety of interests and to come up with a new policy. In August 1993, noting the need to end the "increasingly divisive" debate over federal wetlands policy, Clinton released his compromise plan. Reviving goals of the National Wetlands Forum, the new policy reestablished the aim of no net loss of wetlands. To make amends with the agricultural sector, Clinton clarified that 53 million acres of prior-converted wetlands were exempt from any Section 404 regulation regardless of changes in use. Clinton also put the Soil Conservation Service, renamed as the National Resource Conservation Service (NRCS), in charge of making wetland determinations on all agricultural lands for both the Clean Water Act and Swampbuster, ensuring that farmers would deal with a single familiar agency. Clinton appeased property-rights advocates by creating 404 exemptions for small acreages owned by families who wished to build single-family homes. The president placated industry by endorsing the use of mitigation banks and sought to assuage developers with a speedy appeals process. To satisfy environmentalists, Clinton urged continued support for the Wetlands Reserve Program and wetland restoration, formally adopted the 1987 Corps manual for wetland delineation as recommended by the NAS study, and tightened restrictions for development in Alaska's coastal wetlands.[57]

The Clinton policy succeeded in disappointing developers, farmers, and environmental groups alike, which some regarded as the sign of middle ground. Developers were particularly perturbed by a new rule that allowed the Corps to regulate mechanized land clearing in bottomlands, and they scoffed at the proposed appeals process.

Farm Bureau lobbyist Mark Maslyn described the policy as "pretty weak" but "a step in the right direction."[58] The agricultural community had hoped that "farmed wetlands" (wetlands *partially* drained before December 23, 1985, that retain wetland qualities), such as those in prairie pothole country, would also be exempted from all regulations. Nonetheless, national Farm Bureau president Dean Kleckner praised the effort to end "the past frustrations of contradictory policies."[59]

Finally, environmentalists were disappointed because they expected President Clinton to develop a more aggressive wetland protection plan. They criticized the administration's strong support for mitigation banking

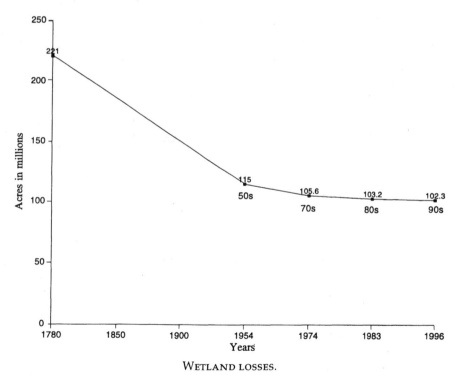

WETLAND LOSSES.

Although the rate of wetland losses has slowed, these important ecosystems continue to be carved up by development and degraded by agriculture, industry, and urbanization. (Courtesy National Wetlands Inventory)

and the quick appeals process for permit applicants, which excluded opportunities for public input. Although the administration officially endorsed restoration as a way to stem losses, environmentalists noted that
Congress had provided only minimal funding in recent years.[60] They were
also skeptical about the lead role of the NRCS in wetlands determinations
on agricultural lands; for decades the agency had encouraged drainage.[61]
While the Clinton administration guarded against the wholesale disman-
tling of wetland protection laws and tried to dampen dissension through
compromise, losses continued and the wetland controversy remained
fundamentally unresolved.

Even though the rate of losses slowed by the mid 1990s, wetlands were
still being carved up at the rate of 117,000 acres per year.[62] And still more
were degraded owing to pollution and water diversions. Seeing little
prospect for more stringent regulations to close in on continuing destruction, environmentalists realized that they must work in imaginative new
ways if they were to maintain the irreplaceable wetlands that remained. And
more than that, they must begin the task of trying to restore what was
already gone.

SEVENTEEN

The Promise of Restoration

> There can be no purpose more enspiriting than to begin
> the age of restoration, reweaving the wondrous diversity
> of life that still surrounds us.
>
> —E. O. Wilson [1]

By the 1990s, restoration was an idea whose time had come. Not only did damaged wetland ecosystems and associated economies desperately need it, but the human spirit needed it. To restore—to literally mend the damaged land—was for many people more satisfying and appealing than regulation and litigation. Restoration was a proactive response that could reestablish lost values and maintain functioning wetland life-support systems. It appeared to be the promising elixir that would help save the natural world in the twenty-first century.

Restoration also had the potential to bridge conflicting attitudes toward wetlands. With Americans stuck between the vision of preserving wetlands and the tradition of property that would ultimately consign wetlands to oblivion, many people involved in the wetland debate saw alternatives to regulation, such as purchasing easements, buying wetlands, and working cooperatively with landowners, as attractive. But to achieve the no-net-loss goal without cracking down on regulation, more wetlands had to be added to the national pool. This prompted scientists and policy makers to think increasingly in terms of restoration.

In the late 1980s and early 1990s, the federal government had initiated several programs offering incentives for private landowners to restore wetlands. For example, the Fish and Wildlife Service Partners for Wildlife Program successfully involved more than twelve thousand farmers to restore 240,000 acres between 1987 and 1994. Many of these farmers had partially drained wetlands during the farm boom but nonetheless enjoyed waterfowl and other values of natural wetlands remaining on their property. Partners for Wildlife provided the help and financial assistance that farmers needed to restore the land. The Department of Agriculture aided restoration efforts through its Wetlands Reserve Program, which enrolled 125,000 acres of marginal farmlands in 1993 and 1994 to be restored as wetlands. Operating on a broader scale, the North American Waterfowl Management Plan, with the assistance of private conservation groups such as Ducks Unlimited and the Nature Conservancy, had successfully restored 400,000 acres of wetlands in the United States since its start.[2] These private groups and others also pursued their own initiatives to restore and safeguard wetlands. For example, in 1995 Ducks Unlimited initiated its River CARE program to restore sizable corridors of wetland habitat along the lower Mississippi. With plans to restore part of the grand Kankakee Marsh, The Nature Conservancy purchased 7,200 acres of farmland along the Indiana–Illinois border in 1997.[3] At the same time that parcels of wetlands continued to be incrementally fragmented and destroyed, other tiny pieces of wetland were being restored in an effort to weave back together some of the ecological integrity lost.

While this promising movement of small-scale restoration proceeded all across the country, other ambitious efforts addressed whole landscapes. For some of the largest wetland ecosystems, restoration offered the only hope.

Louisiana Is Disappearing!

One of the biggest challenges to the federal no-net-loss policy could not be remedied by tougher enforcement of Section 404 or Swampbuster. The coastal marshes of Louisiana were disappearing. This was not more of the same news that wetlands across the nation were being paved under parking lots and carpeted under soybean fields. The Louisiana marshes—forty-three square miles of them each year—were literally sinking into the Gulf of Mexico. At that rate, inland towns would be under water within people's lifetimes.[4] In fact, the delta marshlands had shrunk from about 4 million acres in 1930 to 2.8 million acres by the late 1980s. The sinking Louisiana marshes accounted for 80 percent of the nation's ongoing coastal wetland losses.[5]

Scientists studying the hydrologic regimes of the Mississippi had long recognized that the delta of the Mississippi was dynamic. Over the course of thousands of years, the river had built a series of broad individual lobes of marsh by depositing its rich sediment into shallow coastal waters. Under the weight of the new alluvium, the delta constantly subsided into the gulf, but the arrival of fresh silt kept pace with the subsidence—an equilibrium of sorts between land and sea. When the river's course became too long and inefficient, it jumped to a new route and began forming another delta. A fifty-mile-wide band of golden marshes resulted. All the land forming the tip and sole of the Louisiana "boot" was created in this manner. The present delta represented only the river's most recent path.

But this dynamic process had been disrupted. Dams, plugging all of the Mississippi's main tributaries by the 1960s, held back 60 percent of the silt that had previously gone into delta building.[6] Even more important, the Corps of Engineers had girded the entire lower Mississippi with an enormous levee system to usher floodwaters to the gulf. While these engineered changes safeguarded lands for inhabitation—at least temporarily—they profoundly changed the natural regime of the bottomlands. Before, muddy waters overflowed the river's natural levees and deposited rich sediment that created new lands. Now the river was funneled by engineered levees far into the Gulf of Mexico, where it released its valuable load in waters too deep for accumulation. Sediment-starved marshes, blocked from the river by levees, simply began to sink into the Gulf.[7]

Compounding the problem, the oil and gas industry had gouged nearly ten thousand miles of canals into the coastal marshes since the 1950s.[8] The resulting crisscross increased erosion in much the same way that cutting a bar of soap into smaller pieces hastens its melting. Once dredged, canals continued to widen at a rate of up to 2.5 meters per year. One study blamed canals for 16 percent of delta wetland losses between 1955 and 1978.[9] Canals also acted as conduits, conveying saltwater into freshwater marshes. As a result, bulrushes and reeds died, leaving the peaty soil to erode rapidly. The marshes then became more vulnerable to hurricanes, which routinely blasted the gulf coast, tearing apart lands and pressing saltwater farther up canals.[10]

Although awareness of the coastal-wetland loss became widespread in Louisiana in the late 1970s, little was done.[11] The wide swath of marshes had always fringed the state's coast. It was difficult for most people to imagine that the marshes could actually disappear.

And finding a solution to the herculean problem was daunting. The Mississippi levees protected people and lands from the river's floods; the oil and gas industry supported entire communities and provided revenues that kept the state solvent. On the other hand, the coastal marshes sustained trapping and fishing, industries also traditionally important to Louisiana's economy and identity. The delta marshes nourished a commercial fishery valued at almost $1 billion annually, accounting for nearly 30 percent of the nation's annual fishery harvest.[12] Without the marshes, the catch would plummet. Yet even more than oil and fishery jobs, communities anchored throughout the coastal region needed their land.

Although the federal Coastal Zone Management Act of 1972 had not envisioned problems of such scope as those in Louisiana, the state's Coastal Zone Management Plan had placed a staff in charge of planning for coastal change. Despite its small size and low status, the CZM office managed to bring marsh subsidence problems before the state legislature. Within the three-mile-wide band of gulf under the jurisdiction of Louisiana, the state collected oil and gas royalties. As the shoreline receded, this crucial strip also receded. When legislators realized that the loss of marshes would also result in the loss of significant state revenues, they panicked. If the marshes receded one mile, Louisiana would lose $36.5 million in severance taxes annually.[13] Recognizing the disastrous fiscal and environmental consequences of coastal erosion, Governor David Treen signed the first Coastal Environmental Protection Trust Fund into law in 1981. The $35 million trust was intended to halt saltwater intrusion and to fortify barrier islands, but economic depression subsequently compelled Governor Buddy Roemer to dissolve the fund.[14]

In the early 1980s, the state's Coastal Zone Management Division also began to review activities of the oil and gas industry more stringently. State oversight coupled with a slow economy reduced the number of canals built and encouraged less damaging means of accessing oil well sites, such as directional drilling.[15] But critics charged that the permitting process merely legitimized what oil companies had been doing all along. In one case, both the Corps of Engineers and the state Department of Natural Resources gave an oil company permits to dredge a canal through an ostensibly protected zone just north of Jean Lafitte National Historical Park and Preserve, thereby undermining the wetland park's source of fresh water.[16] As one scientist at the Louisiana State University Center for Wetland Resources observed, "Almost every other coastal state has strong wetland protection laws. With the hard evidence we have, those states would have forbidden dredging by now. But in Louisiana, a lot of it is still permitted."[17]

In the mid 1980s, the Army Corps of Engineers began to reckon with the ecological problems created by its levees and designed three outlets from the mainline system to allow for the controlled release of freshwater (though not sediment) into wetland areas. With the $26 million Caernarvon project, engineers planned to divert water below New Orleans into a 25-square-mile marsh to keep saltwater out. Yet even if all Corps projects were fully operational by the late 1990s as planned, more marsh would be lost in the meantime than the 150 square miles saved by its restoration work.[18] Efforts made by the state and federal government were meager given the monumental scale of the problem.

A breakthrough finally came in 1988 when citizens organized the Coalition to Restore Coastal Louisiana. The group, composed of local governments, churches, environmental groups, chambers of commerce, private landowners, Native Americans, and anglers, pressed for more substantive and thorough action to restore the marshes.[19] The coalition urged the state legislature to set up a cabinet-level position in a new state Office of Coastal Activities with the express purpose of coordinating restoration efforts. In addition, it successfully pushed for a state constitutional amendment that dedicated a scaled percentage of oil and gas revenues to marsh restoration.[20] Most significant, the coalition came up with its own comprehensive plan for restoring and fundamentally reengineering the coastal zone. The coalition's plan became a blueprint for moving forward.

With the strong show of citizen support for coastal restoration, the coalition persuaded Louisiana Senators John Breaux (D) and J. Bennett Johnston (D) to push for federal legislation to help fund the massive restoration. Because marshes in coastal Louisiana accounted for one-third of the coastal wetlands in the continental United States, any resolve to protect wetlands nationally required a significant effort in Louisiana.[21] With the backing of the entire Louisiana delegation, Congress passed the Coastal Wetlands Planning, Protection, and Restoration Act of 1990, which committed $35 million annually, derived from gas production revenues on federal offshore leases, to plan and then implement coastal restoration projects. By 1993, a joint federal state task force had developed a plan and approved thirty-eight projects, ten of which were slated for groundbreaking.[22] Although regulations and conservation management would continue to be important, the ultimate fate of Louisiana's coastal marshes rested upon the success of restoration.

The Mississippi Flood

While levees along the lower Mississippi created subsidence problems at the river's mouth, upriver levees exacerbated flooding all along the river's course. In the spring of 1993, as politicians haggled over wetland regulations in Washington, D.C., the waters of the upper Mississippi and its tributaries began to rise. A persistent storm hovered over the Midwest for two months, dropping more and more rain onto saturated soils. The river swelled and overflowed, carrying at its peak more than one million cubic feet per second of roiling muddy waters, one of the highest flows ever recorded. Riverside residents, most of them veteran flood survivors, boarded up first-story windows and piled sandbags to protect their homes and towns. Although levees girding the rivers were supposed to safeguard floodplain lands, by the end of summer more than one thousand levees had burst, leaving tens of thousands of people homeless and 8.7 million acres of farmland destroyed—some of it buried under many feet of cobbles and new sand.

The floods came in the wake of cool, wet, unusual weather, but many biologists and hydrologists pointed out that widespread channelization, the loss of wetlands, and the increased number and heights of levees were as much to blame for the severity of the flooding as the rain.[23] All told, floodwaters inundated more than 20 million acres in nine midwestern states—states that had lost 57 percent of their original wetlands. The most severely flooded states—Illinois, Iowa, and Missouri—had lost more than 85 percent of their wetlands.[24] Over the course of more than one hundred years of development, water-absorbing bottomland forests and prairie wetlands had been replaced with slickened runoff surfaces such as streets, lawns, and tile-lined farmland. By Fish and Wildlife Service estimates, 19 million acres of wetland had been drained in the upper Mississippi Basin, and as Missouri wildlife biologist Phil Covington explained, "When you replace [wetlands] with an asphalt parking lot or farm field, you lose that sponge."[25]

While more water flowed off these impregnable surfaces, the rivers' flood-carrying capacity was diminished by an extensive system of channels and levees built by farmers, towns, and the federal government for flood control. Following the flood of similar magnitude in 1927, the Army Corps of Engineers had stepped up construction of massive levees designed to keep floodwaters from flowing through floodplains. With levees in place, more farms and communities had sprouted up on the floodplain land; but with more water flowing into the increasingly constrained channels, floodwaters rose higher and higher. Thus, floods of larger magnitude were created with the same amount of precipitation, and more people and property were affected by flooding.

With dozens of communities under water by early summer, demands for disaster relief poured into Washington. Although Congress had designed the National Flood Insurance Program to discourage floodplain development, compliance had always been poor. Of the fifty-six thousand properties damaged by the 1993 floods, only 14 percent were insured. Instead of paying the premiums, which were already heavily subsidized, flood-prone property owners relied on disaster payments—nearly $12,000 a family—to bail them out. The federal government distributed more than $6 billion in disaster aid, two and a half times the amount paid through the flood insurance and crop insurance programs combined, but estimated damages soared to $16 billion.[26]

With the federal deficit soaring, Congress realized that something new must be done. In the Senate, Patrick Leahy (D-VT) criticized the subsidies farmers received as flood relief: one program forgave their farm loans, another paid for crop insurance, and yet another covered field renovations. By helping farmers to reestablish themselves on floodplains, the relief programs perpetuated an expensive and dangerous cycle of disaster. Senator Leahy and others realized that the USDA's Wetlands Reserve Program, which started with the 1990 Farm Bill, might help to break the repeated rebuilding circuit. By acquiring flood prone farmlands, the USDA could prevent new construction. Moreover, by restoring the storage capacity of floodplain wetlands, the reserve program could reduce the severity of future flood damages.[27]

Although the tight-pursed Congress initially balked at the needed appropriations, it eventually approved an Emergency Wetlands Reserve Program (EWRP) to purchase permanent conservation easements for wetlands. The program targeted 100,000 acres for which the cost of reclaiming cropland would exceed the market value of the land.[28]

Timing was critical. As soon as waters subsided, people would clear debris and begin to rebuild their homes and levees if no alternative were available. In order to speed the process, the Soil Conservation Service streamlined sign-up procedures, and a number of conservation organizations, including The Nature Conservancy and the National Fish and Wildlife Foundation, jumped in to purchase easements right away that could be added to the Wetlands Reserve later.[29] By 1994, the Emergency WRP had enrolled 56,516 acres—a substantial area but only a fraction of the 13 million former wetland acres researchers estimated would be necessary to contain floodwaters wholly within the river's banks.[30]

In addition to farmland, some towns were simply tired of dealing with the losses of periodic flooding. Instead of rebuilding again on the floodplain, the citizens of Grafton, Illinois, voted to move a third of the town to dry land. All told, about two hundred communities decided to relocate to higher ground. Though these projects cost U.S. taxpayers $500 million, this would be far cheaper in the long run than repeatedly paying for disaster aid.[31]

Like all grand Mississippi floods, the deluge of 1993 was a powerful reminder of the potent force of nature. For centuries, such reminders had quickly been forgotten; and time and time again, people living in the floodplain had suffered as the river waters rose to higher heights. But this time, the Emergency Wetlands Reserve program and the relocation efforts signified a new response to the Mississippi River flood regime. Instead of working to resist the river, the new approaches accepted the river's natural rise and fall and took advantage of the floodplains' original function. Only by moving out of the most hazardous areas and restoring large tracts of water-absorbing wetlands could people live in accord with the mighty river.

Restoring South Florida

Nowhere was the need to restore wetlands greater than in south Florida. Drastic changes in hydrology caused by flood-control structures, channelization of the Kissimmee, roads, intensive farming, and sprawling urban growth had conspired to degrade the Everglades over the course of a century. But as deterioration worsened, the integral importance of wetlands to the region became clear. The booming Miami metropolis depended on the Everglades to recharge the Biscayne Aquifer that supplied its drinking water. And the tourism industry, which generated more income for the region than agriculture did, relied upon a healthy, bird-filled Everglades National Park and a clean Florida Bay for the Keys' sport fishery. Moreover, people who chose to live in south Florida for its high quality of life didn't want to see that quality compromised. For these reasons, restoring the Everglades enjoyed tremendous popular support and offered the best—if not the only—solution to myriad problems.

Although the Florida legislature first approved restoration of the channelized Kissimmee River in 1976, the project proceeded at a snail's pace. It was far more difficult to put the pieces back together than it had been to take them apart. Between 1978 and 1985, the Corps of Engineers studied possible restoration schemes, but strong state interest prompted the South Florida Water Management District to initiate the first pilot backfilling project. When prechannelization hydrology was restored, wetland vegetation grew back rapidly, and invertebrates, fish, and birds soon started to use the renovated area. Within six years of experimentation, the water management district knew the Kissimmee could be repaired. After follow-up studies by the Corps, partial backfilling of the entire canal was finally scheduled to begin in 1998.[32]

At the receiving end of the Kissimmee watershed, Everglades restoration proved more complicated. When the federal government filed suit against Florida for failing to enforce its water-quality laws in 1989, contention heightened. While lawyers and bureaucrats struggled to smooth the jagged conflicts of lawsuits between the state, the sugar industry, and the federal government, biologists and activists contended that without swift action, the Everglades would die.

In 1993, the Clinton administration took special interest in the region's problems and assigned thirty top federal scientists to develop a comprehensive restoration plan based on returning a sheet flow of water to the Everglades.[33] The Corps of Engineers was also directed to redesign south Florida's plumbing system to restore natural flows to the Everglades while maintaining the Biscayne Aquifer and meeting the needs of the Everglades Agricultural Area (EAA) farms.[34] Given the scope of problems, plans for restoration took on a larger meaning. Secretary of the Interior Bruce Babbitt called the Everglades "the singular, most important, ultimate test of whether we are going to have the capability to do ecosystem restoration."[35] Although the prospect of restoring the glades seemed hopeful, the details of how to do it and especially how to pay for it remained elusive.

The price tag would be high, and many people argued that the EAA farms—mostly sugar growers—should bear the bulk of the costs since they caused the bulk of the pollution. But the growers denied responsibility and blamed problems on the government's water delivery system. Of course, the industry depended on the federal and state water system for its own irrigation, flood control, and wastewater disposal. It was this conflict over who would pay to revive the public values of the Everglades that pushed the issue further up the political ladder.

Both the Clinton administration and Governor Lawton Chiles became closely involved in the settlement negotiations, and in May 1994 the governor signed a compromise law that earmarked $685 million for Everglades cleanup. Relying on the filtration capacities of wetlands, the Foreverglades Act called for the SFWMD to construct 40,000 acres of artificial marshes within the EAA to cleanse polluted runoff before it flowed into water conservation areas and the Everglades. The costs would be paid by taxing both property owners and growers.

Environmentalists, however, argued that the plan unfairly required taxpayers to foot much of the bill. Most troublingly, the act extended the deadline for complying with water-quality standards to the year 2003. According to Joe Podgor of Friends of the Everglades, the new law simply condoned breaking state water-quality rules already on the books. "Environmentalists don't want the pollution to slow down," he explained. "They want it to stop."[36] But Governor Chiles regarded the agreement as a real breakthrough. "The bottom line is this, we're beginning this massive restoration and cleanup effort now."[37] After years of study and years of the recalcitrant sugar industry hamstringing restoration efforts at every chance, lawmakers saw even a tiny step forward as an accomplishment.

In addition to state restoration efforts, the federal government contributed funding and expertise. In 1996, Vice President Al Gore announced a $1.5 billion, seven-year initiative to rehabilitate the Everglades by retrofitting the existing water delivery system.[38] Part of the funding was to come from a one cent reduction in the eighteen-cent-per-pound federal subsidy long reaped by sugar growers, but industry leaders balked and said that they were already paying their fair share through the state law; they refused to pay more.[39] Eventually, the administration backed off from the penny provision. Instead, funding came from U.S. taxpayers through the 1996 Farm Bill and the 1996 Water Resources Development Act, which together authorized spending up to $275 million for Everglades restoration.[40] Florida taxpayers, irked by still bearing the brunt of the state costs, organized a ballot initiative to levy a one-cent-per-pound tax on sugar to pay for more restoration expenses, but the measure was narrowly defeated owing to a last-minute advertising blitz by the sugar industry.[41]

The conflict over who would pay for restoration calls attention once again to wetlands as commons. All the problems had begun when property lines and eventually park boundary lines were drawn atop a natural hydrologic system. Thereafter, people regarded the parcels of land, including the national park, as discrete units. But when scientists learned more about how the Everglades hydrology worked and how birds, fish, and other animals depended on the natural water regime, it became apparent that each unit was in fact part of a larger system.

As south Florida's population swelled to twelve million and beyond, pressure to consume the remaining natural resources grew. New residents required new places to live, pressuring developers to fill in wetlands at the Everglades's edge. At the same time, roughly nine hundred people moving to the state each day demanded 200,000 additional gallons of fresh water daily—water that Florida's wetlands could help to provide but only if restored to a functional state. In order for south Florida to thrive, wetland services had to be preserved. In this context of increasing scarcity, the EAA pollution conflicted sharply with the public good.

Because south Florida depended on the Everglades for its water supply, a better balance needed to be struck between existing land and water uses, growing development, and the life-support system of natural wetlands. The wetlands and the water were essential to all as a resource shared in common, but they were used and degraded as if private ownership of the land was the only wealth that mattered. Whether or not we can restore the Everglades may tell much about our ability to break through barriers of conflict and find solutions that protect and restore wetlands nationwide, solutions that honor the natural wealth once common to all.

EIGHTEEN

The Lessons of History

> When we see land as a community to which we belong, we
> may begin to use it with love and respect.
>
> —Aldo Leopold[1]

The narrow road from Homestead to the Everglades follows along the
edges of tomato farms and strawberry fields where harrowed-up peat soil is
black as night. At the final turn to the west, fields end and swamp begins.
Here at the edge of the Everglades, you can see at once the two trends that
have affected wetlands throughout history: the trend of destruction and the
trend of appreciation.

To the east, farms produce high-priced vegetables on the rich soils of
former sawgrass glades. To the west lies a vast wetland complex protected
as a national park for reasons of biology and wild beauty. Though a property line demarcates the boundary of the private farm and the protected
Everglades, the two still share hydrological connections. For this reason,
the park remains vulnerable to what happens on the farm. The farm and
the park, side by side, represent the persistent paradox of the wetland story.

The trend of destruction began with a cultural disdain for swamps coupled with the recognition that wealth could be extracted from wetland properties. As the commercial economy enlarged, Americans started to log their
swamps and drain them for farms. People believed that by transforming
wetlands, they improved the land from its natural state of wastefulness into
a useful state of cultivation. Moreover, as mosquito-borne diseases spread,
ridding the landscape of wetlands became regarded as a critical public
health measure. When scientific information finally revealed the many
values of wetlands, the age-old disdain for swamps and marshes began to
dissipate. The zeal to remove wetlands for cultural reasons was shorn away,
leaving profit as the prime motive for filling and developing wetlands. After
World War II, a booming economy made the drive to convert wetlands formidable. Thus, for centuries, the trend of wetland destruction dominated.

The trend of appreciation began first when colonists relied on the

sustainable abundance of natural marshes. Then, in the second half of the
nineteenth century, literature and art sparked a fresh regard for wetlands
based on a Romantic aesthetic sensibility and reverence for the waning natural landscape. In the twentieth century, the decline of waterfowl owing to
habitat loss together with scientific evidence about broader values bolstered
stronger appreciation for wetlands. Scientists showed that in addition to
providing habitat, wetlands offered many services, such as purifying water,
providing nursery grounds for important fisheries, storing floodwater, and
recharging groundwater. With the new information, people began to act on
their appreciation for wetlands in the 1960s. Citizen groups worked to protect specific places increasingly threatened by unbridled development. Conservation battles culminated in local, state, and federal laws to protect wetlands through planning, incentives, acquisition, and regulation.

The environmental movement ushered in greater awareness of the natural world and stronger public education about wetland values. Within a
relatively short time, the trend of appreciation gained credence. Back in
1855, Henry Thoreau had claimed to be the only one in his town smitten
by the allure of a natural swamp, but by 1985, public opinion had shifted
dramatically: 85 percent of all Americans believed that wetlands should be
protected. As attitudes toward wetlands changed with greater scientific understanding, governments adopted policies to reflect the new views. As science revealed more clearly that the public benefits of wetlands were a commons shared by all, people saw that government involvement was necessary
to protect endangered values.

Federal protection of wetlands first began with the purchase of refuges
for waterfowl habitat. Then policies encouraged government agencies to
lessen their impacts in wetlands and compensate for losses. In some critical
breeding grounds, the government offered limited incentives to landowners
for leaving their wetlands in a natural state. When these gentle approaches
failed to stem damages, states and then the federal government tried the
tack of regulation to protect wetlands' public values. While the trends of destruction and appreciation had both been at play for more than a century, it
was with regulations that these trends truly confronted each other for the
first time.

Because wetland regulations stood in the way of development projects,
builders and landowners fought new laws fiercely. At the very beginning,
they argued that wetlands were unworthy of special protection. When that
argument didn't work, they disputed technical and legal points, such as jurisdiction and definition. When those arguments didn't work, they shifted
the discourse to property rights.

While the lens of science showed that wetlands offered public services that needed to be protected, a more traditional outlook still consigned wetlands solely to the province of property. Americans were stuck somewhere between the conventional view of wetlands as property and the ecological view of wetlands as a life-support system. Government policies reflected the ambiguity of attitude. By the mid 1990s, two presidents of the two major parties had tried to achieve no net loss of wetlands by setting a firm goal of protection based on science. But federal wetland protection laws were poorly enforced, and the tyranny of small decisions to destroy parcels of remaining wetlands prevailed. Though no one could argue any longer that wetlands were unimportant, no one had come up with a universally accepted way to protect what remained.

This dilemma—society valuing wetlands on one hand but allowing their destruction on the other—perplexed me as I drove farther down the road from Homestead and into Everglades National Park. I pulled out at Payhayokee Overlook and climbed up on a wood platform to view the celebrated glades.

A boundless savanna of golden sawgrass spread before me. The shifting clouds cast dark shadows that seemed to slide through the grass. Here and there, small cypress hammocks dotted the expanse. A fitful wind broke the silence and kept mosquitoes at bay. It was this landscape, once stretching all the way to Lake Okeechobee, that the native people called *Payhayokee*— grassy water.

As I delighted in the beauty of the scene, I wondered if it was this sort of empty, wet expanse that inspired Hamilton Disston to dream of drainage more than a century ago. Was it this same view that caused investors in the Progresso Lottery to despair? Then, looking across endless glades to the east, I imagined the ladies of the Florida Women's Federation driving from Miami in Model Ts on rugged roads through a similar grassy terrain to Paradise Key. And what did the indefatigable Ernest Coe in his white seersucker suit think of this place as he motored across a kindred sawgrass marsh en route to negotiate with wetland owners in the western part of the peninsula?

Then in 1947, President Harry Truman traveled through this sawgrass landscape to dedicate Everglades National Park. The same year, Marjory Stoneman Douglas gave the glades its epithet, "river of grass," and more people began to visit to see for themselves what this extraordinary wetland was all about. In 1948, flood-control levees around Lake Okeechobee stopped the vital flow of water into the Everglades. These sawgrass prairies burned when drought seared through in the 1960s and flooded when excess water abounded in the early 1970s. It was for these unusual wetlands that citizens organized first to stop a jetport, then to stop pollution, and now to seek restoration. It will be in these sawgrass sloughs once again that the drama of our nation's wetland story will be played out.

Although this magnificent scene appeared to be so natural and untouched, it was, in fact, the product of countless human dreams, deliberations, discoveries, and decisions. But what impressed me more, as I gazed across the landscape, was the potent force of nature's resiliency. Here in the heart of the Everglades, I was struck by the broad sweep of sawgrass and the broad sweep of history that this place had survived.

Though not as renowned as the Everglades, each wetland has its own story of endurance. These stories show how people have long benefited from wetlands but also chronicle the unintended and sometimes grim consequences of our use. They explain how we recognized the public services that wetlands have always provided—from clean water to fish and ducks. And they reveal that, beyond the controversy over regulations and technicalities, wetlands are wondrous places that have stirred people's imaginations and spirits for centuries. For these reasons, the question of what to do with our remaining wetlands will continue to provoke intense local, state, and national debate.

As this debate escalates, our society will face a difficult choice: to change our wetlands or to change our culture. Those who would spare the remaining wetlands have gathered strength since the seeds of their movement were planted by William Bartram, Henry Thoreau, and Ding Darling and have now grown into a national force. But while there have been changes in attitudes, policies, and laws, and a marked decrease in the rate of wetlands loss, the destruction of wetlands continues because powerful interests cling to the status quo that calculates its profits in the ledger of short-term private gain with little concern for the common good. As society addresses the difficult question of what to do with wetlands, the lessons of history can serve us well.

Most important, the grand collection of wetland stories reveals again and again that we are fundamentally connected to nature, not apart from it. Informed by history, we can remember the trade-offs already made and turn away from the mistakes and misunderstandings of a time when we knew no better.

Notes

Chapter 1

1. Aldo Leopold, *A Sand County Almanac* (New York: Oxford University Press, 1949; reprint, 1969), 205.
2. Ralph W. Tiner, Jr., *Wetlands of the U.S.: Current Status and Recent Trends* (Washington, D.C.: U.S. Department of the Interior, Fish and Wildlife Service, 1984), 34; Thomas E. Dahl and Craig E. Johnson, *Status and Trends of Wetlands in the Conterminous United States, Mid-1970s to Mid-1980s* (Washington, D.C.: U.S. Fish and Wildlife Service, 1991), 3.
3. Tiner, 18–25.
4. John Mitchell, "Our Disappearing Wetlands," *National Geographic*, Oct. 1992, 8.
5. Arthur E. Morgan, "The Drainage of the Mississippi Delta," *Manufacturers Record*, 8 Sept. 1910, quoted in Robert W. Harrison, *Alluvial Empire: Drainage in the Lower Mississippi Valley* (Little Rock, Ark.: Pioneer Press, in cooperation with the U.S. Department of Agriculture, Economic Research Service, 1961), 227.
6. Theodore Steinberg, *Slide Mountain, or The Folly of Owning Nature* (Berkeley: University of California Press, 1995), passim; Fred P. Bosselman, "Limitations Inherent in the Title to Wetlands at Common Law," *Stanford Environmental Law Journal* 15, no. 2 (June 1996), 247–337.
7. Garrett Hardin, "The Tragedy of the Commons," *Science* (1968). The concept of a "commons" calls to mind Hardin's seminal "tragedy of the commons" essay. When farmers shared a public pasture, Hardin posited, it was in each individual's best interest to graze as many cows as possible. Ultimately, however, too many cows would degrade the pasture and leave the community with a worthless mudpatch. According to Hardin, this metaphor described what would happen as the growing human population consumed the earth's diminishing resources. Because most wetlands have a commons component, their public values are subject to the same tragic degradation. Though most wetlands are privately owned, owners rarely steward the public values of wetlands.
8. U.S. Environmental Protection Agency, Office of Water, *National Water Quality Inventory* (Washington, D.C., 1988), 84.

9. Bill Wilen, telephone interview by author, 26 Sept. 1997.

10. Tiner, 1.

11. Tom Horton, "Chesapeake Bay: Hanging in the Balance," *National Geographic,* June 1993, 23.

Chapter 2

1. John Smith, *The Generall Historie of Virginia, New-England, and the Summer Isles* (London, 1624; reprint, Readex Microprint Corporation, 1966), 169.

2. Thomas E. Dahl, *Wetlands: Losses in the United States, 1780s to 1980s* (Washington, D.C.: U.S. Department of the Interior, Fish and Wildlife Service, 1990), 6. Although the term *wetland* was not coined until the 1950s, I use it throughout the book.

3. Adriaen Van Der Donck, *Description of New Netherlands* (1656), quoted in Percy W. Bidwell, *History of Agriculture in the Northern United States, 1620–1860* (Washington, D.C.: Carnegie Institute, 1925), 7.

4. Isaac DeRasiers (1628), quoted at Hackensack Meadows Interpretive Center display, Hackensack Meadows, Lyndhurst, New Jersey. 1993.

5. Giovanni Verrazzano quoted in Thomas J. Lyon, *This Incomperable Lande: A Book of American Nature Writing* (Boston: Houghton Mifflin, 1989), 24–25.

6. Elizabeth Barlow, *The Forests and Wetlands of New York City* (Boston: Little, Brown, 1971), 5, 31, 64; Bill O. Wilen and Ralph W. Tiner, Jr., "Wetlands of the United States," in *Wetlands of the World I,* ed. D. F. Whigham et al. (Netherlands: Kluwer Academic Publishers, 1993), 586; William Niering, personal correspondence, 14 June 1996.

7. John Teal and Mildred Teal, *Life and Death of the Salt Marsh* (New York: Ballantine, 1969), 84–101; Robert A. Chabreck, *Coastal Marshes: Ecology and Wildlife Management* (Minneapolis: University of Minnesota Press, 1988), 32.

8. George Reiger, "Symbols of the Marsh," *Audubon,* July 1990, 54–55.

9. Robert Beverly, *The History of the Present State of Virginia,* ed. Louis B. Wright (1705; reprint, Chapel Hill: University of North Carolina Press, 1947), 121–27, quoted in Joseph V. Siry, *Marshes of the Ocean Shore: Development of an Ecological Ethic* (College Station: Texas A&M University Press, 1984), 23.

10. Siry, 21.

11. Chabreck, 5; John A. Shimer, *Field Guide to Land Forms in the United States* (New York: Macmillan, 1972), 7–15.

12. Timothy Silver, *A New Face on the Countryside: Indians, Colonists, and Slaves in South Atlantic Forests, 1500–1800* (Cambridge, England: Cambridge University Press, 1990), 26.

13. William A. Niering, *Wetlands,* Audubon Society Nature Guide, 4th ed. (New York: Alfred A. Knopf, 1989), 89; Wilen and Tiner, 599.

14. Silver, 16.

15. Charles F. Carroll, *The Timber Economy of Puritan New England* (Providence: Brown University Press, 1973), 32; Temple and Sheldon, *History of Northfield Massachusetts* (1875), 21, quoted in the *Oxford English Dictionary,* 2d ed., vol. 17 (Oxford: Clarendon Press, 1989), 345.

16. Robert J. Naiman, Carole A. Johnston, and James C. Kelly, "Alteration of North American Streams by Beaver," *BioScience* 38, no. 11 (Dec. 1988): 753–54. The process still occurs on a much smaller scale, but the contribution of beaver-built wetlands is significantly diminished.

17. Henry F. Dobyns, *Native American Historical Demography: A Cultural Bibliography* (Bloomington: Indiana University Press, 1976), 10.

18. Silver, 38–39.

19. Donald R. Whitehead, "Development and Environmental History of the Dismal Swamp," *Ecological Monographs* 42, no. 3 (Summer 1972): 311.

20. This number (41,303,465) was developed by adding up estimated wetland acreages for CT, DE, GA, ME, MD, MA, NH, NY, NC, RI, SC, VT, VA, and 53 percent of Pennsylvania wetlands based on a distribution map of those wetlands in Robert P. Brooks et al., *Wetlands and Wildlife* (State College: Pennsylvania State College of Agricultural Sciences, 1993), 8; Dahl, 6.

21. Jean Ribaut, *The Whole and True Discouerye of Terra Florida: A Facsimile Reprint of the London Edition of 1563*, Florida Facsimile and Reprint Series (Gainesville: University of Florida Press, 1964), 72, 78, 84.

22. U.S. Department of the Interior, *The Impact of Federal Programs on Wetlands*, A Report to Congress, vol. 2, (Washington, D.C., 1994), 126.

23. Ralph W. Tiner, Jr., *Wetlands of the United States: Current Status and Recent Trends* (Washington, D.C., U.S. Department of the Interior, Fish and Wildlife Service, 1984), 17.

24. Bill Lawrence, *The Early American Wilderness: As the Explorers Saw It* (New York: Paragon House, 1991), 43; Barbara A. Purdy, *The Art and Archaeology of Florida's Wetlands* (Boca Raton: CRC Press, 1991), 283; John W. Griffin, *The Archaeology of Everglades National Park: A Synthesis* (Tallahassee: U.S. Department of the Interior, National Park Service Southwest Archaeological Center, 1988), 183.

25. Wilen and Tiner, 557.

26. Wilen and Tiner, 592; Susan M. Galatowitsch and Arnold G. van der Valk, *Restoring Prairie Wetlands: An Ecological Approach* (Ames: Iowa State University Press, 1994), 27.

27. Niering, 53; Arnold G. van der Valk, *Northern Prairie Wetlands* (Ames: Iowa State University Press, 1989), x.

28. Greg Breining, "Rising from the Bogs," *Nature Conservancy,* July–Aug. 1992, 29.

29. Mary K. Whelan, "The Archaeological and Ethnohistoric Evidence for Prehistoric Occupation," in *The Patterned Peatlands of Minnesota*, ed. H. E. Wright, Jr., Barbara A. Coffin, and Norman E. Aaseng (Minneapolis: University of Minnesota Press, 1992), 239–49; Lewis Cecil Gray, *History of Agriculture in the Southern United States to 1860* (New York: Peter Smith, 1941; reprint, Washington, D.C.: Carnegie Institute, 1933), 6; Lewis H. Morgan, *The American Beaver: A Classic of Natural History and Ecology* (New York: Dover, 1986), 190.

30. James Hall, *Statistics of the West* (Cincinnati, 1836), quoted in Percy Wells Bid-

well, *History of Agriculture in the Northern United States, 1620–1860* (Washington, D.C.: Carnegie Institute, 1925), 160.

31. Alfred H. Meyer, "The Kankakee 'Marsh' of Northern Indiana and Illinois," *Papers of the Michigan Academy of Sciences, Arts, and Letters* 21 (1935): 364–67.

32. Roger A. Winsor, "Environmental Imagery of the Wet Prairies of East Central Illinois, 1820–1920," *Journal of Historical Geography* 13, no. 4 (1987): 375–97; *A Century of Farming in Iowa, 1846–1946,* by members of the staffs of Iowa State College and the Iowa Experiment Station (Ames: Iowa State College Press, 1946), 22; Karl E. Bednarik, "Saga of the Lake Erie Marshes," in *Flyways: Pioneering Waterfowl Management in North America,* ed. A. S. Hawkins, R. C. Hanson, H. K. Nelson, and H. M. Reeves (Washington, D.C.: U.S. Department of the Interior, Fish and Wildlife Service, 1984), 423; Martin R. Kaatz, "The Black Swamp: A Study in Historical Geography," *Annals of the Association of American Geographers* 45, no. 1 (Mar. 1955): 1, 18.

33. Brooks, 8; Dahl, 6. This figure was developed by summing estimated wetland acreages for IL, IN, IA, MI, MN, MO, ND, OH, SD, WI, and a percentage of PA based on a wetlands distribution map for that state. It refers to a percentage of wetlands in the lower forty-eight states.

34. Wilen and Tiner, 596; Niering, 102.

35. Le Page DuPratz, *The History of Louisiana or of the Western Parts of Virginia and Carolina Containing a Description of the Countries That Lie on Both Sides of the River Mississippi: With an Account of the Settlements, Inhabitants, Soil, Climate, and Products* (London, 1758; reprint, n.p., 1972), 217; Bill McKibben, "The Wild Wild East," *New York Times Magazine,* 26 Dec. 1993, 29.

36. Lawrence, 34–35; Niering, 107; Silver, 22.

37. Niering, 109.

38. Silver, 28; Tony Fitzpatrick, *Signals from the Heartland* (New York: Walker, 1993), 19–21.

39. Omer Lonie Roberts, Jr., "Cypress Land and Floodway: Environmental Change and the Development of Land Utilization in the Atchafalaya Basin, Louisiana" (Ph.D. diss., University of Tennessee, 1974), 48.

40. Fred B. Kniffen, Hiram F. Gregory, and George A. Stokes, *The Historic Indian Tribes of Louisiana, from 1542 to the Present* (Baton Rouge: Louisiana State University Press, 1987), 20, 49, 137; Vaughn L. Glasgow, *A Social History of the American Alligator* (New York: St. Martin's Press, 1991), 94.

41. Roberts, 21.

42. Silver, 15; Chabreck, 29.

43. Kniffen et al., 20.

44. Harnett T. Kane, *The Bayous of Louisiana* (New York: William Morrow, 1944), 7–8.

45. Louisiana Coastal Wetlands Conservation and Restoration Task Force, "Louisiana Coastal Wetlands Restoration Plan" (Baton Rouge, LA, 1993), 2.

46. Dahl, 6. This number was developed by adding wetlands estimates for AR, LA, MS, AL, FL, and 80 percent of Texas (an estimate of coastal plain wetlands in that state).

47. Jon Farrar, *Lillian Annette Rowe Sanctuary: Way-Station on the Platte,* pamphlet, Nebraska Game and Parks Commission (Omaha, NE, 1989).

48. Reuben Gold Thwaites, ed. *Original Journals of the Lewis and Clark Expedition 1804–1806* (New York: Arno Press, 1969), vol. 1, 343 [Clark, 26 Apr. 1805, Missouri River near mouth of Yellowstone River]; vol. 2, 265 [Lewis, 24 July 1805, Missouri River between Great Falls and Three Forks].

49. Kathleen Rude, "The Playas," *Ducks Unlimited Habitat Series,* Mar.–Apr. 1991, 1–14; Paul L. Rettman, "Theories of Playa Lake Development in the High Plains," Playa Lakes: Symposium Proceedings (Washington, D.C.: U.S. Department of the Interior, Fish and Wildlife Service, Office of Biological Services, 1981), 4–6. In the past, many playa lakes were supplied with water from seeps of the Ogallala Aquifer. This is changing as the aquifer level declines.

50. Chris Madson, "Cheyenne Bottoms," *Nature Conservancy,* May–June 1993, 16–21; Chris Madson, "The Death of a River," *Audubon,* May 1982, 80.

51. Felice F. Furst, "A New Approach to Wetlands Protection for Nebraska's Rainwater Basin," *National Wetlands Newsletter,* July–Aug. 1986, 5.

52. Catherine S. Fowler, *In the Shadow of Fox Peak: An Ethnography of the Cattail-Eater Northern Paiute People of Stillwater Marsh,* Cultural Resource Series, no. 5 (Washington, D.C.: U.S. Department of the Interior, Fish and Wildlife Service, Stillwater National Wildlife Refuge, 1992), 11, 18, 44, passim.

53. Kenneth Thompson, "Historic Flooding in the Sacramento Valley," *Pacific Historical Review* 29 (Nov. 1960): 355; Stephen Johnson, Gerald Haslam, and Robert Dawson, *The Great Central Valley: California's Heartland* (Berkeley: University of California Press, 1993), 6.

54. Gene Rose, *San Joaquin: A River Betrayed* (Fresno: Linrose Publishing, 1992), 11.

55. William Preston, *Vanishing Landscapes: Land and Life in the Tulare Lake Basin* (Berkeley: University of California Press, 1981), 22. Mexico City was once a vast wetland likely vegetated with sedges closely related to tules.

56. Rose, 11.

57. W. E. Frayer, Dennis D. Peters, H. Ross Pywell, *Wetlands of the California Central Valley: Status and Trends, 1939–mid 1980s* (Portland, Ore.: U.S. Department of the Interior, Fish and Wildlife Service, 1989), ii.

58. Dahl, 6; Population Indices from the Midwinter Waterfowl Survey in the Pacific Flyway during January, 1985–1996, unpublished, U.S. Fish and Wildlife Service, Portland, Ore. Because no one can know for sure how many ducks and geese there were, this estimate of Pacific Flyway waterfowl populations is speculative. After consulting with experts, I derived this figure by determining the relationship between California wetland habitat in the mid 1980s with the average winter waterfowl population in California from the mid 1980s through the mid 1990s; then I extrapolated backward using estimated California wetland acreage figures for the 1780s.

59. Rose, 6.

60. Grant D. Werschkull, F. Thomas Griggs, and Jack M. Zaninovich, "Tulare Basin Protection Plan" (San Francisco, The Nature Conservancy, 1983).

61. Rose, 13; Arthur F. McEvoy, *The Fisherman's Problem: Ecology and Law in the California Fisheries 1850–1980* (Cambridge, England: Cambridge University Press, 1990), 19.

62. Johnson, Haslam, and Dawson, 34.

63. Preston, 33–35, 44.

64. San Francisco Estuary Project, *San Francisco Bay–Delta Estuary,* pamphlet (July 1990); San Francisco Estuary Project, *Sacramento–San Joaquin Delta,* pamphlet (Oct. 1990).

65. H. E. Bolton, *Fray Juan Crespi: Missionary Explorer on the Pacific Coast 1769–1774* (Berkeley: University of California Press, 1927) cited in Frederic H. Nichols, James E. Cloern, Samuel N. Luoma, and David H. Peterson, "The Modification of an Estuary," *Science* 231 (7 Feb. 1986): 567.

66. Lansford W. Hastings, *The Emigrant's Guide to Oregon and California* (Princeton, 1932), 76, quoted in Thompson, 356.

67. Jonathan V. Hall, W. E. Frayer, and Bill O. Wilen, *Status of Alaska Wetlands* (Anchorage: U.S. Department of the Interior, Fish and Wildlife Service, 1994), 3, 29.

Chapter 3

1. John Bunyan, *The Pilgrim's Progress from This World to That Which Is to Come,* ed. James Blanton Wharey and Roger Sharrock (Oxford: Oxford University Press, 1960; reprint, 1967), 15.

2. Walter Muir Whitehill, *Boston: A Topographical History,* 2d ed. (Cambridge: Belknap Press of Harvard University Press, 1968), 3–5.

3. Alvan R. Brick, Jr., "The Virgin Swamp: A Chorography of a Primeval Environment in the New World" (Ph.D. diss., Cornell University, 1981), 136–37; Jeremy Purseglove, *Taming the Flood: A History and Natural History of Rivers and Wetlands* (Oxford: Oxford University Press, 1988), 22–29. Purseglove's excellent book chronicles rivers and wetlands in Great Britain.

4. Thomas J. Lyon, *This Incomperable Lande: A Book of American Nature Writing* (Boston: Houghton Mifflin, 1989), 27, 49; *The Planters Plea* (1630), quoted in Percy Wells Bidwell, *History of Agriculture in the Northern United States, 1620–1860* (Washington, D.C.: Carnegie Institute, 1925), 7; Timothy Silver, *A New Face on the Countryside: Indians, Colonists, and Slaves in South Atlantic Forests, 1500–1800* (Cambridge, England: Cambridge University Press, 1990), 141.

5. Peter Matthiessen, *Wildlife in America,* rev. ed. (New York: Viking, 1987), 67.

6. David S. Cohen, *The Dutch American Farm* (New York: New York University Press, 1992), 66.

7. Jedidiah Morse, *American Universal Geography* (1789), cited in Kimberly R. Sebold, *From Marsh to Farm: The Landscape Transformation of Coastal New Jersey* (Washington, D.C.: U.S. Department of the Interior, National Park Service, New Jersey Coastal Historic Trail, 1992), 29.

8. W. Keith Kavenagh, *Vanishing Tidelands: Land Use and the Law in Suffolk County, 1650–1979* (Albany: New York Sea Grant Institute, 1980), 21–22, 135;

Elizabeth Barlow, *The Forests and Wetlands of New York City* (Boston: Little, Brown, 1971), 31; Hackensack Meadows Interpretive Center, Oct. 1994.

9. Henry M. Miller, "An Archaeological Perspective on the Evolution of Diet in the Colonial Chesapeake, 1620–1745," in *Colonial Chesapeake Society*, ed. Lois Green Carr, Philip D. Morgan, and Jean B. Russo, Institute of Early American History and Culture (Chapel Hill: University of North Carolina Press, 1988), 182; Edward T. Price, *Dividing the Land: Early American Beginnings of Our Private Property Mosaic*, Geography Research Paper No. 238 (Chicago: University of Chicago Press, 1995), 123.

10. John Smith, *The Generall Historie of Virginia, New England, and the Summer Isles* (London, 1624; reprint, Readex Microprint Corp., 1966), 162–63; Purseglove, 22–39; Jon Kukla, "Kentish Agues and American Distempers: The Transmission of Malaria from England to Virginia in the Seventeenth Century," *Southern Studies* 25, no. 2 (1986): 140.

11. Quoted in Brian Donahue, "'Dammed at Both Ends and Cursed in the Middle': The 'Flowage' of the Concord River Meadows, 1798–1862," *Environmental Review* 13 (Fall–Winter 1989): 47–50.

12. J. H. Temple, *History of Whately, Massachusetts* (Boston, 1872), 13, quoted in Bidwell, 19–20.

13. Carl Bridenbaugh, *Cities in the Wilderness: Urban Life in America, 1625–1742* (New York: Ronald Press, 1938; reprint, New York: Capricorn Books, 1964), 6.

14. John Teal and Mildred Teal, *Life and Death of the Salt Marsh* (Boston: Little, Brown, 1969), 240–45. The Teals estimate that 2,055 acres were filled.

15. Bridenbaugh, 6.

16. Whitehill, 79–80.

17. Quoted in Bidwell, 102.

18. Sebold, 57–59.

19. David C. Smith, Victor Konrad, Helen Koulouris, Edward Hawes, and Harold W. Borns, Jr., "Salt Marshes As a Factor in the Agriculture of Northeastern North America," *Agricultural History* 3, no. 2 (Spring 1989): 272–81, 289.

20. Nathaniel Saltonstall, *A New and Further Narrative of the State of New England* (London, 1676), in Charles F. Corrall, *The Timber Economy of Puritan New England* (Providence: Brown University Press, 1973), 162; *Oxford English Dictionary*, vol. 17 (Oxford: Clarendon Press, 1989), 345. According to Corrall, Saltonstall felt it necessary in his New England narrative to define the word *swamp* in a glossary of terms as a "moorish place overgrown with woods and bushes, but soft like a quagmire or Irish Bogg, over which Horse cannot at all, nor English Foot, without great difficulty passe."

21. William Bradford, quoted in Samuel Eliot Morrison, ed., *Of Plimouth Plantation* (New York: Modern Library, 1952), 84, quoted in David Cameron Miller, *Dark Eden: The Swamp in Nineteenth-Century American Culture* (Cambridge, England: Cambridge University Press, 1989), 51.

22. Richard Slotkin and James K. Folsom, eds., *So Dreadfull a Judgment: Puritan Responses to King Philip's War, 1676–1677* (Middletown, Conn.: Wesleyan University Press, 1978), 39, 65.

23. Slotkin and Folsom, 3.

24. Quoted in Alan Heivert, "Puritanism, the Wilderness, and the Frontier," *New England Quarterly* 26 (1953): 371–72; Brick, 138.

25. Slotkin and Folsom, 57, 68.

26. Nathaniel Saltonstall, "The Present State of New England with Respect to the Indian War," in *Narratives of the Indian Wars, 1697–1699,* ed. Charles H. Lincoln (New York: Charles Scribner's Sons, 1913), 31. A pike *(Esox lucius*) can grow up to 4½ feet long.

27. Peter N. Carrol, *Puritanism and the Wilderness: The Intellectual Significance of the New England Frontier, 1629–1700* (New York: Columbia University Press, 1969), 77.

28. Bunyan, 15. Another character, "Help," explains this aspect of the slough; even as a sinner recognizes his lost condition, he tells Christian, "there ariseth in his soul many fears, and doubts, and discouraging apprehensions, which all of them get together, and settle in this place: And that is the reason of the badness of this ground."

29. Slotkin and Folsom, 301.

30. Samuel Penhallow, *Penhallow's Indian wars: A facsimile reprint of the first edition printed in Boston in 1726, with the notes of earlier editors and additions from the original manuscript* (Williamstown, Mass. Corner House Publishers, 1973), 36.

31. Mary Rowlandson, "Narrative of the Captivity of Mrs. Mary Rowlandson," in *Narratives of Indian Wars,* ed. Charles H. Lincoln, 112–68. Mary Rowlandson's narrative was published in 1682.

32. Brick, 283–85.

33. William K. Boyd, ed., *William Byrd's Histories of the Dividing Line Betwixt Virginia and North Carolina* (Raleigh: North Carolina Historical Commission, 1929), 70; J. Paul Lilly, "A History of Swamp Land Development in North Carolina," in *Pocosin Wetlands,* ed. C. J. Richardson (Stroudsburg, Penn.: Hutchinson Ross Publishing, 1981), 23.

34. Hubert Davis, *The Great Dismal Swamp: Its History, Folklore, and Science* (Richmond: Cavalier Press, 1962), 48, in Brick, 139.

35. William Wood, *New England's Prospect* (1634), quoted in Lyon, 101.

36. Matthiessen, 99.

37. Robert J. Naiman, Carol A. Johnston, and James C. Kelley, "Alteration of North American Streams by Beaver," *BioScience* 38, no. 11 (Dec. 1988): 753; John Smith, 204; Silver, 98–100; David J. Wishart, *The Fur Trade of the American West 1807–1840: A Geographical Synthesis* (Lincoln: University of Nebraska Press, 1972), 127–28.

38. Brick, 289; Perry Miller, *Errand into the Wilderness* (New York: Harper Torchbooks, 1964), 101.

39. Mark Catesby, *Natural History of South Carolina,* vol. 1 (London, 1731), xvii, cited in *Agriculture in the United States: A Documentary History,* ed. Wayne D. Rasmussen (New York: Random House, 1975), 160; Lewis Cecil Gray, *History of Agriculture in the Southern United States to 1860,* vol. 1 (New York: Peter Smith, 1941), 278; Mildred Kelly Ginn, "A History of Rice Production in Louisiana to 1896," *Louisiana Historical Quarterly* 23, no. 2 (Apr. 1940): 545.

40. Mart A. Stewart, "Rice, Water, and Power: Landscapes of Domination and Resistance in the Lowcountry," *Environmental History Review* 15 (Fall 1991): 47–48.

41. Quoted in Joyce E. Chaplin, *An Anxious Pursuit: Agricultural Innovation and Modernity in the Lower South, 1730–1815* (Chapel Hill: University of North Carolina Press, 1993), 79.

42. Silver, 144, 194; Julia Floyd Smith, *Slavery and Rice Culture in Low Country Georgia, 1750–1860* (Knoxville: University of Tennessee Press, 1985), 100–101; Mart A. Stewart, 52; Chaplin, 85.

43. John Drayton, *A View of South Carolina, As Respects Her Natural and Civil Concerns* (1802), 146–47, quoted in Silver, 194; Dorothy Spruill Redford, *Somerset Homecoming: Recovering a Lost Heritage* (New York: Doubleday, 1988), 131.

44. Price, 115.

45. Gray, 279; François André Michaux, "Travels to the West of the Alleghany Mountains" (Spring 1803) in *Travels West of the Alleghenies*, ed. R. G. Thwaites (Cleveland, 1904), cited in Rasmussen 382; Chaplin, 247–49.

46. Julia Floyd Smith, 130; Mart A. Stewart, 50

47. Julia Floyd Smith, 49, 55; Chaplin, 85. Not to be confused with white overseers, slave drivers were slaves who had the responsibility for overseeing and disciplining other slaves.

48. Julia Floyd Smith, 118; Mart A. Stewart, 56; Vaughn L. Glasgow, *A Social History of the American Alligator: The Earth Trembles with His Thunder* (New York: St. Martin's Press, 1991), 2.

49. Gray, 722.

50. Melvin Herndon, "Timber Products of Georgia," *Georgia Historical Quarterly* 57 (Spring 1973): 57; Julia Floyd Smith, 98; Chaplin, 6.

51. Charles Hately to John Coming Ball, 6 Aug. 1792, Ball Family papers, box 1, folder 10, South Caroliniana Library, University of South Carolina, Columbia, quoted in Chaplin, 244–46, 273–74.

52. Silver, 168.

53. Herndon, 57.

54. Peter C. Stewart, "The Shingle and Lumber Industries in the Great Dismal," *Journal of Forest History* 25 (Apr. 1981): 98; Lilly, 25; Mart A. Stewart, 100.

55. Redford, 106–108; Craig Luken and Lucy Mauger, *Environmental Geologic Atlas of the Coastal Zone of North Carolina: Dare, Hyde, Tyrell, and Washington Counties* (Greenville, N.C.: East Carolina University, Institute for Coastal and Marine Resources, 1983), 49; Lilly, 25–26.

56. Silver, 155–61; Kukla, 135–47; Robert Berkow, ed., *The Merck Manual of Diagnosis and Therapy* (Rahway, N.J.: Merck Research Laboratories, 1992), 229–32.

57. *Animal Husbandry* (London, 1775), quoted in Silver, 78.

58. Quoted in John Capper, Garrett Power, and Frank R. Shivers, Jr., *Governing Chesapeake Waters: A History of Water Quality Controls on Chesapeake Bay, 1607–1972* (Washington, D.C.: U.S. Environmental Protection Agency, Chesapeake Bay Program, 1982), 23.

59. David Ramsey (1809), quoted in Chaplin, 274.

60. Daniel Q. Thompson, Ronald L. Stuckey, and Edith B. Thompson, *Spread, Impact, and Control of Purple Loosestrife* (Lythrum salarica) *in North American Wetlands* (Washington, D.C.: U.S. Department of the Interior, Fish and Wildlife Service, 1987), 13–14.

61. Albert A. Cowdrey, *Land's End: A History of the New Orleans District, U.S. Army Corps of Engineers and Its Lifelong Battle with the Lower Mississippi and Other Rivers Wending Their Way to the Sea* (New Orleans: U.S. Army, Corps of Engineers, 1977), 1; Jeff Hecht, "The Incredible Shrinking Mississippi Delta," *New Scientist,* 14 Apr. 1990, 43.

62. Wetlands Acadian Cultural Center, Thibidoux, Louisiana, interpretive display, Feb. 1994.

63. Harnett T. Kane, *The Bayous of Louisiana* (New York: William Morrow, 1944), 35; Robert W. Harrison, *Alluvial Empire: Drainage in the Lower Mississippi Valley* (Little Rock, Ark.: Pioneer Press, in cooperation with the U.S. Department of Agriculture, Economic Research Service, 1961), 296–97.

64. Ervin Mancil, "Pullboat Logging," *Journal of Forest History* 24 (July 1980): 135.

65. John A. Eisterhold, "Lumber and Trade in the Lower Mississippi Valley and New Orleans, 1800–1860," *Louisiana History* 13 (Winter 1972): 86.

66. John Hebron Moore, *Andrew Brown and Cypress Lumbering in the Old Southwest* (Baton Rouge: Louisiana State University Press, 1967), 10, 33–34.

67. Gray, 749.

68. Kane, 158, 239; Wetlands Acadian Cultural Center display.

69. Estick Evans, "A Pedestrious Tour . . . Through the Western States and Territories," in *Early Western Travels,* vol 8, ed. R. G. Thwaites (Cleveland, 1904–1907), 325–26, quoted in Joseph Carlyle Sitterson, *Sugar Country: The Cane Sugar Industry in the South, 1753–1950* (Lexington: University of Kentucky Press, 1953), 45.

70. Adolph Benson, ed. *Peter Kalm's Travels in North America* (New York: Wilson-Erickson, 1937), 152, quoted in Lyon, 32.

71. Benson, 300, quoted in Lyon, 32; Silver, 119.

72. Le Page DuPratz, *A History of Louisiana or of the Western Parts of Virginia and Carolina Containing a Description of the Countries That Lie on Both Sides of the River Mississippi: With an Account of the Settlements, Inhabitants, Soil, Climate, and Products* (London, 1758; reprint, n.p., 1972), 217.

73. John Drayton (1802), 88, quoted in Silver, 100, 110–11.

74. Whitehill, 90.

75. Bridenbaugh, 159.

Chapter 4

1. Henry Major Tomlinson, *Out of Soundings* (New York: Harper and Bros., 1931), 149.

2. William Bartram, *The Travels of William Bartram,* ed. Mark Van Doren (New York: Macy-Masius, 1928; reprint, Dover, 1955), 82.

3. Alvan Rogers Brick, Jr., "The Virgin Swamp: A Chorography of a Primeval En-

vironment in the New World" (Ph.D. diss., Cornell University, 1981), 120;
William Cronon, *Nature's Metropolis: Chicago and the Great West* (New York:
W.W. Norton, 1991), 267; William Patterson Cumming, *The Southeast in Early
Maps* (Chapel Hill: University of North Carolina Press, 1958), 62.

4. Bartram, 82.

5. N. Bryllion Fagin, *William Bartram: Interpreter of the American Landscape* (Baltimore: Johns Hopkins Press, 1933), 106; Edmund Burke, *A Philosophical Enquiry into the Origin of Our Ideas of the Sublime and Beautiful* (London, 1757), cited in Barbara Novak, *Nature and Culture: American Landscape and Painting, 1825–1875* (New York: Oxford University Press, 1980), 34–35.

6. Bartram, 96, 105, 182, 198–99, 328, 365.

7. Bartram, 94–95, 188, 195, 229–30.

8. Bartram, 166–67.

9. Bartram, 37.

10. Bartram, 114–29; Francis Harper, "Alligators of the Okefenokee," *Scientific Monthly* 31 (1930): 51–67, quoted in Fagin, 94. Although some commentators have criticized Bartram's descriptions of alligators as hyperbolic, biologist Francis Harper, who spent time in the Okefenokee swamp during the first part of the twentieth century, countered that "the fidelity and accuracy of Bartram's account as a whole . . . are impressive." According to Harper, Bartram's description of roaring alligators is the "only genuine, first-hand account by a naturalist . . . which cannot be overlooked by any zoologist."

11. Fagin, 127–93.

12. *Audubon in Louisiana* (New Orleans: Louisiana State Museum, Friends of the Cabildo, 1966).

13. John J. Audubon to G. W. Featherstonhaugh, 7 Dec. 1832, quoted in Kathryn Hall Proby, *Audubon in Florida* (Coral Gables, Fla.: University of Miami Press, 1974), 18.

14. John J. Audubon to Lucy Audubon, 23 Nov. 1831, quoted in Proby, 15.

15. John J. Audubon to Lucy Audubon, 31 Dec. 1831, quoted in Proby, 25–26.

16. John J. Audubon to G. W. Featherstonhaugh, 31 Dec.1831, quoted in Proby, 26, 31.

17. Proby, 33.

18. Cited in Proby, 26.

19. Washington Irving, "The Legend of Sleepy Hollow" (1820) in *The American Landscape: A Critical Anthology of Prose and Poetry,* ed. John Conron (New York: Oxford University Press, 1974), 214–15.

20. Irving, "The Devil and Tom Walker," quoted in David Cameron Miller, "'Desert Places': The Meaning of Swamp, Jungle and Marsh Images in Nineteenth-Century America" (Ph.D. diss., Brown University, 1982), 50.

21. Wirt, *Letters of the British Spy* (New York, 1803; 10th edition, 1832), 105–6, quoted in Miller, 22.

22. Cumming, plate 66. In 1770, for example, John A. Collet published a map of North Carolina ornamented with swamp icons including a panther, an Indian, cattails, and an alligator crawling out from beneath the title box.

23. Frances Anne Kemble, *Journal of a Residence on a Georgia Plantation in 1838–1839,* ed. John A. Scott (New York: Alfred A. Knopf, 1961), 43.

24. Quoted in Martin R. Kaatz, "The Black Swamp: A Study in Historical Geography," *Annals of the Association of American Geographers* 45, no. 1 (Mar. 1955): 7.

25. Quoted in Paul Brooks, ed., *Everglades* (New York: Sierra Club, Ballantine Books, 1970), 42.

26. Nellie Armstrong Robertson and Dorothy Riker, eds., *The John Tipton Papers I* (Indianapolis, 1942), 261–62, quoted in Roger A. Winsor, "Environmental Imagery of the Wet Prairie of East Central Illinois, 1820–1920," *Journal of Historical Geography* 13, no. 4 (1987): 379.

27. U.S. General Land Grant Office, *Annual Reports of the Commissioner and Surveyors General* (1847), quoted in Lowell O. Stewart, *Public Land Surveys: History, Instructions, Methods* (Ames, Iowa: Collegiate Press, 1935), 84.

28. John T. Stewart, *Report on Everglades Drainage Project in Lee and Dade Counties, Florida, January to May 1907* (Washington, D.C.: U.S. Department of Agriculture, 1907), 68.

29. W. H. Keating, "Long's Expedition to the Source of St. Peter's River in 1823," quoted in Erwin H. Ackerknect, *Malaria in the Upper Mississippi Valley, 1760–1900,* Supplements to the Bulletin of the History of Medicine, no. 4 (Baltimore: Johns Hopkins University Press, 1945), 79.

30. Caroline M. Kirkland, *A New Home: Who'll Follow?,* ed. William S. Osborne (New Haven, Conn.: College and University Press, 1965), 40–41.

31. Kirkland, 68.

32. William S. Osborne, "Introduction" in Kirkland, 22–23.

33. Kaatz, 12.

34. John Madson, *Where the Sky Began: Land of the Tallgrass Prairie* (San Francisco: Sierra Club Books, 1982), 60, 92–93.

35 J. M. Peck, *A Guide for Emigrants, Containing Sketches of Illinois, Missouri, and the Adjacent Parts* (Boston: Lincoln and Edmands, 1831), 106, quoted in Cronon, 102.

36. Winsor, 388–89.

37. Quoted in John Duffy, *The Sanitarians: A History of American Public Health* (Urbana: University of Illinois Press, 1990), 63.

38. Isaac Rawlings, *The Rise and Fall of Disease in Illinois* (Springfield, 1927), 39, quoted in Winsor, 389; Ackerknect, 23, 31, 36, 43.

39. Ackerknect, 4–5. Malaria caused by the *Plasmodium Virax* parasite is one of the less-virulent strains of the disease.

40. *Cultivator* 4 (1847), 270, quoted in Percy Wells Bidwell, *History of Agriculture in the Northern United States, 1620–1860* (Washington, D.C.: Carnegie Institute, 1925), 267.

41. John Lewis Peyton, *Over the Alleghenies and across the Prairies* (1848), 327, quoted in Cronon, 57.

42. T. B. Carter, *"Some Facts and Incidents in the Early Life of Thomas Butler Carter from Boyhood and on until 1889"* (1888) quoted in Cronon, 58, 80.

43. Gordon Whitney, *From Coastal Wilderness to Fruited Plain* (Cambridge, England: Cambridge University Press, 1994), 272.

44. Quoted in Brick, 135.

45. Amelia M. Murray, *Letters from the United States, Cuba, and Canada* (New York: G. P. Putnam, 1856), quoted in Florence Roos Brink, "Literary Travellers in Louisiana between 1803 and 1860," *Louisiana Historical Quarterly* 31, no. 2 (Apr. 1948): 9.

46. Kemble, 18–19.

47. Peter C. Stewart, "Man and the Swamp: The Historical Dimension," in *The Great Dismal Swamp*, ed. Paul W. Kirk, Jr. (Charlottesville: University Press of Virginia for Old Dominion University Research Foundation, 1979), 66–67.

48. Peter Pond, "The Journey of Peter Pond," *Connecticut Magazine* 10 (1906), 244–52, reprinted in *Voices from the Wilderness*, ed. Thomas Froncek (New York: McGraw-Hill, 1974), 89.

49. "A Selection of George Croghan's Letters and Journals Relating to Tours into the Western Country, 16 November 1750–November 1765," in Froncek, 61.

50. Chris Madson, "The Death of a River," *Audubon*, May 1982, 80.

51. Quoted in Milton Friend, "Waterfowl Get Sick Too," in *Flyways: Pioneering Waterfowl Management in North America*, ed. A. S. Hawkins, R. C. Hanson, H. K. Nelson, and H. M. Reeves (Washington, D.C.: U.S. Department of the Interior, Fish and Wildlife Service, 1984), 484.

52. Winsor, 375–97.

53. Paul W. Gates, *The Farmer's Age: Agriculture, 1815–1860* (New York: Harper and Row, 1960), 338, 343; James Playsted Wood, *Magazines in the United States*, 3d ed. (New York: Ronald Press, 1971), 169. According to Wood, the *Country Gentleman* alone had a circulation of 250,000 by 1857. Although Gates's and Wood's figures do not correlate, both report that the circulation of agricultural periodicals was very large.

54. "The Present and Future of Products of Louisiana, and the Means for Augmenting Them," *DeBow's Review* 3 (1847), 412–19, in *Agriculture in the United States: A Documentary History*, ed. Wayne D. Rasmussen (New York: Random House, 1975), 760.

55. J. Paul Lilly, "A History of Swamp Land Development in North Carolina," in *Pocosin Wetlands*, ed. Curtis J. Richardson (Stroudsburg, Penn.: Hutchinson Ross Publishing, 1981), 27–29; Jack Temple Kirby, *Poquosin: A Study of Rural Landscape and Society* (Chapel Hill: University of North Carolina Press, 1995), 70–87.

56. Edmund Ruffin, *Agricultural, Geological, and Descriptive Sketches of Lower North Carolina* (Raleigh: Institution for the Deaf and Dumb and the Blind, 1861), 54.

57. Ruffin, *Agricultural, Geological Sketches*, 143–45.

58. Ruffin, *Agricultural, Geological Sketches*, 54; Avery Odelle Craven, *Soil Exhaustion As a Factor in the Agricultural History of Virginia and Maryland, 1606–1860* (Urbana: University of Illinois Press, 1925; reprint, Gloucester, Mass.: P. Smith, 1965), 134–43.

59. Ruffin, *Agricultural, Geological Sketches*, 145–51.

60. Edmund Ruffin, *The Diary of Edmund Ruffin,* vol. 1, ed. William Kauffman Scarborough (Baton Rouge: Louisiana State University Press, 1972), 211.

61. Ruffin, *Agricultural, Geological Sketches,* 206–7.

Chapter 5

1. Congress, Senate, 31st Cong., 2d sess., *Congressional Globe,* vol. 93 (27 Feb. 1851), 739–40.

2. Congress, Senate, 30th Cong., 2d sess., *Congressional Globe,* vol. 91 (26 Feb. 1849), 594; Joseph V. Siry, *Marshes of the Ocean Shore: Development of an Ecological Ethic* (College Station: Texas A&M University Press, 1984), 69. Through the decade of the 1840s, Florida unsuccessfully pressured Congress to cede the Everglades to the state for reclamation.

3. Congress, Senate, 31st Cong., 1st sess., *Congressional Globe,* vol. 93 (2 Sept. 1850), 1729; Congress, Senate, 32d Cong., 1st sess., Senate Exec. Doc. no. 2, "Report on the Overflows of the Delta of the Mississippi," prepared by Charles Ellet, Jr. (21 Jan. 1852), 45, 97; Russell L. Terry, "The Political Career of Solomon Weathersbee Downs" (master's thesis, Louisiana State University, 1935), 52, 63.

4. Congress, Senate, 31st Cong., 1st sess., *Congressional Globe,* vol. 93 (17 Sept. 1850), 1849–50.

5. Congress, Senate, 31st Cong., 1st sess., *Congressional Globe,* vol. 93 (17 Sept. 1850), 1848.

6. Congress, Senate, 30th Cong., 2d sess., *Congressional Globe,* vol. 91 (26 Feb. 1849), 594; Congress, Senate, 31st Cong., 1st sess., *Congressional Globe,* vol. 93 (12 June 1850), 1192; Congress, Senate, 31st Cong., 1st sess., *Congressional Globe,* vol. 93 (17 Sept. 1850), 1849–50; Congress, House, 31st Cong., 1st sess., *Congressional Globe,* vol. 93 (16 Sept. 1850), 1827.

7. Charles E. Rosenberg, *The Cholera Years* (Chicago: University of Chicago Press, 1962; reprint, 1987), 38, 72.

8. Congress, House, 32d Cong., 2d sess., *Congressional Globe,* vol. 101 (14 Sept. 1853), 613; Congress, Senate, 31st Cong., 1st sess., *Congressional Globe,* vol. 93 (17 Sept. 1850), 1849–50.

9. Chester E. Eisinger, "The Freehold Concept in Eighteenth Century American Letters," *William and Mary Quarterly* 4 (Jan. 1947): 42–59; Chester E. Eisinger, "Land and Loyalty: Literary Expressions of Agrarian Nationalism in the Seventeenth and Eighteenth Centuries," *American Literature* 21, no. 2 (May 1949): 160–78; Chester E. Eisinger, "The Influence of Natural Rights and Physiocratic Doctrines on American Agrarian Thought During the Revolutionary Period," *Agricultural History* 21, no. 1 (Jan. 1947): 13–23.

10. William L. Barney, *The Passage of the Republic: An Interdisciplinary History of Nineteenth-Century America* (Lexington, Mass.: D.C. Heath, 1987), 157–58. While 83 percent of the national workforce was self-employed, mostly farmers, in 1800, only 48 percent worked for themselves in 1860.

11. Leo Marx, *The Machine in the Garden: Technology and the Pastoral Ideal in America* (London: Oxford University Press, 1964; reprint, 1967), 26; Henry

Nash Smith, *Virgin Land: The American West As Symbol and Myth* (Cambridge: Harvard University Press, 1950; reprint, 1978), 172–73.

12. Congress, Senate, 31st Cong., 2d sess., *Congressional Globe,* vol. 96 (27 Feb. 1851), 740.

13. Congress, Senate, 31st Cong., 2d sess., *Congressional Globe,* vol. 96 (27 Feb. 1851), 739–41; Congress, Senate, 31st Cong., 1st sess., *Congressional Globe,* vol. 93 (12 June 1850), 1192; Congress, House, 31st Cong., 1st sess., *Congressional Globe,* vol. 93 (16 Sept. 1850), 1826; Ellet, 13, 34. Regarding swamps as evil was not just political parlance; even scientists and engineers equated swamps with evil.

14. Congress, Senate, 31st Cong., 1st sess., *Congressional Globe,* vol. 93 (17 Sept. 1850), 1849–50.

15. Congress, Senate, 31st Cong., 1st sess., *Congressional Globe,* vol. 93 (2 Sept. 1850), 1730.

16. Congress, House, 31st Cong., 1st sess., *Congressional Globe,* vol. 93 (18 Sept. 1850), 1826–27.

17. Robert Bruce, *The Launching of Modern American Science, 1846–1876* (Ithaca: Cornell University Press, 1987), 60–61.

18. Congress, Senate, 31st Cong., 2d sess., *Congressional Globe,* vol. 96 (27 Feb. 1851), 741.

19. Roscoe L. Lokken, *Iowa Public Land Disposal* (Iowa City: State Historical Society of Iowa, 1942; reprint, New York: Arno Press, 1972), 180–82; Stephen F. Strausberg, "Indiana and the Swamp Lands Act: A Study in State Administration," *Indiana Magazine of History* 73 (Sept. 1977): 192–93; Margaret Beattie Bogue, "The Swamp Land Act and Wet Land Utilization in Illinois, 1850–1890," *Agricultural History* 25 (Oct. 1951): 170–71.

20. Joseph Carlyle Sitterson, *Sugar Country: The Cane Sugar Industry in the South, 1753–1950* (Lexington: University of Kentucky Press, 1953), 129.

21. Quoted in Robert W. Harrison, *Swamp Land Reclamation in Louisiana, 1849–1879: A Study of Flood Control and Land Drainage in Louisiana under the Swamp Land Grant of 1849* (Baton Rouge: U.S. Department of Agriculture, Bureau of Agricultural Economics, 1951), 18.

22. Harrison, 21.

23. Harrison, 38.

24. Harrison, 15, 16, 41.

25. Harrison, 39.

26. Sitterson, 21.

27. Harrison, 44–45.

28. Albert A. Cowdrey, *Land's End: A History of the New Orleans District, U.S. Army Corps of Engineers and Its Lifelong Battle with the Lower Mississippi and Other Rivers Wending Their Way to the Sea* (New Orleans: U.S. Army, Corps of Engineers, 1977), 24; Harrison, 58.

29. Harrison, 72.

30. Martin Reuss, *Army Engineers in Memphis District* (Memphis: U.S. Army, Corps of Engineers, 1982), 13–14.

31. Harrison, 78–90.

32. Nollie W. Hickman, *Mississippi Harvest: Lumbering in the Longleaf Pine Belt, 1840–1915* (Montgomery, Ala.: Paragon Press for University of Mississippi Press, 1962), 90, 92.

33. Harrison, 92.

34. Khaled J. Bloom, *The Mississippi Valley's Great Yellow Fever Epidemic of 1878* (Baton Rouge: Louisiana State University Press, 1993), 86.

35. Harrison, 92; Martin Reuss, personal correspondence, July 1996. According to Reuss, Louisiana also disavowed responsibility for the Mississippi in its state constitution.

36. Mary R. McCorvie and Christopher Lant, "Drainage District Formation and the Loss of Midwestern Wetlands, 1850–1930," *Agricultural History* 67, no. 4 (Fall 1993): 22; Thomas E. Dahl, *Wetland Losses in the United States, 1780's to 1980's* (Washington, D.C.: U.S. Department of the Interior, Fish and Wildlife Service, 1990), 6. Eight states are MI, WI, MN, OH, IN, IL, IA, MO.

37. Quoted in Strausberg, 191–92.

38. Dahl, 6.

39. Congress, Senate, 60th Cong., 1st sess., Senate Doc. no. 443, in Ben Palmer, "Swamp Drainage with Special Reference to Minnesota," Studies in the Social Sciences, *Bulletin of the University of Minnesota* (Mar. 1915), 25; James E. Herget, "Taming the Environment: The Drainage District in Illinois," *Journal of the Illinois State Historical Society* 71 (1978): 107; Bogue, "Swamp Land Acts," 171; McCorvie and Lant, 22; Leslie Hewes and Philip E. Frandson, "Occupying the Wet Prairie: The Role of Artificial Drainage in Story Co., Iowa," *Annals of the Association of American Geographers* 42, no. 1 (Mar. 1952): 34.

40. Herget, 109–10.

41. "Draining Wet Lands," *Indiana Farmer and Gardener* (8 Feb. 1845), 24, quoted in Strausberg, 192.

42. McCorvie and Lant, 22–23. Seven midwestern states that received grants are IL, IN, IA, MI, MN, OH, WI. Indiana received 1,265,000 acres; Illinois received 1,493,000 acres.

43. Indiana, *Senate Journal* (1863), 615, quoted in Strausberg, 197.

44. Strausberg, 197.

45. Indiana, *Documentary Journal* (1855), 305, quoted in Strausberg, 199.

46. Indiana, *Senate Journal* (1861), 805–6, quoted in Strausberg, 200.

47. Strausberg, 202–3.

48. Bogue, "Swamp Land Act," 172; Herget, 112; McCorvie and Lant, 28.

49. *Central Illinois Gazette* (Urbana), 13 Oct. 1858, quoted in Bogue, 173.

50. Bogue, "Swamp Land Act," 174.

51. Mel Scott, *The San Francisco Bay Area: A Metropolis in Perspective,* 2d ed. (Berkeley: University of California Press, 1959; reprint, 1985), 35.

52. Robert Kelly, *Battling the Inland Sea: American Political Culture, Public Policy, and the Sacramento Valley, 1850–1986* (Berkeley: University of California Press, 1989), 11–14.

53. Quoted in Gene Rose, *The San Joaquin: A River Betrayed* (Fresno, Calif.: Linrose Publishing, 1992), 14.

54. William C. Preston, *Vanishing Landscapes: Land and Life in the Tulare Lake Basin* (Berkeley: University of California Press, 1981), 56–67; Arthur F. McEvoy, *The Fisherman's Problem: Ecology and Law in the California Fisheries 1850–1980* (Cambridge, England: Cambridge University Press, 1990), 41.

55. Quoted in Rose, 59; Stephen Johnson, Gerald Haslam, and Robert Dawson, *The Great Central Valley: California's Heartland* (Berkeley: University of California Press, 1993), 62. According to Rose, settlers had first named the town of Stockton "Tuleberg" in honor of its swampy site.

56. James Carson, *Recollections of the California Mines and a Description of the Great Tulare Valley* (1852), quoted in Preston, 71.

57. Richard H. Peterson, "The Failure to Reclaim: California State Swamp Land Policy and the Sacramento Valley, 1850–1866," *Southern California Quarterly* 56 (Spring 1974): 47–49; Kelly, *Battling*, 36–37.

58. Quoted in Peterson, 46; Strausberg, 194–96; Lokken, 182–84.

59. Peterson, 49; Robert Kelly, "Taming the Sacramento: Hamiltonianism in Action," *Pacific Historical Review* 34 (1965): 26; Kelly, *Battling*, 42. According to Peterson, in 1880 the state engineer recorded annual discharge of silt in the Yuba River as 22 million cubic yards; in the Feather it was 13 million cubic yards. Where the river passed Marysville, its bed was 15 feet higher than it had been in its natural state.

60. Peterson, 50–51; Kelly, *Battling*, 37–42; John Thompson and Edward A. Dutra, *The Tule Breakers: The Story of the California Dredge* (Stockton, Calif.: Stockton Corral of Westerners, 1983), 24–25. Thompson and Dutra refer to the organization as the state Board of Swamp and Overflowed Land Commissioners.

61. California, *Senate Journal* (1857), Appendix, Doc. 3, 13–14, quoted in Peterson, 52.

62. "Report of the Joint Committee to Inquire into and Report upon the Condition of the Public and State Lands Lying within the Limits of the State," *Senate and Assembly Journal*, vol. 2 (1871–72), Appendix, Doc. 6, 17, quoted in Peterson, 52.

63. John Thompson, "The Settlement Geography of the Sacramento–San Joaquin Delta, California" (Ph.D. diss., Stanford University, 1958), 218, in Peterson, 54; Marvin Breines, "Sacramento Defies the Rivers: 1850–1878," *California History* 58 (Spring 1979): 3.

64. Rose, 41.

65. Kelly, *Battling*, 62, 125–52; Thompson and Dutra, 24–25; Kelly, "Taming," 25.

66. Thompson and Dutra, 25.

67. Quoted in Thompson and Dutra, 26

68. Quoted in Siry, 73–74.

69. Paul W. Gates, *History of Public Land Law Development* (Washington, D.C.: Public Land Law Review Commission, 1968), 328.

70. Gates, 328; Hickman, 90.

71. Quoted in Lokken, 191.

72. Lokken, 192–93.

73. Quoted in Lokken, 196.

74. Margaret Beattie Bogue, *Patterns from the Sod: Land Use and Tenure in the Grand Prairie, 1850–1900,* Collections of the Illinois State Historical Library, vol. 34 (1959), x; Bogue, "Swamp Land Act," 179.

75. *Annual Report of the Commissioner of General Land Office Made to the Secretary of the Interior for the Year 1870* (Washington, D.C.: Government Printing Office, 1872), 184.

76. Hugh H. Wooten and Lewis A. Jones, "The History of Our Drainage Enterprises," *Yearbook of Agriculture, 1955* (Washington, D.C.: U.S. Department of Agriculture, 1955), 479–80.

77. Robert G. LeBlanc, "The Differential Perception of Salt Marshes by the Folk and Elite in the 19th Century," *Proceedings: American Association of Geographers* 5 (1973): 140–41.

78. Quoted in David Montgomery Nesbit, *Tide Marshes of the United States,* U.S. Department of Agriculture Special Report No. 7 (Washington, D.C.: Government Printing Office, 1885), 132, 124.

79. Nesbit, 8–9, 150.

80. Nesbit, 28–29.

81. Nesbit, 133.

82. George M. Warren, "Tidal Marshes and Their Reclamation," U.S. Department of Agriculture, Office of Experiment Stations, Bulletin, no. 240 (Washington, D.C.: Government Printing Office, 1911), 70; Nesbit, 124–29; Nathaniel Southgate Shaler, "Preliminary Report on the Sea-Coast Swamps of the Eastern United States," in *Sixth Annual Report of the U.S. Geological Survey to the Secretary of the Interior, 1884–1885,* ed. John Wesley Powell (Washington, D.C.: Government Printing Office, 1885), 384–88.

83. Quoted in Warren, 72, 67–78, passim.

84. Nesbit, 28.

Chapter 6

1. Henry D. Thoreau, "Walking," in *Thoreau: The Major Essays,* ed. Jeffrey L. Duncan (New York: E.P. Dutton, 1972), 211–12. The essay "Walking" was first published in the *Atlantic* in June 1862.

2. Henry D. Thoreau, *The Journal of Henry D. Thoreau,* vol. 1, ed. B. Torrey and F. H. Allen (New York: Dover Publications, 1962), 141–42.

3. Alvan R. Brick, Jr., "The Virgin Swamp: A Chorography of a Primeval Environment in the New World" (Ph.D. diss., Cornell University, 1981), 156, 160.

4. Thoreau, *Journal,* 449 [4 Jan. 1853].

5. Thoreau, "Walking," 211–12.

6. Barbara Novak, *Nature and Culture: American Landscape and Painting, 1825–1875* (New York: Oxford University Press, 1980), 34–44; Theodore E.

369

Stebbins, Jr., *The Life and Works of Martin Johnson Heade* (New Haven: Yale University Press, 1975), 44.

7. Stebbins, *Life and Works,* 52.

8. *Martin Johnson Heade,* exhibition catalogue, ed. Theodore E. Stebbins, Jr., Museum of Fine Arts, Boston (July–Aug. 1969), University of Maryland Art Gallery (Sept.–Oct. 1969), Whitney Museum of American Art, New York, (Nov.–Dec. 1969); Stebbins, *Life and Works,* 42, 46.

9. David Hunter Strother, "The Great Dismal Swamp," *Harper's New Monthly Magazine,* Sept. 1856, 441–42, quoted in David Cameron Miller, *Dark Eden: The Swamp in Nineteenth-Century American Culture* (Cambridge, England: Cambridge University Press, 1989), 23.

10. Strother, 444, quoted in Miller, 25.

11. John Boyle O'Reilly (1888) in Charles Frederick Stansbury, *The Lake of the Dismal Swamp* (New York: Albert & Charles Beni, 1925), 147–72, quoted in Miller, 30.

12. Thomas Moore, "The Lake of the Dismal Swamp," in *Songs, Ballads, and Sacred Songs* (London: Longman, Brown, Green and Longman's, 1849), 20–21.

13. George Henry Preble, "The Diary of a Canoe Expedition into the Everglades and Interior of Southern Florida in 1842," *The United Service,* 8 Apr. 1883, 363; Novak, 9; John Conron, *The American Landscape: A Critical Anthology* (New York: Oxford University Press, 1974), 25. Merriwether Lewis also alluded to Salvator Rosa when describing the Great Falls of the Missouri in his journal in 1805.

14. *American Whig Review* 16 (July 1852): 12, quoted in Frank Luther Mott, *A History of American Magazines, 1850–1865,* vol. 2 (Cambridge: Belknap Press of Harvard University Press, 1938), 391.

15. Cecil D. Eby, *Porte Crayon: The Life of David Hunter Strother* (Chapel Hill: University of North Carolina Press, 1960), 68–69, 74; *The Diary of Edmund Ruffin,* ed. William Scarborough Kauffman (Baton Rouge: Louisiana University Press, 1972), 156.

16. "Ibis Shooting in Louisiana," *Harper's New Monthly Magazine,* Nov. 1853, 768–72, in *Hunting in the Old South: Original Narratives of the Hunters,* ed. Clarence Gohdes (Baton Rouge: Louisiana State University Press, 1967), 108.

17. Benjamin M. Norman, "Rambles in the Swamps of Louisiana," *Ladies' Magazine of Literature, Fashion and Fine Arts,* Jan. 1844, reprinted in *Louisiana Studies* (Spring 1971), 59; T. W. Higginson, "My Outdoor Study," *Atlantic Monthly,* Sept. 1861, 306–07; William H. Gibson, "Springtime," *Harper's Magazine,* Oct. 1880, 65–80.

18. Harnett T. Kane, *The Bayous of Louisiana* (New York: William Morrow, 1944), 259.

19. Novak, 16–17; Roderick Nash, *Wilderness and the American Mind,* 3d ed. (New Haven: Yale University Press, 1982), 67–73.

20. T. Addison Richards, *Romantic Landscapes* (New York: Leavitt and Allen, 1855), 103.

21. Jack Temple Kirby, *Poquosin: A Study of Rural Landscape and Society* (Chapel Hill: University of North Carolina Press, 1995), 107, 168.

22. Harriet Beecher Stowe, Dred, *A Tale of the Dismal Swamp*, vol. 2 (Boston, 1856), 274, quoted in Miller, 57.

23. Miller, 75.

24. T. W. Higginson, *Out-Door Papers* (Boston, 1863), 129, quoted in Miller, 57.

25. Stowe, *Dred*, vol. 2, 16, quoted in Miller, 100.

26. Miller, 100.

27. Miller, 92.

28. Miller, 90; Kirby, 162.

29. Samuel Warner, *Authentic and Impartial Narrative of the Tragical Scene . . . ,* pamphlet (New York, 21 Oct. 1831), quoted in Miller, 91–92.

30. Frederick Turner, "George Washington Cable's *Old Creole Days*," in *The Spirit of Place: The Making of an American Literary Landscape* (Washington, D.C.: Island Press, 1989), 116–17, 120–21. *The Grandissimes* was published in 1880.

31. Miller, 87.

32. A. R. Waud, "Cypress Swamp in Louisiana," *Harper's Weekly*, 8 Dec. 1866, 769.

33. Waud, 781.

34. Harriet Beecher Stowe, *Palmetto Leaves* (Boston, 1873), 139, quoted in Miller, 68.

35. Charles Edward Stowe, *The Life of Harriet Beecher Stowe* (Boston, 1889), 468, quoted in Miller, 68.

36. A. R. Waud, "On the Mississippi," *Every Saturday Magazine,* 5 Aug. 1871, 141, quoted in Miller, 57–59; Thoreau, *Journal,* 449. In his journal on 4 Jan. 1853, Thoreau wrote: "If there were druids whose temples were the oak groves, my temple is the swamp."

37. C. Reynolds Brown, *Joseph Rusling Meeker: Images of the Mississippi Delta* (Montgomery, Ala.: Montgomery Museum of Fine Arts, 1981), 13, passim; J. A. Dacus and James W. Buel, *A Tour of St. Louis, or The Inside Life of a Great City* (St. Louis: Western Publishing, 1878), 13–14.

38. William Cullen Bryant, ed. *Picturesque America: The Land We Live In,* vol. 1 (New York: Appleton, 1872), 169, quoted in Miller, 62.

39. Edward King, *The Great South* (Hartford, 1875), 384, 370, quoted in Miller, 63.

Chapter 7

1. John C. Gifford, *The Everglades and Other Essays Relating to Southern Florida* (Everglades Land Sales, 1911), 102.

2. Kenneth T. Jackson, *Crabgrass Frontier: The Suburbanization of the United States* (New York: Oxford University Press, 1985), 47; Samuel Hays, *Conservation and the Gospel of Efficiency: The Progressive Conservation Movement, 1890–1920* (Cambridge: Harvard University Press, 1959), 265–66.

3. Kimberly R. Sebold, *From Marsh to Farm: The Landscape Transformation of Coastal New Jersey* (Washington, D.C.: U.S. Department of the Interior, National Park Service, New Jersey Coastal Historic Trail, 1992), 35–36; David

Montgomery Nesbit, *Tide Marshes of the United States*, Special Report No. 7 (Washington, D.C.: U.S. Department of Agriculture, 1885), 20.

4. Frederick Guthheim, *The Potomac* (New York: Rinehart, 1949), 367–70.

5. William C. Preston, *Vanishing Landscapes: Land and Life in the Tulare Lake Basin* (Berkeley: University of California Press, 1981), 94, 135.

6. *Thirty-First Annual Report of the Ohio State Board of Agriculture for the Year 1876* (Columbus: Nevins and Myers, 1877), 509, in Martin R. Kaatz, "The Black Swamp," *Annals of the Association of American Geographers* 45 (1955): 25–26.

7. Albert E. Cowdrey, "Pioneering Environmental Law: The Army Corps of Engineers and the Refuse Act," *Pacific Historical Review* 44, no. 3 (Aug. 1975): 333.

8. Gordon Whitney, *From Coastal Wilderness to Fruited Plain* (Cambridge, England: Cambridge University Press, 1994), 273.

9. George E. Waring, Jr., *Draining for Profit and Draining for Health* (New York: Judd Company, 1890), 191, 208–10.

10. Gordon Harrison, *Mosquitoes, Malaria, and Man: A History of the Hostilities Since 1800* (New York: E.P. Dutton, 1978), 3.

11. John Duffy, *A History of Public Health in New York City, 1866–1966* (New York: Russell Sage Foundation, 1974), 252–53, 532–33.

12. Percy Viosca, Jr., "Engineering Aspects of the Problem of Salt Marsh Mosquito Suppression in Louisiana," *Proceedings of the Louisiana Engineering Society* 12, no. 2 (Apr. 1926): 3; Hackensack Meadows Interpretive Center Display, Lyndhurst, N.J., Oct. 1993; *Report of Metropolitan Drainage Commission* (St. Paul, Minn.: Riverside Press, 1927); John Duffy, *The Sanitarians: A History of Public Health* (Urbana: University of Illinois Press, 1990), 67, 233; State of New Jersey, "Mosquitoes—Prevention of the Breeding of," Laws of 1912, Chapter 104, approved 21 Mar. 1912, in *Public Health Reports* 28, no. 1 (3 Jan. 1913): 23–25; State of Massachusetts, "Prevention of Malaria Drainage of Land in Valley of Neponset River," approved 11 July 1911, in *Public Health Reports* 27, no. 50 (13 Dec. 1912): 2093–94.

13. Viosca, 3.

14. Des Moines, Iowa, "Stagnant Water—Depressions or Excavations to be Drained or Filled," Section 63, Nuisances Ordinance, approved 11 Nov. 1912, in *Public Health Reports* 28, no. 18 (2 May 1913), 883.

15. Gayonne, New Jersey, "Definition of Nuisance," adopted by the Regulation Board of Health, 20 June 1912, in *Public Health Reports* 28, no. 8 (21 Feb. 1913): 376.

16. Orange County, New Jersey, *Public Health Reports* 27, no. 14 (5 Apr. 1912): 494; Hartford, Connecticut, *Public Health Reports* 28, no. 25 (30 June 1913): 1315; Hutchinson, Kansas, *Public Health Reports* 28, no. 26 (27 June 1913): 1392; State of Michigan, *Public Health Reports* 28, no. 23 (6 June 1913): 1174; State of Connecticut, *Public Health Reports* 28, no. 36 (29 May 1913): 1876–77; State of New York, *Public Health Reports* 28, no. 43 (24 Oct. 1913): 2260.

17. Frederick Hoffman, *A Plan and a Plea for the Eradication of Malaria Throughout the Western Hemisphere*, reprint of an address before the Southern Medical

Association, Atlanta, 14 Nov. 1916 (Newark: Prudential Press, 1917), 17, 54–55. Reduction figures given represent a change from the 1900–1904 period to the 1910–1914 period.

18. Quoted in Sebold, 70–71; Paul Eck, *The American Cranberry* (New Brunswick, N.J.: Rutgers University Press, 1990), 10.

19. Sebold, 70–71.

20. Eck, 11; Sebold, 70–71.

21. Eck, 11.

22. Sebold, 75–76.

23. Sebold, 80.

24. Eck, 9.

25. Omer Lonnie Roberts, Jr., "Cypress Land and Floodway: Environmental Change and Development of Land Utilization in the Atchafalaya Basin, Louisiana" (Ph.D. diss., University of Tennessee, 1974), 28, 39.

26. Michael Williams, *Americans and Their Forests: A Historical Geography* (Cambridge, England: Cambridge University Press, 1989), 239.

27. Williams, 240.

28. Williams, 240–41.

29. Thomas D. Clark, *The Greening of the South: The Recovery of Land and Forest* (Lexington: University Press of Kentucky, 1984), 14.

30. Williams, 241.

31. Paul Gates, "Federal Land Policy in the South, 1866–1888," *Journal of Southern History* 6 (1940): 319–25, cited in Williams, 242; Roberts, 33, 36.

32. Williams, 243. The five southern states are LA, MS, AL, AR, and FL.

33. Quoted in Ervin Mancil, "Pullboat Logging," *Journal of Forest History* 24 (July 1980): 134.

34. Rachael Edna Norgress, "The History of the Cypress Lumber Industry in Louisiana," *Louisiana Historical Quarterly* 30, no. 3 (July 1947): 101; Mancil, 134–35.

35. Norgress, 1002; Mancil, 136–37.

36. Williams, 252–63.

37. Norgress, 1021.

38. *The Daily Crescent* (New Orleans) 14 Apr. 1990, cited in Roberts, 40–41.

39. Williams, 269.

40. Roberts, 44, 45.

41. Williams, 271; Anna C. Burns, "Frank B. Williams: Cypress Lumber King," *Journal of Forest History* 24 (July 1980): 132.

42. Williams, 247.

43. Burns, 132.

44. Norgress, 1014–15, 1034.

45. Roberts, 45; Norgress, 1025; Williams, 250.

46. Williams, 268.

47. Roberts, 46.

48. Williams, 282.

49. Louisiana Department of Conservation, *Classification and Uses of Agricultural*

and *Forest Lands in the State of Louisiana and the Parishes,* Bulletin No. 24 (1934), 23, cited in in Norgress, 1047.

50. Marion M. Weaver, *History of Tile Drainage in America Prior to 1900* (Waterloo, N.Y.: self-published, 1964), 12–13, 58–60.

51. *American Agriculturalist* 33 (Apr. 1874): 130, quoted in Albert L. Demaree, *The American Agricultural Press, 1819–1860,* Columbia University Studies in the History of American Agriculture, no. 8 (New York: Columbia University Press, 1941), 41–42.

52. *Cultivator* 6 (Mar. 1849): 89–90, excerpted in Demaree, 239–40.

53. Weaver, 221.

54. *Transactions of the New York State Agricultural Society* (1855), 258, quoted in Weaver, 67.

55. Demaree, 42.

56. Weaver, 263–70.

57. Weaver, 77–79.

58. Weaver, 93–94.

59. Weaver, 229.

60. Hugh H. Wooten and Lewis A. Jones, "The History of Our Drainage Enterprises," in *Yearbook of Agriculture, 1955* (Washington, D.C.: U.S. Department of Agriculture, 1955), 478; Keith Beauchamp, "A History of Drainage and Drainage Methods," in *Farm Drainage in the United States: History, Status, and Prospects,* ed. George Pavelis, Miscellaneous Publication, no. 1455 (Washington, D.C.: U.S. Department. of Agriculture, Economic Research Service, 1987), 20–21.

61. Wooten and Jones, 478.

62. Weaver, 165–82.

63. Beauchamp, 26; John Thompson and Edward A. Dutra, *The Tule Breakers: The Story of the California Dredge* (Stockton, Calif.: Stockton Corral of Westerners, 1983), 33–34, 44.

64. Mary R. McCorvie and Christopher L. Lant, "Drainage District Formation and the Loss of Midwestern Wetlands, 1850–1930," *Agricultural History* 67, no. 4 (Fall 1993): 31–36; *A Century of Farming in Iowa, 1846–1946,* by members of Iowa State College and the Iowa Experiment Station (Ames: Iowa State College Press, 1946), 22.

65. McCorvie and Lant, 33.

66. R. T. Brown, "Tile Drainage As Connected with Progress in Agriculture," *Drainage and Farm Journal* 10, no. 1 (Jan. 1888): 7–9.

67. Wooten and Jones, 485.

68. J. Paul Lilly, "A History of Swamp Land Development in North Carolina," in *Pocosin Wetlands,* ed. Curtis J. Richardson (Stroudsburg, Pa.: Hutchinson Ross Publishing, 1981), 32.

69. McCorvie and Lant, 22, 31–34.

70. Quincy Claude Aires and Daniels Scoates, *Land Drainage and Reclamation* (New York: McGraw-Hill, 1928), 8–10. The 1920 census included for the first time a national accounting of drained lands, though states in the Northeast

were omitted. While this figure gives a sense of the broad extent of drainage, not all land in drainage enterprises was former marsh and swamp, and much of the land within the districts remained wet.

71. Whitney, 277; McCorvie and Lant, 33; Erwin H. Ackerknect, *Malaria in the Upper Mississippi Valley, 1760–1900,* Supplements to the Bulletin of the History of Medicine, no. 4 (Baltimore: Johns Hopkins University Press, 1945), 78–79, 89–91.

72. R. E. Flickinger, *The Pioneer History of Pocahontas County, Iowa, from the Time of Its Earliest Settlement to Present Time* (Fonda, Iowa: Sandborn Publishers, 1904); B. P. Birdsall, *History of Wright County, Iowa: Its Peoples, Industries, and Institutions* (Indianapolis: B. F. Bowen, 1915); R. M. Anderson, "The Birds of Iowa," *Proceedings of the Davenport Academy of Science* 11 (1894): 125–417, cited in Susan M. Galatowitsch and Arnold G. van der Valk, *Restoring Prairie Wetlands: An Ecological Approach* (Ames: Iowa State University Press, 1994), 12.

73. Samuel P. Shaw and C. Gordon Fredine, *Wetlands of the United States,* circular 39 (Washington, D.C.: U.S. Department of the Interior, Fish and Wildlife Service, Office of River Basin Studies, 1956), 7. The seven states are AR, CA, FL, IL, IN, IA, MO.

74. Iowa census reports (1925), in Galatowitsch and van der Valk, 12.

75. *A Century of Farming in Iowa,* 22.

76. Robert Kelly, *Battling the Inland Sea: American Political Culture, Public Policy, and the Sacramento Valley, 1850–1986* (Berkeley: University of California Press, 1989), 1.

77. Kelly, 212–13, 189–235.

78. Kelly, 201–19.

79. Kelly, 203.

80. Ruth Fernwood, "San Francisco Bay—A Living Estuary," *Pacific Discovery* 25, no. 2 (Mar.–Apr. 1972): 4.

81. *Woodruff v. North Bloomfield Mining Co.,* 18F 753 (c.d. Cal 1884); Kelly, 217–18, 223–33.

82. Kelly, 233–46.

83. Kelly, 278–91.

84. Kelly, 292–93.

85. Thompson and Dutra, 26, 33, 208; Stephen Johnson, Gerald Haslam, and Robert Dawson, *The Great Central Valley: California's Heartland* (Berkeley: University of California Press, 1993), 62.

86. Kelly, 302.

87. Kelly, 299.

88. Kelly, 298–99.

89. Kelly, 298–302.

90. U.S. Department of the Interior, *The Impact of Federal Programs on Wetlands,* vol. 2, A Report to Congress (Washington, D.C.: 1994), 13, 192–94.

91. Martin Reuss, *Army Engineers in Memphis District: A Documentary Chronicle* (Memphis: U.S. Army, Corps of Engineers, 1982), xiv–xx. Joseph L. Arnold, *The Evolution of the 1936 Flood Control Act* (Fort Belvoir, Va.: U.S. Army, Corps of Engineers, 1988), 8.

92. Robert W. Harrison, *Alluvial Empire: Drainage in the Lower Mississippi Valley* (Little Rock, Ark.: Pioneer Press, in cooperation with the U.S. Department of Agriculture, Economic Research Service, 1961), 191, 185, 263–71.

93. Robert W. Harrison and Walter M. Kollmorgen, "Past and Prospective Drainage Reclamations in the Coastal Marshlands of the Mississippi River Delta," *Journal of Land and Public Utility Economics* 23, no. 3 (Aug. 1947): 307–8.

94. Louisiana Meadows Investment Company, *Making Rich Black Farms from Louisiana's Wet Lands,* pamphlet (New Orleans, ca. 1915), Louisiana State University, Mississippi River Valley Collection; Lilly, 22.

95. *Making Rich Black Farms.*

96. Harrison, *Alluvial Empire,* 263–71.

97. Edward Wisner, "Reclaimed Lands Would Give Home Sites for 3,000,000; Assessments Would Jump 100 Percent," *New Orleans Item,* 26 July 1909, quoted in Harrison, *Alluvial Empire,* 267.

98. Harrison, *Alluvial Empire,* 205.

99. Harrison and Kollmorgen, 312–13; Harrison, *Alluvial Empire,* 185.

100. Harrison, *Alluvial Empire,* 191–92; Hays, 223–25.

101. Arthur E. Morgan, "The Drainage of the Mississippi Delta," *Manufacturers Record* 8 Sept. 1910, quoted in Harrison, *Alluvial Empire,* 227, also 191, 185, 263–71.

102. Roberts, 48; Arnold, 14.

103. Nelson Manfred Blake, *Land into Water—Water into Land: A History of Water Management in Florida* (Tallahassee: University Presses of Florida, 1980), 43; Thomas E. Dahl, *Wetlands: Losses in the United States, 1780s to 1980s* (Washington D.C.: U.S. Department of the Interior, Fish and Wildlife Service, 1990), 6. Blake offers this figure with the caveat that it is liberal, probably including swamplands ceded to Florida before the actual Swamp Lands Acts. The National Wetlands Inventory estimates that Florida once had 20.3 million acres of wetlands. The disparity is likely due to the different techniques of survey. In any case, the wetland acreage was large.

104. Blake, 73–78.

105. *New York Times,* 18 Feb. 1881, sec. 2, 7, quoted in Blake, 75.

106. Blake, 79–80; Charles W. Finkl, "Water Resource Management in the Florida Everglades: Are 'Lessons from Experience' a Prognosis for Conservation in the Future?" *Journal of Soil and Water Conservation,* Nov.–Dec. 1995, 598.

107. Joseph Carlyle Sitterson, *Sugar Country: The Cane Sugar Industry in the South, 1753–1950* (Lexington: University of Kentucky Press, 1953), 362.

108. Blake, 83.

109. Blake, 80–83. George E. Buker, *Sun, Sand and Water: A History of the Jacksonville District, 1821–1975* (Jacksonville, Fla.: U.S. Army, Corps of Engineers, n.d.), 98.

110. Samuel Proctor, *Napoleon Bonaparte Broward: Florida's Fighting Democrat* (Gainesville, Fla.: University of Florida Press, 1950), 191, quoted in Buker, 100.

111. Blake, 95–96.

112. Blake, 97–98.

113. Blake, 98–99.

114. Blake, 104.

115. Paul S. George, "Land by the Gallon: The Florida Fruitlands Company and the Progresso Land Lottery of 1911," *South Florida History Magazine* 2 (Spring 1989): 8.

116. George, 9.

117. Blake, 109–13.

118. Blake, 121; J. E. Dovell, "A Brief History of the Florida Everglades," in *Proceedings of the Soil Science Society of South Florida*, vol. 4–A (1942): 146.

119. Blake, 122–27; Dovell, 149–50.

120. Blake, 131.

121. Kristine L. Bradof, "Ditching of Red Lake Peatland During the Homestead Era," in *The Patterned Peatlands of Minnesota*, ed. H. E. Wright, Jr., Barbara A. Coffin, and Norman E. Aaseng (Minneapolis: University of Minnesota Press, 1992), 263–74.

122. Lilly, 33; Interpretive Display at Mattamuskeet National Wildlife Refuge, Nov. 1993.

123. Ralph W. Tiner, Jr., *Wetlands of the U.S.: Current Status and Recent Trends* (Washington, D.C.: U.S. Department of the Interior, Fish and Wildlife Service, 1984), 33; W. E. Frayer, Dennis D. Peters, and H. Ross Pywell, *Wetlands of the California Central Valley: Status and Trends, 1939 to mid–1980s* (Portland, Ore.: U.S. Department of the Interior, Fish and Wildlife Service, 1989), 6; Shaw and Fredine, 7. Although acreage figures from early USDA surveys are not directly compatible with modern wetland acreage estimates, they offer the best estimates for the rate of wetland losses during this period.

Chapter 8

1. John C. Van Dyke, *Nature for Its Own Sake: First Studies in Natural Appearances*, 4th ed. (New York: Charles Scribner's Sons, 1900), 250.

2. Rachel Edna Norgress, "The History of the Cypress Lumber Industry in Louisiana," *Louisiana Historical Quarterly* 30, no. 3 (July 1947): 981.

3. Samuel Hays, *Conservation and the Gospel of Efficiency: The Progressive Conservation Movement, 1890–1920* (Cambridge: Harvard University Press, 1959), 198.

4. Norgress, 1047–48.

5. *Forestry Quarterly* 8 (1910): 28–29, quoted in Norgress, 1051; Hays, 203–6. At the time, a scientific controversy raged between those who believed that reservoirs and forest cover affected flooding (Forest Service and USGS engineers) and those who disagreed (Army Corps of Engineers), especially in the lower Mississippi River valley, where the Mississippi River Commission was promoting a solely levee-based system for flood control. The former and correct view was gaining credence and public appeal with the prestige and popularity of Gifford Pinchot.

6. Michael Williams, *Americans and Their Forests: A Historical Geography* (Cambridge, England: Cambridge University Press, 1989), 280–87.

7. Joan Aiken, "Afterword," in Gene Stratton Porter, *A Girl of the Limberlost* (New York: Penguin Books, Signet Classic, 1988), 371–84; Deborah Strom, ed., *Birdwatching with American Women: A Selection of Nature Writings* (New York: W.W. Norton, 1986), 67–70.

8. Porter's conception of the natural world as a font for American character was not all that different from the ideas of her contemporaries historian Frederick Jackson Turner and President Theodore Roosevelt, who believed that the wild West provided Americans with the source of their rugged individuality.

9. Archibald Rutledge, *Wild Life of the South* (New York: Frederick A. Stokes, 1935). There are numerous similar volumes.

10. Joseph Blother, *Faulkner: A Biography* (New York: Random House, 1974; reprint, 1984), 376–77; Alvan Rogers Brick, Jr., "The Virgin Swamp: A Chorography of a Primeval Environment in the New World" (Ph.D. diss., Cornell University, 1981), 196–250.

11. Cynthia Zaitzevsky, *Frederick Law Olmsted and the Boston Park System* (Cambridge: Belknap Press of Harvard University Press, 1982), 18.

12. Walter Muir Whitehill, *Boston: A Topographical History* (Cambridge: Belknap Press of Harvard University Press, 1959), 145; Zaitzevsky, 10.

13. Whitehill, 159, 164.

14. Zaitzevsky, 35–36, 52–54.

15. Zaitzevsky, 57.

16. Quoted in Zaitzevsky, 57.

17. Zaitzevsky, 154–56, 161, 187.

18. F. L. Olmsted to Charles Sprague Sargent, 27 Jan. 1879, Olmsted Papers, Library of Congress, Washington, D.C., quoted in Zaitzevsky, 186–87.

19. Quoted in Zaitzevsky, 186.

20. Zaitzevsky, 154.

21. Zaitzevsky, 57, 156. The Fens project was shortlived. In 1910, the Charles River Dam cut off tidal flows to the park, and many of the plants died. Then the Fens were used as a dumpsite for subway excavations. Only a small part of the park remains.

22. Van Dyke, 249–51.

23. Richard Le Galliene, "Concerning Salt-Marshes," *Harper's,* July 1916, 233–34; see also Lucy Scarborough Conant, "Marshes," *Harper's Monthly,* Oct. 1904, 163–68.

24. *From Outrage to Action: The Story of the National Audubon Society,* pamphlet, 5; Frank Graham, Jr., *The Audubon Ark: A History of the National Audubon Society* (New York: Alfred Knopf, 1990), 24–25.

25. William A. Niering, "Human Impacts on the South Florida Wetlands: The Everglades and Big Cypress Swamp," in *The Earth in Transition—Paths and Processes of Biotic Impoverishment,* ed. George M. Woodwell (New York: Cambridge University Press, 1990), 466.

26. John Madson, *Where the Sky Began: Land of the Tallgrass Prairie* (Boston: Houghton Mifflin, 1982; reprint, San Francisco: Sierra Club Books, 1985), 145.

27. John F. Reiger, *American Sportsmen and the Origins of Conservation,* rev. ed. (Norman: University of Oklahoma Press, 1986), 36–40; Karl E. Bednarik, "Saga of the Lake Erie Marshes," in *Flyways: Pioneering Waterfowl Management in North America,* ed. A. S. Hawkins, R. C. Hanson, H. K. Nelson, H. M. Reeves (Washington, D.C.: U.S. Department of the Interior, Fish and Wildlife Service, 1984), 424. Marsh painter Martin J. Heade frequently contributed conservation editorials under the pen-name Didymus.

28. George Bird Grinnell, "The Audubon Society," *Forest and Stream,* 11 Feb. 1886, 1, reprinted in Reiger, 68.

29. *Outrage to Action,* 5–8.

30. James Trefethen, *An American Crusade for Wildlife* (New York: Winchester Press and the Boone and Crockett Club, 1975), 129–33; Graham, 23.

31. Trefethen, 136.

32. Norman Brydon, "New Jersey Wildlife Conservation and the Law," *New Jersey History* 86, no. 4 (1968): 224–25.

33. Congress, Senate, 63d Cong., 1st sess., *Congressional Record,* 16 Aug. 1913, 3426, quoted in Graham, 81–82.

34. Graham, 93; Arthur Hawkins, "The U.S. Response," in Hawkins et al., *Flyways,* 2–6; Karen Dale Dustman, "The Saga of the Migratory Bird Treaty Act," *Ducks Unlimited,* Jan.–Feb. 1995, 17.

35. Michael J. Bean, *The Evolution of National Wildlife Law* (New York: Praeger, 1983), 19–21.

36. Trefethen, 154–55.

37. Graham, 93, 97.

38. Paradise Key is known to modern Everglades visitors as Royal Palm, the start of the popular Anhinga Trail.

39. Linda Vance, "May Mann Jennings and Royal Palm State Park," *Florida Historical Quarterly* 55, no. 1 (July 1976): 9–10.

40. Vance, 10–12.

41. May Mann Jennings to Mrs. T. M. Shackleford, 4 June 1915, May Mann Jennings Collection, box 6, P. K. Yonge Library, University of Florida, Gainesville, quoted in John C. Paige, *Historic Resource Study for Everglades National Park* (Washington, D.C.: U.S. Department of the Interior, National Park Service, 1986), 178.

42. Vance, 12.

43. Paige, 181–82; Vance, 13.

44. Vance, 15.

45. Paige, 184–85.

46. Vance, 14.

47. Henry M. Reeves, "Wells W. Cooke," in Hawkins et al., *Flyways,* 89.

48. Trefethen, 157–71.

49. David Starr Jordan, *Report on the Fisheries of the Pacific Coast,* U.S. Fisheries

Commission (1888), quoted in Arthur F. McEvoy, *The Fisherman's Problem: Ecology and Law in the California Fisheries, 1850–1980* (Cambridge, England: Cambridge University Press, 1986; reprint, 1990), 78, 85. Of course, commercial fishing also increased during the period Starr referred to and likely contributed to the decline as well.

50. William C. Preston, *Vanishing Landscapes: Land and Life in the Tulare Lake Basin* (Berkeley: University of California Press, 1981), 161.

51. Stephen A. Forbes, "The Investigation of a River System in the Interest of Its Fisheries," *Biological Investigations of the Illinois River,* vol. 2 (Urbana: Illinois State Laboratory of Natural History, 1910), 12, quoted in Daniel W. Schneider, " Science and the Struggle for the Floodplain: The Political Context of Ecological Knowledge on the Illinois River, 1880-1920," unpublished paper, presented at the American Society of Environmental History Biennial Meeting, Baltimore, Md., Mar. 6, 1997, 10

52. Edward A. Goldman, "Conserving Our Wild Animals and Birds," *Yearbook of Agriculture, 1920* (Washington, D.C.: U.S. Department of Agriculture, 1921), 165.

53. E. W. Nelson, "Unwise Drainage," *Bulletin of the American Game Protective Association* (Washington, D.C., 1924), quoted in William Vogt, *Thirst on the Land: A Plea for Water Conservation for the Benefit of Man and Wild Life,* circular no. 32 (National Association of Audubon Societies: ca. 1938), 23, at the U.S. Department of the Interior Library, Washington, D.C.

54. Goldman, 165.

55. V. K. Irion, "Letter of Transmittal," *Louisiana Department of Conservation Bulletin,* no. 14 (May 1926), 2.

56. Percy Viosca, Jr., "Louisiana Wet Lands and the Value of Their Wild Life and Fishery Resources," *Ecology* 9, no. 2 (Apr. 1928): 216–29; Percy Viosca, Jr., "Engineering Aspects of the Problem of Salt Marsh Mosquito Suppression in Louisiana," *Louisiana Department of Conservation Bulletin,* no. 14 (May 1926); Percy Viosca, Jr., "Flood Control in the Mississippi Valley in Its Relation to Louisiana Fisheries," Louisiana Department of Conservation, Technical Paper No. 4 (Apr. 1928); Viosca delivered his papers at conferences of ecologists and fish scientists in both Kansas and Connecticut.

57. Henry M. Reeves, "Frederick C. Lincoln," in Hawkins et al., *Flyways,* 72–73.

58. Reeves, 72–73.

59. John K. Small, *From Eden to Sahara: Florida's Tragedy* (Lancaster, Pa.: Science Press Printing, 1929), 112; John K. Small, "Vegetation and Erosion on the Everglades Keys," *Scientific Monthly* 30 (Jan. 1930): 35–36; Paige, 159, 165.

60. Harold F. Breimyer, "Agricultural Philosophies and Policies in the New Deal," *Minnesota Law Review* 68 (1983): 335; James H. Shideler, *Farm Crisis, 1919–1923* (Berkeley: University of California Press, 1957; reprint, Westport, Conn.: Greenwood Press, 1976), 292–93; T. H. Watkins, *The Great Depression: America in the 1930s* (Boston: Little, Brown, 1993), 44.

61. William J. Berry, "The Influence of Natural Environment in North-Central

Iowa," *Iowa Journal of History and Politics* 25, no. 2 (Apr. 1927): 295; William D. Rowley, *M. L. Wilson and the Campaign for the Domestic Allotment* (Lincoln: University of Nebraska Press, 1970), 61.

62. Arthur Mastick Hyde, "The Agricultural Teeter Board," *Review of Reviews* 84 (Oct. 1931), 41–43; Ray Lyman Wilbur and Arthur M. Hyde, *The Hoover Policies* (New York: Charles Scribner's Sons, 1937), 159–62.

63. Donald Worster, *The Dust Bowl: The Southern Plains in the 1930s* (New York: Oxford University Press, 1979), 184–97.

Chapter 9

1. Franklin D. Roosevelt, "'Men and Nature Must Work Hand in Hand'—A Message to the Congress on the Use of Our National Resources, January 24, 1935," in *The Public Papers and Addresses of Franklin D. Roosevelt*, vol. 4 (New York: Random House, 1938), 60–61.

2. T. H. Watkins, *The Great Depression: America in the 1930s* (Boston: Little, Brown, 1993), 44; Stan Cohen, *The Tree Army: A Pictorial History of the Civilian Conservation Corps, 1933–1942* (Missoula, Mont.: Pictorial Histories Publishing, 1980), 2.

3. Nelson Manfred Blake, *Land into Water—Water into Land: A History of Water Management in Florida* (Tallahassee: University Presses of Florida, 1980), 135.

4. Blake, 133.

5. Blake, 143.

6. Blake, 140.

7. Blake, 140–46.

8. Blake, 147.

9. Joseph L. Arnold, *The Evolution of the 1936 Flood Control Act* (Fort Belvoir, Va.: U.S. Army Corps of Engineers, 1988), 18.

10. Albert E. Cowdrey, *Land's End: A History of the New Orleans District, U.S. Army Corps of Engineers, and Its Lifelong Battle with the Lower Mississippi and Other Rivers Wending Their Way to the Sea* (New Orleans: U.S. Army Corps of Engineers, 1977), 43, 29–57, passim.

11. Robert Kelly, *Battling the Inland Sea: American Political Culture, Public Policy, and the Sacramento Valley, 1850–1986* (Berkeley: University of California Press, 1989), 307.

12. Milton Friend, "Waterfowl Get Sick Too," in *Flyways: Pioneering Waterfowl Management in North America*, ed. A. S. Hawkins, R. C. Hanson, H. K. Nelson, H. M. Reeves (U.S. Fish and Wildlife Service, 1984), 480; Frank Graham, Jr., *The Audubon Ark: A History of the National Audubon Society* (New York: Alfred Knopf, 1990), 108.

13. Quoted in John Farley, *Duck Stamps and Wildlife Refuges*, circular 37 (Washington, D.C.: U.S. Department of the Interior, Fish and Wildlife Service, 1955), 4.

14. James Trefethen, *An American Crusade for Wildlife* (New York: Winchester, and Boone and Crockett Club, 1975), 182–89; Graham, 107–11.

15. Gladys L. Baker, Wayne Rasmussen, Vivian Wiser, and Jane M. Porter, *Cen-*

tury of Service: The First One-Hundred Years of the U.S. Department of Agriculture (Washington, D.C.: U.S. Department of Agriculture, 1963), 143-61.

16. Douglas Helms, "He Loved to Carry the Message," in *Readings in the History of the Soil Conservation Service,* Historical Notes, no. 1 (Washington, D.C.: U.S. Department of Agriculture, Soil Conservation Service, 1992), 33.

17. Baker et al., 195; Donald Worster, *The Dust Bowl: The Southern Plains in the 1930s* (New York: Oxford University Press, 1979), 212-15.

18. Trefethen, 234.

19. Cohen, 90.

20. Keith H. Beauchamp, "A History of Drainage and Drainage Methods," in *Farm Drainage in the U.S.: History, Status, and Prospects,* ed. George A. Pavelis, Miscellaneous Publication, no. 1455 (Washington, D.C.: U.S. Department of Agriculture, Economic Research Service, 1987), 18; Leslie Alexander Lacy, *The Soil Soldiers: The Civilian Conservation Corps in the Great Depression* (Radnor, Pa.: Chilton Book Co., 1976), 161-65, 173-74.

21. Hubert Davis Humphreys, "In a Sense Experimental: The Civilian Conservation Corps in Louisiana" (master's thesis, Louisiana State University, 1964), 23-24, 81-82.

22. Robert W. Harrison, *Alluvial Empire: Drainage in the Lower Mississippi Valley* (Little Rock, Ark.: Pioneer Press, in cooperation with the U.S. Department of Agriculture, Economic Research Service, 1961), 183.

23. Soil Conservation Service, *Annual Reports of the Department of Agriculture, 1939* (Washington, D.C.: U.S. Department of Agriculture, 1939), 57.

24. Cohen, 88, 148; Louis A. Stearns, "Mosquito Work in Delaware During 1933," *Proceedings of the Twenty-First Annual Meeting of the New Jersey Mosquito Extermination Commission* (n.p., 1934), 128-36; Franklin C. Daiber, *Conservation of Tidal Marshes* (New York: Van Nostrand Reinhold, 1986), 95-101; William A. Marshall, "A Teacher," in Hawkins et al., *Flyways,* 52; E. Robert Panzer, Wetland Inventory of Michigan (U.S. Fish and Wildlife Service, Office of River Basin Studies, Apr. 1955), 10.

25. Dan Frances, "The Columbia Slough Bottomlands after Settlement," unpublished manuscript, Portland, Ore., 1995.

26. "Drainage," *WPA Work,* Sept. 1938, passim; Federal Works Agency, Works Projects Administrator, *Report on Progress of the WPA Program* (30 June 1942), 80.

27. Norris Hundley, *The Great Thirst: Californians and Water, 1770s-1990s* (Berkeley: University of California Press, 1992), 248-54; U.S. Department of the Interior, *The Impact of Federal Projects,* A Report to Congress, vol. 2, (Washington, D.C., 1994), 193; W. E. Frayer, Dennis D. Peters, and H. Ross Pywell, *Wetlands of the California Central Valley: Status and Trends, 1939 to mid-1980s,* (Portland, Ore.: U.S. Department of the Interior, Fish and Wildlife Service, 1989), 6.

28. M. J. Clarke, *An Economic and Environmental Assessment of the Florida Everglades Sugarcane Industry* (Baltimore: Johns Hopkins University Press, n.d.), cited in "Wetland Trends: A Historical Perspective," unpublished manuscript from the

files of Bill O. Wilen, n.d., 17; George H. Salley, *A Report on the Florida Sugar Industry* (n.p., 1960), 7; Joseph Carlyle Sitterson, *Sugar Country: The Cane Sugar Industry in the South, 1753–1950* (Lexington: University of Kentucky Press, 1953), 380–81, 383.

29. Arnold, 91–96; Cowdrey, 29–57.

30. Robert Harrison, "Louisiana's State-Sponsored Drainage Program," *Southern Economic Journal* 14, no. 4 (Apr. 1948): 387–99; Harrison, *Alluvial Empire,* 277, 283, 289; John G. Sutton, "Drainage Operations of the Soil Conservation Service," unpublished paper prepared for the American Society of Agricultural Engineers Annual Meeting, at the National Agricultural Library, Beltsville, Maryland, 25 June 1947, 3, 12.

31. News Release from Governor Sam Houston Jones, 10 Jan. 1944, quoted in Harrison, "Louisiana's Drainage Program," 393; Harrison, *Alluvial Empire,* 277, 213.

32. Harrison, "Louisiana's Drainage Program," 394.

33. Ira Gabrielson, *Wildlife Conservation* (New York: Macmillan, 1941; reprint, 1959), 151.

34. David L. Lendt, *Ding: The Life of Jay Norwood Darling* (Ames: Iowa State University Press, 1979), 63–77; J. N. "Ding" Darling Foundation, Inc., *J. N. "Ding" Darling's Conservation and Wildlife Cartoons* (Des Moines, Iowa: 1991), 17, 23; Amy N. Worthen, *The Prints of J. N. Darling* (Ames: Brunnier Gallery and Museum, Iowa State University, 1984), 10.

35. Edna N. Sater, "Federal Duck Stamps and Their Place in Waterfowl Conservation," *Conservation in Action,* no. 3 (Washington, D.C.: U.S. Department of the Interior, Fish and Wildlife Service, 1947), 1–4.

36. Lendt, 75; Trefethen, 221.

37. Quoted in Trefethen, 221–22; Lendt, 76.

38. Philip A. Dumont and Henry M. Reeves, "The Darling–Salyer Team," in Hawkins et al., *Flyways,* 111.

39. Farley, 13.

40. Albert Day, *North American Waterfowl* (New York: Stackpole and Heck, 1949), 161–62.

41. Martha K. McAlister and Wayne H. McAlister, *Guidebook to the Aransas National Wildlife Refuge* (Victoria, Tex.: Mince County Press, 1987), 68–69.

42. Day, 185.

43. Lendt, 79, 85; Trefethen, 225–28.

44. Lonnie L. Williamson, "Evolution of a Landmark Law," in *Restoring America's Wildlife, 1937–1987: The First Fifty Years of the Federal Aid in Wildlife Restoration (Pittman-Robertson) Act,* ed. Harmon Kallman (Washington, D.C.: U.S. Fish and Wildlife Service, 1987), 12.

45. Trefethen, 190.

46. Williamson, 1–12, 281; Trefethen, 228–29; Michael Bean, *The Evolution of National Wildlife Law* (New York: Praeger, 1983), 218–19.

47. Karen Dale Dustman, "The Bakersfield Duck Clubs of the Stars," *Ducks Unlimited,* Nov.–Dec. 1994, 32–33.

48. Mike Beno, "Beginnings: The 1930s and 40s," *Ducks Unlimited,* Sept.–Oct. 1987, 31–37.

49. Trefethen, 233.

50. Charles W. Shipley, "The Fish and Wildlife Coordination Act's Application to Wetlands," in *Environmental Planning: Law of Land and Resources,* ed. Arnold W. Reitze, Jr. (Washington, D.C.: North American International, 1974), sec. 2, 49; Bean, 181.

51. Carol Clayton, "Environmental Protection under the Fish and Wildlife Coordination Act: The Road Not Taken," *Virginia Journal of Natural Resources Law* 2 (1982): 46, 53, 57; Michael Veiluva, "The Fish and Wildlife Coordination Act in Environmental Litigation," *Ecology Law Quarterly* 9 (1981): 489, 315.

52. Randall Gray, "The Evolution of USDA Wetland Policy" (12 Apr. 1991) unpublished manuscript from the files of Douglas Helms, Natural Resources Conservation Service, Washington, D.C.

53. Robert J. Morgan, *Governing Soil Conservation: Thirty Years of the New Decentralization* (Baltimore: Johns Hopkins University Press for Resources for the Future, 1965), 104, 109; Secretary H. A. Wallace, Memorandum 799, in "History of Land Drainage Activities of the Soil Conservation Service," unpublished manuscript from the files of Douglas Helms.

54. "History of Land Drainage Activities of the SCS," 1; Sutton, 1–2.

55. Harrison, "Louisiana's Drainage Program," 401.

56. U.S. Department of Agriculture, Agricultural Stabilization and Conservation Service, "Agricultural Conservation Program: 45-Year Statistical Summary, 1936 through 1980" (Washington, D.C., 1981), 172.

57. William Vogt, *Thirst on the Land: A Plea for Water Conservation for the Benefit of Man and Wild Life,* National Association of Audubon Societies, circular no. 22 (ca. 1938), 6, 15–18, 20–23, 30, at the U.S. Department of the Interior Library, Washington, D.C.

58. Clinton H. Lostetter, "They've Got to Eat Someplace," in Hawkins et al., *Flyways,* 462–65.

59. Farley, 7–8.

60. Day, 163–71.

61. John C. Paige, "Historical Resource Study for Everglades National Park" (Washington, D.C.: U.S. Department of the Interior, National Park Service, 1986), 192.

62. Marjory Stoneman Douglas, "Only Tropics in the U.S. to Be a National Park," *Miami Herald,* 25 May 1930.

63. *Congressional Record,* 24 May 1934, 9497ff., quoted in John Ise, *Our National Park Policy: A Critical History* (Baltimore: Johns Hopkins University Press for Resources for the Future, 1961), 374–75.

64. Marjory Stoneman Douglas with John Rothchild, *Marjory Stoneman Douglas: Voice of the River* (Sarasota: Pineapple Press, 1987), 194.

65. Blake, 169.

66. "Commissioners Opposed to Ceding Fifty Percent of Monroe County Land for National Park Purposes," *Key West Citizen,* 13 June 1936.

67. "Cone Calls for Curbing of Park Plans in Latest Move to Trim Expenses," *Bradenton Herald,* 18 July 1939; Blake, 169.

68. John O'Reilly, "Everglades Canals Soon Deplete Wildlife Heritage of Centuries," *New York Herald Tribune,* 12 Apr. 1939; O'Reilly, "Fire-Swept Everglades a Waste; Drainage Held Cause of Disaster," *NYHT,* 25 Mar. 1939; O'Reilly, "The Everglades Where Drainage Threatens Wildlife with Extinction," *NYHT,* 9 Apr. 1939.

69. Blake, 169.

70. Quoted in Paige, 208.

71. U.S. Department of the Interior, *The Impact of Federal Programs,* vol. 2, 123.

72. Paige, 210.

73. Marjory Stoneman Douglas, *The Everglades: River of Grass* (Marietta, Ga.: Mockingbird Books, 1947; reprint, 1992).

74. Douglas, *Everglades: River of Grass,* 296.

75. Blake, 187.

Chapter 10

1. "Need Land? Then Take a Look at Marshland," *House and Home,* 1 Apr. 1958, 152.

2. Paul L. Errington, *Of Men and Marshes* (New York: Macmillan, 1957), 125–26.

3. Clay Schoenfeld, "Good-By Pot-Holes," *Field and Stream,* Apr. 1949, 36; Walter W. Augustadt, "Drainage in the Red River Valley of the North," *Yearbook of Agriculture,* 1955 (Washington, D.C.: U.S. Department of Agriculture, 1955), 575; "History of Land Drainage Activities of the Soil Conservation Service," unpublished manuscript from the files of Douglas Helms, 1.

4. Schoenfeld, 36.

5. Samuel P. Shaw and C. Gordon Fredine, "Wetlands of the United States: Their Extent and Their Value to Waterfowl and Other Wildlife," circular 39 (Washington, D.C.: U.S. Department of the Interior, Office of River Basin Studies, Fish and Wildlife Service, 1956), 26.

6. U.S. Department of Agriculture, Agricultural Stabilization and Conservation Service, "Agricultural Conservation Program: 45-Year Statistical Summary, 1936 through 1980" (Washington, D.C., 1981), 172. The Agricultural Conservation Program was an entity within the PMA. Nationwide ACP assistance funded drainage on 24,497,956 acres between 1944 and 1950.

7. Schoenfeld, 152.

8. Matthew C. Perry, "The Paxtuxent Team," in *Flyways: Pioneering Waterfowl Management in North America,* ed. A. S. Hawkins, R. C. Hanson, H. K. Nelson, H. M. Reeves (Washington, D.C.: U.S. Department of the Interior, Fish and Wildlife Service, 1984), 169; Laurence Jahn and Cyril Kabat, "Origin and Role," in Hawkins et al., *Flyways,* 383; James Trefethen, *An American Crusade for Wildlife* (New York: Winchester, and Boone and Crockett Club, 1975), 242–43; Lonnie L. Williamson, "Evolution of a Landmark Law," in *Restoring*

America's Wildlife, 1937–1987: The First Fifty Years of the Federal Aid in Restoration (Pittman–Robertson) Act, ed. Harmon Kallman (Washington, U.S. Fish and Wildlife Service, 1987), 13.

9. Clay Schoenfeld, "Welcome Back Potholes," in Hawkins et al., *Flyways,* Grady Mann, "Prairie Marshes Will Not Die," in Hawkins et al., *Flywa,* 412–13.

10. Raymond A. Haik, "Law of the Marsh," *Naturalist,* April, 1962, 31.

11. Russ Dushinske, "Drainage vs. Ducks," *North Dakota Outdoors,* Apr. 1953, 16–17.

12. U.S. Department of the Interior, Fish and Wildlife Service, Bureau of Sport Fisheries and Wildlife, *Waterfowl Production Habitat Losses Related to Agricultural Drainage, North Dakota, South Dakota, and Minnesota, 1954–58* (Washington, D.C., 1961), 16–17.

13. Augustadt, 574; John G. Sutton, "Drainage Operations of the Soil Conservation Service," unpublished paper prepared for the American Society of Agricultural Engineers Annual Meeting, National Agricultural Library, Philadelphia, Pennsylvania, 25 June 1947, 14.

14. Dushinske, 16.

15. Paul L. Errington, *Of Marshes and Men* (New York: Macmillan, 1957), 120; U.S. Department of the Interior, *Waterfowl Production Habitat Losses,* 7, 8, 25.

16. Dushinske, 17.

17. "Report of the Chief of Soil Conservation Service," in *Annual Reports of the Department of Agriculture* (Washington, D.C.: U.S. Department of Agriculture, 1939–1950), passim.

18. "Report of the Chief of Soil Conservation Service," (1949), 63–65.

19. Keith Beauchamp, "A History of Drainage and Drainage Methods," in *Farm Drainage in the United States: History, Status, and Prospects,* ed. George Pavelis, Miscellaneous Publication, no. 1455 (Washington, D.C.: U.S. Department of Agriculture, Economic Research Service, 1987), 27.

20. Robert W. Harrison, *Alluvial Empire: Drainage in the Lower Mississippi Valley* (Little Rock, Ark.: Pioneer Press, in cooperation with the U.S. Department of Agriculture, Economic Research Service, 1961), 290–91; U.S. Department of the Interior, Fish and Wildlife Service, *The Atchafalaya: America's Greatest River Swamp, a Proposal to Establish the Atchafalaya Fish, Wildlife, and Multi-Use Area* (Washington, D.C., Oct. 1978), 11.

21. Douglas Helms, "Small Watersheds and the USDA: Legacy of the Flood Control Act of 1936," in *The Flood Control Challenge: Past, Present, and Future,* proceedings of a national symposium (New Orleans, 26 Sept. 1986), ed. Howard Rosen and Martin Reuss (Chicago: Public Works Historical Society, 1988), 67; Beauchamp, 18; Harrison, *Alluvial Empire,* 284–85; William H. Doucette, Jr., and Joseph A. Phillips, *Drainage in North Carolina's Coastal Zone,* Center for Rural Resource Development (Raleigh, N.C.: Carolina State University, 1978), 4.

22. Shaw and Fredine, 29.

Harmon and Chester A. McConnell, "The Politics of Wetland Conser-
on: A Wildlife View," *Journal of Soil and Water Conservation*, Mar.-Apr.
83, 94; Shaw and Fredine, 29.

Hugh H. Wooten and Lewis A. Jones, "The History of Our Drainage Enterprises," in *Yearbook of Agriculture, 1955* (Washington, D.C.: U.S. Department
of Agriculture, 1955), 479–80; John Madson, "New Budget: Old Threat,"
News from Nilo, newsletter of the conservation department of Winchester-
Western Division, published by Olin Corp., no. 129 (Spring 1974), 1.

25. Wetlands Classification Committee, "Classification of Wetlands of the United
States," Special Scientific Report, no. 20 (Washington, D.C.: U.S. Department
of the Interior, Fish and Wildlife Service, 1953), cited in David Moss, "Historic Changes in Terminology for Wetlands," *Coastal Zone Management Journal*
8, no. 3 (1980): 220.

26. Shaw and Fredine, 9.

27. Shaw and Fredine, 3, 14, 26.

28. R. W. Burwell and L. G. Sugden, "Potholes: Going, Going . . . ," in *Waterfowl
Tomorrow,* ed. Joseph P. Linduska (Washington, D.C.: U.S. Department of the
Interior, Fish and Wildlife Service, 1964), 37; U.S. Fish and Wildlife Service
and North Dakota State University Extension Service, *The Wetland Easement,*
brochure (U.S. Fish and Wildlife Service and North Dakota State University
Extension Service, n.d.).

29. D. A. Williams (administrator, SCS) and P. M. Koger (administrator, ACPS),
Memorandum to SCS State Conservationists, "Guidelines for Applying Policies in Drainage and Biology in the Pothole Section of Minnesota, North
Dakota and South Dakota" (21 Feb. 1957), reprinted in U.S. Department of
the Interior, *Waterfowl Production Habitat Losses,* appendix 17–23.

30. U.S. Department of Agriculture, Economic Research Service, *History of Agricultural Price-Support and Adjustment Program, 1933–1984,* Agricultural Information Bulletin, no. 485 (Washington, D.C,: Dec. 1984), 23.

31. U.S. Department of the Interior, *Waterfowl Production Habitat Losses,* 18,
20–22; Burwell and Sugden, 373; Haik, 32.

32. Errington, viii.

33. U.S. Department of the Interior, *Waterfowl Production Habitat Losses,* 32, 35.

34. Burwell and Sugden, 378; "History of Land Drainage Activities of the Soil
Conservation Service," 3.

35. Shaw and Fredine, 29.

36. Perry, 354; Michael Bean, *The Evolution of National Wildlife Law* (New York:
Praeger, 1983), 216.

37. Shaw and Fredine, 9; U.S. Department of the Interior, *The Impact of Federal
Programs on Wetlands,* A Report to Congress, vol. 2 (Washington, D.C., 1994),
92.

38. "10 Amazing Years: 1947–1957," *U.S. News and World Report,* 27 Dec. 1957,
42–53.

39. Will Johns, *Estuaries—America's Most Vulnerable Frontiers,* pamphlet, rev. ed.
(Washington, D.C.: National Wildlife Federation, 1969), 6; Allan T.

Studholme and Thomas Sterling, "Dredges and Ditches," in Linduska, *Waterfowl Tomorrow*, 359–68; individual state documents of the Fish and Wildlife Service, Office of River Basin Studies, Wetlands Inventory for NY, RI, MA, NJ, DE, MD.

40. "Need Land? Then Take a Look at Marshland," *House and Home*, 1 Apr. 1958, 146–52.

41. Shaw and Fredine, 9.

42. Rezneat M. Darnell, *Impacts of Construction Activities in Wetlands in the United States* (Corvallis, Ore.: Environmental Protection Agency, 1976), xxv–xxvi.

43. Shaw and Fredine, 8; Franklin C. Daiber, *Conservation of Tidal Marshes* (New York: Van Nostrand Reinhold, 1986), 95–101.

44. Rachel Carson, *Silent Spring* (Boston: Houghton Mifflin, 1962; reprint, Fawcett Crest, n.d.), 134–37; Trefethen, 270–72; Gordon Harrison, *Mosquitoes, Malaria, and Man: A History of the Hostilities Since 1800* (New York: E.P. Dutton, 1978), 219.

45. Raymond Arsenault, "The End of the Long Hot Summer: The Air Conditioner and Southern Culture," *Journal of Southern History* 50, no. 4 (Nov. 1984): 610–12, 618.

46. Arsenault, 619–62.

47. Joseph V. Siry, *Marshes of the Ocean Shore: Development of an Ecological Ethic* (College Station: Texas A&M University Press, 1984), 161; John Teal and Mildred Teal, *Life and Death of the Salt Marsh*, (New York: Ballantine, 1969) 225; Tim Palmer, *Lifelines: The Case for River Conservation* (Washington, D.C.: Island Press, 1994), 70–97.

48. "10 Amazing Years," 42.

49. W. H. Conner, *Public Administration of Louisiana's Coastal Wetlands: 1820 to 1976* (Baton Rouge: Louisiana State University Center for Wetland Resources, 1977), 6; William Faulkner Rushton, "Can the Cajuns Survive?" *Environmental Action*, Jan. 1979, 20.

50. Shaw and Fredine, 9; John Naar and Alex J. Naar, *This Land Is Your Land: A Guide to North America's Endangered Ecosystems* (New York: Harper Perennial, 1993), 4; Rushton, 19.

51. "10 Amazing Years," 50.

52. Kenneth T. Jackson, *Crabgrass Frontier: The Suburbanization of the United States* (New York: Oxford University Press, 1985), 248–50.

53. Siry, 161; U.S. Department of the Interior, *The Impact of Federal Programs*, vol. 2, 89.

54. Trefethen 256–58; Peter Matthiessen, *Wildlife in America*, rev. ed. (New York: Viking, 1987), 227. A limited number of refuges had been opened to oil exploration before McKay's tenure.

55. John Kenneth Galbraith, *The Affluent Society* (Boston: Houghton Mifflin, 1958), 251–53.

56. Moss, 220. While Moss identifies the "Classification of Wetlands of the United States" (1953) as the first formal use of the word, it appeared earlier, in 1951, with the Minnesota Wetlands Program.

Ralph W. Tiner, Jr., *Wetlands of the U.S.: Current Status and Recent Trends* (Washington, D.C.: U.S. Department of the Interior, Fish and Wildlife Service, 1984), 31.

Chapter 11

1. Cam Cavenaugh, *Saving the Great Swamp: The People, the Power Brokers, and an Urban Wilderness* (Frenchtown, N.J.: Columbia Publishing Co., Inc., 1978), 157–58.
2. Olga Owen Huckins to Rachel Carson, Jan. 1958, in Paul Brooks, *The House of Life: Rachel Carson at Work* (Boston: Houghton Mifflin, 1972), 231–33; Rachel Carson, *Silent Spring* (Boston: Houghton Mifflin, 1962; reprint Fawcett Crest, ix). Huckins also sent this letter to the *Boston Herald.*
3. Quoted in Brooks, 233.
4. Joseph V. Siry, *Marshes of the Ocean Shore: Development of an Ecological Ethic* (College Station: Texas A&M Press, 1984), 166; Julie Appleby, "How Bay Was Saved by 3 'Too Naive' to Lose," *Sunday Review,* 24 Jan. 1988, reprint.
5. Quoted in "Saving the Bay," *California Monthly,* Apr. 1986, reprint.
6. Appleby, reprint.
7. Samuel P. Hays, *Beauty, Health and Permanence: Environmental Politics in the United States, 1955–1985* (Cambridge, England: Cambridge University Press, 1987), 169.
8. Quoted in Sylvia McLaughlin, "Looking Ahead to the Next 35 Years," *Watershed,* Summer 1996, 2.
9. Joseph E. Bodovitz, "The Shrinking of San Francisco Bay and How It Was Stopped," *California WaterfrontAge* 1, no. 4 (Fall 1985): 21–27.
10. Ralph W. Tiner, Jr., *Wetlands of the United States: Current Status and Recent Trends* (Washington, D.C.: U.S. Fish and Wildlife Service, 1984), 36. Louisiana leads the nation with coastal wetland losses, but most are not categorized as "human-induced." Rather, they result from the changed hydrologic regime of the Mississippi River coupled with sea level rise. Of course, the change in the Mississippi is entirely caused by the "human-induced" levee system that girdles it. This issue will be covered separately in chapter 17.
11. Louis Darling, "The Death of a Marsh: The Story of Sherwood Island Marsh and Its Political Consequences," in *Connecticut's Coastal Marshes: A Vanishing Resource,* Connecticut Arboretum Bulletin, no. 12 (New London: Connecticut College, Feb. 1961), 21–27.
12. Frank B. Golley, *A History of the Ecosystem Concept in Ecology: More Than the Sum of the Parts* (New Haven: Yale University Press, 1993), 62–69, 106.
13. Eugene Odum, interview by author, 20 Dec. 1993, telephone.
14. Alice Chalmers, interview by author, 13 Dec. 1993, Sapelo Island, Georgia.
15. Eugene Odum, "The Role of Tidal Marshes in Estuarine Production," reprint from the *Proceedings of the MAR Conference,* sponsored by IUCN, ICBP, and IWRB, Les Saintes-Maries-de-la-Mer, 12–16 Nov. 1962, 71–72; William E. Odum and Stephen S. Skjei, "The Issue of Wetlands Preservation and Management: A Second View," *Coastal Zone Management Journal* 1, no. 2 (Winter

1974): 153. Odum and Skjei have criticized popular writers for using the ten-ton/acre/year figure to represent the productivity of all North American marshes. The figure is valid only for gulf and south Atlantic marshes with large tidal amplitude—like those in Georgia. A more typical marsh would produce a still impressive five to six tons, though some produce upwards of fifteen tons. For historical purposes, it is most significant that the ten-ton figure became widely quoted and used as evidence to support wetland conservation.

16. Alice Chalmers, interview by author, 13 Dec. 1993, Sapelo Island, Georgia; Tiner, 19.

17. James Gosselink, Eugene Odum, and R. M. Pope, *The Value of the Tidal Marsh* (Baton Rouge: Louisiana State University Center for Wetland Resources, 1973;) Joel B. Hagen, *An Untangled Bank: The Origins of Ecosystem Ecology* (New Brunswick, N.J.: Rutgers University Press, 1992), 126.

18. James E. Kundell and S. Wesley Woolf, *Georgia's Wetlands: Trends and Policy Options* (Athens: Carl Vinson Institute of Government, University of Georgia, 1986), 14–16.

19. K. D. Woodburn, "Biological Survey of North Lake Worth (Palm Beach Co.) with Special Reference to Bulkhead Lines," *Florida State Board of Conservation Bulletin*, no. 61–11 (Sept. 1961): 1–15; C. R. Mock, "Natural and Altered Estuarine Habitats of Penaeid Shrimp," in *Proceedings of Gulf and Caribbean Fisheries Institute* 19 (1967): 86–97, cited in Odum and Skjei, 156–57.

20. Congress, Senate, 90th Cong., 2d sess., *Estuarine Areas*, Senate Report 1419 (17 July 1968), cited in Siry, 170.

21. Ross L. Leffler, from address given at the National Fisheries Institute Convention, Chicago (30 Apr. 1957), reprinted in *Connecticut's Coastal Marshes: A Vanishing Resource*, 36.

22. J. L. McHugh, "Management of Estuarine Fisheries," in *A Symposium on Estuarine Fisheries*, American Fisheries Society Special Publication, no. 3 (1966): 133–54; R. E. Turner, "Louisiana's Coastal Fisheries and Changing Environmental Conditions," in *Proceedings of the Third Coastal Marsh and Estuary Management Symposium*, ed. J. W. Day, Jr.; D. D. Culley, Jr.; R. E. Turner; and A. J. Mumphrey (6–7 Mar. 1978, Louisiana State University, Baton Rouge), 363–70, in Tiner, 13.

23. Quoted in Will Johns, *Estuaries—America's Most Vulnerable Frontiers*, pamphlet, rev. ed. (National Wildlife Federation, 1969), 11–12.

24. Charles H. W. Foster et al., "Coastal Wetlands Protection Program in Massachusetts," in *Eco-solutions: A Handbook for the Environmental Crisis*, ed. Barbara Woods (Cambridge, Mass.: Schenkman Publishing, 1972), 157–61, 167; "The Massachusetts Wetlands Protection Program," in *Environmental Planning: Law of Land and Resources*, ed. Arnold W. Reitze, Jr. (Washington, D.C.: North America International, 1974), 260–66.

25. William A. Niering, *The Life of the Marsh: The North America Wetlands* (New York: McGraw-Hill, 1966; reprint, 1969); John Teal and Mildred Teal, *Life and Death of the Salt Marsh* (Boston: Little, Brown, 1969); Ron Powers, "The Medium Is the Message," *Audubon*, Sept.–Oct. 1994, 79.

). Eugene Odum, interview by author, 20 Dec. 1993; Eugene Odum, personal correspondence, 31 May 1996; Kundell and Woolf, 35, 85; Gregory W. Blount, "From Marshes to Mountains: Wetlands Come Under State Regulation," *Mercer Law Review* 41 (Spring 1990): 869.

27. R. R. Grant and R. Patrick, "Tinicum Marsh As a Water Purifier," in *Two Studies of Tinicum Marsh* (Washington, D.C.: Conservation Foundation, 1970), 105–23, in Gosselink, Odum, and Pope, 10.

28. *John Heinz National Wildlife Refuge at Tinicum,* pamphlet (Washington, D.C.: U.S. Department of the Interior, Fish and Wildlife Service, 1992); Tom Walker, assistant refuge manager, personal correspondence, 27 June 1996.

29. Environmental Protection Agency, *The Hackensack River and Its Meadowlands: A Water Quality Success Story* (Washington, D.C., 1978), 4, cited in Rowan Baker and Richard Roos-Collins, *Successes in River Management* (San Francisco: Friends of the River Foundation, 1983), 3.

30. Baker and Roos-Collins, 2–7; Hackensack Meadows Development Corporation, Lyndhurst, New Jersey, "Background/History of the 'District,'" information sheet, 1991; Virginia S. Albrecht, "Special Area Management Planning in the Hackensack Meadowlands," *National Wetlands Newsletter,* Mar.–Apr. 1989, 5.

31. J. Claiborne Jones and M. P. Lynch, "Local Environmental Management— Can It Work? A Case Study of the Virginia Wetlands Act," *Coastal Zone Management Journal* 4 (1978): 127–28; William N. Hedeman, Jr., "The Maryland Wetlands: A Study in Corruption and the Law," in Reitze, 275–82; Siry, 174.

32. Noel Grove, *Preserving Eden: The Nature Conservancy* (New York: Harry N. Abrams, 1992); Cavenaugh, 23–48, 157–70; Carl Cahill, "The Great Dismal Swamp Plan," *American Forests* 80, no. 12 (Dec. 1974): 19; Federal Aviation Administration, *FAA Statistical Handbook* (Washington, D.C., 1967, 1969, 1972).

33. Nelson Manfred Blake, *Land into Water—Water into Land: A History of Water Management in Florida* (Tallahassee: University Presses of Florida, 1980), 218.

34. Quoted in Blake, 219.

35. Quoted in Frank Graham, *The Audubon Ark: A History of the National Audubon Society* (New York: Alfred A. Knopf, 1990), 236.

36. Quoted in Blake, 219.

37. Quoted in Blake, 220.

38. Blake, 216–22; Steve Yates, "Marjory Stoneman Douglas and the Glades Crusade," *Audubon,* Mar. 1983, 121.

39. Elliott McCleary, "Will 10,000,000 People Ruin All This?" *National Wildlife,* June–July 1971, reprinted in *Florida's Disney World: Promises and Problems,* ed. Leonard E. Zehnder (Tallahassee: Peninsula Publishing, 1975), 198–203; William E. Potter, *Engineer Memoirs: Major General William E. Potter,* interview by Martin Reuss, Feb. 1980 (Washington, D.C.: U.S. Army Corps of Engineers, 1983), 190–98.

40. Arthur L. Putnam, *Summary of Hydrologic Conditions and Effects of Walt Disne_ World Development in the Reedy Creek Improvement District, 1966–73*, report no. 79 (Tallahassee: Florida Department of Natural Resources, 1975), 1–9. Putnam attributes 75 percent of the aquifer decline to increased water use and 25 percent to drought. The Corps of Engineers' Four River Basins flood-control project also interfered with aquifer recharge. The figure refers to potentiometric aquifer surface decline.

41. Blake, 238–41.

42. Tiner, 23.

43. Jon A. Kusler, "Regulating Sensitive Lands: An Overview of Programs," in *Land Use Issues of the 1980s*, ed. James H. Carr and Edward E. Duensing (New Brunswick, N.J.: Rutgers University Center for Urban Policy Research, 1983), 129.

44. Thomas R. Dunlap, *DDT: Scientists, Citizens, and Public Policy* (Princeton, N.J.: Princeton University Press, 1981), 143–46.

45. Robert Gottlieb, *Forcing the Spring: The Transformation of the Modern Environmental Movement* (Washington D.C.: Island Press, 1993), 135–38.

46. Thomas E. Dahl and Craig E. Johnson, *Status and Trends of Wetlands in the Conterminous United States, Mid-1970s to Mid-1980s* (Washington, D.C.: U.S. Department of the Interior, Fish and Wildlife Service, 1991), 8.

Chapter 12

1. Gilbert F. White, *Water Resources People and Issues: Interview with Gilbert F. White,* interview by Martin Reuss, 25 June 1985, Boulder, CO (Washington, D.C.: U.S. Army Corps of Engineers, 1993), 63.

2. Quoted in Paul Brooks, *The Pursuit of Wilderness* (Boston: Houghton Mifflin, 1971), 82, quoted in Tim Palmer, *Endangered Rivers and the Conservation Movement* (Berkeley: University of California Press, 1986), 89.

3. Quoted in Palmer, 89.

4. A. Starker Leopold and Justin W. Leonard, "Alaska Dam Would Be Resources Disaster," *Audubon*, May–June 1966, 177.

5. Clare Conley, "Rampart Dam and the Perpetual Engineers," *Field and Stream*, June 1966, 34–36.

6. Palmer, 88–90; Stephen H. Spurr, "Rampart Dam: A Costly Gamble," *Audubon*, May–June 1966, 173–75, 179; Leopold and Leonard, 177–78; "The Rampart Project," *Natural History*, Jan. 1966, 12; Martin Reuss, personal correspondence, 10 June 1996.

7. Sam Mase, "In Wake of Cuban Ban—Millions Invested in New Plants and Plantings for Sugar in the Everglades Area," *Tampa Tribune*, 20 Mar. 1961; Sam Mase, "Price of Mucklands Soaring—Glades Land Boom Develops in Wake of Sugar Industries," *Tampa Tribune*, 22 Mar. 1961; George H. Salley, *A Report on the Florida Sugar Industry* (n.p., n.d.); *Florida's Sugar Industry* (Clewiston: Florida Sugar Cane League, 1979).

U.S. Department of the Interior, *The Impact of Federal Programs on Wetlands,* A Report to Congress, vol. 2 (Washington, D.C., 1994), 127.

9. Nelson Manfred Blake, *Land into Water—Water into Land: A History of Water Management in Florida* (Tallahassee: University Presses of Florida, 1980), 187.

10. Joan Browder, "Don't Pull the Plug on the Everglades," *American Forests,* Sept. 1967, 14; Peter Farb, "Disaster Threatens the Everglades," *Audubon,* Sept.–Oct. 1965, 308.

11. Blake, 187.

12. Blake, 188–89.

13. Blake, 190–93.

14. Blake, 187–94.

15. Blake, 260–61.

16. Quoted in Arthur Marshall, et al., *The Kissimmee-Okeechobee Basin: A Report to the Cabinet of Florida* (Miami, 12 Dec. 1972), 12, quoted in Blake, 261.

17. Blake, 262–64.

18. Blake, 264–65.

19. Blake, 268; William R. Barada, "Restoring the Kissimmee River May Be Florida's Environmental Armageddon," *ENFO* (Florida Conservation Foundation newsletter) (1977), 8.

20. Martin Reuss, "Engineers, Science, and the Public Interest: Water Resources Planning in the Atchafalaya Basin," *Journal of Policy History* 3, no. 3 (1991): 284–87.

21. Omer Lonnie Roberts, Jr., "Cypress Land and Floodway: Environmental Change and the Development of Land Utilization in the Atchafalaya Basin, Louisiana" (Ph.D. diss., University of Tennessee, 1974), 81–83.

22. "A Louisiana Swamp Story," *National Wetlands Newsletter,* Jan.–Feb. 1980, 12–13; Sam Iker, "Look What We've Done to Our Wetlands," *National Wildlife,* June–July 1992, 44.

23. Martin Reuss, "Along the Atchafalaya: The Challenge of a Vital Resource," *Environment* 30, no. 4 (May 1988): 6–11, 36–44; Oliver A. Houck, "The Atchafalaya," *National Wetlands Newletter,* Mar.–Apr. 1985, 11–13.

24. Reuss, "Engineers, Science," 288.

25. Reuss, "Engineers, Science," 298–299.

26. Reuss, "Engineers, Science," 300–301.

27. Rowan Baker and Richard Roos-Collins, *Successes in River Management* (San Francisco: Friends of the River Foundation, 1983), 14–15; U.S. Army Corps of Engineers, New England Division (Waltham, Mass.), "Natural Valley Storage: A Partnership with Nature," *Public Information Fact Sheet* (Spring 1976), 2–3.

28. U.S. Army Corps of Engineers, *Charles River, Massachusetts* (Jan. 1976), H-17, cited in Baker and Roos-Collins, 11.

29. U.S. Army Corps of Engineers, New England Division (Waltham, Mass.), "Natural Valley Storage: A Partnership with Nature," *Public Information Fact Sheet* (Spring 1977), 1.

30. U.S. Army Corps of Engineers, New England Division (Waltham, Mass.),

"Natural Valley Storage: A Partnership with Nature," *Public Information Fact Sheet* (Spring 1976, Spring 1977, Spring 1978); Baker and Roos-Collins, 14–16; Rita Barron, "Protecting the Charles River Corridor," *National Wetlands Newsletter,* May–June 1989, 8–9; Martin Reuss, personal correspondence, 10 June 1996.

31. John Madson, "A Plague on Your Rivers," *Audubon,* Sept. 1972, 41.

32. Quoted in "Spare That Stream," *Newsweek,* 3 Apr. 1972, 87.

33. Peter Harnik, "Channelization: Streamlining Our Nation's Rivers," *Environmental Action,* 4 Mar. 1972, 3–6.

34. "Stream Channelization: Conflict between Ditchers, Conservationists," *Science* 176 (1972): 892. It's probably no coincidence that Georgia, Louisiana, Mississippi, and North Carolina, with more than fourteen hundred miles of approved projects awaiting action, all had senior congressmen and senators seated on agricultural appropriations committees.

35. Kenneth E. Grant, "Re: Background Statements on Key Issues," advisory memorandum, ADM-2, 7 Apr. 1972, from the files of Douglas Helms, Natural Resources Conservation Service, Washington D.C.

36. Tom Herman, "Waterway Wrangle: Federal Soil Service Stirs Ecologists' Ire by Altering Streams," *Wall Street Journal,* 19 July 1971, 1; Ben Blackburn, "Where Conservation Is a Bad Word," *Field and Stream* (Dec. 1969), 14, 58.

37. Jeff Nesmith, "Ecologist Puts Alcovy Swamp's Worth at $7 Million Annually," *Atlanta Constitution,* 11 June 1970, 6-a; "Alcovy Swamp Report," *Atlanta Constitution,* 14 June 1970, 18-a; Ralph W. Tiner, Jr., *Wetlands of the United States: Current Status and Recent Trends* (Washington, D.C.: U.S. Fish and Wildlife Service, 1984), 14, 19.

38. Bob Hurt, "Alcovy River Project Blasted by Private Report," *Atlanta Constitution,* 25 May 1970, 3-a.

39. *Central Atlantic Environment News* 1, no. 7 (30 July 1971): 6.

40. Denton L. Watson, "Reuss Raps Swamp Project," *Washington Sunday Star,* 13 June 1971.

41. Kenneth E. Grant, "Re: Congressman Reuss Asks for Moratorium on Appropriations for Stream Channelization," advisory memorandum, INF-48, 19 May 1971, from the files of Douglas Helms.

42. Harnik, 4; Herman, 1.

43. George R. Bagley, "Statement to the Conservation and Natural Resources Sub-Committee, House Committee on Government Operations," 10 June 1971, 5, reprinted in Hubert W. Kelley, "Re: June 9, 10, and 14 Hearings on Channelization," advisory memorandum, INF-59, 17 June 1971, from the files of Douglas Helms.

44. "Stream Channelization: Conflict between Ditchers, Conservationists," 890.

45. Kenneth E. Grant, "Re: WS-PL-566 Channel Improvement," advisory memorandum, WS-12, 1 May 1970, from the files of Douglas Helms.

46. "Stream Channelization: Conflict between Ditchers, Conservationists," 890.

47. "Stream Destruction by Channelization," *Sport Fishing Institute Bulletin,* July 1971, 1.

8. Kenneth E. Grant, Watersheds Memorandum 108, Feb. 1971, cited in Harnik, 5.

49. Don Kendall, "Fight Continues on Channelization," *Atlanta Constitution,* 25 June 1972; Kenneth E. Grant, "Re: Background Statements on Key Issues," advisory memorandum, ADM-2, 7 Apr. 1972, from the files of Douglas Helms; Madson, 38.

50. Harnik, 6.

51. Albert Coffey, "Stream Improvement: The Chicod Creek Episode," *Journal of Soil and Water Conservation,* Mar.–Apr. 1982, 80–82; Robert R. Mason, Jr., Clyde E. Simmons, and Sharon A. Watkins, "Effects of Channel Modifications on the Hydrology of the Chicod Creek Basin, North Carolina, 1975–1987," USGS Water Resources Investigator, Report 90–4031 (Raleigh, N.C.: U.S. Geological Survey, 1990), 10; "Stream Channelization: A Problem in Land Abuse," in Reitze, 3–5.

52. Ronald E. Erickson, Raymond L. Linder, and Keith W. Harmon, "Stream Channelization (P.L. 83–566) Increased Wetland Losses in the Dakotas," *Wildlife Society Bulletin* 7, no. 2 (1979): 71–78.

53. Keith W. Harmon and Chester A. McConnell, "The Politics of Wetland Conservation: A Wildlife View," *Journal of Soil and Water Conservation,* Mar.–Apr. 1983, 92.

54. Oliver A. Houck, "Uncle Sam: Split Personality," *National Wildlife,* Feb.–Mar. 1973, reprinted in *Congressional Record,* 1 Feb. 1973, E570–71.

55. Quoted in Houck, E570.

56. Gary L. Pearson, "Draining the Great Marsh," *USA Today,* Nov. 1985, 83–89, reprint.

57. Elinor Lander Horwitz, *Our Nation's Wetlands: An Interagency Task Force Report* (Washington, D.C.: Council on Environmental Quality, 1978), 67–69.

58. *Impact of Federal Programs on Wetlands,* vol. 2, 29, 83, 270–272; Harmon and McConnell, 94.

Chapter 13

1. *New York Times,* 1 Feb. 1970, sec. 10, 1, quoted in Nelson Manfred Blake, *Land into Water—Water into Land* (Tallahassee: University Presses of Florida, 1980), 221.

2. 33 C. F. R. §209.120(d) (1968), in Michael C. Blumm and D. Bernard Zahela, "Federal Wetlands Protection under the Clean Water Act: Regulatory Ambivalence, Intergovernmental Tension, and a Call for Reform," *University of Colorado Law Review* 60 (1989): 695, 701–2; Lance D. Wood and John R. Hill, Jr., "Wetlands Protection: The Regulatory Role of the U.S. Army Corps of Engineers," *Coastal Zone Management Journal* 4, no. 4 (1978): 378.

3. Wood and Hill, 379.

4. Christopher B. Myhrum, "Federal Protection of Wetlands through Legal Process," *Boston College Environmental Affairs Law Review* 7 (1979): 577; Harold Semling, "Nixon Likely to Veto Water Pollution Control, but Congress

Will Override," *American City,* Nov. 1972, 14; Edmund Muskie, *Journ.* (Garden City, N.Y.: Doubleday, 1972), 79–83, 95.

5. Charles D. Ablard and Brian Boru O'Neill, "Wetlands Protection and Section 404 of the Federal Water Pollution Control Act Amendments of 1972: A Corps of Engineers Renaissance," *Vermont Law Review* 1 (1976): 67–74.

6. Quoted in J. Dicken Kirschten, "Corps' Wetlands Control Survives Trip through Legislative Swamp," *National Journal,* 23 Oct. 1976, 1507.

7. Quoted in Kirschten, 1507.

8. Blumm and Zahela, 704–5; Thomas Addison and Timothy Burns, "The Army Corps and Nationwide Permit 26: Wetlands Protection or Swamp Reclamation?" *Ecology Law Quarterly* 18 (1991): 627; Lee Evan Caplin, "Is Congress Protecting Our Water? The Controversy Over Section 404, Federal Water Pollution Control Act Amendments of 1972," *University of Miami Law Review* 31, no. 3 (Spring 1977): 448.

9. Caplin, 449.

10. *Congressional Record,* vol. 118, daily ed., 4 Oct. 1972, 9124–25, quoted in "Comprehensive Wetlands Protection: One Step Closer to Full Implementation of §404 of the FWPCA," *Environmental Law Reporter* 5 (July 1975): 10100.

11. Jeffrey K. Stine, "Regulating Wetlands in the 1970s: U.S. Army Corps of Engineers and the Environmental Organizations," *Journal of Forest History* 27 (Apr. 1983): 64; Garrett Power, "The Fox in the Chicken Coop: The Regulatory Program of the U.S. Corps of Engineers," *Virginia Law Review* 63 (1977): 503, 559.

12. "A Constituency of the Corps," *Audubon,* Sept. 1973, 144.

13. "Comprehensive Wetlands Protection," 10103.

14. *Natural Resources Defense Council v. Callaway,* 392 F. Supp. 685 (D.D.C. 1975); Stine, 66.

15. Stine, 66–67.

16. U.S. Army Corps of Engineers, "Federal Control of Dredge and Fill Operations Expands," news release, 6 May 1975, quoted in Stine, 67.

17. Quoted in Kirschten, 1508; Stine, 68.

18. U.S. Department of Agriculture, news release, 18 Aug. 1975, quoted in Caplin, 454.

19. "Wetlands and the Corps of Engineers," *Washington Post,* 3 June 1975, quoted in Stine, 68.

20. Stine, 68.

21. Quoted in Stine, 68.

22. Lt. Gen. William C. Gribble, Jr., "Memorandum for All Division Engineers," 25 Nov. 1975, Civil Works Environment File, Historical Division, Office of the Chief of Engineers, quoted in Stine, 70.

23. Stine, 75.

24. Ralph W. Tiner, Jr., *Wetlands of the United States: Current Status and Recent Trends* (Washington, D.C.: U.S. Department of the Interior, Fish and Wildlife Service, 1984), 32.

25. Stine, 71; William E. Odum, "Pathways of Energy Flow in a South Florida

Estuary" (Ph.D. diss., University of Miami, 1970), in William A. Niering, "Human Impacts on the South Florida Wetlands: The Everglades and Big Cypress Swamp," in *The Earth in Transition—Patterns and Processes of Biotic Impoverishment*, ed. George M. Woodwell (Cambridge, England: Cambridge University Press, 1990), 468.

26. Stine, 71–73.
27. Stine, 73.
28. Russell Peterson to Martin Hoffman, 30 Apr. 1976, Marco Island Permit Folder, Council on Environmental Quality office files, quoted in Stine, 74.
29. Don Moser, "Mangrove Island Is Reprieved by Army Engineers," *Smithsonian*, Jan. 1977, 75; Stine, 74.
30. Stine, 75.
31. Wood and Hill, 401; Moser, 69.
32. Caplin, 455–57.
33. 33 C.F. R. § 323.2 (a)(5) quoted in Myhrum, 609–10.
34. Wood and Hill, 374; Keith W. Harmon and Chester A. McConnell, "The Politics of Wetland Conservation: A Wildlife View," *Journal of Soil and Water Conservation*, Mar.–Apr. 1983, 93.
35. Michael C. Blumm, "The Clean Water Act's Section 404 Permit Program Enters Its Adolescence: An Institutional and Programmatic Perspective," *Ecology Law Quarterly* 8 (1980): 420.
36. Blumm and Zahela, 707–8.
37. Blumm, 424.
38. Brock Evans, "Call Them 'Water Meadows,'" *Audubon*, Nov. 1983, 32.
39. Suzanne Schwartz, Environmental Protection Agency, interview by author, 13 Nov. 1993, Washington D.C.; Blumm, 709–10.
40. Jamie W. Moore and Dorothy P. Moore, *The Army Corps of Engineers and the Evolution of Federal Flood Plain Management Policy*, Program on Environment and Behavior, special publication no. 20 (Boulder: University of Colorado, Institute of Behavioral Science, 1989), 104.
41. John E. Costa, "The Dilemma of Flood Control in the United States," *Environmental Management* 2 (July 1978): 313–22, cited in Moore and Moore, 104.
42. Moore and Moore, 74–75; Rutherford H. Platt, *Land Use and Society: Geography, Law and Public Policy* (Washington, D.C.: Island Press, 1996), 420–25. Congress created the federal flood insurance program with the National Flood Insurance Act of 1968. Provisions of the Flood Disaster Protection Act of 1973 strengthened the program.
43. Moore and Moore, 113–14.
44. Julie Durel Livudais, "Conflicting Interests in Southern Louisiana's Wetlands: Private Developers Versus Conservationists, and the State and Federal Regulatory Roles," *Tulane Law Review* 56 (1982): 1009.
45. Tim Palmer, *Lifelines: The Case for River Conservation* (Washington, D.C.: Island Press, 1994), 167–68.
46. *Floodplain Management in the United States: An Assessment Report*, prepared by

the National Hazards Research and Applications Information Center at the University of Colorado at Boulder, for the Federal Interagency Floodplain Management Task Force (Washington, D.C.: Federal Emergency Management Agency, 1992), 16.

47. U.S. Department of the Interior, *The Impact of Federal Programs on Wetlands,* A Report to Congress, vol. 2 (Washington, D.C.: 1994), 97; National Research Council, *Wetlands: Characteristics and Boundaries* (Washington, D.C.: National Academy Press, 1995), 152–55.

48. Sarah Chasis, "Problems and Prospects of Coastal Zone Management: An Environmental Viewpoint," *Coastal Zone Management Journal* 6, no. 4 (1979): 277; Tiner, *Status and Trends,* 33, 36.

49. Zigurds L. Zile, "A Legislative-Political History of the Coastal Zone Management Act of 1972," *Coastal Zone Management Journal* 1, no. 3 (Winter 1974): 238.

50. Timothy Beatly, David J. Brower, and Anna K. Schwab, *An Introduction to Coastal Zone Management* (Washington, D.C.: Island Press, 1994), 67–68; Zile, 255–59.

51. Zile, 254–55.

52. Zile, 235–74; Samuel P. Hays, *Beauty, Health and Permanence: Environmental Politics in the United States, 1955–1985* (Cambridge, England: Cambridge University Press, 1987), 52, 168–69; Platt, 412–13.

53. Robert W. Knecht, "Coastal Zone Management: The First Five Years and Beyond," *Coastal Zone Management Journal* 6, no. 4 (1979): 261.

54. Daniel R. Mandelker, *Environmental and Land Controls Legislation* (New York: Bobbs-Merrill, 1976), 223, 262; Chasis, 275; Beatly, Brower, and Schwab, 104–5, 127.

55. Grays Harbor Regional Planning Commission, "Grays Harbor Estuary Management Plan: Preliminary Draft," (1978), 46–48, cited in Blumm, 465.

56. Evans, 32–33.

57. Knecht, 265; Chasis, 273.

58. Steven Lewis Yaffee, *The Wisdom of the Spotted Owl: Policy Lessons for a New Century* (Washington, D.C.: Island Press, 1994), 12–13; Alston Chase, *In a Dark Wood: The Fight over Forests and the Rising Tyranny of Ecology* (Boston: Houghton Mifflin, 1995), 79–93.

59. T. H. Watkins, "What's Wrong with the Endangered Species Act?" *Audubon,* Jan.–Feb. 1996, 38.

60. David W. Lowe, John R. Matthews, and Charles J. Moseley, eds., *The Official World Wildlife Fund Guide to Endangered Species of North America,* vol. 2 (Washington, D.C.: Beacham Publishing, 1990), 728. The American alligator remains listed as threatened under a special classification because it so closely resembles the still endangered American crocodile. The alligator's threatened status gives the FWS authority to monitor hunting to ensure that no crocodiles are affected.

61. U.S. Department of the Interior, Fish and Wildlife Service, *Salt Marsh Harvest*

Mouse and California Clapper Rail Recovery Plan (Portland, Ore.: Fish and Wildlife Service, 1984), 45–100.

62. Nathaniel P. Reed and Dennis Drabelle, *The United States Fish and Wildlife Service* (Boulder: Westview Press, 1984), 98.

63. Reed and Drabelle, 94.

64. *Endangered Species Technical Bulletin* 3, no. 6 (June 1978): 11.

65. *WWF Guide to Endangered Species,* vol. 2, 653–55.

66. Watkins, 40.

67. *Life on the Edge: A Guide to California's Endangered Natural Resources: Wildlife* (Santa Cruz: Biosystems Books, 1994), 80–81; Peter Steinhart, *Tracks in the Sky: Wildlife and Wetlands of the Pacific Flyway* (San Francisco: Chronicle Books, National Audubon Society, 1987), 33–34.

68. *Endangered Species Technical Bulletin* 2, no. 1 (Dec. 1976–Jan. 1977): 7; Thomas B. Allen, *Guardian of the Wild: The Story of the National Wildlife Federation, 1936–1986* (Bloomington: Indiana University Press, 1987), 199.

69. J. Nelson, "Agriculture, Wetlands, and Endangered Species: The Food Security Act of 1985," *Endangered Species Technical Bulletin* 14 (1989): 1, 6–8, cited in Reed F. Noss and Allen Y. Cooperrider, *Saving Nature's Legacy: Protecting and Restoring Biodiversity* (Washington, D.C.: Island Press, 1994), 65.

70. Larry Anderson, "The Evolution of a Movement," *Sierra,* Sept.–Oct. 1987, 85–89; Hays, 7; Jon Kusler, interview by author, 4 Nov. 1993, Washington, D.C.; David G. Davis, "Wetlands Conservation Since 1970: One Observer's Reflections," *National Wetlands Newsletter,* Nov.–Dec. 1988, 2–3.

71. Lewis M. Cowardin, Virginia Carter, Frank Golet, and Edward T. LaRoe, *Classification of Wetlands and Deepwater Habitats of the United States* (Washington, D.C.: U.S. Department of the Interior, Fish and Wildlife Service, 1979).

72. Bill Wilen, personal correspondence, 28 June 1996.

73. Bill Wilen, interview by author, 12 Nov. 1993, Washington, D.C.; Bill O. Wilen and Ralph W. Tiner, Jr., "The National Wetlands Inventory: The First Ten Years," reprint, 1–12, in *Wetlands: Concerns and Successes,* American Resources Association, Sept. 1989, 1–12; *Overview of the National Wetlands Inventory,* pamphlet (Washington, D.C.: U.S. Fish and Wildlife Service, 1993).

74. John Montanari, interview by author, 20 Jan. 1994, St. Petersburg, Florida; Bill Wilen, interview by author, 12 Nov. 1993; Bill Wilen, personal correspondence, 18 June 1996.

75. Tiner, *Status and Trends,* 32; James Watt, interview by author, 23 Aug. 1996, telephone. Although generally considered an ardent opponent of conservation, James Watt was a strong supporter of the NWI. He believed that maps could eliminate confusion by letting landowners know ahead of time what lands were wetlands and thereby subject to regulation. In that way, Watt believed, sound business decisions could be made quickly and accurately.

76. Ralph Tiner, interview by author, 16 Dec. 1994, Newton Corner, Massachusetts.

77. John Montanari, interview by author, 20 Jan. 1994.

Chapter 14

1. Senator Edmund Muskie (1973), quoted in Norman J. Vig and Michael E. Kraft, eds. *Environmental Policy in the 1980s: Reagan's New Agenda* (Washington, D.C.: Congressional Quarterly Press, 1984), 54.

2. Keith Harmon and Chester McConnell, "The Politics of Wetland Conservation: A Wildlife View," *Journal of Soil and Water Conservation*, Mar.–Apr. 1983, 95.

3. Quoted in the *New York Times*, 29 Mar. 1981, 1, quoted in Robert V. Bartlett, "The Budgetary Process and Environmental Policy," in Vig and Kraft, 121–23.

4. Quoted in Hope Ryden, "Conflict and Compatibility: When Does Use Become Abuse?" *Wilderness*, Fall 1983, 26.

5. Quoted in Ryden, 27.

6. Ryden, 27.

7. Dennis Drabelle, "Going It Alone: An Inside Look at a Vulnerable System," *Wilderness*, Fall 1983, 23; "Environmental Organizations' Attack on Reagan Program Includes Wetland Policies," *National Wetlands Newsletter*, Mar.–Apr. 1982, 2–3.

8. James Watt, interview by author, 23 Aug. 1996, telephone; U.S. Department of the Interior, "A Year of Enrichment for *All* Americans" (Washington, D.C., 1983), 9.

9. Steve Huntley, "After Burford—What Next for EPA?" *U.S. News and World Report*, 21 Mar. 1983, 27; Helen M. Ingram and Dean E. Mann, "Preserving the Clean Water Act: The Appearance of Environmental Victory," in Vig and Kraft, 268; Louis S. Clapper, "EPA Funds Slashed," *National Wildlife*, Apr. 1982, 28A; Suzanne Schwartz, interview by author, 12 Nov. 1993, Washington, D.C.; Robert Alder, Jessica C. Landman, and Diane M. Cameron, *The Clean Water Act 20 Years Later* (Washington, D.C.: Island Press, 1993), 109.

10. Lawrence Mosher, "When Is a Prairie Pothole a Wetland? When the Federal Regulators Get Busy," *National Journal*, 6 Mar. 1982, 412–13; William R. Gianelli, *Water Resources People and Issues: An Interview with William R. Gianelli, Assistant Secretary of the Army (Civil Works)*, interview by Martin Reuss, 20 June 1984, Pebble Beach, California (Washington, D.C.: U.S. Army Corps of Engineers, 1985), 1.

11. Quoted in Harmon and McConnell, 94.

12. Michael C. Blumm and D. Bernard Zahela, "Federal Wetlands Protection under the Clean Water Act: Regulatory Ambivalence and a Call for Reform," *University of Colorado Law Review* 60 (1989): 699.

13. William R. Gianelli, "Regulatory Reform Equals Good Government," *National Wetlands Newsletter*, July–Aug. 1983, 6–7; Harmon and McConnell, 94; Blumm and Zahela, 710; Thomas Addison and Timothy Burns, "The Army Corps of Engineers and Nationwide Permit 26: Wetlands Protection or Swamp Reclamation?" *Ecology Law Quarterly* 18 (1991): 659.

14. Blumm and Zahela, 734; "EPA and FWS Sign New §404(q) MOAs With Army," *National Wetlands Newsletter*, Jan.–Feb. 1986, 2–3; *An Interview with William R. Gianelli*, 29–32. According to William Gianelli, this memorandum

eliminated a system in which appeals could be filed indefinitely up the chain of command to the secretary of the army, a process that took far too long. The new system made it possible for the Fish and Wildlife agencies to appeal once, but if the assistant secretary of the army decided against their appeal, there would be no further recourse. Because there was no recourse, and because Gianelli was not sympathetic to the idea of protecting wetlands with the Section 404 program, environmentalists had justifiable fears.

15. Blumm and Zahela, 711.

16. Vig and Kraft, ix.

17. John McLaughlin, "From Washington Straight: The EPA Debacle," *National Review*, 18 Mar. 1983, 304; Huntley, 25–27. Ann Gorsuch married during her tenure as EPA administrator and changed her name to Ann Gorsuch Burford.

18. Vig and Kraft, 57; Harris Poll, 1982, in *Floodplain Management in the United States: An Assessment Report*, vol. 1 prepared for the Federal Interagency Floodplain Management Task Force by the National Hazards and Applications Information Center (Washington, D.C.: Federal Emergency Management Agency, 1992), 53.

19. Michael E. Kraft, "A New Environmental Policy Agenda: The 1980 Presidential Campaign and Its Aftermath," in Vig and Kraft, 46.

20. James T. B. Tripp and David W. Hoskins, "Implementation of a §404 Bottomland Hardwoods Regulatory Program: Rethinking Lower Mississippi Valley Resource Objectives and Priorities," *National Wetlands Newsletter*, Mar.–Apr. 1985, 8; *Avoyelles Sportsmen's League v. Marsh* , 715 F. 2d 897 (5th Cir. 1983).

21. U.S. District Court for the District of Columbia, 1984, *National Wildlife Federation v. Marsh*, Civil No. 82–3632 (D.D.C. 1984), settlement agreement, cited in William Want, *Law of Wetlands Regulation* (New York: Clark Boardman, 1991), 2–10; "Environmental Organizations Sue to Undo Reagan Administration Changes in Sec. 404 Program," *National Wetlands Newsletter*, Nov.–Dec. 1982, 4–6; William Y. Brown, "Corps Proposals Are Further Retreat from Wetlands Protection," *National Wetlands Newsletter*, July–Aug. 1983, 7–8; Office of Technology Assessment, *Wetlands: Their Use and Regulation* (Washington, D.C.: Government Printing Office, 1984), 71–72; Thomas B. Allen, *Guardian of the Wild: The Story of the National Wildlife Federation, 1936–1986* (Bloomington: Indiana University Press, 1987), 199.

22. Blumm and Zahela, 714–16; Want, 2–10; *United States v. Riverside Bayview Homes, Inc.*, 474 U.S. 121 (1985).

23. Blumm and Zahela, 742–44; Thomas Eggert, "Out with the Old, In with the New: The Corps' Controversial Interpretation of the §404 (b)(1) Guidelines," *National Wetlands Newsletter*, Sept.–Oct. 1985, 2–4; "EPA Issues Final §404(c) Determination Prohibiting Filling of Sweedens Swamp," *National Wetlands Newsletter*, July–Aug. 1986, 10–13; *Bersani v. United States Environmental Protection Agency*, 850 F. 2d 36 (2d Cir. 1988).

24. Quoted in Blumm and Zahela, 761.

25. Quoted in "Congressional Update: Dawson Confirmation," *National Wetlands Newsletter*, Jan.–Feb. 1986, 4.

26. Quoted in "Dawson Confirmation," 5.

27. Quoted in "Dawson Confirmation," 5.

28. "EPA and FWS Sign New §404(q) MOAs with Army," *National Wetlands Newsletter,* Jan.–Feb. 1986, 2–3.

29. Mosher, 410–12; Louis S. Clapper, "Army Proposes Weaker Wetlands Law," *National Wildlife,* Apr. 1982, 28A.

30. Office of Technology Assessment, *Wetlands: Their Use and Regulation* (Washington, D.C.: Government Printing Office, 1984); General Accounting Office, *Wetlands: The Corps' Administration of the Section 404 Program* (Washington, D.C.: Government Printing Office, 1988).

31. Blumm and Zahela, 729.

32. Alder, Landman, and Cameron, 210–12, 214.

33. U.S. Department of the Interior, *The Impact of Federal Programs on Wetlands,* A Report to Congress, vol. 2 (Washington, D.C., 1994), 129; Blumm and Zahela, 730, 747; *Impact of Federal Programs,* vol. 2, 295; *Audubon Wildlife Report* (New York: National Audubon Society, 1986), 387–88. The OTA's estimate was based on corps data for 1980 and 1981.

34. Blumm and Zahela, 748; Addison and Burns, 656. In 1991 the Corps had a regulatory staff of 2,500 with an annual budget of approximately $70 million; the EPA wetlands staff totaled 150.

35. Ted Williams, "The Wetlands-Protection Farce," *Audubon,* Mar.–Apr. 1995, 34.

36. *Floodplain Management,* 53.

37. Congressional Research Service, "Wetland Management: A Report for the Committee on Environment and Public Works" (1982), in *Impact of Federal Programs,* vol. 1, 36.

38. Suzanne Schwartz, interview by author, 12 Nov. 1993, Washington, D.C.

39. *Impact of Federal Programs,* vol. 2, 101–2. Although CBRA protected wetlands behind pristine coastal barriers, it did nothing for those tucked behind already developed areas. CBRA was amended by the Coastal Barrier Improvement Act of 1990, which extended the subsidy free zone to 1.25 million acres of shoreline.

40. Martin Reuss, *Reshaping National Water Politics: The Emergence of the Water Resources Development Act of 1986* (Washington, D.C.: U.S. Army Corps of Engineers, 1991), 1–2.

41. *Impact of Federal Programs,* vol. 2, 74; "Congressional Update: Water Resources Projects," *National Wetlands Newsletter,* Jan.–Feb. 1987, 4.

42. Martin Reuss, interview by author, 7 Nov. 1993, Arlington, Virginia; *Impact of Federal Programs,* vol. 2, 71.

43. "House and Senate Subcommittees Hold Hearings on Wetlands Protection Legislation," *National Wetlands Newsletter,* July–Aug. 1983, 2–3.

44. Hope Babcock, "Federal Wetlands Regulatory Policy: Up to Its Ears i᠁ tors," *Pace Environmental Law Review* 8, no. 2 (Spring 1991): 3᠁

45. "House and Senate Subcommittees Hold Hearings," 2–3.

46. "House and Senate Subcommittees Hold Hearings," 3; Russ Peterson, "Watt's Wetlands Fraud," *Audubon,* May 1983, 4.

47. "House and Senate Committees Approve Wetlands Conservation Legislation," *National Wetlands Newsletter,* Nov.–Dec. 1983, 9; "Congressional Update: Wetlands Acquisition," *National Wetlands Newsletter,* Jan.–Feb. 1987, 2–3; Dale A. Pierce, "The Emergency Wetlands Resources Act: Status Report on Implementation," *National Wetlands Newsletter,* Sept.–Oct. 1987, 11; "Wetlands Preservation," *National Hazards Observer,* 9 Mar. 1987, 6.

48. U.S. Department of the Interior, Fish and Wildlife Service, "Wetlands of International Importance Fact Sheet" (n.d.); "Congressional Update: International Wetlands Treaty," *National Wetlands Newsletter,* Jan.–Feb. 1987, 3.

49. Harvey Nelson, interview by author, 21 Feb. 1995, telephone; Laurence Jahn and Cyril Kabat, "Origin and Role," in *Flyways: Pioneering Waterfowl Management in North America,* ed. A. S. Hawkins, R. C. Hanson, H. K. Nelson, H. M. Reeves (Washington, D.C.: U.S. Department of the Interior, Fish and Wildlife Service, 1984), 382–83.

50. Scott Sutherland (Ducks Unlimited), interview by author, 8 Nov. 1993, Washington, D.C.; Mexico did not sign the plan at that time but participated under a separate agreement.

51. U.S. Department of the Interior, Fish and Wildlife Service and Environment Canada, Canadian Wildlife Service, *North American Waterfowl Management Plan: A Strategy for Cooperation* (Washington, D.C., 1986), ii.

52. David Smith, U.S. Fish and Wildlife Service, interview by author, 9 Nov. 1993, Washington, D.C.

53. David Smith, interview by author, 9 Nov. 1993.

54. *North American Wetlands Conservation Act, 1989–1991 Progress Report* pamphlet (North American Wetlands Conservation Council, 1992), 18–19; "North American Waterfowl Management Plan," in *Fish and Wildlife '91: A Report to the Nation* (Washington, D.C.: U.S. Department of the Interior, Fish and Wildlife Service, 1991), 67; Harvey Nelson, interview by author, 21 Feb. 1995.

55. Mike Prevost, interview by author, 3 Dec. 1993, Hollywood, South Carolina.

56. Mike Prevost, interview by author, 3 Dec. 1993.

57. U.S. Fish and Wildlife Service, North American Waterfowl and Wetlands Office and the Canadian Wildlife Service, "North American Waterfowl Management Plan: A Review of the First Five Years" (Washington, D.C.: U.S. Department of the Interior, 1993), 10–13. The three accomplished joint ventures (JVs) include Atlantic Coast JV, Central Valley Habitat JV, and the Eastern Habitat JV in Canada. The other five important areas are the Gulf Coast JV, the Lower Great Lakes–St. Lawrence Basin JV, the Lower Mississippi Valley JV, the Prairie Pothole JV, and the Pacific Habitat JV in Canada.

58. Alder, Landman, and Cameron, 217; "Congressional Update: Clean Water Act Amendments," *National Wetlands Newsletter,* Jan.–Feb. 1987, 4–5.
    Alder, Landman, and Cameron, 206; Thomas E. Dahl and C. E. Johnson, *⌐tus and Trends of Wetlands in the Conterminous United States, mid-1970s to mid-*

1980s (Washington, D.C.: U.S. Department of the Interior, Fish and Wildlife Service, 1991), 1, 8, 15.

Chapter 15

1. Congress, Senate, Committee on Appropriations, Subcommittee on Rural Development, and Related Agencies, *Implementation of the Swampbuster Provision of the 1985 Farm Act: Hearing before a Subcommittee of the Committee of Appropriations,* 100th Cong., 2d sess., special hearing, 26 Jan. 1988, 29.

2. Ralph W. Tiner, Jr., *Wetlands of the United States: Current Status and Recent Trends* (Washington, D.C.: U.S. Department of the Interior, Fish and Wildlife Service, 1984), 32.

3. Joseph M. Petulla, *American Environmental History* (San Francisco: Boyd & Fraser, 1977), 374–75; Douglas Helms, "The Soil Conservation Service: A Historical Note," in *Readings in the History of the Soil Conservation Service,* ed. Douglas Helms (Washington, D.C.: U.S. Department of Agriculture, Soil Conservation Service, 1992), 9; U.S. Department of Agriculture, Economic Research Service, "History of Agricultural Price-Support and Adjustment Programs, 1933–1984," *Agricultural Information Bulletin,* no. 485 (Dec. 1984), 23, 25.

4. Helms, 9; Ralph E. Heimlich, "Soil Erosion on New Cropland: A Sodbusting Perspective," *Journal of Soil and Water Conservation,* July–Aug. 1985, 323. Between 1972 and 1982, 60 million acres of new cropland came into production; most of it was range and pastureland.

5. Leonard Shabman, "Economic Incentives for Bottomland Conversion: The Role of Public Policy and Programs," in *Proceedings of the Forty-Fifth North American Wildlife Conference* (1980), 402–12.

6. Wayne Rasmussen, "New Deal Agricultural Policies after Fifty Years," *Minnesota Law Review* 68 (1983): 353–77.

7. Earl L. Butz, "Produce and Protect," *Journal of Soil and Water Conservation,* Nov.– Dec. 1973, 250–252, quoted in Helms, 158.

8. Quoted in Tim Palmer, *Endangered Rivers and the Conservation Movement* (Berkeley: University of California Press, 1986), 189.

9. Jon R. Luoma, "Twilight in Pothole Country," *Audubon,* Sept. 1985, 77; U.S. Department of the Interior, *The Impact of Federal Programs on Wetlands,* A Report to Congress, vol. 1 (Washington, D.C., 1988), 18.

10. Earl L. Butz, "Produce and Protect," quoted in Helms, 158–59.

11. General Accounting Office, *To Protect Tomorrow's Food Supply, Soil Conservation Needs Priority Attention* (Washington, D.C.: Government Printing Office, 1977) and Comptroller General, *Agriculture's Soil Conservation Programs Miss Full Potential in the Fight against Soil Erosion,* report no. 84–48 (Washington, D.C.: Government Printing Office, 1983), cited in Linda A. Malone, "A Historical Essay on the Conservation Provisions of the 1985 Farm Bill: Sodbusting, Swampbusting, and the Conservation Reserve," *Kansas Law Review* 34 (1986): 577–97.

12. Dick Lindberg, interview by author, 7 Nov. 1993, telephone; Tiner, 42; *Impact of Federal Programs,* vol. 1, 91–92.

13. Timothy Bremicker, "United States Department of Agriculture Programs—a Need for New Direction," *Naturalist,* Autumn 1984, 27.

14. Kristin L. Bradof, "Ditching of Red Lake Peatland during the Homestead Era," in *The Patterned Peatlands of Minnesota,* ed. H. E. Wright, Jr., B. A. Coffin, and N. E. Aaseng (Minneapolis: University of Minnesota Press, 1992), 278.

15. Gary Pearson, "Draining the Great Marsh," *USA Today,* Nov. 1985, reprint ed., July 1986, 84–85.

16. Tiner, 21.

17. J. P. Furst, "Court Hears State Wetlands Case," *Jamestown Sun* (North Dakota), 25 Oct. 1982; Pearson, 86; "North Dakota Wetlands—Update," *National Wetlands Newsletter,* Nov.–Dec. 1980, 10; Luoma, 72.

18. Shabman, 402–12; *Impact of Federal Programs,* vol. 1, 3, 41, 52, 60.

19. U.S. Fish and Wildlife Service, *The Atchafalaya: America's Greatest River Swamp: A Proposal to Establish the Atchafalaya Fish, Wildlife, and Multi-Use Area* (Washington, D.C.: U.S. Department of the Interior, Fish and Wildlife Service, 1978), 11.

20. U.S. Fish and Wildlife Service, *The Atchafalaya,* 11; Randall A. Kramer and Leonard Shabman, "The Effects of Agricultural and Tax Policy on the Economic Return to Wetland Drainage in the Mississippi Delta Region," *Land Economics* 69, no. 3 (Aug. 1993), 249: Y. Abernethy and R. E. Turner, "U.S. Forested Wetlands: 1940–1980," *BioScience* 37, no. 10 (Nov. 1987): 726, 721–27.

21. Bob Anderson, "The Swamp Bear's Last Stand," *Nature Conservancy,* Sept.–Oct. 1991, 22, 16–22; Kramer and Shabman, 251, 249–62.

22. Anderson, 20.

23. Congress, House, Committee on Government Operations, Subcommittee on Conservation and Natural Resources, *Stream Channelization, Part II,* 92d Cong., 1st sess., 3 June 1971, 533.

24. Craig G. Lukin and Lucy L. Mauger, *Environmental Geologic Atlas of the Coastal Zone of North Carolina: Dare, Hyde, Tyrrell, and Washington Counties,* Raleigh, North Carolina Department of Natural Resources, Coastal Energy Impact Report, no. 32 (Nov. 1983), 49–50; R. W. Skaggs, J. W. Gilliam, T. J. Sheets, and J. S. Barnes, "Effect of Agricultural Land Development on Drainage Waters in the North Carolina Tidewater Region," University of North Carolina, Water Resources Research Institute, report no. 159 (Aug. 1980), 1; Jan DeBlieu, *Hatteras Journal* (Golden, Colo.: Fulcrum Press, 1987), 66; *Impact of Federal Programs,* vol. 2, 23; Douglas Helms, "Soil and Soil Conservation," in *Readings in the History of the Soil Conservation Service,* ed. Douglas Helms, 12.

25. Peter H. Lindert, "Long-Run Trends in American Farmland Values," *Agricultural History* 62 (Summer 1988): 45–85, cited in Douglas Helms, "New Authorities and New Roles," in *Readings in the History of the Soil Conservation Service,* 162.

26. Pearson, 85; Luoma, 82. In 1983, nearly 5.4 million acres of wheatland were idled. In 1985, 85 percent of North Dakota wheat farmers participated in PIK compared with 46 percent nationwide.

27. Pearson, 85.

28. *Impact of Federal Programs,* vol. 1, 4, 22, 91.

29. Keith Harmon and Chester A. McConnell, "The Politics of Wetland Conservation: A Wildlife View," *Journal of Soil and Water Conservation,* Mar.–Apr. 1983, 94; Office of Technology Assessment, *Wetlands: Their Use and Regulation* (Washington, D.C.: Government Printing Office, 1984), 78; Norman A. Berg, "Envir-Coord-Proposed Amendment to SCS Rule on Protection of Wetlands," Soil Conservation Service, *National Bulletin,* no. 220–1–5, 6 Mar. 1981.

30. Malone, 577–97; Jeffrey Zinn, "Swampbuster: Status and Issues," *CRS Report for Congress,* Washington, D.C.: Congressional Research Service, 1 Apr. 1993, 2; Douglas Helms, "New Authorities and New Roles," 163; *Impact of Federal Programs,* vol. 1, 11.

31. Clayton Ogg, "Addressing Environmental Needs in Farm Programs," *Agricultural History* 66, no. 2 (Spring 1992): 275–76.

32. Helms, "New Authorities and New Roles," 161–62.

33. U.S. Department of Agriculture, Agricultural Stabilization and Conservation Service, "Water Bank Program: From Inception of Program through Sept. 30, 1992," (Washington, D.C., 1993); Jeffrey Zinn, Congressional Research Services, personal correspondence, June 1996. According to Zinn, less than half the land in the water bank is wetland.

34. Jeffrey Zinn, personal correspondence, June 1996. According to Zinn, this was especially true in the early 1980s, when support payments were high.

35. Malone, 587.

36. Ralph E. Heimlich, "Economics of Wetland Conversion: Farm Programs and Income Tax," *National Wetlands Newsletter,* July–Aug. 1986, 8.

37. Maureen Hinkle, National Audubon Society, interview by author, 25 Oct. 1993, Washington D.C.; Jeffrey Zinn, interview by author, 9 Nov. 1993; Robert Misso, U.S. Fish and Wildlife Service, interview by author, 28 Oct. 1993; Jeffrey Zinn to Sen. Quentin Burdick, "Swampbuster Provisions of the 1985 Food Security Act," memorandum (15 Jan. 1988), from the files of Jeffrey Zinn.

38. Ken Cook, "Pinch Me, I Must be Dreaming!" *Journal of Soil and Water Conservation,* Mar.–Apr. 1986, 94.

39. Peter Kilian Weber, National Audubon Society, "Statement Submitted to the Senate Committee on Appropriations, Subcommittee on Agriculture, Rural Development and Related Agencies, for Inclusion in the Record of the January 26, 1988, Hearing on the Implementation of the Swampbuster Provision of the Food Security Act of 1985," 5, from files of Maureen Hinkle.

40. James T. B. Tripp and Daniel J. Dudek, "The Swampbuster Provisions of the Food Security Act of 1985: Stronger Wetland Conservation If Properly Implemented and Enforced," *Environmental Law Reporter* 16 (May 1986): 10122; Helms, "New Authorities and New Roles," 164.

41. Wayne "Skip" Baron, National Wildlife Federation, interview by author, 19 Sept. 1994, pothole country, North Dakota; Dale Hennegar, interview by author, 20 Sept. 1994, Bismarck, North Dakota; Weber, 10.
42. *Impact of Federal Programs*, vol. 1, 18.
43. Luoma, 81.
44. Quoted in Luoma, 80–81.
45. Gary Pearson, interview by author, 20 Sept. 1994, Jamestown, North Dakota.
46. Gary Pearson, interview; Dale Hennegar, interview; *Impact of Federal Programs*, vol. 1, 103; Wayne "Skip" Baron, interview.
47. *Impact of Federal Programs*, vol. 1, 106.
48. Ward Sinclair, "'Swampbuster' Penalties Irk Farmers," *Washington Post*, 27 Jan. 1988, 18; Congress, Senate, Committee on Appropriations, Subcommittee on Rural Development, and Related Agencies, *Implementation of the Swampbuster Provision of the 1985 Farm Act: Hearing before a Subcommittee of the Committee of Appropriations*, 100th Cong., 2d sess., special hearing, 26 Jan. 1988, 30–31.
49. Weber, appendix 3; James Bovard, *The Farm Fiasco* (San Francisco: ICS Press, 1991), 219; Ann Y. Robinson, "Wetland Protection: What Success?" *Journal of Soil and Water Conservation*, July–Aug. 1993, 270; Gary Pearson, interview.
50. Wayne "Skip" Baron, interview; Ducks Unlimited Private Lands Program, *The Good Life Is Getting Even Better: Partners Helping Partners*, pamphlet (Memphis, TN: n.d.); "Farming in the Flyways," *Successful Farming* (Feb. 1990), reprint; Kathleen Rude, "Cultivating Cooperation," *Ducks Unlimited*, May–June 1992, 47–51.
51. Robert Misso, interview; Robinson, 268–70.
52. *Impact of Federal Programs*, vol. 2, 62, 79; Peter Steinhart, "No Net Loss," *Audubon*, July 1990, 20.
53. Ralph E. Heimlich, "Costs of an Agricultural Wetland Reserve," *Land Economics* 70, no. 2 (May 1994): 234.
54. Ralph E. Heimlich, "The Swampbuster Provision: Implementation and Impact," paper presented at the National Symposium on Protection of Wetlands from Agricultural Impacts, Colorado State University, Fort Collins, Colorado (Apr. 25–29, 1988), cited in *Impact of Federal Programs*, vol. 1, 106; *Impact of Federal Programs*, vol. 2, 55.
55. Matthew Keefer, "Wetland Drainers Stymied," *NWF Leader*, Oct. 1991, 5.
56. Associated Press, "'Swampbuster' Enforcement Inadequate, Inspectors Say," *Jamestown Sun* (North Dakota), 29 Mar. 1993.
57. "'Swampbuster' Enforcement Inadequate."
58. Robinson, 268–70; Greg Breinig, "Growing Crops, and Wildlife Too," *National Wildlife*, Dec.–Jan. 1995, 43.
59. Jeffrey Zinn, "Conservation Provisions in the 1996 Farm Bill: A Summary," *CRS Report for Congress*, Washington, D.C., Congressional Research Service, 11 Apr. 1996, 2–3.
60. Robert Misso, interview.
61. *Impact of Federal Programs*, vol. 2, 13, 195; W. E. Frayer, Dennis D. Peters, and H. Ross Pywell, *Wetlands of the California Central Valley, Status and Trends, 1939*

to mid-1980s (Portland, Ore: U.S. Department of the Interior, Fish and Wildlife Service, 1989), ii.

62. *Impact of Federal Programs,* vol. 2 , 196; Moira McDonald, "Getting Water to the Wetlands," *National Wetlands Newsletter,* July–Aug. 1995, 15.

63. Tom Harris, *Death in the Marsh* (Washington, D.C.: Island Press, 1991), 1–13, passim; Peter Steinhart, "Empty the Skies," *Audubon,* Nov. 1987, 71–95; Marc Reisner, "California's Vanishing Wetlands," *Headwaters,* Mar.–Apr. 1988, 12–14.

64. Harris, 30, 123.

65. Steinhart, "Empty the Skies," 78; Michael A. Rozengurt, "Alteration of Fresh-water Flows," in *Stemming the Tide of Coastal Fish Habitat Loss: Proceedings of a Symposium on Conservation of Coastal Fish Habitat, Baltimore, Maryland, Mar. 1991,* ed. Richard Stroud, ed., Marine Recreational Fisheries Report No. 14 (Savannah, Ga: National Coalition for Marine Conservation, 1992), 76.

66. *Impact of Federal Programs,* vol. 2, 14, 78.

67. *Impact of Federal Programs,* vol. 2, 72; "It's Back: The San Luis Drain," *Bay Watcher,* Oct. 1994, 6.

68. "Waters of Change for California," *Bay Watcher,* Jan. 1993, 5–8; "The End of California Water Policy Gridlock," *Bay Watcher,* Jan. 1994, 5–8; Tim Palmer, *Lifelines: The Case for River Conservation* (Washington, D.C.: Island Press, 1994), 150. According to Palmer, Bush favored the act for water projects it authorized elsewhere.

69. *Impact of Federal Programs,* vol. 2, 209.

70. Ruth Norris and Cynthia Lenhart, "The National Wildlife Refuge System," in *Audubon Wildlife Report* (New York: National Audubon Society, 1987), 241; Ted Williams, "Death in a Black Desert," *Audubon,* Jan.–Feb. 1994, 24–31.

71. "Turning on the Tap at Stillwater," *Nature Conservancy,* July–Aug. 1990, 28–29; Don Vetter, "Teeming Oasis or Desert Mirage? Bringing a Wildlife Refuge Back to Life," *Nature Conservancy,* Sept.–Oct. 1991, 22–27.

72. U.S. Department of the Interior, Fish and Wildlife Service, *Fish and Wildlife '91: A Report to the Nation* (Washington, D.C., 1991), 38–39.

73. D. E. Brown, C. H. Lowe, and J. F. Hausler, "Southwestern Riparian Communities: Their Biotic Importance and Management in Arizona," in *Importance, Preservation, and Management of Riparian Habitat: A Symposium,* ed. R. R. Johnson and D. A. Jones, General Technical Report, RU-43 (Washington, D.C.: U.S. Department of Agriculture, Forest Service, 1977), 201–11.

74. U.S. Department of the Interior, Fish and Wildlife Service, *Regional Wetland Concept Plan: Emergency Wetlands Resources Act* (Lakewood, Colo., n.d.), cited in Douglas N. Gladwin and James E. Roelle, "Nationwide Permits: Case Studies Highlight Concerns," *National Wetlands Newsletter,* Mar.–Apr. 1992, 9.

75. Connie Young, "Wetlands Targeted for Endangered Fish," *Newsletter of the Recovery Program for the Endangered Fishes of the Upper Colorado* (Vernal, Utah, Spring 1993), 1.

76. *Impact of Federal Programs,* vol. 2, 16.

77. Palmer, 129–30. Diversion of water reduced the width of the river channel by

80 to 90 percent and encouraged woody growth, but sandhill and whooping cranes prefer expansive cobble bars and marshes.

78. John L. Zimmerman, *Cheyenne Bottoms: Wetland in Jeopardy* (Lawrence: University Press of Kansas, 1990), 7. Between 1973 and 1985, the water table declined an average of three feet per year in southwestern Kansas.

79. William W. Kirby-Smith and Richard T. Barber, *The Water Quality Ramifications in Estuaries of Converting Forest to Intensive Agriculture,* University of North Carolina, Water Resources Research Institute, report no. 148 (Dec. 1979), 3; J. W. Gilliam and R. W. Skaggs, "Drainage and Agricultural Development: Effects on Drainage Waters," in *Pocosin Wetlands,* ed. C. J. Richardson (Stroudsberg, Pa.: Hutchinson Ross Publishing, 1981), 110. DeBlieu, 61–79. Plans in the late 1970s and early 1980s to mine peat for power generation also raised concern for pocosin wetlands.

80. *Impact of Federal Programs,* vol. 2, 281–83; Michael W. Street and Joseph D. McClees "North Carolina's Coastal Fishing Industry and the Influence of Coastal Alterations," in *Poscosin Wetlands,* ed. C. J. Richardson, 238–247.

81. Bruce Galloway, *Chesapeake Bay Program: A Work in Progress, a Retrospective on the First Decade of the Chesapeake Bay Restoration* (Annapolis: Chesapeake Bay Program, 1993), 4–6; Tom Horton and William Eichbaum, *Turning the Tide: Saving the Chesapeake Bay* (Washington, D.C.: Island Press, 1991), 128–30, passim.

82. "The Chesapeake Bay Conference: A Study in Intergovernmental Cooperation," *National Wetlands Newsletter,* Jan.–Feb. 1984, 8–9; Galloway, 7; Tom Horton, "Chesapeake Bay: Hanging in the Balance," *National Geographic,* June 1993, 4; Tiner, 39–40; Marjorie Sun, "The Chesapeake Bay's Difficult Comeback," *Science,* 15 Aug. 1986, 715–17.

83. Joseph L. Arnold, *The Baltimore Engineers and the Chesapeake Bay, 1961–1987* (U.S. Army Corps of Engineers, Baltimore District, 1988), 9–10.

84. "The Chesapeake Bay Conference," 8–9; Erik Meyers, Robert Fischman, and Anne Marsh, "Maryland Chesapeake Bay Critical Areas Program: Wetlands Protection and Future Growth," in *Collaborative Planning for Wetlands and Wildlife: Issues and Examples,* ed. Douglas R. Porter and David A. Salvesen (Washington, D.C.: Island Press, 1995), 182–85, 190; Horton and Eichbaum, 161–65.

85. Joseph A. Mihursky, "Overview of Political, Science, and Management Issues in the Chesapeake Bay Region," in *Proceedings of the Conference: Wetlands of the Chesapeake,* ed. Hazel A. Groman (Washington, D.C.: Environmental Law Institute, 1985), 277; Patricia Ross McCubbin, "Consensus through Mediation: A Case Study of the Chesapeake Bay Land Use Roundtable and the Chesapeake Bay Preservation Act," *Journal of Law and Policy* 5, no. 4 (1989): 829; John P. Wiley, "The Drive to Save the Chesapeake Has Moved Up . . . ," *Smithsonian,* Nov. 1993, 24.

86. Paul Parks, "Will the Everglades Be Saved?" *Newsletter of the Sierra Club Public Lands Committee,* Dec. 1991, 12; *Impact of Federal Programs,* vol. 2, 6; Joe Podgor, Friends of the Everglades, interview by author, 13 Jan. 1994, Miami.

87. William A. Niering, "Human Impacts on the South Florida Wetlands: The Everglades and Big Cypress Swamp," in *The Earth in Transition—Patterns and Processes of Biotic Impoverishment,* ed. George M. Woodwell (Cambridge, England: Cambridge University Press, 1990), 467.

88. W. B. Robertson, Jr., and J. A. Kushlan, "South Florida Avifauna," in *Environments of South Florida: Present and Past,* ed. P. J. Gleason (Miami: Miami Geological Society, 1984), 257, cited in *Impact of Federal Programs,* vol. 2, 127.

89. Quoted in Rose Mary Meachem, "In Florida, the Grass Is No Longer Greener," *National Wildlife,* 11 Oct. 1982, 55; Norman Boucher, "Smart As Gods: Can We Put the Everglades Back Together Again?" *Wilderness,* Winter 1991, 12.

90. Steve Yates, "Marjory Stoneman Douglas and the Glades Crusade," *Audubon,* Mar. 1983, 114.

91. Mark Derr, "Redeeming the Everglades," *Audubon,* Sept.–Oct. 1993, 128.

92. Quoted in Yates, 120.

93. Derr, 128–29; Jeffrey P. Cohn, "Restoring the Everglades," *BioScience* 44, no. 9 (Oct. 1994): 579; Ted Levin, "Immersed in the Everglades," *Sierra,* May–June 1996, 63.

94. Niering, 469–70.

95. Tiner, 40.

96. Governor's Office of Planning and Budgeting, *Save Our Everglades, Tenth Anniversary, 1983–1993* (Tallahassee, Fla., 1993), 18.

97. G. Thomas Bancroft, *Water for People and Wildlife: Principles for Restoring the Endangered Everglades System,* (n.p.: National Audubon Society, 1993), 4; Alan Mairson, "The Everglades: Dying for Help," *National Geographic,* Apr. 1994, 18–19.

98. Quoted in Phillip Shabecoff, *A Fierce Green Fire: The American Environmental Movement* (New York: Hill and Wang, 1993), 152.

99. Kathleen Shea Adams, with Hugh Gladwin, Mary Jean Matthews, and Barbara McCabe, "The East Everglades Planning Study," in *Collaborative Planning,* 247; Boucher, 19–21.

100. Derr, 128; Boucher, 18.

101. Don Hinchman, "Waterworld," *Amicus Journal* 17 (Summer 1995): 27.

Chapter 16

1. "Proposals Urged to Save Wetlands," *Oregonian,* 16 Nov. 1988, a-10, quoted in Michael C. Blumm and D. Bernard Zaleha, "Federal Wetlands Protection Under the Clean Water Act: Regulatory Ambivalence, Intergovernmental Tension, and a Call for Reform," *University of Colorado Law Review* 60 (1989): 695.

2. *Protecting America's Wetlands: An Action Agenda, The Final Report of the National Wetlands Policy Forum* (Washington, D.C.: Conservation Foundation, 1988). The group included three governors; a state legislator; chief executive officers from conservation groups, oil and gas, forest products, agriculture, and development industries; state agency heads; a town supervisor; farmers and ranchers; academic experts; and senior officials from the five principal federal agencies involved in wetlands protection and management.

3. Hope Babcock, "Federal Wetlands Regulatory Policy: Up to Its Ears in Alligators," *Pace Environmental Law Review* 8, no. 2 (Spring 1991): 334–35.

4. Quoted in U.S. Department of the Interior, Fish and Wildlife Service, *Wetlands: Meeting the President's Challenge, Wetlands Action Plan* (Washington, D.C., 1990), 1.

5. U.S. Department of the Interior, *The Impact of Federal Programs on Wetlands*, A Report to Congress, vol. 2 (Washington, D.C., 1994), 91.

6. Suzanne Schwartz, interview by author, 12 Nov. 1993, Washington, D.C.; Timothy Beatly, David K. Brower, and Anna K. Schwab, *An Introduction to Coastal Zone Management* (Washington, D.C.: Island Press, 1994), 71; Barbara Rosewicz, "Wetlands Plan May Leave Bush on Soft Ground," *Wall Street Journal*, 12 Aug. 1991, b-4; Frank Graham, Jr., "Of Broccoli and Marshes," *Audubon*, July 1990, 105; U.S. Department of the Interior, Fish and Wildlife Service, *A Legacy for the Future: Accomplishments and Highlights, 1989–1993*, (Washington, D.C., 1994), 3.

7. Babcock, 338–39.

8. Quoted in Peter Steinhart, "Mud Wrestling," *Sierra*, Jan.–Feb. 1993, 148.

9. Steinhart, 150.

10. Quoted in Steinhart, 58.

11. Frank Clifford, "Raising the Price of Protecting Nature," *Los Angeles Times*, 25 May 1995, a-32.

12. Steinhart, 148–49; Jean Seligmann and Mary Hager, "What on Earth Is a Wetland?" *Newsweek*, 26 Aug. 1991, 48–49; Lori Nordstrom, "Section 404 Gets Bad Rap," *National Wildlife Federation Leader*, Apr. 1991, 1.

13. Steinhart, 149.

14. Quoted in Michael Weisskopf and D'Vera Cohn, "60 Million Farm Acres Lose Wetlands Protection Status," *Washington Post*, 29 Sept. 1990, a-2; Babcock, 346.

15. Paul Rauber, "Political Science: What Happens to Government Researchers Who Reach the "Wrong" Conclusions?" *Sierra*, Sept.–Oct. 1992, 38; Jon Kusler, "Wetlands Delineation: An Issue of Science or Politics?" *Environment* 34, no. 2 (Mar. 1992): 8; Michael Weisskopf, "Wetlands Protection and the Struggle over Environmental Policy," *Washington Post*, 8 Aug. 1991, a-17. This change in policy prompted the controversial resignation of EPA senior biologist William Sipple.

16. Quoted in Rosewicz, b-1.

17. Kusler, 8.

18. Matthew Keefer, "Wetlands: Going, Going, Going," *National Wildlife Federation Leader*, Oct. 1991, 5; Kusler, 34; Warren E. Leary, "In Wetlands Debate, Acres and Dollars Hinge on Definitions," *New York Times*, 15 Oct. 1991, b-8; Rosewicz, b-4. Not only was the burden of proof shifted to the government, but the new definition required far more evidence that was difficult to obtain for all wetland sites.

19. John Turner, personal correspondence, 12 June 1996.

20. Richard S. Stenger, "All Wet," *Environmental Action*, Nov.–Dec. 1991, 13.

21. Quoted in Leary, b-8; Bill O. Wilen, "The Folly of the Numbers Game," *National Wetlands Newsletter,* May–June 1995, 8–10.

22. Michele Leslie, "Mitigation Policy," in *Issues in Wetlands Protection: Background Papers Prepared for the National Wetlands Policy Forum* (Washington, D.C.: Conservation Foundation, 1990), 173.

23. Joseph L. Arnold, *The Baltimore Engineers and the Chesapeake Bay, 1961–1987* (Baltimore: U.S. Army, Corps of Engineers, Baltimore District, 1988), 45, 60; Stephen W. Broome, "Creation and Restoration of Tidal Wetlands of the Southeastern United States," in *Wetland Creation and Restoration,* ed. Jon A. Kusler and Mary E. Kentula (Washington, D.C.: Island Press, 1990), 41–42.

24. William L. Kruczynski, "Mitigation and the Section 404 Program: A Perspective," in Kusler and Kentula, 551.

25. Mark S. Dennison and James F. Berry, *Wetlands: Guide to Science, Law, and Technology* (Park Ridge, N.J.: Noyes Publications, 1995), 1, 18–21.

26. Leslie, 174.

27. *New York Times,* 8 Aug. 1985, 9, quoted in John David Brady, "Mitigation of Damage to Wetlands in Regulatory Programs and Water Resource Projects," *Mercer Law Review* 41, no. 3 (Spring 1990): 898.

28. Margaret S. Race, "San Francisco Bay Experience," in *Proceedings: Northwest Wetlands: What Are They? For Whom? For What?* November 1–2, 1985, ed. Polly Dyer (Seattle: University of Washington, Institute for Environmental Studies, 1987), 201–9.

29. Dennison and Berry, 1, 18–21.

30. Frank Golet, "Critical Issues in Wetland Mitigation: A Scientific Perspective," *National Wetlands Newletter,* Sept.–Oct. 1986, 3, 6.

31. Margaret S. Race and Donna Christie, "Coastal Zone Development: Mitigation, Marsh Creation, and Decisionmaking," *Environmental Management* 6 (1982): 7, cited in Brady, 924.

32. Jon A. Kusler, "Views on Scientific Issues Relating to the Restoration and Creation of Wetlands," in *Issues in Wetlands Protection,* 217–30; Kusler and Kentula, xviii.

33. Rosewicz, b-4; General Accounting Office, *Wetlands Overview: Federal and State Policies, Legislation, and Programs* (Washington, D.C.: Government Printing Office, 1991), 31; Peter A. A. Berle, "A New Threat to Wetlands," *Audubon,* July 1991, 4; Clark Williams, Environmental Working Group, personal correspondence, 12 Oct. 1996.

34. John Echeverria and Raymond Booth Eby, *Let the People Judge: Wise Use and the Private Property Rights Movement* (Washington, D.C.: Island Press, 1995), 163.

35. Susan Sward, "Illegal Filling Threatens Bay's Last Wetlands," *San Francisco Chronicle,* 22 Jan. 1990; Steinhart, "Mud Wrestling," 87–89.

36. Quoted in Ted Williams, "The Wetlands Protection Farce," *Audubon,* Mar.–Apr. 1995, 31.

37. Echeverria and Eby, 148.

38. Congress, House, Committee on Merchant Marine and Fisheries, Subcommittee on Fisheries and Wildlife Conservation and the Environment, *Takings,*

Compensation, and Pending Wetlands Legislation: Hearing on the Future Course of the Federal Wetlands Program, 102d Cong., 2d sess., 21 May 1992, 4–5.

39. *Takings, Compensation, and Pending Wetlands Legislation,* 74.

40. Jerold S. Kayden, "Private Property Rights, Government Regulation, and the Constitution: Searching for Balance," in *Land Use in America,* ed. Henry L. Diamond and Patrick F. Noonan (Washington, D.C.: Island Press, 1996), 297–98; *Pennsylvania Coal Co. v. Mahon,* 260 U.S. 393, 43 S. Ct. 158 (1922), quoted in Kathleen C. Zimmerman and David Abelson, *Takings Law: A Guide to Government, Property, and the Constitution,* (Boulder, Colo.: Land and Water Fund of the Rockies, 1993), 5–6. The full quotation is a little difficult to follow: "Government could hardly go on if to some extent value incident to property could not be diminished without paying for every such change in the general law."

41. Richard C. Ausness, "Regulatory Takings and Wetlands Protection in the Post-*Lucas* Era," *Land and Water Law Review* 30, no. 2 (1995): 401.

42. Quoted in Ausness, 31–32, 35–37.

43. Quoted in Ausness, 104–105.

44. Kristin Siemann, "Wetlands Campaign Off to Fast Start," *National Wildlife Federation Leader,* Feb. 1993, 1, 8; "Wetlands Protection," *National Wildlife Federation Leader,* Sept. 1993, 1; Clark Williams, "Senate Environment Leaders Tackle Wetlands Legislation," *National Audubon Society Fact Sheet,* Sept. 1993; Steinhart, "Mud Wrestling," 150.

45. LaJuana S. Wilcher, "Wetlands and the Constitutional Balance," *National Wetlands Newsletter,* Mar.–Apr. 1995, 17.

46. Ann Robinson, "Small and Seasonal Does Not Mean Insignificant: Why It's Worth Standing Up for Tiny and Temporary Wetlands," *Journal of Soil and Water Conservation,* Nov.–Dec. 1995, 589; Clark Williams, *Swamped with Cash* (Washington, D.C.: Environmental Working Group, 1996), 6.

47. Joy B. Zedler, "Reinventing Wetland Science," *National Wetlands Newsletter,* July–Aug. 1995, 17, italics added for emphasis.

48. Quoted in Louise Lavathes, "Science Gets Swamped," *Audubon,* July–Aug. 1995, 112.

49. Committee on Characterization of Wetlands, National Research Council, *Wetlands: Characteristics and Boundaries* (Washington, D.C.: National Academy Press, 1995), xiv; Jon Kusler, interview by author, 4 Nov. 1993, Washington, D.C.

50. Michael L. Davis, "A More Effective and Flexible Section 404," *National Wetlands Newsletter,* July–Aug. 1995, 9.

51. Quoted in "Clinton Promises Veto," *National Wetlands Newsletter,* July–Aug. 1995, 21.

52. "House Approves Budget Cut and Restrictive Riders for EPA," *National Wetlands Newsletter,* Sept.–Oct. 1995, 23; Roberta Ulrich, "Congress' Attack on Environment May Hurt Oregon's Quality of Life," *Oregonian,* 12 Oct. 1995, 1. In particular, the bill prohibited implementing and enforcing several water-quality programs.

53. William D. Ruckelshaus, "Stopping the Pendulum," *Environmental Forum,* Nov.–Dec. 1995, 25–26.

54. Ken Miller, "Democrats Gag on Bitter Budget Pills," *High Country News,* 15 Apr. 1996, 5; Bill Wilen, personal correspondence, June 1996; Gary Pearson, personal correspondence, July 1996.

55. "Water Reform Fight Looms," *Bay Watcher,* July 1995, 4; Moira Mcdonald, "Getting Water to the Wetlands," *National Wetlands Newsletter,* July–Aug. 1995, 14–16; Barry Nelson, "Congress Clashes over Central Valley Water," *Watershed,* Fall 1995, 3.

56. Clark Williams, *Swamped with Cash,* 2. These figures understate true contributions because they include only PAC money, not personal contributions.

57. Michael L. Davis, "A More Effective and Flexible Section 404," *National Wetlands Newsletter,* July–Aug. 1995, 8; "Clinton Administration Wetlands Policy: Talking Points for the Secretary," Aug. 1993, 5; "A Summary of 'Protecting America's Wetlands: A Fair, Flexible, and Effective Approach,'" 24 Aug. 1993; White House Office on Environmental Policy, "New Federal Wetlands Policy Offers Fair, Flexible Approach, Ends Agency Infighting and Gridlock with Strong Agreement," press release, 24 Aug. 1993; Stephen Barr, "Clinton to Revise Wetlands Policy," *Washington Post,* 25 Aug. 1993, a-1; Hazel Groman, Environmental Protection Agency, personal correspondence, 20 Sept. 1996; Robert H. Wayland, "The Clinton Administration's Perspective on Wetlands Protection," *Journal of Soil and Water Conservation,* Nov.–Dec. 1995, 581–84.

58. Quoted in Kenneth Pins, "Clinton's Wetlands Policy: Will It Resolve Stalemate?" *Des Moines Register,* 12 Oct. 1993, 8.

59. Quoted in Barr, a-1.

60. Barr, a-14.

61. Ann Robinson, "New Name, New Direction," *National Wetlands Newsletter,* Jan.–Feb. 1995, 4.

62. Bill Wilen, telephone interview by author, 26 Sept. 1997; Ralph Heimlich and Jeanne Melanson, "Wetlands Lost, Wetlands Gained," *National Wetlands Newsletter,* May–June 1995, 1.

Chapter 17

1. E. O. Wilson, *The Diversity of Life* (1992), quoted in Reed F. Noss and Allen Y. Cooperrider, *Saving Nature's Legacy: Protecting and Restoring Biodiversity* (Washington, D.C.: Island Press, 1994), 86.

2. Jonathan Tolman, "Achieving No Net Loss," *National Wetlands Newsletter,* May–June 1995, 6–7.

3. Matt Young, "River CARE," *Ducks Unlimited,* May–June 1996, 59–61; John Kinch, "Resurrecting the Kankakee," *National Conservancy,* May–June 1997, 33.

4. Julie Durel Livaudais, "Conflicting Interests in Southern Louisiana's Wetlands: Private Developers versus Conservationists, and the State and Federal Regulatory Roles," *Tulane Law Review* 56 (1982): 1008. Plaquemines Parish would be under water in less than fifty years.

5. "The Coalition to Restore Coastal Louisiana," background sheet, n.d.; U.S. Department of the Interior, *The Impact of Federal Programs on Wetlands,* A Report to Congress, vol. 2 (Washington, D.C., 1994), 144; Ralph W. Tiner, Jr., *Wetlands of the United States: Current Status and Recent Trends* (Washington, D.C.: U.S. Department of the Interior, Fish and Wildlife Service, 1984), 37–38; Louisiana Coastal Wetlands Conservation and Restoration Task Force, "Louisiana Coastal Wetlands Restoration Plan," Nov. 1993, 2.

6. *Impact of Federal Programs,* vol. 2, 144.

7. James M. Coleman, Harry H. Roberts, and Robert S. Tye, "Causes of Louisiana Land Loss," A Report Prepared for the Louisiana Mid-Continent Oil and Gas Association, 1985, 5, 11.

8. Jeff Hecht, "The Incredible Shrinking Mississippi Delta," *New Scientist* 14 (Apr. 1990): 44; Coalition to Restore Coastal Louisiana, *Coastal Louisiana: Here Today and Gone Tomorrow? A Citizens' Program for Saving the Mississippi River Delta Region to Protect Its Heritage, Economy, Environment* (Baton Rouge, La.: 1989), 35.

9. R. E. Turner and D. R. Cahoon, eds. *Causes of Wetland Loss in the Coastal Central Gulf of Mexico* (1988), cited in *Coastal Louisiana,* 17.

10. Coleman, Roberts, and Tye, 4–5, 11–12.

11. *Coastal Louisiana,* 38; W. H. Conner, *Public Administration of Louisiana's Coastal Wetlands:* 1820 to 1976 (Baton Rouge: Louisiana State University Center for Wetland Resources, 1977), 14. As early as 1971, the governor established an Advisory Commission on Coastal and Marine Resources to investigate the situation. Its report, *Louisiana Wetlands Prospectus,* formed the foundation of the work to be done under the CZMA.

12. *Coastal Louisiana,* 5; Louisiana Coastal Wetlands Conservation and Restoration Task Force, 5.

13. *Times Picayune* (New Orleans), 28 Nov. 1981, 11, cited in Livaudais, 1008.

14. Livaudais, 1008; Donald G. Schueler, "Losing Louisiana," *Audubon,* July 1990, 85.

15. Hecht, 46; *Coastal Louisiana,* 35–36.

16. Schueler, 85.

17. John Day, quoted in Schueler, 85

18. Hecht, 47; *Coastal Louisiana,* 27–29; Schueler, 86.

19. *Coastal Louisiana,* 1.

20. Schueler, 86; Paul Kemp, "Commentary," *Coastwise,* May–June 1990, 1.

21. Tiner, 37–38; Louisiana Coastal Wetlands Conservation and Restoration Task Force, 2.

22. "CWPRA Update," *Coastwise,* Mar.–Apr. 1993, 2.

23. William Allen, "Return of the Great River Debate," *BioScience* 43, no. 11 (Dec. 1993): 734; G. E. Galloway, "New Directions in Flood Plain Management," *Water Resources Bulletin* 31, no. 3 (1995): 351–57.

24. Rae Zimmerman, "After the Deluge," *Sciences* 34 (July–Aug. 1994): 18–22; Ted Williams, "The River Always Wins," *Audubon,* July–Aug. 1994, 86.

25. Quoted in Ann Robinson, "Small and Seasonal Does Not Mean Insignificant: Why It's Worth Standing Up for Tiny and Temporary Wetlands," *Journal of Soil and Water Conservation,* Nov.–Dec. 1995, 588; Allen, 734.

26. Tim Palmer, *America by Rivers* (Washington, D.C.: Island Press, 1996), 127; Rutherford H. Platt, *Land Use and Society: Geography, Law, and Public Policy* (Washington, D.C. Island Press, 1996), 418; Paul Hoversten, "Flood Control System under a Microscope," *USA Today,* 9 Aug. 1993; Zimmerman, 22; Jerry Adler, "Troubled Waters," *Newsweek* 26 July 1993, 26.

27. Michael A. Lev, "In Flood's Wake Wetlands Idea Surfaces Again," *Chicago Tribune,* 1 Aug. 1993, 4.

28. Mark Marturello, "A Set Up for Disaster?" *Des Moines Register,* 5 Sept. 1993, j-1; Kenneth Pins, "Some Flooded Farmland Will Convert to Wetlands," *Des Moines Register,* 8 Oct. 1993, m-6.

29. Bringing the Big Muddy to Life," *Nature Conservancy,* May–June 1996, 31.

30. William K. Stevens, "Restored Wetlands Could Ease Threat of Mississippi Floods," *New York Times,* 8 Aug. 1995, c-1, 4; Martha Naley, Natural Resources Conservation Service, personal correspondence, 14 June 1996.

31. Williams, 82.

32. Joseph W. Koebel, Jr., "An Historical Perspective on the Kissimmee River Restoration Project," *Restoration Ecology* 3, no. 3 (Sept. 1995): 152–53, 156.

33. Heather Dewar, "Prescription Posed for Ailing Glades," *Miami Herald,* 13 Jan. 1994, 1, 10.

34. Don Hinrichsen, "Waterworld: A Hundred Years of Plumbing, Plantations, and Politics in the Everglades," *Amicus Journal* 17, no. 2 (1995): 23.

35. Quoted in John H. Cushman, Jr., "U.S. and Florida Lean on Sugar Producers to Restore Polluted Everglades," *New York Times,* 15 Jan. 1994.

36. Quoted in Randy Lee Loftis, "Massive Recovery Effort Targets Everglades," *Dallas Morning News,* 20 Feb. 1994; "Everglades: One Step Forward or Several Steps Back?" *Wilderness,* Summer 1994, 6.

37. Quoted in Deborah Sharp, "River of Discontent Swirls around 'River of Grass,'" *USA Today,* 4 May 1994, a-8.

38. Peter Katel, "Letting the Water Run into 'Big Sugar's' Bowl: A Federal Plan to Restore Part of the Everglades," *Newsweek,* 4 Mar. 1996, 56; Kim A. O'Connell, "Gore Unveils Everglades Plan," *National Parks,* May–June 1996, 13.

39. Will Lester, "Replumbing the 'River of Grass,'" *USA Today,* 20 Feb. 1996, a-4.

40. Jeffrey Zinn, "Conservation Provisions in the 1996 Farm Bill: A Summary," *CRS Report for Congress,* 11 Apr. 1996, 6; Todd S. Purdum, "$3.8 Billion Water Projects Bill Is Signed," *New York Times,* 13 Oct. 1996.

41. John H. Cushman, Jr., "Environmental Groups Had Mixed Results," (Boise) *Idaho Statesman* (New York Times News Service), 8 Nov. 1996.

Chapter 18

1. Aldo Leopold, *A Sand County Almanac* (New York: Oxford University Press, 1949; reprint, 1969), viii.

Appendix

Some Common and Scientific Names of Wetland Plants

American baldcypress (*Taxodium distichum*)
American sycamore (*Plantanus occidentalis*)
ash (*Fraxinus spp.*)
black grass (*Spartina pectinata*)
black mangrove (*Avicennia germinans*)
black spruce (*Picea mariana*)
black tupelo (*Nyssa sylvatica*)
blueberry (*Vaccinium angustifolium*)
bulrush (*Scirpus spp.*)
cattail (*Typha latifolia*)
common reed (*Phragmites australis*)
cordgrass (*Spartina spp.*)
cottonwood, eastern (*Populus deltoides*), plains (*Populus sargentii*), swamp (*Populus heterophylla*)
fetterbrush (*Lyonia lucida*)
iris or flag (*Iris spp.*)
leatherleaf (*Chamaedaphne calyculata*)
liquidambar, see sweetgum
loblolly bay (*Gordonia lasianthus*)
needle rush (*Juncus roemerianus*)
overcup oak (*Quercus lyrata*)
paperbark (*Melaleuca quiquenervia*)

pitcher plant (*Sarracenia purpurea*)
pond pine (*Pinus serotina*)
prairie cordgrass (*Spartina pectiana*)
purple loosestrife (*Lythrum salarica*)
red bay (*Persea borbonia*)
saltgrass (*Distichlis spicata*)
sawgrass (*Cladium jamaicensis*)
sheep laurel (*Kalmia latifolia*)
sloughgrass (*Spartina michauxiana*)
smartweed (*Polygonum amphibium*)
swamp chestnut oak (*Quercus michauxii*)
swamp white oak (*Quercus bicolor*)
sweetgum (*Liquidambar styraciflua*)
tamarack (*Larix laricina*)
three-cornered grass (*Scirpus olneyi*)
titi (*Cyrilla racemiflora*)
tule (*Scirpus acutus Muhl.*)
water hickory (*Carya aquatica*)
water lily tuber (*Nymphaea odorata*)
water oak (*Quercus nigra*)
water tupelo (*Nyssa aquatica*)
waxmyrtle (*Myrica cerifera*)
wild rice (*Zizania aquatica*)
wild turnips (*Nuphar advena*)
willow (*Salix spp.*)

Acknowledgments

In 1993, I began research with a grand tour through many wetland regions of the country from Maine to Florida, then west across the gulf, working in libraries, talking with wetland experts, and visiting swamps, bogs, and marshes. During this trip, many people opened their homes to me and my husband. I would like to thank Marc and Janet Taylor, Jim and Lois Palmer, Trex and Beth Proffitt, Steve and Janet Anderson, the Schmitz family, Vita Vileisis, Jane and Chuck May, and Charles Fryling and Doris Faulkenheiner. I was thoroughly impressed by the many people I met who work full-time on wetland conservation; without their dedication the outcome of this story would be very different. Thanks to those who shared expertise and knowledge (their names can be found in my endnotes), but in particular, I would like to thank Bill Wilen, William Niering, Glenn Eugster, Mark Burget, and Wayne Baron. I am also indebted to many excellent scholars and researchers who helped along the way and whose work I drew upon, in particular Jeffrey Stine, Martin Reuss, Douglas Helms, Robert Kelly, Nelson M. Blake, Robert Harrison, and David C. Miller.

In the years of research and writing that followed that first trip, other friends offered help. Thanks to Jack and Nancy Shea and the Teton Science School for enabling me and my husband to spend a winter as writers-in-residence. I would also like to thank Alan and Margo Hunt who graciously invited us to live and work at their cabin in Jackson Hole, Wyoming, for six productive months. Kaz Thea let us live at her apartment in Portland while my husband worked on a book about the Columbia River, and John McCarthy shared his Boise home with us. Thanks also to Terry Pritchard and Nancy Mertz, Diane Ronayne and Gary Richardson, Jamie Williams and Florence Williams, Julie Holding, Mike Medberry, Tim Lotina, Beth Jacobi and Stephen Junkins, John and Lil Gremer, Greg and Mary Bettencourt, Dave and Janet Murray, Jonathan and Jenny Murray, the Roberts

420   DISCOVERING THE UNKNOWN LANDSCAPE

family, Ben and Betsy Sayler, Sean Hecht and Rebecca Weiker, and Birute
Anne Vileisis, who all welcomed into their homes and assisted in various
ways. I am also grateful to Terry Krumdick and Suzanne Morlock, who
amiably honored my interlibrary loan requests while I lived in Wyoming.

When a draft was complete, Jeffrey Stine, Florence Williams, Tiffany
Bingham, and Tim Palmer gave me the generous gift of reading the entire
manuscript and offered excellent suggestions. Many others reviewed ex-
cerpts and made thoughtful comments: Martin Reuss, Douglas Helms,
Diana Selig, Jamie Williams, Tom Siccama, John Kuzloski, William
Niering, Bill Wilen, Daniel McInerney, David Lendt, Harvey Nelson, Eu-
gene Odum, Hazel Groman, Mike Prevost, Clark Williams, Gary Pearson,
Norton Nickerson, Jeffrey Zinn, Ann Burruss, Sue Hawes, and John
Turner. In the end, Jill Mason helped with a careful copyedit, and Thomas
Dahl and Valeree King assisted with illustrations. Thanks also to the many
people at Island Press who have worked on this project, especially to Bar-
bara Dean for her belief that my proposal could become an important book.

My years of research and writing would not have been possible without
generous grants from the J.N. "Ding" Darling Foundation, the National
Fish and Wildlife Foundation, the Compton Foundation, and the Gilbert
and Ildiko Butler Foundation. I am especially grateful to Chris Koss, Jim
Compton, Gil Butler, Sara Nichols, and Lucy Wallace for their help and
support.

In addition, I want to give heartfelt thanks to the many teachers who
nourished my inquisitive spirit before this project began. In particular,
William Cronon first taught me to think about environmental issues from a
historical perspective and encouraged me to pursue this study.

Thanks also to members of my family (especially those who sent newspaper clippings) for their interest and moral support. My mother deserves
a gold medal for faithfully forwarding mail and messages while I worked in
so many different places.

Finally, thanks to my husband, Tim Palmer, who helped me in every way
through the journey of writing this book. His inspiraton, insight, encour-
agement, humor, and love have enriched my life as well as this work.

Index